A PRINCIPLED FRAMEWORK FOR THE AUTONOMY OF RELIGIOUS COMMUNITIES

It is a popular view that there is tension between religious freedom and equality. Both are essential to a free society but sometimes appear to pursue competing objectives. Against those who despair that conflict is intractable, many scholars from across the spectrum yearn for a resolution.

This book gives substantive content to such calls through applying theological virtues such as love, dignity, patience, humility, forgiveness and kindness. Among others, these virtues acknowledge the inherent worth of all humans while simultaneously cultivating a willingness to permit genuine difference, even profound moral disagreement.

Drawing on these virtues to analyse legal and theoretical approaches to religious freedom and discrimination in Australia, the US, and England, the book constructs a principled framework for reconciling religious freedom and discrimination. Based on this framework, the book provides specific theoretical and legal policy principles to create a peaceful coexistence of difference which values and upholds both religious freedom and equality.

A Principled Framework for the Autonomy of Religious Communities

Reconciling Freedom and Discrimination

Alex Deagon

·HART·

OXFORD · LONDON · NEW YORK · NEW DELHI · SYDNEY

HART PUBLISHING

Bloomsbury Publishing Plc

Kemp House, Chawley Park, Cumnor Hill, Oxford, OX2 9PH, UK

1385 Broadway, New York, NY 10018, USA

29 Earlsfort Terrace, Dublin 2, Ireland

HART PUBLISHING, the Hart/Stag logo, BLOOMSBURY and the Diana logo are
trademarks of Bloomsbury Publishing Plc

First published in Great Britain 2023

A catalogue record for this book is available from the British Library.

Library of Congress Cataloging-in-Publication data

Names: Deagon, Alex, author.

Title: A principled framework for the autonomy of religious communities :
reconciling freedom and discrimination / Alex Deagon.

Description: Oxford ; New York : Hart, 2023. | Includes bibliographical references and index. |
Summary: "This book engages in a theological critique of the legal frameworks and theoretical approaches
of Australia, the US and England to create a peaceful coexistence of difference which supports both religious
freedom and equality. It develops a new framework for reconciling religious freedom and discrimination in
Western liberal democracies and presents a unique approach to practically supporting both religious freedom
and equality as fundamentally important objectives which promote more compassionate and cohesive
communities. The book applies the idea of peaceful coexistence of difference by assuming the dignity
and goodwill of different people and perspectives, and proceeds upon shared virtues such
as love which are affirmed by all"—Provided by publisher.

Identifiers: LCCN 2022049005 | ISBN 9781509950638 (hardback) | ISBN 9781509950676 (paperback) |
ISBN 9781509950652 (pdf) | ISBN 9781509950645 (Epub)

Subjects: LCSH: Freedom of religion—Australia. | Freedom of religion—England. |
Freedom of religion—United States.

Classification: LCC K3258 .D43 2023 | DDC 342.08/52—dc23/eng/20230103

LC record available at https://lccn.loc.gov/2022049005

ISBN: HB: 978-1-50995-063-8
        ePDF: 978-1-50995-065-2
        ePub: 978-1-50995-064-5

Typeset by Compuscript Ltd, Shannon

FOREWORD

This book by Alex Deagon addresses what many consider to be one of the most important issues in the field of law and religion studies. Is there a principled way of reconciling the autonomy of religious communities with the right to equality and non-discrimination?

Deagon offers a startling line of argument: he proposes that a theological approach is able to offer a principled basis for reconciling the deep differences that characterise public debates about these issues. Deagon's goal is also ambitious: he wishes to maintain the autonomy of religious communities without compromising the right to equality. He proposes this can be done by grounding the accommodation of difference on the principle of peaceful coexistence. For Deagon, this principle derives from the Christian precept of loving one's neighbour, which he says entails a radical and selfless compassion for others, regardless of their religion, culture, race, gender or sexuality. It is an approach that eschews anger, wrath, malice and slander, and pursues kindness, humility, meekness and patience, so that we relate to others with honesty, forbearance, compassion and forgiveness. His hope is that such an approach will help to diffuse many of the tensions in our contemporary societies and will help to promote the development of more compassionate and cohesive communities.

Why would a specifically Christian approach appeal to the non-religious and persons of other faiths? Deagon proposes, among other things, that the Christian virtues he identifies (ie, love, kindness, humility, patience) are universally attractive, and have become foundational to modern western societies precisely as a consequence of the influence of Christianity. These virtues, he argues, are conducive to the formation of loving communities of interdependence in which religious freedom is not understood as a subjective right which can be asserted at the expense of another, but as the expression of a culture marked by gratitude, generosity, and mutual trust.

Deagon proposes that this approach is not intrinsically incompatible with liberal conceptions of freedom and equality. He argues that liberalism brought to light elements of the Christian ethical tradition that had been obscured in medieval Christianity. As a consequence, liberalism and Christianity share premises which can mutually inform and strengthen each other. Deagon maintains that the law of love fully realises, while it also transcends, the liberal virtues of freedom, neutrality and equality. As the Apostle Paul put it, 'whoever loves others has fulfilled the law' (*Romans* 13:8). Deagon thus understands his position to be 'post-secular', not 'post-liberal'.

Deagon examines the Australian, US and UK legal systems, assessing the extent to which each regime promotes a peaceful coexistence of difference which reconciles the autonomy of religious communities with the right to equality and non-discrimination. The result, on his argument, is a need for compromises and accommodations on both sides. On one hand, he argues, Australia's antidiscrimination laws provide excessively broad exemptions to religious bodies to enable them to discriminate on the basis of sex-related attributes in a manner that is specifically targeted at sexual minorities. On the other hand, he maintains that these laws should be amended to provide a positive right to religious organisations to regulate their membership so that they can cultivate the particular communal ethos that is appropriate to the religion. Similarly, he argues that the ministerial exception rule developed in the US is too broad because it allows discrimination on the basis of attributes unrelated to religion, potentially allowing malicious discrimination unrelated to upholding the organisation's religious ethos. The principle should therefore be narrowed to protect decisions genuinely based on the religious principles of the organisation. Likewise, Deagon rejects as misconceived the view that religious organisations that engage in public or commercial activities, or provide public services such as education and welfare, must lose their rights to religious freedom. He points out that many religious groups do not draw a sharp distinction between the public and the private, but rather see their public and commercial activities as intrinsic to their religious beliefs and practices. Deagon believes that too much public debate on these topics has been conducted on a zero-sum basis in which one's political opponents are seen more like enemies to be defeated than fellow human beings of equal dignity and worth. This problem has been manifested, he says, when the autonomy of religious communities has been framed as necessarily in conflict with equality principles, closing out the possibility of mutual accommodations which acknowledge the dignity and value of all concerned. Deagon calls for genuine attempts at reconciliation, understanding and compromise, so that reasonable and proportionate accommodations can occur for the good of the community as a whole.

Deagon evaluates the various theoretical perspectives which have been said to undergird the approaches adopted in Australia, the US and the UK. His view is that there is no one model that is appropriate for all peoples and places. For some societies, various types of establishment may be appropriate to best protect the autonomy of religious communities and the equality of individuals. In other societies, pluralism may be more suitable. However, he considers that secularist separationism should be rejected because it marginalises religion and undercuts the proper autonomy of religious communities.

Deagon's striking conclusion is that a mild establishment of religion can actually provide a more robust foundation for a peaceful coexistence of difference compared with other models of the religion-state relationship. This is particularly the case, he argues, where the establishment is based on the widely recognised Christian virtues of love, dignity, forgiveness and patience. Deagon believes that such an approach will not necessarily exclude or alienate those who are not religious or of the same religion because these virtues, which are generally acknowledged, entail strong protections for the freedom of all religions and for those who are not religious. Rather, he maintains that the moderate form of establishment implemented in the UK actually encourages pluralism and religious diversity because the Church of England uses its privileged position to make room for majority and minority religions in public affairs. He therefore advocates moderate, liberty-enhancing forms of religious establishment, particularly for the UK but also in a milder form for Australia. However, the situation in the US is different. Deagon argues that a secularist 'wall of separation' approach is not an appropriate framework in that country because it tends to privilege secularist beliefs and practices over religious ones. He maintains that pluralism is a better model for the US, because it allows for an accommodation of religious and non-religious perspectives in which the religious is not relegated to the 'private' while secularist beliefs dominate the 'public' sphere.

For Deagon, a principled approach to these issues needs always to acknowledge the intrinsic dignity and value of all people, whether religious or irreligious, and irrespective of their particular religious, cultural, ethnic or sexual identities. His hope is that a principled approach will help to build the trust and common ground necessary for a peaceful coexistence of difference which is protective of both religious freedom and equality. What matters, he concludes, is that the forms of protection consistently frame religious freedom and equality as important goods to be pursued together, albeit in diverse ways, rather than entering a zero-sum game in which one side dominates the other.

One of the significant merits of Deagon's book is that it combines theological and philosophical assessment of religious freedom issues with close examination of technical issues of law and policy across three distinct, but related, jurisdictions. One of the questions that arise for further investigation is the application of Deagon's approach to the same sorts of issues as they arise in a more diverse array of national settings. What would his approach mean for the increasingly post-Christian societies of western and northern Europe, or for the countries of southern, central and eastern Europe where religion retains a more significant cultural and political influence? What of the countries of Latin America, as well as of Africa, Asia and the Middle East, for that matter? To what extent is Deagon's approach tailored specifically to English-speaking countries whose traditions of law and governance are shaped by the common law and whose religious inheritance is predominantly Protestant? How would it apply – indeed, can it apply – to countries whose legal, governmental and religious inheritance is Roman Catholic or Eastern Orthodox, let alone Sunni Muslim, Hindu or Buddhist? Does it have any purchase on countries that do not have the same or similar cultural moorings?

These sorts of questions lie beyond the scope of Deagon's admirable book. It is a mark of its quality that one's mind is drawn towards them.

Professor Nicholas Aroney
Professor of Constitutional Law
TC Beirne School of Law
University of Queensland

ACKNOWLEDGEMENTS

I first became interested in religious freedom as an intellectual pursuit during my PhD, which was in jurisprudence and theology. As a fresh-faced PhD Candidate I presented my first paper outside my PhD topic on theocracy and secularism in Australia. That foolhardy gamble paid off and I made my first connections in the field, including Professor Nicholas Aroney, who became an informal academic mentor. Professor Aroney has generously offered his counsel and assistance with respect to academic matters too numerous to count, including through the writing of this book. Professor Aroney honours me by writing the foreword.

After I completed my PhD, religious freedom became my focus. I initially concentrated on the freedom of religion provision in section 116 of the Australian Constitution, and moved to religious freedom and anti-discrimination more broadly as the debate gained political traction in the US through the *Masterpiece Cakeshop* case, in the UK through the *Asher's Bakery* case, and in Australia through the Ruddock Review, and divided opinions regarding the religious exemptions in anti-discrimination law. The debate continues today around the Religious Discrimination Bill.

As I continued to write and speak about these issues in formal and informal forums, it struck me that despite an apparently intractable debate with entrenched sides, there also seemed to be a desire for reconciliation expressed as a pursuit of mutual understanding and compromise. My aim in this book has been to provide a robust standard which can be used to evaluate the extent to which Australia, the US and the UK has provided and can provide such reconciliation, which I conceive as a peaceful coexistence of difference. I leave the reader to judge whether I have advanced us forward in this respect.

A secondary function of this book has been the reconciliation of my ostensibly competing research agendas. On one hand, I have developed an abstract theological approach to jurisprudence. On the other, I have engaged in the minutiae of freedom of religion case law. For many years I compartmentalised these two pursuits in separate work, yet always with a view to working out how I could bring them together. This book represents a culmination of that process through the deployment of my theological approach as a standard to critique how the legal frameworks of different jurisdictions protect the autonomy of religious communities while upholding equality.

For a work of this magnitude I owe many academic debts. First, I thank the QUT School of Law for providing space to research, and I thank my supportive colleagues at the QUT School of Law for making this a fun and vibrant place to work. I particularly acknowledge Professor Afshin Akhtar-Khavari, Professor Kieran Tranter, and Dr Nigel Stobbs for their enthusiastic support of my research and constructive feedback along the way. For my many academic colleagues around the world who have supported me and my research in ways too numerous and significant to detail, thank you. I have benefited from engagement and collaboration with, among others, Professor Nicholas Aroney, Professor Rex Ahdar, Professor Iain Benson, Dr Stephen Chavura, Associate Professor Joshua Neoh, Professor Paul Babie, Dr Constance Lee, Professor Patrick Parkinson, Associate Professor Neil Foster, Professor Augusto Zimmermann, Associate Professor Benjamin Saunders, Dr Neville Rochow QC, Dr Jeremy Patrick, Mark Fowler, Dr Joel Harrison, Professor John Milbank and Professor Marc DeGirolami. I particularly thank Professor Helen Alvare for contacting me out of the blue from across the world to compliment my first book and organise an ultimately successful conference exploring ideas in it.

Early versions of ideas found in this book have already appeared in various contexts. I thank Professor Janet Epp-Buckingham for inviting me to contribute an article on Secularism in Free Exercise Jurisprudence to a special issue of the *International Journal for Religious Freedom*, Professor Helen Alvare for inviting me to contribute a paper on Theological Virtues and the First Amendment to the *Beyond Defensive Crouch Religious Freedom Conference* at George Mason University, and Dr Joel Harrison for inviting me to contribute a paper on Framing a Post-Liberal Christian Approach to Religious Freedom and Equality to the *Post-Liberal Christian Jurisprudence Workshop* at the University of Sydney. These experiences helped refine my thinking on different issues covered in the book.

I have thus far described my intellectual journey in writing this book. My personal journey has been no less eventful, and certainly more difficult for reasons which I do not burden the reader with here. I am thankful to family and friends who provided support when I needed it most. To Neil, Constance, Afshin, Mark, Augusto – I hope the feeling is mutual when I say that you are more than esteemed colleagues in pursuit of the good for all – you are also good friends. To Tim, Jerram, Paul, Daniel and Louisa – I appreciate you reaching out and meeting with me. To Rose, my favourite cousin (and in a Greek family that is no small feat!) – your empathy and presence has been invaluable. To my parents and my brother and his family, thank you for always being available for advice and as an outlet for stress. All of you think higher of me than I deserve.

To my children and Emma-Lee, I love you, and thank you for your constant support. I hope this work of mine contributes to a more harmonious society for you all.

Most importantly, I thank the Lord Jesus Christ for his faithfulness in hard times. It is His work on the cross, his death and resurrection for the forgiveness of my sins, which in every sense provides the foundation for this book.

Alex Deagon
June 2022

CONTENTS

PART III
THEORETICAL FRAMEWORKS

PART IV
A PRINCIPLED FRAMEWORK

PART I

Religious Freedom versus Anti-Discrimination?

Introduction

I. The Purpose of this Book: Reconciling Freedom and Discrimination

Religious freedom is essential to a free society. It is often called a 'fundamental' freedom, for it goes to the very foundation of a person's dignity as they identify with particular religious beliefs and live ethically as an individual and as part of a community of belief.[1] For many, religion provides a conceptual basis for political, moral, cultural and social beliefs and religious freedom grounds other important freedoms like freedom of speech and freedom of association, leading people to practise and speak about their beliefs by associating with like-minded people to influence the community as a whole towards their view of the good. Religion can therefore be constitutive of a person and a community.[2] The idea of equality is also central to the functioning of the modern liberal democracy. If public or private entities discriminate by treating a person or group unequally in an arbitrary way which unjustly targets particular intrinsic attributes of that person or group, this too is an affront to dignity which undermines fundamental freedoms all people ought to enjoy by virtue of who they are as people.[3]

There is, for all practical purposes, universal agreement that freedom and equality are fundamentally important imperatives which should be pursued. The problem is these imperatives can conflict. The idea of religious freedom and its complex relationship with discrimination has divided Western liberal democracies. There is deep disagreement about whether religious individuals or groups should order their lives and conduct their affairs in accordance with their religious convictions when this may involve discrimination on the basis of protected attributes such as sex, sexual orientation and gender identity.[4] In this book for ease of

---

[1] See eg M McConnell, 'Why is Religious Liberty the First Freedom?' (1999) 21 *Cardozo Law Review* 1243; B Bussey, 'Blazing the Path: Freedom of Conscience as the Prototypical Right' (2020) *Supreme Court Law Review* 145.

[2] See R Ahdar and I Leigh, *Religious Freedom in the Liberal State,* 2nd edn (Oxford University Press, 2013) 1–2.

[3] J Doomen, *Freedom and Equality in a Liberal Democratic State* (Bruylant, 2014).

[4] See eg Ferrari, 'Who is Afraid of Religious Freedom? The Right to Freedom of Religion and Belief and its Critics' (2016) 11(3) *Religion and Human Rights* 224–49. I focus on sex and LGBT discrimination because the topic is popular, controversial, and is relevant in many of the legal issues which arise. However, I will consider other manifestations such as religious discrimination, or religious freedom and disability in significant US cases on the ministerial exception under the First Amendment like *Hosanna-Tabor Evangelical Lutheran Church and School v Equal Employment Opportunity Commission,* 565 U.S. 171 (2012) and, more recently, *Lady of Guadalupe School v Morrissey-Berru* 140 S. Ct. 2049 (2020).

reference I broadly designate religious individuals (including vendors), businesses, organisations (including charities), institutions (including churches and schools), groups, associations and so forth as 'communities'. I call the ability of 'religious communities' to freely order their lives and conduct their affairs in accordance with their own understanding of their religious doctrine (religious convictions) the 'autonomy of religious communities'. This references classical debates regarding church autonomy and the freedom of the church; these classical debates take on new meaning in a context where the freedom or autonomy of religious communities is directly challenged because it may conflict with equality norms.[5]

Fundamentally, the claim from religious freedom advocates is that religious freedom requires the ability to organise and associate in a way consistent with the religious beliefs or convictions of the community. Equality advocates respond that religious freedom is not absolute and ought to be balanced against equality considerations, and the ability of religious communities to discriminate should not be overly broad. The counter-argument from the religious freedom perspective is discrimination in this context is not unjust, but the necessary consequence of having an association based around an ethos. The ability to associate by definition requires the ability to exclude. This operates as a function not only of freedom, but also of equality – for the law provides accommodations and exemptions allowing all kinds of discrimination for all kinds of reasons (such as on the basis of race and sex through affirmative action policies, or on the basis of political belief for maintaining the ideological integrity of political parties). Why should religion be treated differently? The rejoinder from the equality perspective is religion is not the same as politics or race or sex in a secular, democratic society, and so should not be given special treatment.[6] And on it goes.[7]

My articulation of the debate is merely illustrative. It contains some elements of truth and distortion, and does not cover every aspect of all the arguments. More importantly for my purpose here, it contains many theoretical and legal assumptions about the nature and aims of religious freedom and equality in a secular liberal state, and assumptions about the nature and perspective of secular liberal democratic states in terms of how they attempt to reconcile religious freedom with discrimination in a diverse community.[8] Though tension is an inevitable feature

---

[5] *cf* eg G Robbers (ed), *Church Autonomy: A Comparative Survey* (Peter Lang, 2001); J Calderwood Norton, *Freedom of Religious Organisations* (Oxford University Press, 2016); R Garnett, 'The Freedom of the Church' (2007) 4(1) *Journal of Catholic Social Thought* 59–86. See also the 'Freedom of the Church in the Modern Era' symposium papers, published in (2013) 21 *Journal of Contemporary Legal Issues*.

[6] See especially B Leiter, *Why Tolerate Religion?* (Princeton University Press, 2012), though Leiter chiefly discusses religious exemptions for individuals (focusing on individual conscience) rather than groups.

[7] See eg J Corvino, R Anderson and S Girgis, *Debating Religious Liberty and Discrimination* (Oxford University Press, 2017), where the authors engage in an internal debate about these issues within the book.

[8] For articulation and critique of some of these assumptions see my work in A Deagon, 'Liberal Secularism and Religious Freedom in the Public Space: Reforming Political Discourse' (2018) 41(3)

of a democratic society in which different views exist, views are so polarised and often acrimonious that advocates simply talk past each other and do not deeply consider these assumptions, and do not charitably engage to work out a solution.[9] Our highly pluralistic culture not only disagrees about specific moral issues, but also about the fundamental normative conceptions and premises regarding moral- ity which are necessary to resolve specific moral issues.[10] This indicates that the pragmatically pluralist or liberal *laissez-faire* 'live and let live' approach is no longer sufficient. A new, conceptually robust, principled approach that provides shared premises for more beneficial interactions, and explicitly engages with the some- times competing imperatives of religious freedom and equality, is necessary to facilitate harmonious relations between religious and non-religious communities in a liberal democracy.[11]

This book consequently develops the principled theoretical and legal frame- work of a 'proportionate, reasonable accommodation of difference' for the autonomy of religious communities and protection against discrimination, which relies on shared premises and mutual compassion. It helps resolve the challenge of reconciling religious freedom and non-discrimination norms by investigating different jurisdictional approaches to reconciling these fundamental but some- times competing imperatives, revealing current structures and relationships between religious freedom and antidiscrimination law, and critiquing these within a broader theological context which can inform a principled approach to promot- ing a peaceful coexistence of difference. By suggesting avenues that reconcile the fundamental norms of religious freedom and equality, the book is designed to provide a set of specific theoretical and legal policy principles to help facilitate the autonomy of religious communities without compromising equality, produc- ing peaceful coexistence through a principled framework: the proportionate, reasonable accommodation of difference. To be clear, the goal of the book is to use peaceful coexistence as a standard to construct a principled framework for the autonomy of religious communities which reconciles freedom with equality. Peaceful coexistence may well have a broader ambit than religious freedom and equality but I do not focus on that in the book. So I am not presenting a theoretical argument in favour of the peaceful coexistence framework or using the tensions between religious freedom and equality to test the merits of peaceful coexistence.

Harvard Journal of Law and Public Policy 901; A Deagon, 'Liberal Assumptions in Section 116 Cases and Implications for Religious Freedom' (2018) 46 *Federal Law Review* 113.

[9] As noted in the Australian context by N Aroney, J Harrison, and P Babie, 'Religious Freedom Under the Victorian Charter of Rights' in M Groves and C Campbell (eds), *Australian Charters of Rights a Decade On* (Federation Press, 2016).

[10] See eg S Smith, 'Equality, Religion and Nihilism' in R Ahdar (ed), *Research Handbook on Law and Religion* (Edward Elgar, 2018); A MacIntyre, *After Virtue: A Study in Moral Theory*, 3rd edn (Duckworth, 2007).

[11] For example see J Inazu, *Confident Pluralism: Surviving and Thriving Through Deep Difference* (University of Chicago Press, 2016).

Rather, peaceful coexistence is used as a standard to evaluate the tensions in different jurisdictions and create a principled framework for reconciling them.

Peaceful coexistence derives from the Christian idea to 'love your neighbour as yourself'. This entails a radical and selfless compassion for others in your community, regardless of religious, cultural, racial or sexual boundaries, as Christ explains in the Parable of the Good Samaritan. It privileges all people as dignified, unique individuals within the context of a loving community characterised by shared virtues such as humility, sacrifice, forgiveness and patience.[12] Such an approach seeks to cultivate these virtues as a means to promoting harmonious coexistence, despite the complex, ideologically divided and sometimes emotionally charged nature of these issues. It will be shown how the constitutive virtues of peaceful coexistence can contribute to defusing much of the political tension and social fracture, providing avenues for the pursuit of the good of pluralism and diversity through a proportionate, reasonable accommodation of difference, but by using Christian perspectives to promote a more compassionate and cohesive community.[13]

The remainder of the Introduction constructs the context for the book through outlining the tensions between religious freedom and anti-discrimination with reference to internationally prominent case examples such as *Masterpiece Cakeshop* in the US. It also identifies the shortcomings of the current scholarly literature in terms of the twin failures to seek a solution based on shared premises which is informed by an analysis of multiple jurisdictions. The Introduction explains the rationale for the book and overviews key terms and concepts, particularly the theological framework of 'peaceful coexistence' and models of the religion-state relationship, as well as outlining the structure of the book and indicating the contours of the principled framework – a proportionate, reasonable accommodation of difference – which the book develops.

II. Religious Freedom and Equality: A Tense Relationship

The modern Western liberal democracy is a religiously diverse secular state. This religious diversity, and in particular the resurgence of a more devout and political kind of religious practice, can lead to troubling conflict on issues of social significance which have moral or religious dimensions.[14] Social consensus over

---

[12] As I articulate in A Deagon, *From Violence to Peace: Theology, Law and Community* (Hart Publishing, 2017).

[13] As indicated in J Milbank and A Pabst, *The Politics of Virtue: Post-Liberalism and the Human Future* (Rowman & Littlefield, 2016). See also R Finke and D Mataic, 'Promises, Practices and Consequences of Religious Freedom' (2019) 15(3) *University of St Thomas Law Journal* 587.

[14] See Ahdar and Leigh (n 2) 1–23.

the role of religion in public life is fraying.[15] A recent example is the same-sex marriage debate in Australia during 2017 which eventually resulted in the legal recognition of same-sex marriage. When Australia publicly debated legalising same-sex marriage, people were often bitterly divided along cultural, religious and secular lines. This controversy often manifested as a tension between religious freedom and anti-discrimination law, or more broadly between religious freedom and equality.[16] Many religions expressed concern about their religious freedom to continue advocating and teaching 'traditional' marriage, while advocates for same-sex marriage argued that equality must be fundamental and people cannot discriminate on the basis of religion.[17] The objections to religious freedom as a basis for discrimination were often grounded in theoretical views about the nature of religion and religious freedom within the secular state. Thornton and Luker, for example, assert that religious belief is 'concerned with interior life', 'paradigmatically private and subjective', as opposed to law which is 'concerned only with the outward manifestation of a belief or prejudice'.[18]

This book takes a broad approach to the idea of equality.[19] It is not a study on anti-discrimination law, but it does use anti-discrimination law to illustrate equality interests, while also acknowledging that equality and anti-discrimination law are not necessarily equivalent.[20] In Australia, for example, multiple national reviews and inquiries over the past five years have raised the urgent issue of how to reconcile the autonomy of religious communities with anti-discrimination law in the context of equality concerns.[21] There is a need to better protect religious freedom but there is no clarity or consensus on how a liberal democracy such as Australia can effectively promote peaceful coexistence in this context when religious freedom may entail discrimination. The tense debates around religious freedom and discrimination illustrate the importance of enhancing public engagement, understanding and constructive dialogue around religion. The contemporary significance and challenge of reconciling religious freedom and

---

[15] See generally S Chavura, J Gascoigne and I Tregenza, *Reason, Religion and the Australian Polity: A Secular State?* (Routledge, 2019).

[16] See eg J Harrison, 'Debating Rights and Same-Gender Relationships' (2016) 4 *Journal of Law, Religion and State* 194; A Gray, 'Reconciliation of Freedom of Religion with Anti-Discrimination Rights' (2016) 42(1) *Monash University Law Review* 72. Of course, religious freedom and equality do not *necessarily* conflict: see the material corresponding with fns 141–45.

[17] See the accounts in R Barker, *State and Religion: The Australian Story* (Routledge, 2018) 146–60; Chavura et al (n 15) 244–48.

[18] M Thornton and T Luker, 'The Spectral Ground: Religious Belief Discrimination' (2009) 9 *Macquarie Law Journal* 71, 72–73.

[19] See eg S Segall, 'What's So Bad About Discrimination?' (2012) 24 *Utilitas* 82; P Shin, 'The Substantive Principle of Equal Treatment' (2009) 15 *Legal Theory* 149.

[20] See eg E Holmes, 'Anti-Discrimination Rights Without Equality' (2005) 68(2) *Modern Law Review* 175.

[21] As detailed in the most recent 'Religious Freedom Review' conducted in 2018, Department of Prime Minister and Cabinet, accessed 19 February 2019, https://pmc.gov.au/domestic-policy/religious-freedom-review.

anti-discrimination was particularly exposed through the recommendations of the Religious Freedom Review (known colloquially as the 'Ruddock Review' because it was chaired by a former Government Minister, Philip Ruddock) which allowed religious schools to continue legally 'discriminating against' (or on another view, 'positively selecting') prospective staff and students through religious exemptions in the Commonwealth Sex Discrimination Act. This sparked further public and parliamentary debates and proposed legislation to remove or alter the exemptions, which produced two further Senate inquiries and eventually a stalemate. The issue has been referred to the Australian Law Reform Commission. In 2019 the Commonwealth Attorney-General released two exposure drafts of a Religious Discrimination Bill designed to implement a recommendation from the Ruddock Review to protect religious communities from discrimination, which has been broadly supported by religious communities but largely rejected by LGBT and human rights groups because of the perception that the bill privileges religion above equality. Eventually the bill was introduced to Parliament in 2022 but failed to pass before an election resulted in a change of government, and the bill lapsed.

In the UK, there have been some prominent cases which seemingly pit religious freedom against equality. For example, in *Asher's Baking* (one of the infamous 'vendor' cases), the owners of a bakery who consistently operated the bakery in accordance with Christian principles were asked to bake a cake proclaiming a message supporting same-sex marriage.[22] They refused to do so because of a religious objection to the message, and were sued for discrimination. The case eventually went to the UK Supreme Court, who overturned the findings of sexual orientation discrimination by lower courts (but held there may have been discrimination on the basis of political opinion), and decided in favour of Asher's on the basis that the law in question should not be read as compelling providers of goods and services to express religious or political messages with which they disagree. A different outcome occurred in *Bull v Hall*,[23] where the Christian owners of a bed and breakfast who had consistently refused to provide accommodation to those engaged in 'sinful lifestyles' (including unmarried heterosexual couples) refused to provide accommodation to a gay couple. In that case they were found guilty of direct discrimination on the basis of sexual orientation. The Supreme Court conceded that religious beliefs had been interfered with, but concluded religious freedom must be appropriately limited to protect the rights of others (in this case a right not to be discriminated against). Finally, the autonomy of religious associations is directly challenged by 'the promotion of British values' in schools, which includes sexual orientation equality. The British Government's programme to insert promotion of sexual orientation equality into the curriculums of all schools, including private religious schools, raises the issue of the extent to which these

---

[22] *Lee v Asher's Baking Company Ltd* [2018] UKSC 49.
[23] *Bull & Bull v Hall & Preddy* [2013] UKSC 73.

religious schools will be required to endorse teachings which run contrary to their religious ethos.[24]

Of course, in the US, one of the more famous international cases was *Masterpiece Cakeshop*.[25] In this case, the Christian owner of a cake business was asked to bake a cake to celebrate a same-sex marriage, and refused because this would conflict with his Christian beliefs about marriage.[26] Masterpiece Cakeshop was sued by the state of Colorado for breaching anti-discrimination laws, and relied (among other claims) on free exercise of religion under the First Amendment. In the end Masterpiece Cakeshop was successful, but only because Colorado had displayed religious animus. The Supreme Court sidestepped the question of whether religious freedom protections under the First Amendment trump generally applicable state anti-discrimination laws. In other situations the Supreme Court has interpreted the First Amendment and religious freedom protections more generously, providing a 'ministerial exception' for religious organisations as a function of church autonomy which prevents them from being sued under anti-discrimination laws such as the Civil Rights Act,[27] and holding in the infamous *Hobby Lobby* decision that close corporations can have legal personality capable of possessing religious freedom rights under the Religious Freedom Restoration Act, which enlivens religious exemptions to general healthcare funding requirements.[28] Adding to the complexity of this interplay between religious freedom and equality in the US are the exemptions for religious organisations in the Civil Rights Act itself.[29]

The details of these situations and the legal and theoretical principles undergirding them will be more fully explored in Parts II and III of the book. I outline them here merely to provide examples of the tensions involved. There are at least four kinds of tensions. First, there is a tension between the religious freedom of individuals and the religious freedom of groups, as well as between individual and collective approaches to anti-discrimination law. Aroney has persuasively argued that religious freedom is by its very nature a group or associational freedom, and rights attaching to religious associations are not merely an aggregate of individual rights.[30] Conversely, Calderwood Norton grounds the freedom of religious

---

[24] See eg R Vanderbeck and P Johnson, 'The Promotion of British Values: Sexual Orientation Equality, Religion, and England's Schools' (2016) 30(3) *International Journal of Law, Policy and the Family* 292–321.

[25] *Masterpiece Cakeshop v Colorado Civil Rights Commission* 138 S. Ct. 1719 (2018).

[26] These cases are starting to become more common in the US: for example in *State of Washington v Arlene's Flowers* 441 P.3d 1203 (2019) and *Elane Photography, LLC v Willock* 309 P.3d 53 (2013), Christian vendors were sued for discrimination after refusing to supply their services for a same-sex marriage on the basis of their Christian beliefs about marriage.

[27] *Hosanna-Tabor Evangelical Lutheran Church and School v Equal Employment Opportunity Commission*, 565 U.S. 171 (2012). In this case the equality issue was disability rather than sex or sexual orientation.

[28] *Burwell v Hobby Lobby*, 573 U.S. 682 (2014).

[29] For further detail see eg M Breidenbach and O Anderson (ed), *The Cambridge Companion to the First Amendment and Religious Liberty* (Cambridge University Press, 2020).

[30] N Aroney, 'Freedom of Religion as an Associational Right' (2014) 33(1) *University of Queensland Law Journal* 153.

organisations in individual autonomy and rights.[31] Significant debates remain in anti-discrimination literature as to its collective dimensions.[32] This debate is significant because the weight given to the rights of religious associations affects what a reasonable or proportional balance might be between those rights and the rights of individuals versus groups who may be discriminated against.

Second, there is a tension involved in deciding whether religious vendors and businesses are actually religious 'bodies' capable of attracting religious freedom protections in the way churches and religious schools tend to do. Some argue that since vendors and businesses exist for commercial gain and are not engaging in 'religious' practice or offering 'religious' services, they should not be categorised as religious bodies (and consequently, they should not attract protection under exemptions to anti-discrimination law or religious freedom statutes).[33] However, others (including myself) have argued that this is a narrow view of religion and for many vendors and businesses, religion is the motivating factor for their existence and significantly influences how they conduct their activities.[34] So the categorisation should be a question of fact rather than a blanket inclusion or exclusion.

Third, there is a tension regarding how far the autonomy of religious communities extends. This involves consideration of whether religious freedom is public or private, and relatedly, whether the state should interfere with internal ordering of lives and the conduct of affairs within religious organisations when this may involve discrimination against proposed members or consumers in public contexts.[35] Related to this, the final tension is the relative weight which should be given to religious freedom concerns compared to equality concerns. Some have argued that religious liberty gives way to equality too often.[36] Others contend that the principle of exemptions from anti-discrimination law gives religion a special privilege and implies equality is a goal of limited value.[37]

Each of these tensions are interrelated and important in their own right, and ought to attract detailed examination. This book explicitly focuses on the latter two tensions in seeking to reconcile the autonomy of religious communities with equality. But, as we have seen in some of the case examples, considering the latter two tensions entails at least some consideration of the former two tensions.

---

[31] Calderwood Norton (n 5).

[32] See eg T Khaitan, *A Theory of Discrimination Law* (Oxford University Press, 2015).

[33] See eg M Schwartzman, C Flanders and Z Robinson (eds), *The Rise of Corporate Religious Liberty* (Oxford University Press, 2016); Leiter (n 6).

[34] A Deagon, 'Religious Schools, Religious Vendors and Refusing Services After Ruddock: Diversity or Discrimination? (2019) 93(9) *Australian Law Journal* 766–77; R Ahdar, 'Companies as Religious Liberty Claimants' (2016) 5(1) *Oxford Journal of Law and Religion* 1; Aroney, 'Freedom of Religion' (n 30).

[35] See eg A Deagon, 'Equal Voice Liberalism and Free Public Religion: Some Legal Implications' in M Quinlan, I Benson and K Thompson (eds), *Religious Liberty in Australia: A new* Terra Nullius? (Connor Court Publishing, 2019) 292–332.

[36] R Trigg, *Equality, Freedom and Religion* (Oxford University Press, 2012).

[37] C Evans and L Ujvari, 'Non-Discrimination Laws and Religious Schools in Australia' (2009) 30 *Adelaide Law Review* 31.

In this book all four tensions will be deeply examined as relevant in the course of developing a principled framework for the autonomy of religious communities – a proportionate, reasonable accommodation of difference – in the context of equality concerns.

III. Shortcomings in the Literature

This book uses the theological framework of 'peaceful coexistence of difference' to engage in a sustained exploration of different theoretical and jurisdictional approaches to the autonomy of religious communities in liberal democracies committed to equality. Though there is a voluminous literature on the relationship between religious freedom and equality, this book breaks new ground in three significant ways. First, it examines the autonomy of religious communities specifically rather than religious freedom generally. Second, there is limited research which engages in a multi-jurisdictional evaluation of both legal and theoretical approaches to the autonomy of religious communities. Finally, the book adopts a novel and robust theoretical approach designed to cut through the apparent stalemate between religious freedom and equality advocates in this specific area by affirming the dignity and good of people from different perspectives, and proceeding upon shared premises which can be agreed to by all.

A. A Focus on Specific Jurisdictions

Much scholarship on religious freedom and equality often only focuses on the individual legal frameworks of specific jurisdictions.[38] Of course, this is not in itself a vice. Detailed analyses of specific jurisdictions are necessary and valuable. This kind of scholarship explores the legal framework for the protection of religious freedom in individual jurisdictions and interaction with equality legislation such as anti-discrimination law, but does not consider the context of different jurisdictions. In particular, there has been very little consideration of the differences between jurisdictions in terms of legal and theoretical frameworks, and what can be learnt (or rejected) from other jurisdictions to effectively promote a peaceful coexistence of communities in this context. As Strong notes, 'the literature reflects a number of gaps, most notably in the area of jurisprudence.

---

[38] See eg J Rivers, *The Law of Organised Religions: Between Establishment and Secularism* (Oxford University Press, 2010) (UK); C Evans, *Legal Protection of Religious Freedom in Australia* (Federation Press, 2012) (Australia); D Laycock, *Volumes on Religious Liberty* (Eerdmans, 2010) (US). However, Rivers does adopt a more collective approach to religious freedom, noting that religious freedom 'is not merely individual'; it is an associational freedom and has a collective and communal orientation (31–32, 37–39, 317–18, 322, 338–39).

Indeed, comprehensive, cross-border theoretical analyses of religio-legal concerns are virtually non-existent'.[39] Consequently, this book investigates how the US, UK and Australia attempt to reconcile the autonomy of religious communities with preserving equality. Comparison enables a deep analysis of the competing conceptualisations that underlie particular jurisprudential approaches. These conceptualisations can then be scrutinised and built upon to develop a principled framework.

B. Lack of Focus on Autonomy of Religious Communities

The burgeoning literature on religious freedom and equality may discuss institutional religious freedom and associational freedoms, but it generally does not engage with the insights of different jurisdictions at the specific level of the autonomy of religious communities. For example, Luke Sheahan has recently articulated the importance of associational autonomy, but only focuses on the US and does not specifically focus on religious communities.[40] Bader and Inazu adopt persuasive pluralistic theoretical models but do not consider the insights of different jurisdictions or focus specifically on the autonomy of religious communities.[41] Trigg and Ten Napel do consider the autonomy of religious communities and different jurisdictions in some detail, but not in a sustained or principled way which is undergirded by a robust theoretical approach.[42] Hence, there is yet to be a specific, substantial study informed by different jurisdictions of how to theoretically conceptualise and legally implement a principled framework for the autonomy of religious communities without compromising equality (while also recognising that the very terms freedom, equality and discrimination are themselves conceptually contested and need to be put within a theoretical framework).[43] While Calderwood Norton and Aroney do focus on the autonomy of religious communities, they do not specifically engage with different jurisdictions or adopt an innovative theoretical perspective designed to reconcile the autonomy of religious communities with equality.[44]

Some analysis has also considered the complex relationship between religion and state using different theoretical models such as secularism versus pluralism,

---

[39] SI Strong, *Transforming Religious Liberties: A New Theory of Religious Rights for National and International Legal Systems* (Cambridge University Press, 2018) 7.

[40] L Sheahan, *Why Associations Matter: The Case for First Amendment Pluralism* (University Press of Kansas, 2020).

[41] V Bader, *Secularism or Democracy? Associational Governance of Religious Diversity* (Amsterdam University Press, 2007); Inazu (n 11).

[42] Trigg (n 36); H-M Ten Napel, *Constitutionalism, Democracy and Religious Freedom* (Routledge, 2017).

[43] See eg Doomen (n 3).

[44] Calderwood Norton (n 5); Aroney, 'Freedom of Religion' (n 30).

and in different jurisdictional contexts – but these do not focus specifically on the autonomy of religious communities and equality, and many focus on one jurisdiction. For example, Durham and Scharffs and Monsma and Soper cover different jurisdictions, but there is no deep consideration of the autonomy of religious communities undergirded by a principled theoretical perspective.[45] Similarly, Adenitire engages in deep jurisdictional analyses in a theoretically informed way, but there is no specific or consistent theoretical analysis focused on the autonomy of religious communities.[46] Barker, and Chavura, Gascoigne and Tregenza, do not specifically consider the autonomy of religious communities in depth and only focus on Australia.[47] Laborde's work is theoretically robust and considers different jurisdictions and the autonomy of religious communities, but does not specifically critique particular jurisdictions or exclusively focus on the autonomy of religious communities.[48] McConnell, in various works, takes a Christian perspective on issues of defining the relationship between religion and the secular, but does not explicitly refer to Christian theology or standards in his extensive legal analysis of religious freedom in the US (and he does not engage in detail with other jurisdictions).[49] Finally, Ahdar and Leigh adopt a consistent self-proclaimed Christian perspective and consider the autonomy of religious communities and different jurisdictions in some detail, but do not exclusively focus on the autonomy of religious communities using a robust theoretical perspective informed by the insights of different jurisdictions. Ahdar and Leigh reach many conclusions which would be consistent with the peaceful coexistence perspective (and these will be explored later in the book), but they do not have an explicitly theological framework to provide a more robust foundation for those conclusions.[50] As such, this book differs from McConnell and Ahdar and Leigh primarily by adopting the explicitly theological perspective of peaceful coexistence as an evaluative standard to analyse theoretical principles and legal infrastructure pertaining to the autonomy of religious communities in different jurisdictions. This provides a deep and vigorous normative perspective to buttress what may ultimately be conclusions similar to or consistent with those propounded by other sympathetic scholars who do not adopt an explicitly theological perspective.

---

[45] C Durham and B Scharffs, *Law and Religion: National, International and Comparative Perspectives* (Wolters Kluwer, 2010); SV Monsma and JC Soper, *Church and State in Five Democracies,* 2nd edn (Rowman and Littlefield, 2017).

[46] J Adenitire, *A General Right to Conscientious Exemption* (Cambridge University Press, 2020).

[47] Barker (n 17); Chavura et al (n 15).

[48] C Laborde, *Liberalism's Religion* (Harvard University Press, 2017).

[49] See eg M McConnell, 'The Origins and Historical Understanding of the Free Exercise of Religion' (1990) 104 *Harvard Law Review* 1409; M McConnell, 'Why is Religious Liberty the First Freedom?' (1999) 21 *Cardozo Law Review* 1243; M McConnell, 'Why Protect Religious Freedom?' (2013) 123(3) *Yale Law Journal* 770.

[50] Ahdar and Leigh (n 2) 18–19.

C. Lack of a Deep, Robust Theoretical Perspective which Relies on Shared Premises

Again, to use Australia as an example, the leading scholarship on religious freedom has traditionally discussed the cases and legislation relevant to section 116 of the Constitution.[51] There has been some general exploration of the legal framework for the protection of religious freedom and its interaction with anti-discrimination law, but these do not articulate or apply an innovative or robust theoretical perspective in an attempt to reconcile the two.[52] Nelson Tebbe takes a substantive (though ultimately secular) 'social coherence' approach to questions of religious freedom and equality, but does not focus exclusively on religious communities and only considers the US context.[53] While this book also adds greater jurisdictional diversity and focus on religious communities, more fundamentally this book takes a theological approach which is friendlier to religion. Similarly, Kozinski and Harrison suggest new theoretical approaches based in theological ideas which this book builds on, but they do not consider the insights of different jurisdictions or focus on the autonomy of religious communities specifically. Fundamentally though, this book largely adopts a framework similar to Harrison in terms of an ecclesiological account which aims to develop communities of charity (the reader will see numerous references to his work throughout the book), but builds upon it by focusing specifically on religious communities and incorporating an analysis of different jurisdictions.[54] Overall then, there have been no previous attempts to use the theoretical approach of peaceful coexistence to analyse the autonomy of religious communities in the context of anti-discrimination law in different jurisdictions. This book therefore extends the previous work of other scholars, and extends my previous work in constructing theological critiques of the secular state, studying the limits of purely secular approaches to peaceful coexistence and public good, and considering the implications for religious freedom and the relationship between religion and the state.[55]

---

[51] See eg Aroney, 'Freedom of Religion' (n 30); R Mortensen, 'The Establishment Clause: A Search for Meaning' (2014) 33(1) *University of Queensland Law Journal* 109; L Beck, *Religious Freedom and the Australian Constitution* (Routledge, 2018); N Aroney and B Saunders, 'Freedom of Religion in Australia' in M Groves, D Meagher and J Boughey (eds), *The Legal Protection of Rights in Australia* (Hart Publishing, 2019).

[52] See eg C Evans, *Legal Protection of Religious Freedom in Australia* (Federation Press, 2012); N Foster, 'Freedom of Religion and Balancing Clauses in Discrimination Legislation' (2016) 5(3) *Oxford Journal of Law and Religion* 385; A Deagon, 'Defining the Interface of Freedom and Discrimination: Exercising Religion, Democracy and Same-Sex Marriage' (2017) 20 *International Trade and Business Law Review* 239.

[53] N Tebbe, *Religious Freedom in an Egalitarian Age* (Harvard University Press, 2017).

[54] T Kozinski, *The Political Problem of Religious Pluralism: And Why Philosophers Can't Solve It* (Rowman & Littlefield, 2010); J Harrison, *Post-Liberal Religious Liberty* (Cambridge University Press, 2020).

[55] See eg Deagon, *From Violence to Peace* (n 12); A Deagon, 'Secularism as a Religion? Questioning the Future of the "Secular State"' (2017) 8 *Western Australian Jurist* 31; Deagon, 'Liberal Secularism and Religious Freedom' (n 8); Deagon, 'Equal Voice Liberalism' (n 35); A Deagon, 'Reconciling

IV. Peaceful Coexistence, Shared Premises and Political Virtues

A. A Principled Theological Context

Some narratives assume intrinsic conflict between, for example, Christian and LGBT communities.[56] However, this is no longer helpful for resolving tensions. Koppelman successfully recognises that compromise is a more effective way of living together, but does not articulate a substantive theoretical framework undergirding this view.[57] According to leading LGBT activist Chai Feldblum, such conflicts can only be resolved through 'generosity of spirit'.[58] Numerous other scholars from across the spectrum have echoed these calls. Brady argues that the goal should always be to seek solutions which minimise burdens on both sides, rather than focus on one at the expense of the other. 'Mutually acceptable compromises' are possible but require listening and working together 'in good faith'.[59] Wilson suggests that the 'Utah Compromise', which consists of state laws made to accommodate the needs of the LGBT community and religious communities simultaneously, affirms the good and dignity of all persons and can serve as a model for reconciling freedom and discrimination.[60] In fact, Eskridge and Wilson devote an entire edited collection to bridging the differences between LGBT and faith communities through dialogue and negotiation to reach mutually acceptable laws.[61] For example, Brownstein observes that for a genuine reconciliation of tensions, the fears, concerns and harms on both sides need to be taken seriously; he advocates 'empathy' and 'compromise'.[62] Against those who despair that the conflict is intractable, many scholars from different perspectives yearn for a resolution.

John Milbank and Religious Freedom: "Liberalism" through Love' (2019) 34(2) *Journal of Law and Religion* 183; A Deagon, 'The Name of God in a Constitution: Meaning, Democracy and Political Solidarity' (2019) 8(3) *Oxford Journal of Law and Religion* 473.

[56] See eg Smith, *Pagans and Christians in the City: Culture Wars from the Tiber to the Potomac* (Eerdmans, 2018).

[57] A Koppelman, *Gay Rights vs Religious Liberty: The Unnecessary Conflict* (Oxford University Press, 2020).

[58] C Feldblum, 'Religious Liberty and LGBT Rights: Finding the Right Balance (Ginsburg Lecture)' (2019) 41(2) *Thomas Jefferson Law Review* 163, 164–65.

[59] K Brady, 'Religious Accommodations and Third-Party Harms: Constitutional Values and Limits' (2018) 106(4) *Kentucky Law Journal* 717, 727, 730.

[60] R Fretwell Wilson, 'Common Ground Lawmaking: Lessons for Peaceful Coexistence from *Masterpiece Cakeshop* and the Utah Compromise' (2019) 51(3) *Connecticut Law Review* 483.

[61] WN Eskridge, Jr and R Fretwell Wilson, 'Prospects for Common Ground: Introduction' in WN Eskridge, Jr and R Fretwell Wilson (eds), *Religious Freedom, LGBT Rights, and the Prospects for Common Ground* (Cambridge University Press, 2018) 1.

[62] A Brownstein: 'Choosing Among Non-Negotiated Surrender, Negotiated Protection Of Liberty And Equality, Or Learning And Earning Empathy' in WN Eskridge, Jr and R Fretwell Wilson (eds), *Religious Freedom, LGBT Rights, and the Prospects for Common Ground* (Cambridge University Press, 2018) 12–15, 19–20.

In this book I give substantive content to such calls through applying theological virtues such as dignity, humility, patience, generosity, kindness, forgiveness and compassion. Particularly relevant to this conflict are dignity and forgiveness, which respectively recognise the inherent worth of all humans as created in the image of God, and a willingness to permit genuine difference, even profound moral disagreement, loving neighbour as self by aiming to persuade to what is true and good as Jesus did, while also accepting freedom to reject and disagree with our most deeply held convictions. As such, my hope is all parties who seek to live together in peace will see this as a desirable, robust and principled framework which will catalyse the reconciliation of freedom and discrimination.

In previous research, I have used a theologically informed evaluative framework to explore the idea of religious freedom in secular liberal states, which is 'the reconciliation of virtue with difference', or a 'peaceful coexistence of difference' which is oriented to pursuing the good. I developed this innovative theoretical approach through expanding and applying John Milbank's seminal work.[63] Applying peaceful coexistence to the challenging question of reconciling equality with the autonomy of religious communities uniquely begins by assuming the possibility of a peaceful coexistence between different communities (such as Christian and LGBT communities, as far as they are distinct), and recognises the dignity and good of the members of those communities, acknowledging how these communities can exist together harmoniously with their differences – rather than adopting a divisive and hostile posture which assumes the worst.

To articulate an alternative Christian foundation for a community based on true peace and reconciliation rather than conflict and violence, Milbank proposes the model of the Trinity, God as three divine persons: Father, Son and Holy Spirit; this is an 'infinite relation' of love and perfect peace, since God as Trinity is both unity and 'himself community' – which can therefore be a 'differential ontology', or a mode of being which allows the harmonious existence of difference in a community.[64] So put crudely, ontological peace is the affirmation of Being as the harmonious ordering of difference. Peace itself therefore also is beyond virtue because peace is the final end and condition in which virtue can flourish, the culmination of Being itself – or, as above, the harmonious ordering of difference.[65] Thus, the new Christian imagination of peace is more elegantly defined as 'the reconciliation of virtue with difference'.[66] So Christian Trinitarian ontology reconciles difference, promoting peace through the unity of individuals in the community.

---

[63] Deagon, *From Violence to Peace* (n 12); J Milbank, *Theology and Social Theory: Beyond Secular Reason*, 2nd edn (Blackwell, 2006); J Milbank, *Beyond Secular Order: The Representation of Being and the Representation of the People* (Blackwell, 2013); J Milbank and A Pabst, *The Politics of Virtue: Post-Liberalism and the Human Future* (Rowman & Littlefield, 2016).

[64] J Milbank, 'Postmodern Critical Augustinianism: A Short *Summa* in Forty-Two Responses to Unasked Questions' in G Ward (ed), *The Postmodern God: A Theological Reader* (Blackwell Publishers, 1997) 274.

[65] J Milbank, *Theology and Social Theory: Beyond Secular Reason* (Blackwell, 1990) 367.

[66] ibid 332–33.

Harmonious, relational community is the end goal, the peaceful transmission of difference, or differences in a continuous harmony.[67] Christianity consequently provides a more peaceful framework which does not merely 'permit' difference if it meets arbitrarily imposed criteria, but creates a space for the harmonious co-existence of difference. The particular nature of divine gift(s) allows difference to be harmonised and promoted, producing peace through virtue in the body as the Apostle Paul describes in 1 Corinthians 12.[68]

As mentioned earlier, the idea of peaceful coexistence derives from the Christian idea to 'love your neighbour as yourself'.[69] This entails a radical and selfless compassion for others in your community as articulated by Christ in the Parable of the Good Samaritan.[70] It privileges both self and neighbour as dignified, unique individuals which constitute a loving community characterised by shared virtues such as humility, sacrifice, forgiveness and patience, with each member of the community relying on and responsible for each other member.[71] This idea goes far beyond the traditional *laissez-faire* liberalism which adopts a 'live and let live' or 'agree to disagree' approach; it positively and actively seeks the good of self and other, recognising that we live in an interdependent community.[72] As discussed below, this is not merely personal ethics; to act virtuously is to truly act politically. For example, the peaceful coexistence approach transforms political discourse by considering it as the interaction of different perspectives made harmonious by loving one's neighbour. Practically, this means properly listening and engaging rather than judging (patience), interpreting charitably (trust), asking questions to clarify and learn (humility), and avoiding malice (kindness).[73]

The virtue of trust constitutes a more fundamental mode of eternal law.[74] It is mutual dependence between each member of the community, which provides a structure for harmonious existence and the embrace of difference without assimilation or alienation. Milbank reasons:

> It may appear that trust is weak recourse compared to the guarantees provided by law, courts, political constitutions, checks and balances, and so forth. However, since all these processes are administered by human beings capable of treachery, a suspension of distrust, along with the positive working of tacit bonds of association, is the only real source of reliable solidarity for a community. Hence to trust, to depend on others, is in reality the only reliable way in which the individual can extend his or her own power … the legitimate reach of one's own capacities, and also the only reliable way to attain a collective strength.[75]

---

[67] ibid 422.
[68] J Milbank, 'Paul Against Biopolitics' in J Milbank et al (eds), *Paul's New Moment: Continental Philosophy and the Future of Christian Theology* (Brazos Press, 2010) 42–43.
[69] Romans 13:8–10.
[70] Luke 10:25–37. See Deagon, *From Violence to Peace* (n 12) 188–93.
[71] See generally Deagon, 'The Name of God in a Constitution' (n 55) 472.
[72] See generally Deagon, 'Reconciling John Milbank' (n 55) 183.
[73] ibid.
[74] Milbank, 'Paul Against Biopolitics' (n 68) 49–50.
[75] ibid 53.

This application of the law of love consequently encourages love for one's neighbour in terms of humility and sacrifice. Importantly, this is not forced or coerced, but rather freely volunteered as an imitation of Christ in trust that the action will be reciprocated. Through the paradigm of the law of loving your neighbour as yourself, which is the unity and diversity in the community of the Trinity, a model is provided from Christian theology which allows harmonious relationship between the individuals and the society, providing for a peaceful community which privileges one's neighbour as an individual and therefore strengthens the community as a composite of unique individuals.[76] Charity (love) or 'doing good' requires going beyond boundaries or precedents, something 'creative'.[77] As Milbank exhorts, 'to act charitably we must break through the existing representation of what is our duty towards our neighbour and towards God', and 'break through the bounds of duty which "technically" pre-defines its prescribed performance'; this constitutes a real political community of peaceful coexistence characterised by virtue.[78]

In particular, we need to go beyond mere legal duty (for example, to just avoid hate speech, blasphemy, vilification or discrimination) and selfish interest (the aggressive pursuit of our own agenda without due consideration for alternative views, or the prideful need to be seen as right), desiring to truly act with humility, love and sacrifice just like Christ did in humbling himself to death on a cross for our forgiveness:

> Do nothing from selfish ambition or conceit, but in humility count others more significant than yourselves. Let each of you look not only to his own interests, but also to the interests of others. Have this mind among yourselves, which is yours in Christ Jesus, who, though he was in the form of God, did not count equality with God a thing to be grasped, but emptied himself, by taking the form of a servant, being born in the likeness of men. And being found in human form, he humbled himself by becoming obedient to the point of death, even death on a cross.[79]

In this practical sense love of neighbour means properly listening and engaging rather than judging, interpreting expressed views charitably and asking questions to clarify and learn rather than assuming or misrepresenting the views of others, seeking ways to compromise as much as possible even at the cost of sacrificing our own ideal preferences, and not engaging in malicious or contemptuous conduct. Love of neighbour here eschews 'anger, wrath, malice, slander' and lying,

---

[76] Deagon, *From Violence to Peace* (n 12) 8–9.

[77] J Milbank, *The Word Made Strange: Theology, Language, Culture* (Blackwell, 1997) 134.

[78] ibid 134. See Deagon, *From Violence to Peace* (n 12) 188–93. To clarify, the need to go beyond mere legal duty is in the context of articulating what it means to personally act in accordance with the law of love in a political community. It does not imply anything specific about the kinds of legal duties that could or should exist in the broader context of the work of the book. As outlined later in the Introduction, the book will engage in a detailed legal analysis in conjunction with a theoretical analysis. The result will be practical principles to help inform law and policy – but with the acknowledgement that harmonious personal conduct (ie going beyond legal duty) is just as important and can often forestall litigation, helping to create peaceful coexistence.

[79] See Philippians 2:3–8.

and pursues 'kindness, humility, meekness and patience' with honesty, forbearance, compassion and forgiveness.[80] The law of love, constituted by virtues such as humility, sacrifice, forgiveness and trust, enables the peaceful transmission of difference, or differences in a continuous harmony – an inclusive space where different perspectives are acknowledged and coexist harmoniously such that there is freedom for people to equally choose how they live.[81]

The desirability of this theological framework is further entrenched by its unique ability to recognise and accommodate difference by peaceful rather than violent means. 'Christianity … pursued from the outset a universalism which tried to subsume rather than merely abolish difference: Christians could remain in their many different cities, languages, and cultures, yet still belong to one eternal city ruled by Christ, in whom all "humanity" was fulfilled.'[82] Following this Augustinian aspect however, Christianity does not

> … imply mere mutual tolerance, far less any resignation to a regulated conflict … while it is open to difference … it also strives to make of all these differential additions a harmony … true community means the freedom of people and groups to be different, not just to be functions of a fixed consensus, yet at the same time it totally refuses *indifference*.[83]

In this way, Christianity acknowledges the necessity of difference. Rather than trying to deny difference or regulate it with violence, at the ontological level Christian theology seeks a universal harmony of difference through incorporating the virtues which constitute the law of love, thereby enabling a community of peace at the political level.[84]

B. Compatibility and Application in Liberal Democracies: Religious Diversity and Shared Virtues

There may, understandably, be some concerns about using such an explicitly Christian theological framework as the basis for reconciling religious freedom with equality in religiously diverse secular liberal democracies. First, the astute reader may have noticed a heavy focus on 'Christian' communities. This is partly a function of my own research expertise and experience, which is in Christian communities – but more importantly, the majority of religious communities in the three jurisdictions this book considers are Christian communities, and the corresponding autonomy issues mainly occur in Christian communities. So in effect the book will focus on Christian communities, but it will also consider other

---

[80] See Colossians 3:8–9, 12–13.
[81] Milbank, *Theology and Social Theory* (n 63) 422.
[82] ibid 267–68.
[83] ibid 268.
[84] Deagon, *From Violence to Peace* (n 12) 17.

religious communities (and differing views within Christian communities) where relevant as a necessary aspect of peaceful coexistence, which involves considering all different kinds of religious communities.[85] Related to this point is an objection that the book may not consider the experiences and impacts on those who are discriminated against, including non-Christian religious communities. However, while it is not the method of this theoretical framework to develop theory based on experiences, the principled theoretical framework for the autonomy of religious communities will be developed in the context of equality concerns. Evaluating approaches using peaceful coexistence involves consideration of diverse perspectives, including those experiencing discrimination. The book will engage in a close reading of the law and scholarly literature, which includes relevant empirical studies and the experiences of different communities.[86]

Second, there may be concerns about the theory's basis in Christian thought, and whether it can account for religious diversity and appeal to non-Christian communities. This connects to a concern regarding how the theory can address the problems of a multi-religious liberal democracy. However, there are significant challenges for the traditional secular liberal approach to addressing these problems as well.[87] This book adopts a new theological approach which proceeds on the basis of shared premises. The theological virtues which underpin a peaceful coexistence of difference are also shared political virtues that all perspectives can agree with eg love, kindness, humility and patience. The appeal for non-Christian religious communities is a conceptual approach which is friendly to religion (unlike the secular liberal account) and aims to promote harmonious coexistence, which addresses the problem of religious diversity. The appeal for non-religious communities is a framework which provides a more deeply coherent (and so more universally sustainable and acceptable) account of shared political virtues than the secular liberal account, and concrete ways to implement these in areas of political tension. Even a religion-friendly secular approach which has the objective of a shared harmonious space is actually just the secular outworking of the theological peaceful coexistence approach. As I explain below, 'secular' liberal virtues actually have their foundation in Christian virtues.[88] The peaceful coexistence approach in this context merely makes explicit what is implicit, providing greater scope for theological critique according to a thick normative standard which the limited secular approach cannot have.

[85] See Ahdar and Leigh (n 2) 1–23, where the authors provide similar observations.
[86] See eg G Bouma, *Being Faithful in Diversity: Religions and Social Policy in Multifaith Societies* (ATF Press, 2011).
[87] As I have extensively argued in eg Deagon, *From Violence to Peace* (n 12); Deagon, 'Liberal Secularism and Religious Freedom' (n 8); Deagon, 'Liberalism through Love' (n 55); Deagon, 'Name of God' (n 55).
[88] See eg P Zagorin, *How the Idea of Religious Toleration Came to the West* (Princeton University Press, 2003); B Ward, *Redeeming the Enlightenment: Christianity and Liberal Virtues* (Eerdmans, 2010); J Witte Jr and F Alexander (eds), *Christianity and Human Rights* (Cambridge University Press, 2010).

For example, Hunter-Henin identifies an 'epistemological concern' as moti-vating a view which accommodates religious claims in a democratic context: 'the inability of liberal laws and courts to truly understand religious normative systems.'[89] Secular institutions cannot fully grasp or understand the complexity of religious doctrine and practice due to its special transcendence and relation between God and creation. This inability is also 'tainted by suspicions of illegitimacy', and the recognition that the liberal system has been largely shaped by Christian theol-ogy and culture, and hence any framing of minority religious concerns in liberal or secular language would distort those concerns.[90] 'Against those liberals who would dissolve, disaggregate and dilute religious freedom into underlying secular values of liberty and equality, I argue that such an approach would not solve but just divert the epistemological problems associated with the category of religion and unduly undermine the importance of the religious self-definition of religious citizens.'[91] So Hunter-Henin argues that retaining the specific category of reli-gion is important for maintaining democratic diversity, while also drawing limits around religious practice in order to maintain diversity with reference to Britain and France.[92] This book pursues a similar goal, yet provides a more robust theo-retical framework in the form of the specific theological approach of peaceful coexistence – giving substantive content to the laudable goal of democratic diver-sity through the idea of a harmonious ordering of difference.

Third, and following from the previous point, the promotion of Christian virtues as an evaluative framework does not alienate or restrict those who are not Christians or not even religious. Such virtues (humility, kindness, sacri-fice, forgiveness, love etc.) are universally desirable and universally achievable regardless of one's particular perspective. Rather than Christianity undermining religious freedom and equality in a democracy, it ensures it by promoting practices that facilitate genuine religious freedom and genuine democracy – fundamentally, the refusal of coercive violence and the use of peaceful persuasion. Milbank calls this the 'democratisation of virtue', where 'the most important human goods are in principle achievable by all', which 'is itself also a Christian legacy'.[93] Milbank argues 'that the viability of democracy itself depends upon a continued consti-tutional commitment to "mixed government"', which is a blend of 'the life and implicit wisdom of the social many with the guidance of the virtuously rational few and the unifying artifice of the personal one, under the orientation of all to the transcendent Good and final vision of the Godhead'.[94] Moreover, the 'Christian democratisation of virtue as charity [love] implies a transfigured version of mixed

---

[89] M Hunter-Henin, *Why Religious Freedom Matters for Democracy* (Hart Publishing, 2020) 10–11.
[90] ibid 11–12.
[91] ibid 14.
[92] ibid 14.
[93] Milbank, *Beyond Secular Order* (n 63) 264.
[94] ibid 10.

government that newly promotes the creative flourishing of all and the combined shaping of an earthly city that might remotely image the eternal.'[95]

In other words, genuine democracy entailing true religious freedom and equality promotes the individual and communal good so that the earthly polity might echo the eternal one. Such democracy is premised upon the universal practice of virtue, particularly love, which peacefully persuades the community to the good. As Milbank clarifies in later work, 'virtue is democratic because its practice is open to all, especially the supreme virtues of love, trust, hope, mercy, kindness, forgiveness and reconciliation, which we have all in the West, whether avowedly Christians or not, inherited from the teachings of the Bible'.[96]

Therefore the better approach is not a subjective 'right' to religious freedom which can be asserted at the expense of another, but a loving community of interdependence grounded in virtue which will reconcile religious freedom with equality.[97] This is a 'politics of virtue' which eschews selfish, Machiavellian modes of discourse in favour of charity, humility and sacrifice. We need to act with 'more receptive gratitude, more communicated generosity, and in such a way that in turn opens up the possibility of trust and further self-giving on the part of others'.[98] 'Thus politics is a shared demand for a manifest mutual recognition and regard, since justice and friendship are co-original and inseparable', and the politics of virtue is then really a superfluous phrase – as mentioned above, to act virtuously is really to truly act politically.[99]

Fourth, and directly related to the previous two points, this framework is not intrinsically incompatible with or in conflict with traditional liberal conceptions of freedom and equality, or liberal legal principles such as proportionality and accommodation.[100] Indeed, Christianity has been the major influence on the formation of liberal democracies with religious freedom and equality, and Christian theology importantly contributes to addressing religious pluralism.[101] Relatedly, Christian theology itself underpins modern Western legal systems. As painstakingly demonstrated in Berman's celebrated work, Christian theology, structure and content irrevocably informed the development of legal ideas and frameworks, particularly through papal revolutions and canon law.[102] Following Berman, Zimmermann has specifically explained how Christianity formed the

---

[95] ibid.

[96] Milbank and Pabst, *Politics of Virtue* (n 63) 7.

[97] See J Milbank, 'Against Human Rights: Liberty in the Western Tradition' (2012) 1(1) *Oxford Journal of Law and Religion* 201.

[98] Milbank and Pabst, *Politics of Virtue* (n 63) 6–7.

[99] ibid 7.

[100] See eg Trigg (n 36); Ten Napel (n 42); Deagon, 'Equal Voice Liberalism' (n 35).

[101] See eg Kozinski (n 54); R Woodberry, 'The Missionary Roots of Liberal Democracy' (2012) 106(2) *American Political Science Review* 244; Milbank, *Beyond Secular Order* (n 63); F Oakley, *The Watershed of Modern Politics: Law, Virtue, Kingship, and Consent* (Yale University Press, 2015); Milbank and Pabst, *The Politics of Virtue* (n 63); Ten Napel (n 42).

[102] H Berman, *Law and Revolution: The Formation of the Western Legal Tradition* (Harvard University Press, 1983).

foundation of the common law in the US, England and Australia.[103] Another example is Samuel Moyn's careful and attentive exposition of how Christianity underpins modern human rights discourse – not only through vague appeals to Christian conceptions of dignity which overlook inimical Christian conduct over the centuries, but more compellingly through the concrete anxieties of World War II atrocities which led to human rights being a project more of the Christian right than of secular liberals.[104] For this reason – the historical connection between Christianity and the liberal western ideology which undergirds the jurisdictions this book considers, in conjunction with the fact the majority of religious communities in those jurisdictions are Christian, and my own expertise is in Christian theology and communities – a Christian theological approach is appropriate.[105] Though it is true Christianity made use of existing concepts, it fundamentally transformed those concepts so that they became essentially unique and new – and this in turn was the primary influence in the ethical developments of the Enlightenment. For example, respect for the dignity of the individual, human rights, a commitment to equality, and concern for the poor are largely foreign to ancient religions, and reflect the uniquely biblical claims that humans were created in the image of God and that God sacrificed himself for the good of humans through Christ.[106] The fundamental point is the virtues of modern liberalism are themselves distorted versions of Christian virtues; and, simultaneously, it is the liberal project which privileged these Christian virtues largely obscured in medieval Christianity.[107] The almost symbiotic development of modern legal liberalism and Christianity means the theological approach of this book is able to apply to and be valuable for a pluralistic liberal legal context, especially with the ostensibly liberal 'proportionate, reasonable accommodation of difference' framework I develop – a framework nevertheless firmly grounded in the theological virtues which constitute peaceful coexistence.

Hence, liberal and Christian conceptions share premises which mutually inform and strengthen each other through connecting the liberal virtues with theological virtues. The theological law of love fulfils the liberal virtues of religious freedom, neutrality and equality, in conjunction with the Christian virtues of faith, hope, love, humility and sacrifice, by transcending them.[108] The theological framework has been integrated with more traditional liberal legal ideas such

---

[103] A Zimmermann, *The Christian Foundations of the Common Law, Volume I: England* (Connor Court, 2018); A Zimmermann, *The Christian Foundations of the Common Law, Volume II: United States* (Connor Court, 2018); A Zimmermann, *The Christian Foundations of the Common Law, Volume III: Australia* (Connor Court, 2018).

[104] S Moyn, *Christian Human Rights* (University of Pennsylvania Press, 2015).

[105] Of course, many other sources and religious traditions could also be referred to as a basis for compassion and peaceful coexistence: see eg K Lampert, *Traditions of Compassion* (Palgrave MacMillan, 2005).

[106] S Smith, *Pagans and Christians in the City* (Eerdmans, 2018) 206–07.

[107] Deagon, 'Liberalism through Love' (n 55).

[108] As explained in Deagon, 'Liberalism through Love' (n 55).

as freedom, equality and accommodation, so it can apply to different theories and legal models.[109] In this sense my approach is more properly post-secular liberal rather than post-liberal, enriching liberal concepts through a theological framework and explicitly rejecting the secularism of Rawlsian liberalism. The 'peaceful coexistence of difference' idea therefore provides an innovative and robust political theology for a liberal society which aims to facilitate pluralism, diversity, freedom and equality through accommodation of difference. This political theology will be used to critique the conceptualisations underlying particular jurisprudential approaches.

Finally, religious community is more than the simple expression of shared religious beliefs. It is an exercise in solidarity and broader community-building which mediates between the extremes of collectivism and individualism, strengthening both the individual and the community within a society governed by liberal-democratic constitutionalism.[110] Here solidarity takes its classical meaning of deeper relationality and mutual love as a bond between citizens of a community through what Joel Harrison calls a 'cooperative order', a framework for a community of harmonious being where self and other (neighbour) are loved and built up together.[111] In this 'cooperative order', 'all persons are given their appropriate positions', an ordered harmony in the community of the city where all citizens contribute and fulfil their role.[112] The coordination of different communities and individuals within those communities is attentive to the dignity of persons and their place within a created order, enabling the pursuit of shared goods in different ways.[113] These relationships are perfected in a life of charity – selfless affection which is recognised by mutual dependence and responsibility, and demonstrated through offering ourselves as gifts of service.[114] Such a harmonious human community is ultimately grounded in the highest Good, the object of our desires and satisfaction of our anxieties: God Himself. In relating to God in this way, we also deepen our horizontal relationships: 'Love the Lord your God, and love your neighbour as yourself'.[115]

Augustine argues that to love a person for the sake of God invests them with a 'transcendental significance' as loved by God.[116] A harmonious social and

---

[109] ibid; Deagon, 'Equal Voice Liberalism' (n 35).

[110] See eg A Menuge, 'The Secular State's Interest in Religious Liberty' in A Menuge (ed), *Religious Liberty and the Law: Theistic and Non-Theistic Perspectives* (Routledge, 2018); V Bader, 'Post-Secularism or Liberal-Democratic Constitutionalism?' (2012) 5(1) *Erasmus Law Review* 5.

[111] J Harrison, 'Dworkin's Religion and the end of religious liberty' in R Ahdar (ed), *Research Handbook on Law and Religion* (Edward Elgar, 2018) 94–98.

[112] ibid 96. See Augustine, *The City of God Against the Pagans* (Penguin, 2008) 876.

[113] See J Harrison, '"A Communion in Good Living": Human Dignity and Religious Liberty Beyond the Overlapping Consensus' in C McCrudden (ed), *Understanding Human Dignity* (Oxford University Press, 2014).

[114] Harrison, 'Dworkin's Religion' (n 111) 97.

[115] ibid. See also Luke 10:25–27.

[116] Harrison, 'Dworkin's Religion' (n 111) 94.

political order is predicated upon common agreement on the objects of love. Where the love of the earthly city is disordered, focusing on self, ambition and conflict, the love of the heavenly city focuses on God, and therefore reconciliation with the other. 'Orienting oneself to God commits one to a deeper relationality with others'.[117] These 'networks of charity' extend throughout social, economic and political contexts, manifesting in the freedom of the church, economic and political associations, trade unions, educational bodies and families.[118] For Augustine they are grounded in a love of God and neighbour and displayed in right and virtuous living – a life of charity.[119]

All this entails understanding, mutual dependence and responsibility, culminating in communities of mercy, grace and generosity. It suggests an enduring, mutually beneficial connection between citizens of different religions and non-religion, and more generally between the state and religion, as part of a desirable democratic process. Joshua Neoh calls this a 'transcendental politics', which makes no metaphysical claims about the reality of the transcendent but rather opens politics up to the possibility of the transcendent, and thus 'enriches the political process'.[120] For example, in England religious minorities such as Muslims and Jews actually support Anglican establishment because it gives religion a seat at the public table, which facilitates dialogue between religious groups and represents shared religious values. The established Church of England helps members of other faiths 'feel at home' by including, acknowledging, and welcoming faith as part of the democratic community.[121]

Domingo also observes that the acknowledgement of God more generally has political implications in terms of the promotion of human solidarity. Just as God desired to share the good with creatures by creating the universe, 'human solidarity embodies sharing spiritual and material goods; it transcends reciprocity … [and] helps explain natural interdependence as a source of political collaboration and social fraternity'.[122] By recognising God as the provider of all things, it assists humans to 'feel responsible to one another, increasing individual awareness and collective responsibility … it promotes an equitable distribution of the goods of the universe in a spirit of solidarity'.[123] The presence of God as a transcendent symbol motivates people to act in a more virtuous fashion towards their fellow citizens, enhancing the goods of the democratic process by entrenching their higher origin and manifesting their practice as the fulfilment of the view that each citizen is a

---

[117] ibid 95–96.

[118] ibid 97.

[119] ibid 97–98. Harrison extends these ideas in detail with specific regard to religious freedom in J Harrison, *Post-Liberal Religious Liberty* (Cambridge University Press, 2020).

[120] J Neoh, 'The Good of Religion' (2019) 93(9) *Australian Law Journal* 791, 796–97.

[121] P Dane, 'Establishment and Encounter' in R Ahdar (ed), *Research Handbook on Law and Religion* (Edward Elgar, 2018) 141–42.

[122] R Domingo, *God and the Secular Legal System* (Cambridge University Press, 2016) 41.

[123] ibid.

connected and valued member of the community.[124] It follows that these bonds of mutual obligation grounded in transcendent principles of human dignity facilitate human action which reflects this reality (at least for religious citizens, if not for non-religious citizens – which improves the environment for non-religious citizens as well). As Schulz observes:

> religion can, in an existential and motivational respect, elevate the operating temperature of a democratic society insofar as it motivates one to act virtuously. This function is very helpful and even crucial for a democratic society. Religions can impart worth and attitudes that support the active participation of the citizen in the democratic process.[125]

In other words, the cultivation of higher virtues by reference to religion enhances the democratic process for all people of all religions and none, through consideration of the welfare of a citizen both as a unique and dignified individual, and as a valuable member of a community.

C. A Principled Framework for Peaceful Coexistence in Liberal Democracies: Pluralism, Diversity, Accommodation

Harrison, Aroney and Parkinson have provided recent contributions to how peaceful coexistence and shared virtues may manifest in modern liberal democracies through pluralism, diversity and accommodation, but without the explicit theological grounding. This book provides that grounding in conjunction with a multi-jurisdictional theoretical analysis to develop a principled framework of a proportionate, reasonable accommodation of difference which facilitates pluralism and diversity. For example, Harrison and Parkinson eschew a simplistic and ultimately false liberal public-private divide in favour of recognising a 'social pluralist' account comprised of multiple pluralities of authority and a 'federation of cultures'.[126] This account entails the accommodation of community identity, in which individuals can 'cultivate a more genuine sense of citizenship' and 'develop an interest in shared goods', contributing to political virtue and the common good through diverse means.[127] Building on this work, Aroney and Parkinson reject the

---

[124] It may be objected that this would not hold true for atheist secularists and atheistic religions who are opposed to Christian domination of public discourse and politics, or even symbolic representation of God in politics. However, if 'God' is broadly conceived as the transcendent, ultimate end of religion (rather than an explicitly Christian or even monotheist representation) then this would be more acceptable to non-Christian religions, and potentially even the atheist secularist who nevertheless acknowledges the existence or the possibility of the existence of transcendence or some 'higher power'. Conceived this way, it may really only alienate a pure dogmatic materialist, and they are relatively rare (certainly much rarer than those who are religious or believe in the transcendent in some form). See the discussion in Deagon, 'Name of God' (n 55).

[125] M Schulz, 'The Existential and Semantic Truth of Religion in Jurgen Habermas's Political Philosophy and the Possibility of a Philosophy of Religion' (2017) 31(3) *Journal of Speculative Philosophy* 457, 459.

[126] J Harrison and P Parkinson, 'Freedom Beyond the Commons: Managing the Tension between Faith and Equality in a Multicultural Society' (2014) 40(2) *Monash University Law Review* 413, 438–42.

[127] ibid 440.

atomistic and individualistic social ontology of liberalism, arguing that a communal social ontology is required which endorses a 'community of communities'
containing 'intermediate associations'.[128] This requires a more open dialogue and
encounter between different communities and the state, with a presumption in
favour of maximum diversity and accommodation of different communities.[129]

As Harrison, Aroney and Parkinson all note,[130] this plural and communal
approach 'is not feasible without generous protection of the more associational
and institutional dimensions of the right to freedom of religion or belief' – or,
in other words, legal protection for the autonomy of religious communities.[131]
Thinkers such as Nicholas Wolterstorff who believe in the need for societal pluralism therefore give much weight to freedoms of religion, association and assembly.
They claim that 'in order for different voices to be heard, there is a need for places
where people can find their voice'.[132] Wolterstorff argues his equal political voice
liberalism is consequently dependent on there being 'moral or religious communities in society that nourish the kind of convictions put forward by citizens and
their political representatives'.[133] The implication is if these communities are not
allowed to self-regulate, their ideas will dissipate and politics will be impoverished
as a result. Consequently all the state should do is facilitate the adaptation and
development of the convictions of moral and religious communities by guaranteeing the freedoms of religion, expression, assembly and association.[134]

The principled framework of a proportionate, reasonable accommodation of
difference, informed by peaceful coexistence which is constituted by the theological virtues such as love, forgiveness, humility and patience, broadens the notion of
politics beyond the political process to the advancement of human development
and the common good, or what might also be termed a harmonious community in
the Pauline sense discussed above. Since religious groups in particular provide the
associational structures (including visionary and didactic resources) for training
in discourse concerning advancement of human development in virtue, and the
common good, it is essential for moral engagement and civic virtue (and democracy itself) that these groups be protected by and from the state.[135] As Ten Napel
argues, 'it is precisely within such faith and other communities that mature visions
of the good life can develop, which simultaneously contribute to the notion of the
common good'.[136] Thus the state must have a role in preserving the freedom of

---

[128] N Aroney and P Parkinson, 'Associational Freedom, Anti-Discrimination Law and the New
Multiculturalism' (2019) 44 *Australasian Journal of Legal Philosophy* 1, 14, 21–23.
[129] ibid 23.
[130] Harrison and Parkinson (n 126) 443–50; Aroney and Parkinson (n 128) 23–28.
[131] Ten Napel, (n 42) 10. See also Deagon, 'Equal Voice Liberalism' (n 35).
[132] Ten Napel, (n 42) 10.
[133] ibid 92–93; N Wolterstorff, *Understanding Liberal Democracy: Essays in Political Philosophy*
(Oxford University Press, 2012) 141.
[134] Ten Napel, (n 42) 93.
[135] ibid 94.
[136] ibid 97.

such groups because of the natural human tendency to form groups with common interests. The 'liberal society is itself sustained and protected by such groups'.[137]

Social divisions, differences and fragmentation along religious and cultural lines can lead to conflict which undermines democratic freedom and equality. But this is only if the state fails to 'recognise and accommodate the various ethnicities, religions, languages and values in a particular country'.[138] Ten Napel proceeds to note that since 'religion is of profound importance to one's identity, from the point of view of cultural liberty, guaranteeing religious freedom in the best possible way is of foremost importance'.[139] A principled framework which entails negotiation, reasonableness and accommodation is needed to preserve freedom and equality in difference. 'Reasonable accommodation' is the way forward, including a 'proportionality principle' to reconcile differing interests, as opposed to an 'inadequately blunt' hierarchy of rights.[140] This can be more concisely expressed as a proportionate, reasonable accommodation of difference.

Indeed, this kind of open, inclusive liberal democracy is a means of making it possible for groups to harmoniously exist despite deep difference, rather than coercing uniformity. No doubt equality legislation is an essential aspect of liberal democracy. But if administered in a coercive fashion without good faith attempts to reconcile this with the autonomy of religious communities so peaceful coexistence is possible, it could burden religious communities unnecessarily and inequitably.[141] However, at the same time, this does not mean religious freedom should be pursued at the expense of other fundamental rights such as equality. Believers must recognise and respect opposing interests in a liberal democracy, especially if these are protected as fundamental rights.[142] It is also worth noting that religion and equality are not necessarily in conflict. Religion is often protected in equality law through explicit anti-discrimination provisions.[143] It is also protected in this way through exemptions which have the effect of preserving equality between religious and non-religious communities where anti-discrimination provisions apply disproportionately or unequally to religious communities.[144] As Trigg emphasises, 'the idea of reasonable accommodation highlights the need to adjust rules when they bear down unfairly on some categories, including religious believers'.[145] That is why a proportionate, reasonable accommodation of difference

---

[137] ibid 123. See also Trigg (n 36) 43–44.

[138] Ten Napel (n 42) 98.

[139] ibid 99.

[140] ibid 126.

[141] ibid 127. See also T Berg, 'What Same-Sex Marriage Claims and Religious Liberty Claims Have in Common' (2010) 5(2) *Northwestern Journal of Law and Social Policy* 206.

[142] Ten Napel (n 42) 127.

[143] See eg L Vickers, *Religious Freedom, Religious Discrimination and the Workplace* (Hart Publishing, 2016), K Alidadi, *Religion, Equality and Employment in Europe: The Case for Reasonable Accommodation* (Hart Publishing, 2017).

[144] See Deagon, 'Equal Voice Liberalism' (n 35) 325–27.

[145] Trigg, (n 36) 124.

which holistically reconciles equality with the autonomy of religious communities for peaceful coexistence is appropriate as a principled framework, rather than unfettered religious autonomy or mandated uniformity – either extreme would tend to intensify tension and conflict.

Similarly, John Inazu expresses a principled framework comprised of a proportionate, reasonable accommodation of difference as a 'confident pluralism' of 'mutual respect and coexistence'.[146] Such confident pluralism 'allows genuine difference to coexist without suppressing or minimising our firmly held convictions. We can embrace pluralism precisely because we are confident in our own beliefs, and in the groups and institutions that sustain them'.[147] 'Confidence without pluralism misses the reality of politics. It suppresses difference, sometimes violently. Pluralism without confidence misses the reality of people. It ignores or trivialises our stark differences for the sake of feigned agreement and false unity'.[148] Confident pluralism 'proposes the future of our democratic experiment requires finding a way to be steadfast in our personal convictions' while also allowing fundamental disagreement; we must have a 'principled commitment' to 'mutual respect' sufficient for peaceful coexistence and flourishing.[149] This framework includes the premises of 'inclusion' (we seek for those within our boundaries to be part of the political community) and 'dissent' (we allow for people to dissent from the norms established by that community).[150] Confident pluralism also includes three 'civic practices': 'tolerance' (people are free to pursue their own beliefs and practices even if we find them morally objectionable), 'humility' (others will find our beliefs and practices morally objectionable and we can't always prove we are right and they are wrong), and 'patience' (restraint, persistence and endurance in our engagements across difference).[151] What this book adds to Inazu's analysis is a more robust theoretical framework which grounds Inazu's constitutional commitments and civic practices – a peaceful coexistence of difference informed by the theological virtues. Indeed, Inazu's notions of patience and humility explicitly reflect theological virtues such as patience and humility discussed earlier.

So broadly speaking, a principled framework of a proportionate, reasonable accommodation of difference in accordance with the theological virtues would advocate for various conclusions in the controversial cases mentioned above, depending on the unique factual circumstances of each case and the parties involved. For example, in *Masterpiece Cakeshop*, the vendor had a consistent policy determining the kind of cakes he would supply, including the rejection of Halloween-themed cakes. He did not reject people on the basis of their identity, but rather because they requested a cake which indicated a message with which

---

[146] Inazu (n 11) 8.
[147] ibid 7.
[148] ibid 6–7.
[149] ibid 8.
[150] ibid 9.
[151] ibid 10–11.

he disagreed. He did so consistently with his religious beliefs and without insult, malice or anger, directing the customer to another vendor which would have been happy to supply the product, loving the customer by ensuring their needs could be met even though he could not meet them himself. A proportionate, reasonable accommodation of difference recognises that differences exist and seeks a peaceful coexistence between those differences. So the vendor can continue serving the community in accordance with their religious beliefs as a function of inclusion, dissent and tolerance, benefiting that community, while consumers can exercise humility, trust, sacrifice and patience, acknowledging the convictions of the vendor (that they are genuine, not identity-based, and not malicious) and obtaining the supplies they need from other vendors as may be necessary.[152]

However, there are two aspects which require further discussion. First, as mentioned earlier, some argue that religious persons engaged in commercial enterprise (religious vendors) should not receive religious freedom protections which allow them to discriminate.[153] However, a proportionate, reasonable accommodation of difference does not simplistically exclude religious vendors from religious freedom protections because they are not part of the category of 'religious communities'. This fails to love our religious neighbours because it fails to exercise humility, trust and patience; such an exclusion does not recognise that running a business for commercial enterprise can be just as religiously meaningful as traditional religious activities.[154] More broadly then, in a proportionate, reasonable accommodation of difference there is no concrete rule upon which purported religious sub-groups of the community (eg vendors, schools, or churches) are included or excluded. There are not necessarily different approaches. Rather, this is more appropriately a question of fact, exercising love of neighbour and the golden rule by allowing the religious group to identify the nature and extent of their religious belief and practice in the circumstances, supported by evidence as needed.[155] This will involve discerning and careful analysis.

Second, this proportionate, reasonable accommodation of difference must also impose limits on the religious vendor. So for example a vendor cannot feign religion in order to attract protection. This would be a lie, inconsistent with the theological virtues of honesty and trust. The business must be genuinely and consistently religious in nature. The vendor also cannot refuse to supply a product on the basis of the identity of the customer. This would be inconsistent with the

---

[152] I discuss the various balancing acts in these circumstances, arguing that this is the best compromise for both parties here: Deagon, 'Religious Schools and Religious Vendors' (n 34).

[153] See Schwartzman et al (n 33); Leiter (n 6).

[154] I expand on this argument with further references in Deagon, 'Religious Schools and Religious Vendors' (n 34).

[155] See A Deagon, 'The "Religious Questions" Doctrine': Addressing (Secular) Judicial Incompetence' (2021) 47(1) *Monash University Law Review* 60–87. I have argued that individuals/vendors should be understood as 'religious bodies' for the purposes of attracting religious associational protections if they are factually similar to other bodies/institutions such as schools in Deagon, 'Religious Schools and Religious Vendors' (n 34).

theological virtues of love, trust, kindness, avoidance of malice, and not undermining the dignity of a fellow human. Instead any refusal must be on the basis of an objection to the nature of the product itself and/or the message it supplies.[156] Even where the vendor is genuinely and consistently religious in nature, and refuses to supply a product due its nature or message being inconsistent with the ethos of the business, in circumstances where a refusal is malicious, or would impose substantive damage or hardship because there is no equivalent product or service reasonably available, a proportionality analysis in accordance with the theological virtues which is attentive to the dignity of both parties (especially selfless sacrifice and kindness) may yield the result that protection should not be granted for that refusal.[157] The book will explore these kinds of issues in the context of the legal frameworks and theoretical perspectives of different jurisdictions, evaluating them in accordance with the theological virtues constituting peaceful coexistence, in the process of developing the specific details of a principled framework for the autonomy of religious communities.

Hence this book develops the principled framework of a proportionate, reasonable accommodation of difference informed by the theological virtues for reconciling the autonomy of religious communities with equality to produce a peaceful coexistence of difference. A proportionate, reasonable accommodation of difference in a liberal democracy involves respecting difference by providing reasonable, proportionate accommodations for religious communities. As a function of loving neighbour as self, it requires facilitating peaceful coexistence in deep difference by enabling the autonomy of religious communities to build shared identity and pursue goods which enrich liberal democracy, while simultaneously prohibiting disproportionate or unjust discrimination to support equality as a function of the intrinsic dignity and good of all people. The capacity of theoretical models and specific legal frameworks to promote peaceful coexistence will therefore be evaluated by considering whether they support freedom and equality in accordance with the theological virtues. For example, I will analyse religious exemptions to anti-discrimination law to work out whether this legal structure, and underlying theory, best promotes peaceful coexistence between religious communities and those who may be discriminated against. What this looks like specifically will turn on the theoretical and legal context of individual jurisdictions.

In other words, the principled framework of a proportionate, reasonable accommodation of difference is distinct from the theological perspective of 'peaceful coexistence' which is composed of the theological virtues and their liberal counterparts – but the principled framework is informed by the theological perspective and related to it. This book uses the theological perspective to evaluate the legal frameworks and theoretical approaches of the different jurisdictions.

---

[156] See Deagon, 'Religious Schools and Religious Vendors' (n 34).
[157] I explore this in Deagon, 'Defining the Interface' (n 52). *cf* J Harrison, 'Towards Re-thinking "Balancing" in the Courts and the Legislature's Role in Protecting Religious Liberty' (2019) 93(9) *Australian Law Journal* 734.

That theological perspective, in conversation with and critique of the different legal frameworks and theoretical approaches, is what will produce the development of the detailed principled framework (legal and theoretical) of a proportionate, reasonable accommodation of difference. The above discussion of a religious vendor is a brief example.

V. Models of the Religion-State Relationship

Part of the theoretical context for each jurisdiction is the model of the religion-state relationship it implements. This book addresses a significant problem because the autonomy of religious communities in a liberal democracy depends on complex and contested conceptions of religious freedom which differ between jurisdictions. Conceptions of religious freedom within a liberal, democratic state can differ depending on the particular political context and constitutional principles arranging that state, often expressed through and influencing particular legislation.[158] The jurisdictional analyses will consider all these aspects to facilitate a comprehensive capture of the differences between jurisdictions with respect to equality and religious freedom. In the midst of such complexity any principled framework for the autonomy of religious communities must preserve freedom and equality (as 'freedom' and 'equality' are understood in those jurisdictions) through a proportionate, reasonable accommodation of difference, facilitating peaceful coexistence among different communities while bearing in mind that this may look different in different jurisdictions.

At the outset one could more rigidly attempt to distinguish between religion-state relations generally and the autonomy of religious communities specifically. However, the autonomy of religious communities exists within the context of the relationship between religion and the state.[159] For the purposes of this book I will adopt the theoretical categorisation of the models of the religion-state relationship which are well established and cited in the literature: theocracy, establishment, neutrality, pluralism, soft secularism and hard secularism.[160] To briefly define these, 'Theocracy' assumes supreme rule by religion, where the religious leaders are also the political leaders and seek to enforce religious doctrine as the law of the land. 'Establishment' is where the state singles out a religion for special recognition and support, while also exerting some influence over the affairs of that religion. State and religion therefore exist in a symbiotic relationship for mutual advantage and with mutual obligations (the state officially endorses and materially supports the religion, and the religion provides the state with the aura of legitimacy

---

[158] See Barker (n 17) 13–42.
[159] See Robbers (n 5).
[160] See eg Durham and Scharffs (n 45); Ahdar and Leigh (n 2); Monsma and Soper (n 45); Deagon, 'Secularism as a Religion' (n 55); Barker (n 17).

and a unifying sense of purpose). 'Neutrality' (including formal and substantive versions) entails that a state essentially ignores religion and treats religious communities exactly the same as other communities – no better and no worse. More substantive versions also take the consequences of a 'religion-blind' policy into account, minimising state interference with religion and leaving religion, as much as possible, as a purely private matter. 'Pluralism' (including principled and pragmatic approaches) recognises the public dimension of religion and its importance to religious communities and the state as a whole, and therefore facilitates the state working together with different religions for the common good, but in a non-preferential and non-discriminatory way (that is, in a way which does not privilege any one religion above others).[161]

Finally, secularism involves at least an institutional separation between church and state, and between religious and political power. In soft secularism the state does not explicitly regulate private religion and provides legal protections for freedom of religion, but the state also does not support religion in any way. In hard secularist regimes the state does not protect freedom of religion; such a state expressly promotes atheism and demands that individuals and social institutions be anti-religious.[162] Bearing in mind these theoretical models, all the dimensions of theoretical perspectives and legal frameworks in different jurisdictions need to be examined to tease out what it means for any individual jurisdiction to be a liberal democracy which reconciles the autonomy of religious communities with equality. The legal framework of every jurisdiction is necessarily undergirded by a theoretical model of some kind, even if it is implicit or otherwise unacknowledged. For example, pragmatism is itself a theoretical model. Barker argues that Australia's general approach to religion and state is a 'pragmatic pluralism'.[163] Conversely, the US arguably has a more principled soft secularism approach, while the UK arguably has a principled legal establishment which pragmatically has become weaker.[164] Speaking for the moment at a highly abstract level, these models and distinct constitutional principles may translate into different legal frameworks for the autonomy of religious communities. A pragmatically pluralist approach will provide a considerable level of autonomy for religious communities, but without a principled basis this may decrease for pragmatic reasons as the scope of anti-discrimination laws increase. A soft secularist approach provides some protection for the autonomy of religious communities that falls short of state support, but is not likely to provide a shield from the operation of facially neutral, generally applicable laws such as anti-discrimination laws. An establishment approach might provide robust autonomy for the 'established' religious community, limiting the scope of anti-discrimination law, but this may impact on the equal treatment of other religious communities. Parts II and III of the book will analyse these issues

---

[161] See eg Ahdar and Leigh (n 2) 87–124.
[162] See eg Deagon, 'Secularism as a Religion' (n 55) 36.
[163] Barker (n 17) 325.
[164] See Barker (n 17) 13–42. These claims will be further explored in Part III of the book.

in detail, identifying problems and issues using the standard of peaceful coexistence in the process of articulating a principled framework for the autonomy of religious communities which is a proportionate, reasonable accommodation of difference.

VI. Structure of the Book

Building on my earlier work examining religious freedom in legal contexts in both Australia and the US,[165] Part II of the book examines the legal approaches to the autonomy of religious communities in three jurisdictions and explores the extent to which these different approaches promote a peaceful coexistence of difference. This involves considering the legal framework of constitutional principles and arrangements, legislation and case law relating to the autonomy of religious communities in each jurisdiction, elucidating the legal infrastructure which enables religious communities to conduct their affairs in accordance with their religion, and assessing the extent to which this infrastructure promotes peaceful coexistence using the fully developed theological perspective explained above. Australia, the US and UK (with a focus on England) have been chosen as liberal democracies similar to each other, yet all with different theoretical approaches as currently understood. The US and England have also historically influenced Australian law and politics, unlike other alternatives such as Canada and New Zealand. Choosing three similar jurisdictions enables the analysis to have more explanatory power, keeping the general liberal framework constant, and allowing a detailed evaluation of the theoretical and legal variables in each jurisdiction. This produces greater insights which we can learn from. Only three jurisdictions are considered because this provides enough scope for meaningful analysis but ensures the book retains focus.

The federal and constitutional structures of the US and Australia provide complexity here, because the legislative powers of the national governments are limited by a written constitution and the states have some legislative power. In contrast the unitary structure of England and its unwritten constitution means the legislative power of the national parliament is significant. Any comprehensive analysis of a federalist jurisdiction would require some consideration of the state contexts, and this would provide a useful point of contrast between federalist and unitary structures in the context of considering whether and how this affects the peaceful coexistence of religious and other communities.[166] However, with 50 states in the US, this could quickly become unwieldy. Thus, in the legal context, the book analyses legislation and cases from each jurisdiction, but will for reasons

---

[165] See Deagon, 'Defining the Interface' (n 52); Deagon, 'Liberal Secularism and Religious Freedom' (n 8); Deagon, 'Liberal Assumptions' (n 8); Deagon, 'Religious Schools and Religious Vendors' (n 34).

[166] See N Aroney, *The Constitution of a Federal Commonwealth* (Cambridge University Press, 2009).

of feasibility focus on legal materials at the national level only. With the exception of English law which incorporates aspects of the European Convention of Human Rights, generally the book will also only consider domestic law, and not engage in detail with human rights protections under international or European law.

Chapter one evaluates the legal doctrine surrounding section 116 of the Australian Constitution and the religious exemptions in Commonwealth legislation such as the Sex Discrimination Act to determine if their structure and content promotes a peaceful coexistence between religious and other communities such as the LGBT community, to the extent that these communities are distinct. The chapter will also consider the proposed (at the time of writing) Religious Discrimination Act in this context. It argues that to preserve peaceful coexistence, section 116 should be given an interpretation which enables the beneficial interaction of religion and government, and that the religious exemptions in the Sex Discrimination Act should be removed and replaced with positive associational rights. Chapter two evaluates the case law which stems from the First Amendment of the Constitution of the United States of America, focusing on the free exercise and establishment clauses to determine if their content promotes a peaceful coexistence between religious and other communities. It will also consider the federal Religious Freedom Restoration Act, the federal Religious Land Use and Institutionalised Persons Act, and the religious exemptions in Title VII of the federal Civil Rights Act in this context. It argues that the First Amendment should also be given an interpretation which enables the beneficial interaction of religion and government, acknowledging the public importance of religion while also providing some limitations for the autonomy of religious communities to protect both freedom and equality. Chapter three considers the UK with a focus on English law. In the context of England's unique position as a unitary state with an established religion, this chapter evaluates the legislation and case law relating to the autonomy of religious communities and potential tensions with equality under the Human Rights Act and the Equality Act to determine if their content promotes a peaceful coexistence of difference, including any relevant applications of ECtHR jurisprudence. It argues that the ECtHR should explicitly articulate a robust jurisprudence for the autonomy of religious communities, and this should be incorporated into English law to provide positive associational rights for religious groups alongside equality protections.

Part III of the book explores the theoretical approach to the autonomy of religious communities in each jurisdiction with respect to promoting a peaceful coexistence of difference. It will identify underlying implicit philosophical and theological presuppositions and conceptualisations (for example Australia's pragmatic pluralism mentioned above), and evaluate these by determining whether and how they promote peaceful coexistence using the fully developed theological perspective explained above. It does this by drawing on Part II and the theoretical models of the religion-state relationship outlined above, conceptually identifying which theoretical perspective best captures the legal framework for the autonomy of religious communities in that jurisdiction. This combination of legal framework and theoretical perspective constitutes a jurisdiction's theoretical approach.

Though a jurisdiction may incorporate aspects of multiple approaches and may not be entirely coherent, the book will isolate and explore particular approaches by examining specific laws in conjunction with the general legal framework. The book will then evaluate each theoretical approach by determining whether and how they promote peaceful coexistence. This evaluation will involve consideration of how they reconcile freedom and equality through producing a proportionate, reasonable accommodation of difference in accordance with the theological virtues described above, noting the strengths and weaknesses of each theoretical approach in this context.

Chapter four argues that mild establishment, rather than pragmatic pluralism, best captures Australia's legal framework for the autonomy of religious communities and best protects the peaceful coexistence of difference. Following chapter one, this indicates positive associational rights for religious organisations in conjunction with existing equality protections is a reasonable accommodation which best promotes the peaceful coexistence of difference. Chapter five rejects secularism as the legal framework for the autonomy of religious communities in the US, arguing that pluralism is the historical and jurisprudential background to the First Amendment and preserves social peace. Chapter six defends English substantive establishment as capturing England's legal framework for the autonomy of religious communities, arguing that it also preserves peaceful coexistence. English law may then incorporate protections for the autonomy of religious communities and equality which acknowledge the mutual and intrinsic good of both goals.

The final part, developing a principled framework, draws upon the theological analysis in Parts II and III to articulate a new theoretical approach (theoretical perspective and legal framework) for the autonomy of religious communities which preserves a peaceful coexistence of difference: a reasonable accommodation of difference. This new approach draws from the strengths and mitigates the weaknesses of the different theoretical approaches considered in Parts II and III to best promote peaceful coexistence of religious communities in a liberal democratic context committed to both religious freedom and equality. The principled framework is flexible to account for religious diversity, acknowledges the intrinsic dignity and value of all people from all kinds of communities, and recognises the mutual public benefit of both religious freedom and equality as enabling the diverse pursuit of the common good. As such, both religious freedom and equality support each other and ought to be protected together, rather than having one goal dominate or marginalise the other. The book concludes by explaining how the development of this new theoretical approach over the course of this work addresses the tensions and issues identified in the Introduction by reconciling freedom and discrimination. The chapter delineates a set of practical principles, as indicated above, to help inform policy and legislation for the autonomy of religious communities without compromising equality to support the peaceful coexistence of difference and a more harmonious society.

PART II

Legal Frameworks

1

Australia

I. Introduction

Part II of this book examines the legal approaches to the autonomy of religious communities in Australia, the US, and the UK (focusing on England), exploring the extent to which these different approaches promote a peaceful coexistence of difference in accordance with the theological virtues. This involves considering the legal framework of constitutional principles and arrangements, legislation and case law relating to the autonomy of religious communities in each jurisdiction, elucidating the legal infrastructure which enables religious communities to conduct their affairs in accordance with their religion, and assessing the extent to which this infrastructure promotes peaceful coexistence using the fully developed theological perspective explained in the Introduction. In terms of scope, this book will focus on legal materials at the national level only. Part II will not engage with the broader theoretical principles undergirding religious autonomy and its interaction with equality in detail. That will be covered in Part III. This part focuses exclusively on analysing the relevant law in each jurisdiction.

This chapter focuses on Australia, evaluating the relevant Constitutional and Commonwealth law to determine if their structure and content promotes a peaceful coexistence between religious and other communities, to the extent that such communities are distinct. The chapter will also consider the proposed Religious Discrimination Bills in the same way. Freedom of religion holds a place of high value in Australian law. The Constitution contains an acknowledgement of God and limits the power of the Commonwealth to curtail free exercise of religion. Although Australians enjoy a high degree of religious freedom, increasing secularisation and political pressures are challenging this, especially in the area of tension between the autonomy of religious communities and equality (eg the ability of religious schools to discriminate in the employment of teachers). Currently this ability is provided through exemptions to anti-discrimination law.[1] The challenge is exacerbated by the fact that the Australian legal framework for the autonomy of religious communities is poor; it allows significant scope for governmental

---

[1] N Aroney and B Saunders, 'Freedom of Religion in Australia' in M Groves, D Meagher and J Boughey (eds), *The Legal Protection of Rights in Australia* (Hart Publishing, 2019).

and social interference, and provides little informed guidance to the judiciary when they may need to resolve conflicts between freedom of religion and other interests.[2] Hobbs and Williams observe that 'Australian law provides only ad hoc and incomplete protection for freedom of religion'.[3] Protection is 'inadequate' and 'limited' at the Commonwealth level.[4] Multiple national reviews and inquiries over the past five years have raised the urgent issue of how to reconcile the autonomy of religious communities with anti-discrimination law.[5] There is a need to better protect religious freedom but there is no clarity or consensus on how Australia can effectively promote peaceful coexistence in this context when religious freedom may entail discrimination.

This chapter elucidates the legal infrastructure which governs the autonomy of religious communities in Australia, and evaluates this infrastructure to determine the extent to which it promotes a peaceful coexistence of difference in accordance with the theological virtues. It begins by examining the associational elements of the freedom of religion provision (section 116). Moving on to existing Commonwealth legislation, the chapter focuses on outlining the legal effect of the exemptions for religious bodies and religious educational institutions in the Sex Discrimination Act, while also considering proposed but ultimately unsuccessful amendments to these exemptions in the wake of recommendations by the Ruddock Review. The chapter also briefly notes minor supporting Commonwealth legislation before examining how Commonwealth legislation interacts with section 116 to support the autonomy of religious communities in Australia. Finally, the chapter explains the proposed Religious Discrimination Bills (also the implementation of a recommendation by the Ruddock Review) and their potential effect on the autonomy of religious communities in Australia.

The chapter subsequently evaluates the legal infrastructure outlined above using peaceful coexistence and the theological virtues as a standard. It argues that section 116 has the capability to protect the autonomy of religious communities but only in a limited and partial way which does not promote peaceful coexistence. The proposed Religious Discrimination Bills assist in this capacity, providing positive rights for religious communities to order their affairs so they can peacefully coexist alongside other communities. Most importantly, the exemptions in the Sex Discrimination Act provide significant protection for the autonomy of religious communities, but not in a way that promotes peaceful coexistence. The exemptions are problematic because they divide religious communities from those

---

[2] H Hobbs and G Williams, 'Protecting Religious Freedom in a Human Rights Act' (2019) 93(9) *Australian Law Journal* 721, 721–22.

[3] Hobbs and Williams (n 2) 721.

[4] ibid 726. See generally C Evans, *Legal Protection of Religious Freedom in Australia* (Federation Press, 2012).

[5] As detailed in the most recent 'Religious Freedom Review' conducted in 2018, Department of Prime Minister and Cabinet, accessed 19 February 2019, https://pmc.gov.au/domestic-policy/religious-freedom-review ('Ruddock Review').

who may be discriminated against, giving the impression of an unconstrained and exceptional freedom to discriminate. Fundamentally, this chapter suggests that Australia's legal framework promotes peaceful coexistence of difference in accordance with the theological virtues to a limited extent, but there are some areas which require change – in particular, the exemptions in the Sex Discrimination Act need to be reframed. The nature of this reconceptualisation and practical suggestions (such as using the language of positive associational rights) will be articulated through Parts III and IV of the book.

II. The Australian Constitution

A. Section 116: Freedom of Religion

Section 116 of the Australian Constitution provides:

> The Commonwealth shall not make any law for establishing any religion, or for imposing any religious observance, or for prohibiting the free exercise of any religion, and no religious test shall be required as a qualification for any office or public trust under the Commonwealth.[6]

Section 116 is subject to a number of limitations.[7] First, section 116 only applies to laws (including laws which authorise executive acts amounting to a breach) rather than general executive or personal action.[8] This means section 116 is not an individual right but a limit on legislative power.[9] Second, section 116 only applies to Commonwealth laws and does not apply to the states.[10] Finally, the High Court of Australia has given section 116 a very conservative and limited interpretation, such that the boundaries of free exercise and issues of discrimination have largely been left to political and democratic processes. The Court has been generous and inclusive in defining religion, but very narrow in defining the scope of religious freedom.[11]

---

[6] For a recent detailed examination of the provision, see L Beck, *Religious Freedom and the Australian Constitution: Origins and Future* (Routledge, 2018).

[7] See N Aroney, 'Freedom of Religion as an Associational Right' (2014) 33 *University of Queensland Law Journal* 153, 155–56; Hobbs and Williams (n 2) 725.

[8] *Minister for Immigration and Ethnic Affairs v Lebanese Moslem Association* (1987) 17 FCR 373.

[9] *Attorney-General (Vic); Ex rel Black v Commonwealth (DOGS Case)* (1981) 146 CLR 559, 605 (Stephen J).

[10] *Grace Bible Church v Reedman* (1984) 36 SASR 376.

[11] See in particular *Krygger v Williams* (1912) 15 CLR 366, 369; *Adelaide Company of Jehovah's Witnesses Inc v Commonwealth* (1943) 67 CLR 116, 149–50; *Church of the New Faith v Commissioner of Pay-Roll Tax (Vic)* (1983) 154 CLR 120, 135–36. See also C Evans, 'Religion as Politics not Law: the Religion Clauses in the Australian Constitution' (2008) 36(3) *Religion, State and Society* 283, 284. Mortensen also observes the very narrow interpretation given to the free exercise clause, though he acknowledges that questions over s 116's applicability to the Territories and the fact that it only applies to Commonwealth legislation have also contributed to its restricted operation. See R Mortensen,

In regard to the scope of religious freedom, Chief Justice Latham in the *Jehovah's Witnesses* case argues that since the 'free exercise' of religion is protected, this includes but extends beyond religious belief or the mere holding of religious opinion; the protection 'from the operation of any Commonwealth laws' covers 'acts which are done in the exercise of religion' or 'acts done in pursuance of religious belief as part of religion'.[12] However, subsequent cases noted these acts must be religious conduct, or 'conduct in which a person engages in giving effect to his [sic] faith in the supernatural'.[13] Religious conduct protected by section 116 extends to 'faith and worship, to the teaching and propagation of religion, and to the practices and observances of religion'.[14] This is a narrow definition which restricts 'free exercise' to that conduct which is overtly religious and normally considered private in nature, such as prayer and church attendance.

In the first case considering the free exercise clause, the High Court glibly dismissed a claim that Commonwealth legislation infringed free exercise of religion by compelling a person who was a pacifist for religious reasons to engage in military training. According to Griffith CJ in the 1912 case of *Krygger v Williams*, section 116 protects religious opinion or the private holding of faith, and also protects 'the practice of religion – the doing of acts which are done in the practice of religion' (which was followed by Latham CJ in *Jehovah's Witnesses*, as above).[15]

'The Unfinished Experiment: A Report on Religious Freedom in Australia' (2007) 21 *Emory International Law Review* 167, 170–71. The vast majority of eminent scholars in the field continue to hold this view: see eg Beck, *Religious Freedom* (n 6); A Deagon, 'Defining the Interface of Freedom and Discrimination: Exercising Religion, Democracy and Same-Sex Marriage' (2017) 20 *International Trade and Business Law Review* 239; N Aroney and P Taylor, 'The Politics of Freedom of Religion in Australia: Can International Human Rights Standards point the way forward?' (2020) 47(1) *University of Western Australia Law Review* 42, 45; BB Saunders and D Meagher, 'Taking Seriously the Free Exercise of Religion under the Australian Constitution' (2021) 43(3) *Sydney Law Review* 287–314.

[12] *Adelaide Company of Jehovah's Witnesses Inc v Commonwealth* (1943) 67 CLR 116, 124–25. So the free exercise clause likely protects religious speech which is expressed as part of a religious act. For further discussion and questions regarding the current applicability of this 'action-belief dichotomy', see G Moens, 'Action-Belief Dichotomy and Freedom of Religion' (1989) 12 *Sydney Law Review* 195. The implied freedom of political communication, which is a protection for political communication implied from the constitutional requirement for freely informed representative government, also protects religious communication which has relevance to political matters. See *Brown v Tasmania* (2017) 261 CLR 328; *Attorney-General (SA) v Corporation of the City of Adelaide* (2013) 249 CLR 1. For this reason, it is likely the free exercise clause and the implied freedom of political communication simultaneously operate to protect the expression of religious speech or opinion with respect to political matters. See eg N Aroney, 'The Constitutional (In)Validity of Religious Vilification Laws: Implications for their Interpretation' (2006) 34 *Federal Law Review* 287, 297–303; A Zimmermann, 'The Unconstitutionality of Religious Vilification Laws in Australia: Why Religious Vilification Laws Are Contrary to the Implied Freedom of Political Communication Affirmed in the Australian Constitution' (2013) *Brigham Young University Law Review* 457, 493–503. However, the High Court has not recognised an independent implied freedom of association, stating that such a freedom would only exist as a corollary of the implied freedom of political communication: *Wainohu v New South Wales* (2011) 243 CLR 181 [212], [72], [186].

[13] *Church of the New Faith v Commissioner of Pay-Roll Tax (Vic)* (1983) 154 CLR 120, 136.

[14] ibid 135–36.

[15] (1912) 15 CLR 366, 369.

However, 'to require a man to do a thing which has nothing at all to do with religion is not prohibiting him from a free exercise of religion'.[16] On this view, again, section 116 protects private, overtly religious conduct such as prayer or attending church, but not the doing of public/political acts which are ostensibly separate from religious beliefs.[17] Finally, the last time the High Court considered the free exercise clause was the 1997 case of *Kruger v Commonwealth*.[18] In *Kruger*, the plaintiffs argued that a Northern Territory ordinance which authorised the forced removal of Indigenous children from their tribal culture and heritage was invalid as a law prohibiting the free exercise of religion. The majority held that the impugned law did not mention the term 'religion' and was not 'for' the purpose of prohibiting the free exercise of religion in its terms, and so the law was upheld. Only laws could breach section 116, not the administration of laws.[19] Chief Justice Brennan, Gummow and McHugh JJ (in separate majority judgments) reinforced the traditional narrow approach, stating that to be invalid under section 116 the impugned law 'must have the purpose of achieving an object which s 116 forbids', and upholding the law on the basis that 'no conduct of a religious nature was proscribed or sought to be regulated in any way'.[20]

Furthermore, not every interference with religion is a breach of section 116, but only those which 'unduly infringe' upon religious freedom.[21] At a minimum, the High Court has stated that the narrowest limitations on free exercise of religion are appropriate – that required for the 'maintenance of civil government' or 'the continued existence of the community'.[22] Thus the current High Court approach is narrow and focused on the explicit purpose of the legislation: if the impugned law does not restrict free exercise of religion as part of its purpose, it will be valid.[23] In *Church of the New Faith*, Mason ACJ and Brennan J even go so far as to say that 'general laws to preserve and protect society are not defeated by a plea of religious obligation to breach them'.[24]

Despite this narrow interpretation of religious freedom, the definition of religion has been interpreted generously.[25] According to the High Court, the

---

[16] ibid.

[17] See A Deagon, 'Liberal Assumptions in Section 116 Cases and Implications for Religious Freedom' (2018) 46(1) *Federal Law Review* 113–36.

[18] (1997) 190 CLR 1.

[19] Evans, 'Religion as Politics not Law' (n 11) 296.

[20] *Kruger* (1997) 190 CLR 1, 40, 161.

[21] *Jehovah's Witnesses* (1943) 67 CLR 116.

[22] ibid 126, 131, 155.

[23] The result is foreseen by Moens: see G Moens, 'Church and state relations in Australia and the United States: The purpose and effect approaches and the neutrality principle' (1996) 4 *Brigham Young University Law Review*, 788–89, 809–10. For a more recent critique see L Beck, 'The Case Against Improper Purpose as the Touchstone for Invalidity under Section 116 of the Australian Constitution' (2016) 44(3) *Federal Law Review* 505.

[24] *Church of the New Faith v Commissioner of Pay-Roll Tax (Vic)* (1983) 154 CLR 120, 136.

[25] For a detailed overview see A Deagon, 'Towards a Constitutional Definition of Religion: Challenges and Prospects' in P Babie, N Rochow and B Scharffs (eds), *Freedom of Religion or Belief: Creating the Constitutional Space for Fundamental Freedoms* (Edward Elgar, 2020).

definition of religion in the Australian constitutional context extends beyond monotheistic or even theistic religions, and includes belief in a supernatural thing or principle, where supernatural means that which is beyond perception by the five natural senses. The category of religion is not closed.[26] In the seminal *Jehovah's Witnesses* case, Latham CJ outlined the broad and dynamic nature of what constitutes religion, and the consequent reluctance of the High Court to impose a precise definition.[27] He stated that religion may include a set of beliefs, code of conduct, or some kind of ritual observance. It is not for the High Court to 'disqualify certain beliefs as incapable of being religious in character'.[28] However, in the more recent *Church of the New Faith* ('Scientology') case, Mason ACJ and Brennan J clarified this general position and articulated more specific indicia to be referenced in the determination of whether particular conduct and/or beliefs is classified as religion:

> We would therefore hold that, for the purposes of the law, the criteria of religion are twofold: first, belief in a supernatural Being, Thing or Principle; and second, the acceptance of canons of conduct in order to give effect to that belief.[29]

Justices Wilson and Deane stated similar principles, though they provided more detailed indicia or guidelines:

> One of the more important indicia of 'a religion' is that the particular collection of ideas and/or practices involves belief in the supernatural, that is to say, belief that reality extends beyond that which is capable of perception by the senses. If that be absent, it is unlikely that one has 'a religion'. Another is that the ideas relate to man's nature and place in the universe and his relation to things supernatural. A third is that the ideas are accepted by adherents as requiring or encouraging them to observe particular standards or codes of conduct or to participate in specific practices having supernatural significance. A fourth is that, however loosely knit and varying in beliefs and practices adherents may be, they constitute an identifiable group or identifiable groups. A fifth, and perhaps more controversial, indicium is that the adherents themselves see the collection of ideas and/or practices as constituting a religion.[30]

On this basis the High Court concluded 'Scientology' is a religion for constitutional purposes. Hence, the definition of religion in Australia is broad and dynamic; a definition has not been explicitly prescribed by the High Court and will be largely dependent on the flexible application of the indicia in each unique circumstance. Most significantly for the purposes of this book, all four justices were 'explicit about the group character of religion' in the sense that protection for freedom of religion in Australia extends to the autonomy of religious communities.[31]

---

[26] L Beck, 'Clear and Emphatic: The Separation of Church and State Under the Australian Constitution' (2008) 27(2) *University of Tasmania Law Review* 161, 164–67.

[27] *Adelaide Company of Jehovah's Witnesses Inc v Commonwealth* (1943) 67 CLR 116.

[28] ibid 123–24.

[29] *Church of the New Faith v Commissioner of Pay-Roll Tax (Vic)* (1983) 154 CLR 120, 137.

[30] ibid 173–74.

[31] Aroney, 'Freedom of Religion' (n 7) 163.

Aroney argues that section 116 protects religious freedom as an associational right as a function of its text, clear acknowledgement in the case law, and the nature of Australian religious practice as communal in the late nineteenth century. This means section 116 protects religious organisations and communities.[32] The text of section 116 operates as a limit on Commonwealth power, which means persons (whether natural or artificial – including corporations and associations) are protected from laws which breach section 116. For example, if the free exercise of any religion includes 'conducting religious services, disseminating religious teachings, determining religious doctrines, establishing standards of religious conduct, identifying conditions of membership, appointing officers, ordaining religious leaders and engaging employees,' these practices are all protected regardless of whether they are engaged in by individuals or associations.[33]

In *Jehovah's Witnesses*, the impugned regulations prohibited the advocacy of doctrines which were prejudicial to the prosecution of the war in which the Commonwealth was engaged. It provided for the dissolution of associations propagating such doctrines and vested their property in the Commonwealth. The Jehovah's Witnesses challenged the constitutional validity of these regulations. The Court found that the regulations exceeded the purported head of power and were therefore invalid, but, following the narrow approach in *Krygger*, they held that the regulations did not breach section 116 because freedom of religion is not absolute.[34] This means they did not directly decide whether religious groups are protected by section 116, though a majority held that the Witnesses were competent to bring the action as an incorporated organisation – which implies the majority assumed the protection granted to section 116 extends to groups.[35]

Finally, in *Kruger* as discussed above, despite the existence of legislation which in effect prevented Indigenous Australians from practicing their culture and values in a community which formed their religion, there was no breach of section 116. Kerruish notes that the *Kruger* case concerns 'forcible removal of children from their families and culture on such a scale as to have the tendency to destroy the culture and cause serious harm to its bearers'.[36] The plaintiffs, five of whom were among the children taken and the sixth whose mother was taken, also framed this in terms of a law prohibiting the free exercise of religion, particularly given the importance of land, culture and community to the religious practice of Indigenous Australians. However, only Gaudron J was prepared to assume that the empowering legislation 'prevented certain people from freely exercising their aboriginal

---

[32] ibid 154–55. See 169–71, 176–78 for the history.

[33] ibid 156–57.

[34] *Jehovah's Witnesses* (1943) 67 CLR 116, 149–50.

[35] Aroney, 'Freedom of Religion' (n 7) 159–61, 166. This is further reflected in *Minister for Immigration & Ethnic Affairs v Lebanese Moslem Association* (1987) 17 FCR 373, where it was 'taken for granted' that the LMA could bring the action as a group to protect its right to select its religious leaders.

[36] V Kerruish, 'Responding to *Kruger*: The Constitutionality of Genocide' (1998) 11(1) *Australian Feminist Law Journal* 65, 67–8.

religious practices in association with other members of their community.[37] The majority rejected this on the basis that the legislation did not explicitly or purposefully target the free exercise of religion, even if they acknowledged (as Gummow J did) that a potential effect of the legislation was to deny 'instruction in the religious beliefs of their community.[38] However, these statements still clearly support the view that the religious practices protected by section 116 may be 'pervasively communal.[39]

This chapter has so far considered only the 'free exercise' clause. However, the 'establishment' clause has actually offered some protection through the High Court's narrow interpretation of 'establish', with the effect that the Commonwealth can fund religious bodies for secular purposes in a non-discriminatory way. The major case dealing with the question of establishment is *Attorney-General (Vic); Ex rel Black v Commonwealth*, or the 'Defence of Government Schools' (*DOGS*) case.[40] Commonwealth legislation which provided for grants to the States for distribution amongst denominational schools was challenged on the grounds that they amounted to an establishment of religion. However, the High Court held that section 116 is not a strict separation of church and state like in the US. The Commonwealth can support religion in a non-discriminatory and non-preferential way. The limit only stops a law for establishing any religion.

The High Court took a narrow view of what it means to 'establish any religion', stating that this clause of section 116 prohibits the 'statutory recognition of a religion as a national institution' or a 'state church', and a 'deliberate selection of one to be preferred before others' which creates a 'reciprocal relationship imposing rights and duties on both parties'.[41] This may include the 'entrenchment of a religion as a feature of and identified with the body politic', and the 'identification of the religion with a civil authority so as to involve the citizen and the Commonwealth in the observance and maintenance of it'.[42] Therefore the legislation was constitutional because the grants law was not a law which was specifically designed to establish a religion. Rather, it was specifically designed to improve the education in church related schools, which has the effect of supporting religious schools to continue operating autonomously as a community. Aroney thus argues the 'core meaning' of establishment is 'institutional' – the political preference or favouring of a particular group.[43] Hence, though it sometimes has not been borne out in

---

[37] S Joseph, '*Kruger v Commonwealth*: Constitutional Rights and Stolen Generations' (1998) 24 *Monash University Law Review* 486, 496.

[38] *Kruger* (1997) 190 CLR 1, 161.

[39] Aroney, 'Freedom of Religion' (n 7) 167.

[40] (1981) 146 CLR 559.

[41] ibid 653 (Wilson J).

[42] *DOGS* (1981) 146 CLR 559, 582 (Barwick CJ), 604 (Gibbs J), 612 (Mason J), 653 (Wilson J).

[43] Aroney, 'Freedom of Religion' (n 7) 164–65.

the results of the cases, as a matter of principle section 116 provides some protection for the autonomy of religious communities – at least from the operation of Commonwealth laws.

III. Commonwealth Legislation

A. Sex Discrimination Act

The Commonwealth anti-discrimination legislation considered will be the Sex Discrimination Act 1984 (Cth) ('the Act'). Section 5A of the Act, for example, states that discrimination occurs on the ground of sexual orientation where, in equal circumstances, the aggrieved person is treated less favourably than a person of a different sexual orientation by reason of the aggrieved person's sexual orientation. Sections 5 to 7A of the Act provide an equivalent provision for discrimination on other grounds. Sections 14 to 27 of the Act provide for instances of discrimination in specific areas. For example, section 14(1) of the Act states 'it is unlawful for an employer to discriminate against a person on the ground of the person's … sexual orientation' in 'determining who should be offered employment or in the terms and conditions on which employment is offered', or 'by dismissing the employee'. Section 22(1) of the Act provides that 'it is unlawful for a person who, whether for payment or not, provides goods or services, or makes facilities available, to discriminate against another person on the ground of the other person's … sexual orientation' by 'refusing to provide the other person with those goods or services or to make those facilities available to the other person'.

Sections 14 and 16 of the Act provide that it is not lawful to discriminate against employers or contract workers on the basis of protected attributes (such as sex, sexual orientation, gender identity, pregnancy, and so on) in the context of employment. Section 21 of the Act provides that it is not lawful to discriminate in the provision of education on the basis of these attributes. Sections 37 and 38 of the Act provide exemptions for religious bodies and educational institutions established for religious purposes. Section 37(1) states that none of the sections outlined above affect the ordination, appointment, training or selection of members of any religious order, or any other act or practice of a body established for religious purposes which conforms to the doctrines of that religion or is necessary to avoid injury to the religious susceptibilities of adherents of that religion. This effectively means any religious body or community has the autonomy to select, appoint and train a person without constraint from anti-discrimination law, which is a robust protection for the autonomy of a religious community. Aged care is explicitly excluded from exemption on the basis that aged care facilities should not be able to deny services to older same-sex couples. This qualification only applies in the context of service provision, not employment – so aged care facilities remain free to make employment decisions on the basis of their religious ethos, again reinforcing the autonomy of this religious community.[44]

The more contentious religious exemptions are contained in section 38 of the Act:

(1)   Nothing in paragraph 14(1)(a) or (b) or 14(2)(c) renders it unlawful for a person to discriminate against another person on the ground of the other person's sex, sexual orientation, gender identity, marital or relationship status or pregnancy in connection with employment as a member of the staff of an educational institution that is conducted in accordance with the doctrines, tenets, beliefs or teachings of a particular religion or creed, if the first-mentioned person so discriminates in good faith in order to avoid injury to the religious susceptibilities of adherents of that religion or creed.

(2)   Nothing in paragraph 16(b) renders it unlawful for a person to discriminate against another person on the ground of the other person's sex, sexual orientation, gender identity, marital or relationship status or pregnancy in connection with a position as a contract worker that involves the doing of work in an educational institution that is conducted in accordance with the doctrines, tenets, beliefs or teachings of a particular religion or creed, if the first-mentioned person so discriminates in good faith in order to avoid injury to the religious susceptibilities of adherents of that religion or creed.

(3)   Nothing in section 21 renders it unlawful for a person to discriminate against another person on the ground of the other person's sexual orientation, gender identity, marital or relationship status or pregnancy in connection with the provision of education or training by an educational institution that is conducted in accordance with the doctrines, tenets, beliefs or teachings of a particular religion or creed, if the first-mentioned person so discriminates in good faith in order to avoid injury to the religious susceptibilities of adherents of that religion or creed.

Similar to section 37, section 38(1) specifies that nothing in the relevant paragraphs of section 14 renders it unlawful for a person to discriminate on the ground of sexual orientation in connection with employment as a member of an education institution conducted in accordance with the doctrines of a particular religion. Section 14 does not apply if the discrimination occurs in good faith and is necessary to avoid injury to the religious susceptibilities of adherents of that religion. Essentially, this means religious schools can 'discriminate' on the basis of any sex-related attribute (or put positively, select and regulate) for their communities in order to uphold the religious ethos of that school. Neither section 37 nor section 38 provide any protection for religious individuals or religious vendors.

The contention regarding religious freedom and discrimination in the schools context only makes sense if we take into account the 2017 same-sex marriage

---

[44] S Moulds, 'Drawing the Boundaries: The Scope of the Religious Bodies Exemptions in Australian Anti-Discrimination Law and Implications for Reform' (2020) 47(1) *University of Western Australia Law Review* 112, 131.

debate.[45] During that debate religious freedom was raised as an issue. Marriage has traditionally been understood as a religious institution with particular immutable characteristics, including that it is by definition only between a man and a woman.[46] Religious freedom advocates were concerned about the freedom of religious ministers and religious associations (including schools) to continue teaching this traditional understanding of marriage if the legal definition were to be altered to recognise same-sex marriage.[47] When the law recognising same-sex marriage was being considered in Parliament, many amendments to strengthen religious freedom protections in the wake of the change were voted down. To placate those concerned, then Prime Minister Malcolm Turnbull ordered a review into whether the human right to freedom of religion is adequately protected in Australian law. The panel conducting the review was chaired by Philip Ruddock, a senior minister in the economically and socially conservative government led by John Howard from 1996–2007. The review consequently became known as the 'Ruddock Review'.

The Ruddock Review found that there was no systemic, imminent danger to religious freedom in Australia, but there is inadequate legal protection for religious freedom and there are isolated occasions where religious freedom is violated or curtailed, as well as a rising social hostility to and ignorance of religion in general.[48] The Panel made a number of recommendations to address this, most of which will not be considered here. One of the most contentious recommendations was that religious schools should retain the freedom to discriminate against staff and students through religious exemptions to anti-discrimination law. As mentioned in the Introduction, there was significant public objection to this recommendation – with many apparently unaware that these exemptions for religious schools have existed for decades and were actually reaffirmed and extended in 2013 by the progressive Labor Government.[49] This sparked further public and parliamentary debates and proposed legislation to remove or alter the exemptions, which produced two further Senate inquiries and eventually a stalemate.

As mentioned above, the Ruddock Review recommended that the religious exemptions in the Sex Discrimination Act be retained. Under section 38, educational institutions established for religious purposes can directly discriminate against staff and students if they do so in good faith and in accordance with their

---

[45] See generally S Chavura, J Gascoigne and I Tregenza, *Reason, Religion and the Australian Polity: A Secular State?* (Routledge, 2019).

[46] See J Witte, Jr, *From Sacrament to Contract: Marriage, Religion, and Law in the Western Tradition* (Westminster John Knox Press, 2012).

[47] See eg N Rochow, 'Speak Now or Forever Hold Your Peace – The Influence of Constitutional Argument on Same-Sex Marriage Legislation Debates in Australia' (2013) 3 *Brigham Young University Law Review* 521, 526–27.

[48] See *Religious Freedom Review*, Department of Prime Minister and Cabinet, accessed 19 February 2019, https://pmc.gov.au/domestic-policy/religious-freedom-review.

[49] See Sex Discrimination Amendment (Sexual Orientation, Gender Identity and Intersex Status) Act 2013 (Cth). Section 50 extended the exemptions in s 38 of the Sex Discrimination Act 1984 (Cth) to cover the new protected attributes of sexual orientation, gender identity and intersex status.

religion to avoid injury to the religious susceptibilities of adherents to that religion. The Panel recommended that any discriminatory decision on the part of the school be in accordance with a publicly available policy document, and any decision made in relation to child students must have the best interests of the child as a primary consideration. In fact, therefore, the recommendation actually *narrows* the ability of faith-based schools to discriminate – the school must have a publicly available policy which complies with the Act, and any discrimination must be in accordance with that policy (and for children, in their best interests).[50] The main bill seeking to remove or alter the exemptions reflected the strong view that religious schools should not have the ability to directly discriminate against students or teachers at all. However, the specific amendments proposed in the bill failed to adequately protect the autonomy of religious schools in several respects.

First, if section 38(3) was repealed (removing direct discrimination), schools would only be able to generally regulate student conduct if it is 'reasonable in the circumstances' under section 7B (indirect discrimination). However, unless it is made clear that this determination is up to the school, it gives secular courts effective theological power to determine if a particular school policy based in religion is 'reasonable'. This is an unwise intrusion of the state in the church and consequently it undermines religious freedom.[51] Second, a uniform rule imposed on students which regulates their conduct may still be interpreted to be directly discriminatory. For example, a rule that a student cannot bring a same-sex partner to a school social is directed at conduct, not orientation (it applies to heterosexual students as well as homosexual ones). But in cases such as *CYC v Cobaw* courts have not made this distinction between orientation and conduct, stating that the conduct is indissolubly linked to the orientation.[52] As such, under the mere protection of section 7B schools may actually not be able to impose general rules on students which are reasonably based in the religious ethos of that school. Third, the amendments had unduly broad and unforeseen repercussions which could severely undermine religious freedom in Australia. The proposed repeal of section 38(3) extended to any educational institution where education or training is provided, including tertiary theological colleges with an explicitly religious approach, not just religious primary and secondary schools. Furthermore, since section 37 deals with religious bodies, the proposed insertion of section 37(3) (removing the exemption for teaching of religious bodies) went far beyond educational institutions and literally extended to any 'body' established for religious purposes which provides education. This includes places of worship, and therefore plausibly covers church sermons, Sunday schools, mosques and synagogues – any context where education and

---

[50] See Aroney and Taylor, 'The Politics of Religious Freedom in Australia' (n 11) 54–55.

[51] See eg N Foster, 'Respecting the Dignity of Religious Organisations: When is it Appropriate for Courts to Decide Religious Doctrine?' (2020) 47 *University of Western Australia Law Review* 175.

[52] See *Christian Youth Camps Limited v Cobaw Community Health Services Limited* [2014] VSCA 75.

training are provided. Such an amendment would have prevented these bodies from legal protection in the process of providing religious education and training. The Parliamentary Committee which considered the bill found (for these and other reasons) that the bill was rushed, flawed and a more detailed consideration was needed.[53] The Committee recommended that the bill not be passed and the issue be referred to the Australian Law Reform Commission for further consideration.[54] Consequently, the Senate did not pass the bill. The issue has been referred to the Australian Law Reform Commission, which is now due to report back one year after the passing of the Religious Discrimination Bills. As discussed below, these have not yet passed Parliament at the time of writing.

The proposed changes to the exemptions did not promote a peaceful coexistence of difference in accordance with the theological virtues. First, giving secular courts the power to make theological pronouncements about the reasonableness of a religious school's general policy is contrary to the golden rule ('do unto others as you would have them do unto you') and loving one's neighbour ('love your neighbour as yourself') in the sense that any group or ideology would object to the condescending treatment of having a potentially ignorant outsider determine the reasonableness of the application of their beliefs through their practices.[55] Indeed, tolerance and humility would indicate that it is not unreasonable or disproportionate to expect a particular community with certain ethical commitments to not engage with or provide services to persons or groups which contradict those commitments. Rather, the religious body should be provided with autonomy to define their own doctrine and what that doctrine entails for their practice.[56] Completely removing the ability for religious communities to preference and select their leaders, members and method of teaching does not reflect trust, humility, patience and tolerance on the part of the broader community, for the result is to coerce uniformity (ie compel other communities to conform to a particular version of the good) rather than to accept that there are diverse approaches to pursuing the good, and peacefully coexist in dialogue with those approaches to maximise the common good.[57] The chapter will follow this line of thought to specifically evaluate the recommendation of the Ruddock Review to introduce greater transparency, in conjunction with the exemptions in their current form, below. For now the chapter turns to a constitutional issue and other Commonwealth legislation, before considering the proposed Religious Discrimination Bills.

---

[53] See 'Sex Discrimination Report', *Senate Legal and Constitutional Affairs Legislation Committee* [3.68]. The Report can be accessed (19 February 2019) here: www.aph.gov.au/Parliamentary_Business/Committees/Senate/Legal_and_Constitutional_Affairs/Sexdiscrimination/Report?fbclid=IwAR1TqKRJ5EA5I7o3D2cv_Wc2qlr_vhaSIrK-NsZCKRHSzr5rr_2iIZ0SEzk.

[54] ibid [3.80]–[3.84].

[55] Luke 6:31; Romans 13:9.

[56] See A Deagon, 'The "Religious Questions" Doctrine': Addressing (Secular) Judicial Incompetence' (2021) 47(1) *Monash University Law Review* 60–87.

[57] As explored in J Harrison, *Post-Liberal Religious Liberty* (Cambridge University Press, 2020).

B. The Religious Exemptions and Free Exercise

It is also worth noting that any attempt to remove the exemptions for religious educational institutions in the Commonwealth Sex Discrimination Act, without equivalent replacements, may breach the free exercise clause of section 116 of the Constitution and consequently be invalid. As discussed above, free exercise includes religious conduct such as 'faith and worship', 'the teaching and propagation of religion', and 'the practices and observances of religion'.[58] Since staff and students of religious educational institutions engage in or receive, at the very least, the teaching and propagation of religion, the ability of these institutions to select staff consistent with their religious convictions and regulate their teaching of students comes within the ambit of free exercise.

Furthermore, as discussed above, not every interference with religion is a breach of section 116, but only those which 'unduly infringe' upon religious freedom.[59] Free exercise should only be limited where it is required for the maintenance of civil government or the continued existence of the community.[60] More precisely, freedom of religion should extend to protect all external actions which are not dangerous to society or democracy, even if those views or actions are deemed unpopular according to community values.[61] As Latham CJ observes, 'section 116 is required to protect the religion (or absence of religion) of minorities, and in particular, of unpopular minorities'.[62] Given that exemptions for religious educational institutions appear to be unpopular according to community values (whether this unpopularity is warranted or not – they are certainly not dangerous to society or democracy), this supports the argument that they are protected by section 116.[63]

Even on the narrow interpretation in *Kruger*, any proposal to remove religious exemptions for religious educational institutions directly targets these institutions and restricts their free exercise in its terms by preventing them from selecting staff consistent with their religious convictions.[64] Section 116 does extend to protect acts done in the practice of religion by religious bodies, and this includes teaching of students, and staff selections, of educational institutions.[65] Section 116 was

---

[58] *Church of the New Faith* 135–36 (Mason ACJ and Brennan J).

[59] See generally *Adelaide Company of Jehovah's Witnesses Inc. v Commonwealth* (1943) 67 CLR 116.

[60] ibid 126, 131 (Latham CJ), 155 (Starke J).

[61] ibid 149–50 (Rich J).

[62] ibid 124 (Latham CJ).

[63] See eg ML Rasmussen, A Singleton, A Halafoff and G Bouma, 'There's no argument or support for allowing schools to discriminate against LGBTIQ teachers', *The Conversation* (16 October 2018): https://theconversation.com/theres-no-argument-or-support-for-allowing-schools-to-discriminate-against-lgbtiq-teachers-104765.

[64] *Kruger* (1997) 190 CLR 1, 40, 161.

[65] See *Adelaide Company of Jehovah's Witnesses Inc. v Commonwealth* (1943) 67 CLR 116; N Aroney, 'Freedom of Religion as an Associational Right' (2014) 33 *University of Queensland Law Journal* 153. It could be objected, following the narrow interpretation in *Krygger*, that teaching is a secular activity rather than a religious activity, and therefore not part of free exercise. However, putting aside this

designed precisely to prevent the direct targeting of religious practice by religious entities through Commonwealth laws, and since the provision of education by a religious institution is a religious practice in accordance with religious convictions, and any removal of exemptions would directly prohibit that practice in accordance with those convictions, it follows that the removal of exemptions would be likely to breach the free exercise clause. Thus, if the exemptions are no longer tenable, some equivalent replacement would be necessary for the repeal to not infringe section 116.

C. Other Legislation

Though many amendments to protect religious freedom in the wake of same-sex marriage were unsuccessful as mentioned above, some were included in the legislation which legally recognised same-sex marriage: the Marriage Amendment (Definition and Religious Freedoms) Act 2017 (Cth). The main one for religious communities is a protection for bodies established for religious purposes. This inserted section 47B into the Marriage Act, which provides that bodies established for religious purposes may refuse to make facilities available or to provide goods or services for the purpose of or purposes reasonably incidental to solemnising a marriage where the refusal conforms to the religious doctrine of the body or is necessary to avoid injury to the religious susceptibilities of adherents of the religion. This provision uses the same language and definitions as section 37 of the Sex Discrimination Act. In other words, it allows religious bodies such as churches to refuse to be involved in marriages they have a religious objection to, preserving the autonomy of that community to practise in accordance with its religious beliefs.

There are some other minor protections for the autonomy of religious communities in miscellaneous Commonwealth legislation. Sections 7 and 12 of the Charities Act 2013 (Cth) provides that 'advancing religion' is a charitable purpose presumed to be of public benefit, along with associated purposes such as advancing social or public welfare, advancing culture, promoting or protecting human rights (which includes freedom of religion), and promoting reconciliation, mutual respect and tolerance. This allows religious charities to freely operate for the purposes of advancing religion and sundry purposes which have public benefit, protecting the autonomy of these communities. Sections 351 and 772 of the Fair Work Act 2009 (Cth) prohibit employers, including religious bodies, from taking adverse action against, or terminating the employment of, employees on the basis of certain protected attributes, including religion – with exemptions which

---

narrow and highly questionable secular/religious dichotomy, even on that view, removing exemptions will curtail the ability of religious schools to exist as genuinely religious, and therefore curtail their ability to engage in religious activities (eg home groups and chapel services) which are also part of the teaching curriculum. So free exercise would still be prohibited by the Commonwealth passing a law to remove the exemptions.

permit religious institutions to avoid these requirements if the action meets the 'good faith' and 'religious susceptibilities' tests (which are in effect the same as those in the Sex Discrimination Act). The prohibition in section 351 is further limited in its application to religious bodies and religious educational institutions as it does not apply if the action is not unlawful under the relevant jurisdiction's anti-discrimination law. These provisions provide further robust protection for the autonomy of religious institutions which employ staff, allowing them to take various actions relevant to staff if those actions are in accordance with the religion of the institution.[66] Finally, the Racial Discrimination Act 1975 (Cth) prohibits discrimination on the basis of race or ethnicity, which potentially provides protection against discrimination for religions which are closely connected to ethnicity, such as Sikhism and Judaism. However, given the ambiguity of the connection between race, religion and ethnicity, this protection is tenuous at best – and in any case only extends to those religions which are closely connected to ethnicity, excluding ethnically diverse religions such as Christianity and Buddhism.[67] So this is very limited, and there is no general protection against religious discrimination in Commonwealth law. That is the subject of the Religious Discrimination Bills.

D. Proposed Commonwealth Legislation: The Religious Discrimination Bills

Finally, amongst the other recommendations relevant to the autonomy of religious communities such as amending the religious exemptions in the Sex Discrimination Act discussed above, the Ruddock Review also recommended that the Commonwealth pass laws which protect against religious discrimination. The subsequent conservative Morrison Government implemented this recommendation by proposing the Religious Discrimination Bills ('the Bill').[68] In 2019 the Commonwealth Attorney-General released two exposure drafts of the bills, designed to protect religious communities from discrimination. It has been broadly supported by religious communities but largely rejected by LGBT and human rights groups because of the perception that the Bill privileges religion above equality.[69] The Government did plan to introduce the Bill to Parliament

---

[66] See Moulds (n 44) 131–32; G Walsh, 'The Right to Equality and the Employment Decisions of Religious Schools' (2014) 16 *University of Notre Dame Australia Law Review* 107, 108.

[67] See Evans (n 4) 65–67.

[68] See *Religious Freedom Bills – First Exposure Drafts* (Attorney-General's Department, 2019): Available at   www.ag.gov.au/rights-and-protections/consultations/religious-freedom-bills-first-exposure-drafts; *Religious Freedom Bills – Second Exposure Drafts* (Attorney-General's Department, 2020): Available at www.ag.gov.au/rights-and-protections/consultations/religious-freedom-bills-second-exposure-drafts.

[69] See R Sarre, 'Legislating for Religious Freedom in Australia: Navigating the Long and Winding Road' (2020) 47(1) *University of Western Australia Law Review* 15 for a more detailed overview.

early in 2020, but this was delayed due to the Government rightly prioritising their response to COVID-19. The Bill was introduced in the Lower House (the House of Representatives) in 2022, but only passed with controversial amendments (removing some of the religious exemptions in the Sex Discrimination Act, which for the reasons discussed above were poor amendments) supported by moderate Government members who voted with the progressive Opposition and other non-government members.[70] The Bill then languished in the Upper House (the Senate) after the Morrison Government withdrew it from consideration due to the rogue amendments, and the Government subsequently lost the May 2022 election, resulting in the lapse of the Bill. The incoming Albanese Government has indicated they want to pass the bill with significant amendments in the new term, but at the time of writing have not provided any more specific details or a timeline. This section outlines the provisions of the Bill relevant to religious communities, and these will be evaluated in subsequent sections.

The primary provision is section 7 of the Bill, so it is worth reproducing this in detail:

Religious bodies may generally act in accordance with their faith etc.

What this section is about

(1)   This section sets out circumstances in which a religious body's conduct is not discrimination under this Act. Because the conduct is not discrimination, it is therefore not unlawful under this Act in any area of public life, including work, education, access to premises and the provision of goods, services and accommodation.

Note 1: For example, because of subsection (4), it is not discrimination for a religious primary school to require all of its staff and students to practice that religion, if such a requirement is necessary to avoid injury to the religious susceptibilities of people of that religion.

Conduct that is not discrimination by a religious body

(2)   Subject to subsection (6), a religious body does not discriminate against a person under this Act by engaging, in good faith, in conduct that a person of the same religion as the religious body could reasonably consider to be in accordance with the doctrines, tenets, beliefs or teachings of that religion.

Note 1: Subsection (6) contains an additional requirement for religious educational institutions in relation to conduct in the context of employment.

Note 2: Conduct that is not discrimination under this Act may still constitute direct or indirect discrimination under other anti-discrimination laws of the Commonwealth including, for example, the Sex Discrimination Act 1984.

---

[70] See Religious Discrimination Bill 2022 – Parliament of Australia (www.aph.gov.au/Parliamentary_Business/Bills_Legislation/Bills_Search_Results/Result?bId=r6821).

(3)　Without limiting subsection (2), conduct mentioned in that subsection includes giving preference to persons of the same religion as the religious body.

(4)　Subject to subsection (6), a religious body does not discriminate against a person under this Act by engaging, in good faith, in conduct to avoid injury to the religious susceptibilities of adherents of the same religion as the religious body.

Note 1: Subsection (6) contains an additional requirement for religious educational institutions in relation to conduct in the context of employment.

Note 2: Conduct that is not discrimination under this Act may still constitute direct or indirect discrimination under other anti-discrimination laws of the Commonwealth including, for example, the Sex Discrimination Act 1984.

(5)　Without limiting subsection (4), conduct mentioned in that subsection includes giving preference to persons of the same religion as the religious body. Religious educational institutions must have a publicly available policy in relation to conduct in the context of employment.

(6)　The Minister may, by legislative instrument, determine requirements for the purposes of paragraph (5).

As indicated in section 5 of the Bill which defines a religious body, this provision has a broad application to religious schools, charities and churches. It will in principle provide those bodies with some autonomy to regulate themselves according to a religious ethos through staffing decisions, in accordance with a policy which must be made publicly available. However, the provision relies on a questionable 'reasonableness' test and specifically excludes bodies that engage solely or primarily in commercial activities from its protection.

The Religious Discrimination Bills also included the Human Rights Legislation Amendment Bill, which has three relevant provisions. The first is an amendment to the Charities Act, which clarifies that a charitable purpose of promoting or supporting traditional marriage is not a disqualifying purpose. This preserves the autonomy of religious charities to continue advocating for traditional marriage as a charitable institution, implementing a recommendation in the Ruddock Review. The second is a further amendment to the Marriage Act, which inserts section 47C (a provision the same as section 47B discussed above, except it applies to 'educational institutions established for religious purposes' rather than 'religious bodies'). This extends protection to religious schools to refuse to be involved in marriages they have a religious objection to in the context of making facilities available or providing goods and services, preserving the autonomy of that community to practise in accordance with its religious beliefs. This also implements a recommendation of the Ruddock Review. Finally, the bill inserts objects clauses in other Commonwealth discrimination legislation which state that regard must be had to the indivisibility and universality of human rights and their equal status in international law, and the principle that every person is free and equal in their dignity and rights. This also implements a recommendation of the Ruddock Review and ensures that religious freedom is viewed alongside equality rather than being subservient to it.

IV. Summary: The Legal Infrastructure for the Autonomy of Religious Communities in Australia

In regard to the Constitution, section 116 provides some limited protection for the autonomy of religious communities. In principle the free exercise clause would operate to invalidate Commonwealth laws which remove the ability of religious bodies and religious educational institutions to select and preference staff and members who adhere to their beliefs and expected conduct in accordance with the ethos of the organisation. However, though free exercise is plausibly viewed as associational in the cases, in practice the narrow interpretation of the scope of free exercise means religious associational autonomy has not been effectively protected by section 116. Section 116 also does not protect against actions by the executive, the states, or individuals. The establishment clause also provides some protection for the autonomy of religious communities by allowing non-discriminatory Commonwealth support for religious educational institutions.

In regard to Commonwealth law, the Sex Discrimination Act provides fairly robust protections for the autonomy of religious communities, allowing religious bodies and religious educational institutions to discriminate in the process of selecting or preferring staff and members of their communities. Even if the Ruddock recommendation for transparency is implemented, this only narrows the protection slightly. However, there is no protection in Commonwealth law for religious individuals or religious vendors which would allow them to (potentially) discriminate in the process of upholding a religious ethos. The recent and proposed amendments to the Marriage Act and the Charities Act also provide significant protection to religious bodies (including charities and educational institutions) to continue advocating for positions some view as discriminatory, and to only use their facilities, goods and services for purposes which are in accordance with their religious ethos. The Fair Work Act religious exemptions also provide protection to religious institutions which are employers to make staffing decisions that are in accordance with their religious ethos. Finally, the proposed Religious Discrimination Bill provides some protection for the autonomy of religious communities, allowing some religious bodies to engage in (what may be) discriminatory conduct which is reasonably regarded as being in accordance with a religious ethos.

V. Evaluation of the Law: Peaceful Coexistence and the Theological Virtues

This section evaluates the legal infrastructure for the autonomy of religious communities elucidated in the chapter so far to determine the extent that this legislation promotes a peaceful coexistence of difference in accordance with the theological virtues. The evaluation in this Part II of the book is based purely on the law itself. Underlying theoretical perspectives will be evaluated and incorporated into the analysis in Part III of the book.

A. Section 116: Free Exercise and Establishment

As mentioned above, section 116 of the Constitution provides some limited protection for the autonomy of religious communities, at least in principle. The free exercise clause may well extend to invalidating Commonwealth laws which directly target the autonomy of religious communities, and the establishment clause protects at least the non-discriminatory financial support of religious schools by the Commonwealth. To the extent these protections are effective, they promote a peaceful coexistence of religious bodies, accepting and even facilitating their differences which demonstrates humility and tolerance. It is love of neighbour as self in the sense of promoting the existence of diverse communities in the same way as your own community.

However, the main problem with section 116 (and specifically the free exercise clause) is these in-principle protections have not been effective in practice. Despite at least two cases which directly threatened the autonomy of religious communities, the free exercise clause has never been successfully litigated. In *Jehovah's Witnesses*, the impugned legislation actually *dissolved* the religious community on the spurious basis that the advocacy of a small religious minority may undermine the Australian war effort. Similarly, in *Kruger* the impugned legislation prevented Indigenous Australians from participating in the religious and other practices of their community without just cause. The failure of section 116 to protect these groups is inconsistent with peaceful coexistence and did not demonstrate humility or tolerance of diverse approaches to the good. In particular, it failed to adhere to the golden rule and the law of love in the sense that any group would object to interference with their associational autonomy without compelling reasons which uphold diverse approaches to the good. These are issues involving the interpretation of the free exercise clause rather than its text, and therefore any advocacy for change in this space must be directed to the judiciary.[71] Of course, since section 116 is only a limit on Commonwealth law, even if a broader interpretation is forthcoming the scope of protection for the autonomy of religious communities is necessarily bound.

---

[71] See eg Deagon, 'Defining the Interface' (n 11); Deagon, 'Liberal Assumptions in Section 116 Cases' (n 17).

B. The Sex Discrimination Act: Religious Schools and Discrimination

Australia has a broad legal and normative commitment (in principle) to protect the right of religious organisations and individuals to freely express, practise and act upon their beliefs. This is evidenced through section 116 of the Constitution and various protections in anti-discrimination law.[72] These protections can give rise to conflict in the context of protections against discrimination on the basis of other attributes, such as sexual orientation. However, allowing discrimination against (for example) LGBT people can result in actual mistreatment, the fear of mistreatment, and a debilitating perception (arguably corresponding to a reality) that their dignity is undermined. Moulds notes that the two guiding principles for legal frameworks designed to address these tensions are religious freedom and equality. When these clash, the aim is to bring these rights into 'practical concordance' through 'reasonable accommodation'.[73]

For example, a religious person may run a small business which normally provides services in accordance with their religious beliefs, and then refuse to provide a requested marriage-related service to a same-sex couple because it will conflict with their religious beliefs. This would be discrimination under section 22(1). However, such a person cannot rely on the exemptions under sections 37(1) or 38(1) of the Sex Discrimination Act. Though they may have a consistent practice of refusing jobs which would tend to injure their religious susceptibilities in accordance with the teaching of their religion, the business would probably not be viewed as an educational institution or a body established for religious purposes.[74] The religious individual running a business might attempt to invoke the free exercise clause to claim that this Commonwealth legislation restricts their free exercise of religion. However, based on the majority judgment in *Kruger*, the High Court would probably hold that the Sex Discrimination Act in general does not have the restriction or regulation of religion as part of its purpose (as opposed to specific legislation amending or repealing the religious exemptions). Certainly a lack of existence of exemptions for individuals is not a Commonwealth law targeting religion, and therefore the validity of the legislation would be upheld. The fact that general religious exemptions are included in the legislation would also support that finding because free exercise has arguably been catered for. So the 'reasonable accommodation' in this context is general religious exemptions which apply to religious bodies as traditionally conceived. Nevertheless, the legislation has the

---

[72] Moulds (n 44) 114–15.
[73] ibid 115–18.
[74] *cf* A Deagon, 'Religious Schools, Religious Vendors and Refusing Services After Ruddock: Diversity or Discrimination? (2019) 93(9) *Australian Law Journal* 766–77, where I argue that whether religious vendors are religious bodies is better considered as a question of fact.

effect of restricting the autonomy of a religious vendor by not allowing them to conduct their affairs in accordance with their religious ethos. There is a lack of protection in Commonwealth anti-discrimination law for religious vendors, and the narrow interpretation of the free exercise clause allows Commonwealth anti-discrimination legislation to indirectly restrict the autonomy of such vendors, undermining peaceful coexistence by failing to promote diverse approaches to the good of public service according to the virtues of humility and tolerance.[75]

Conversely, a minister of religion, as an agent for a religious community, might refuse to provide a marriage-related service to a same-sex couple. Their reason is providing such a service is not in accordance with their religion. Following the Sex Discrimination Act, such a case would be relatively straightforward. The minister would have discriminated in accordance with section 22(1), but because their action conforms to the doctrine of the religion and falls within the exemption, a claim would not be successful. This is an example of the Commonwealth's attempt to reasonably accommodate religious freedom and equality, and the exemption is a generous protection for the autonomy of religious communities in this context. However, these generous exemptions exist only for bodies or organisations (educational or other) established for religious purposes, and even these exemptions have been questioned.[76] The consensus which once supported religious exemptions no longer exists. Many have called for the repeal of all exemptions as enshrining unjust discrimination.[77] It must be emphasised that the claim from religious bodies is not a right to discriminate, but a right to positively select such that religious communities are treated equally to other communities that may have legitimate reasons to only have members with beliefs and behaviour consistent with the ethos of the organisation (eg political parties).[78] Nevertheless, Parkinson notes that the exemptions have come under sustained attack recently as, in the view of opponents, giving religion a licence to unjustly discriminate which is inconsistent with the virtues of love and tolerance.[79]

In the specific context of religious schools, as mentioned above there is currently no requirement for a publicly available policy on the matter, so the public document requirement recommended by the Ruddock Review actually, in effect, narrows the exemptions. The public outcry was due to the perception that discrimination because of religion is exclusive and immoral, an affront to the dignity of members of the LGBT community, and therefore unloving. The exemptions, on

---

[75] See Deagon, 'Defining the Interface' (n 11).

[76] See eg C Evans and L Ujvari, 'Non-Discrimination Laws and Religious Schools in Australia' (2009) 30 *Adelaide Law Review* 31, 56.

[77] N Aroney and P Parkinson, 'Associational Freedom, Anti-Discrimination Law and the New Multiculturalism' (2019) 44 *Australasian Journal of Legal Philosophy* 1, 4–6.

[78] Hobbs and Williams (n 2) 728. See P Parkinson, 'Christian Concerns about an Australian Charter of Rights' (2010) 15 *Australian Journal of Human Rights* 83.

[79] Patrick Parkinson, 'The Future of Religious Freedom' (2019) 93(9) *Australian Law Journal* 699, 701–02.

this view, undermine peaceful coexistence because they contradict the golden rule and the law of love by treating members of the LGBT community with a lack of kindness and compassion, and possibly even with malice.[80] Termination for being in a same-sex relationship, for example, leads to 'serious harm' for the employee because 'they may experience this not only as a rejection of their sexuality and the worth of their relationship, but also as a rejection by their religious community'.[81] Walsh argues that the public document requirement is likely to play 'a significant role in reducing the harm that can be caused by the general exception approach', for the school can specifically advise potential employees of 'the school's religious commitments and the relevant expectations that the school has of their staff members'.[82] This will mean individuals who disagree with those commitments and/or expectations may not apply for the position, or if they do, they are aware they may be subject to an adverse employment decision and can even prepare in advance by having back-up employment.[83] In this sense the public document requirement accords with the virtue of honesty, which helps to promote peaceful coexistence.

However, Moulds notes that the Ruddock Review's Recommendation that schools may continue to discriminate against children as long as it is in accordance with an available policy document and the best interests of the child is a primary consideration is 'inconsistent', for it is 'not clear' 'on what basis a religious school would be able to justify a policy that discriminates against students on the basis of their gender identity but is also developed having regard to the "best interest of the child" as its primary consideration'.[84] This lack of clarity is inconsistent with the virtue of honesty and may increase the harm any child may be subjected to, undermining peaceful coexistence. Moreover, Evans and Ujvari contend that even the present exemptions as they stand go too far, acknowledging that religious schools 'play an important role' and are 'deserving of some protection of their distinctive worldview', but stating that such protection is 'consistent with the idea that that they should be subject to more aspects of discrimination law than is currently the case in Australia'.[85] In particular, they criticise permitting discrimination to avoid 'injuring religious susceptibilities' on the basis that the phrase is 'rather vague', 'provides little guidance', and that 'religious freedom does not normally protect religious sensibilities'.[86] Again, this ambiguity and lack of clarity undermines peaceful coexistence by reducing honesty and therefore increasing the probability of harm because an employee or student is unable to know the circumstances in which they may be discriminated against.

---

[80] See Colossians 3:8–9, 12–13.
[81] Walsh, 'Right to Equality' (n 66) 135.
[82] ibid 134–35.
[83] ibid.
[84] Moulds (n 44) 148–49.
[85] Evans and Ujvari (n 76) 56.
[86] ibid 53.

In addition, Hilkemeijer and Maguire also argue that the section 38 exemptions are inconsistent with international human rights law, particularly that of the European Court of Human Rights. Though international law is outside the scope of an analysis of Australia's legal framework, their argument is relevant in terms of evaluating whether the exemptions promote peaceful coexistence in accordance with the theological virtues. First, as already referenced above, the law is imprecise because 'injury to religious susceptibilities' is a broad and vague basis upon which the power to discriminate can be legitimately exercised.[87] Second, the scope of religious institutional autonomy to regulate members depends on whether the member is part of the religious community and employed for religious purposes, or whether they are merely an employee engaged in 'secular' activities. The exemptions do not allow for such distinctions, and also do not allow for any balancing of rights to privacy and equality for the employee with the religious autonomy of the organisation.[88] They 'allow a religious school to dismiss a teacher on the ground of their sexual orientation where the sexual orientation of that teacher has no negative impact on the church's ability to teach its religious doctrine'.[89] The fact that it may be difficult for dismissed teachers to find employment must also be taken into account.[90] The lack of precision in the exemptions, as already noted, undermines peaceful coexistence by increasing the probability of harm suffered by those who may be discriminated against – including not only a dignity harm, but also a material harm in terms of needing to find other employment.

Aroney and Parkinson suggest that the exemptions are problematic because they do not acknowledge institutional autonomy or the communal rights of people of faith to set up and operate such institutions how they see fit. Instead they frame these rights as 'concessions' to religious 'susceptibilities' as a grudging exception to a general prohibition against any kind of discrimination.[91] Neil Foster has also persuasively contended that framing religious freedom protections as 'exemptions' from anti-discrimination laws might give the impression that powerful religious lobby groups are simply bullying politicians into giving them a special privilege to engage in otherwise unlawful conduct (which is not an unfounded concern).[92] In this sense, even those friendlier to the exemptions in principle question whether they are the best means of promoting peaceful coexistence, for the exemptions not only fail to articulate the proper basis for the autonomy of religious communities in the sense of patiently and humbly supporting diverse pursuits of the good,

---

[87] A Hilkemeijer and A Maguire, 'Religious Schools and Discrimination against Staff on the Basis of Sexual Orientation: Lessons from European Human Rights Jurisprudence' (2019) 93(9) *Australian Law Journal* 752, 757.

[88] ibid 757–60. It should be noted that this criticism relies on the problematic religious/secular distinction.

[89] ibid 760.

[90] ibid 760–61.

[91] Aroney and Parkinson, 'Associational Freedom' (n 77) 23.

[92] Neil Foster, 'Freedom of Religion and Balancing Clauses in Discrimination Legislation' (2016) 5 *Oxford Journal of Law and Religion* 385, 389.

but they also create a perception of religious bodies such as schools engaging in 'unloving' behaviour by seeking special privileges to discriminate based simply on prejudice, undermining the virtues of humility, kindness, love and the golden rule. There seems to be a common reluctance to maintain the exemptions in their current form.[93] Yet there must be an alternative.

As already seen in the above analysis of the proposed amendments to the Sex Discrimination Act, eliminating or narrowing the exemptions without an equivalent replacement would 'reduce greatly the freedom of religious organisations to have staffing policies consistent with their identity and ethos'.[94] Some schools may not have a strong religious identity and may not mind, but others see their religious ethos as critical to the identity and operation of the school. Freedom of religion contains a corporate dimension which, in such circumstances, needs to be accommodated.[95] Any association or community cannot exist without the ability to define the terms and character of the association and its members, including in matters of ideology (eg political parties) and practices (eg sexual morality). This is not a blanket freedom for people of faith to discriminate. In the setting of schools, as already mentioned, transparency, clarity and consistency are essential to convey expectations of belief and conduct to prospective staff so they can make an informed decision whether they accept the employment with its attendant conditions.[96] This accords with the virtue of honesty and helps to promote peaceful coexistence.

Ultimately, the exemptions are offensively and irrelevantly targeted at sexual minorities, undermining peaceful coexistence, when what religious schools really need is a

> ... freedom to conduct their educational functions through a curriculum and in a manner which is consistent with their religious ethos, delivered by and within a community of like-minded others. Their wish is to make suitable appointments based on the alignment of fundamental beliefs and practices ... Substitution of legislation to similar effect, in place of the existing schools exemptions, could remove some of the impassioned hostility from current debate, in particular by enabling them to require employees to act in a manner that demonstrates loyalty to their religious ethos, rather than misplaced sexuality-focused exceptions and exemptions.[97]

It is true that those who are discriminated against clearly 'suffer significant harm to their dignity, emotional well-being and in some cases their economic security'.[98] However, Walsh notes that the religious community who incidentally engages in

---

[93] Aroney and Saunders (n 1).
[94] Parkinson, 'Future of Religious Freedom' (n 79) 702.
[95] ibid 702–03.
[96] Aroney and Parkinson, 'Associational Freedom' (n 77) 25.
[97] Aroney and Taylor, 'Politics of Religious Freedom' (n 11) 61–62.
[98] G Walsh, 'Same-Sex Marriage and Religious Liberty' (2016) 35(2) *The University of Tasmania Law Review* 106, 126. Walsh expands on the specific nature of such harms in Walsh, 'Right to Equality' (n 66) 127–36.

discrimination in the process of maintaining a particular ethos consistent with their religious beliefs 'will typically suffer much greater harm' if there are no laws protecting their ability to do this, including 'severe emotional distress from the violation of their faith commitments', potentially the 'impairment of their relationship' with the rest of their faith community, and being the subject of 'protests, boycotts and complaints to anti-discrimination tribunals with the frequent result' that they will be forced to cease either their religious ethos or their activities – both fatal to the existence and nature of the community.[99] In the vast majority of cases the party discriminated against can simply choose another option at minimal cost, and given increasing support for vulnerable persons and groups (especially among the young) and potential financial incentives for the religious party to accept their requests, it is increasingly unlikely that discrimination will occur. The failure to realise that harm to the religious party from not protecting their autonomy overrides harm to the party from being discriminating against only results from simply refusing to give the religious party's beliefs and interests any significant weight.[100] So providing religious schools with alternative legal infrastructure to operate in accordance with a religious ethos is loving because it promotes diverse approaches to the good and upholds the virtues of humility, patience and tolerance, while also avoiding the unkind nature of the current exemptions which undermine peaceful coexistence by explicitly and unnecessarily targeting sexual minorities.

Facilitating the religious autonomy of schools to select and regulate their community is loving in another sense. It is important to note the incidental ability to 'discriminate' in this context actually preserves equality between religious and non-religious communities. An example already mentioned to illustrate this principle is political parties. Political parties, by their nature, discriminate on the basis of political opinion. It would be absurd for the law to compel a particular political party to hire someone who repudiates the ethos of the party in thought or conduct, and the law has long recognised this ability for political parties to 'discriminate'.[101] The same notion applies to religious schools.[102] So, in other words, since loving your neighbour as yourself entails affirming their dignity by treating them equally, and the golden rule entails treating others as you would like to be treated, it is loving for religious communities to have autonomy to select and regulate their members in the same way other ideological groups have the autonomy to select and regulate their members.

Hence, the exemptions in the Sex Discrimination Act rightly provide significant autonomy for religious communities, but not in a way which promotes peaceful coexistence. The exemptions unfairly and unnecessarily target sexual

---

[99] Walsh, 'Religious Liberty' (n 98) 127.

[100] ibid 127–28. See Aroney and Saunders (n 1) who also argue that there needs to be greater recognition of the wrongness and harm which results from compelling religious parties to act contrary to their conscience.

[101] Aroney and Saunders (n 1).

[102] See Deagon, 'Defining the Interface' (n 11) 276–78.

minorities, giving the impression of a special privilege to maliciously discriminate. New legal infrastructure broadly in the form of positive associational rights is required to remove this impression while simultaneously maintaining the ability for religious communities to select and regulate their members in accordance with their religious ethos – promoting a peaceful coexistence of difference informed by the theological virtues. The precise nature of this proposed infrastructure will be informed by further analysis in Part III of the book and articulated in Part IV.

C. Other Legislation

The provisions in the Charities Act relating to the advancement of religion and sundry purposes being of public benefit is in accordance with the theological virtues of humility, generosity and compassion, enabling religious charities to continue operating in accordance with their religious ethos, and upholding peaceful coexistence by facilitating diverse pursuits of the good. Similarly, the provisions in the Fair Work Act provide protection both for employees who may be discriminated against on the basis of religion, and religious employers who may wish to make employment decisions to uphold their religious ethos. However, these provisions (in particular the exemptions for religious employers) are in the same form as the religious exemptions in the Sex Discrimination Act so they are subject to the same analysis. Some form of legal protection framed as positive rights would better promote peaceful coexistence.

In regard to the recently inserted section 47B of the Marriage Act, this is framed as a positive right of religious bodies which gives them the autonomy to choose how to use their facilities and services in accordance with their religious ethos. This upholds peaceful coexistence in accordance with the virtues of honesty, patience and kindness, limiting any potential discrimination to a marriage issue specifically yet also enabling genuine difference to peacefully coexist so such religious bodies can pursue their distinctive religious version of the good. However, as I have argued elsewhere, if religious vendors are religious bodies which are truly and consistently religious in nature, and they are offering a service directly connected to marriage (these will be questions of fact in individual cases), then it logically follows that religious vendors should also be entitled to this protection for the same reasons religious bodies are entitled to it.[103] The provisions in the Fair Work Act mitigate this shortfall to an extent in the sense that they would in principle protect a religious vendor (employer) when they make staffing decisions to uphold a religious ethos, but this would only apply to employment within the religious business rather than to the provision of services more broadly. An amendment (or an explanatory note clarifying that religious bodies could encompass specific

---

[103] See the detailed argument in Deagon, 'Religious Schools and Religious Vendors' (n 74).

kinds of religious vendors) would help promote the peaceful coexistence of businesses which operate from a distinct religious perspective, contributing to the common good.

D. Religious Discrimination Bills

Despite the criticism directed towards the Religious Discrimination Bills, they do preserve a peaceful coexistence of difference to a limited extent, at least in the specific context of religious communities. For example, the proposed amendment to the Charities Act (supporting traditional marriage is not a disqualifying purpose) and the proposed insertion of section 47C of the Marriage Act (providing the same protection to religious educational institutions as section 47B does for religious bodies) support a peaceful coexistence of difference for the reasons already discussed above in relation to the Charities Act and section 47B of the Marriage Act. However, some improvements to the Bill can be made.

Section 7 of the Religious Discrimination Bill supports peaceful coexistence in accordance with the theological virtues for a number of reasons. It is a provision with a broad application to religious schools, charities and churches, and as the explanatory notes indicate this will in principle allow those bodies to regulate themselves according to a religious ethos through staffing decisions, and to regulate who can attend its premises and what particular events may be held there. This upholds the virtues of honesty, patience and tolerance, enabling religious communities to peacefully coexist in accordance with their beliefs.

Section 7 clearly allows religious bodies to give preference to persons that share their religion in staffing and student decisions. One could imagine, for example, a vocally Atheist student who seeks to publicly undermine the religious ethos of a school. One could similarly imagine a Jewish or Muslim school which desires to only enrol Jewish or Muslim students due to the connection between religion and ethnicity/culture in those religions. Allowing bodies to regulate students and members provides autonomy to these communities, which will uphold the theological virtues of humility, patience, love and tolerance, thus promoting peaceful coexistence. Section 7 also states that conduct which is designed to avoid injury to the religious susceptibilities of adherents of that faith is not discrimination. This accords with other known legislation such as the exemptions in the Sex Discrimination Act, and (notwithstanding the ambiguity of 'susceptibilities') decreases the chances that secular courts will impose their own views about whether conduct is discrimination – now they will need to have reference to the adherents of that faith. Similarly, section 7 clarifies that a court will now need to consider whether a person of the same religion could reasonably consider conduct to be in accordance with the doctrine of a religion in considering whether that conduct is discriminatory. This emphasises that it is not for the court to decide what religious doctrine requires or allows in terms of religious conduct, but rather it is for the religion and its adherents to determine. Having a secular court determine what a religious belief reasonably requires and imposing this on the religious body contrary to their own view undermines peaceful coexistence. There is still the possibility of a court imposing a view as to what a person from the same religion would believe is reasonable, and the wording allowing the Minister to impose requirements is problematically broad, even potentially extending to content. The best approach would be to allow the religious body to articulate, with supporting evidence, how their beliefs inform their practices, and the Minister can mandate that this explanation be made available without mandating the content of that explanation.[104]

The definition of religious body extends to any religious body including registered charities. Hence these charities can engage in staffing and other decisions to uphold a religious ethos, regardless of commercial activities. Other religious charities will also be religious bodies under the section, unless they are solely or primarily engaged in commercial activities. This will be measured by an activities test rather than an income test, so that even if a religious charity funds themselves primarily through commercial income, if the activity which produces that income is less than their charitable non-income activities, they are still entitled to the protection. Though this is a broader scope for protecting religious bodies which engage in commercial activities and helps preserve peaceful coexistence in accordance with the theological virtues of honesty, humility and patience as discussed above, the fundamental point remains that any religious body engaging in commercial activities is no less a religious body deserving of protection. This applies not only to charities, hospitals and aged care facilities, but also to religious vendors which genuinely conduct themselves as 'religious bodies'. The commercial activities of a religious body are not relevant to whether they are in fact a religious body deserving of protection. For example, religious hospitals operate commercially but are clearly designed to implement religious perspectives on healthcare for the vulnerable. Many religiously-based charities charge fees or sell products in order to operate. To exclude these kinds of bodies from protection of their associational autonomy undermines peaceful coexistence and the common good because such an exclusion is inconsistent with humility, patience and tolerance – it does not allow religious communities to pursue their diverse version of the good (which in this case also enables tangible public good in the form of hospitals and charities).

Section 40 of the Bill also allows religious camps and conference sites to make hiring decisions that reflect their religious ethos and history. Decisions not to hire out accommodation or facilities for religious reasons will not be discrimination. These are similar protections in effect as those in section 47B and the proposed section 47C of the Marriage Act, and protect the autonomy of religious groups and thus protect peaceful coexistence in the same way as discussed in that context.[105]

---

[104] See text accompanying fns 51–57.
[105] With the slight differences that this protection is general and not limited to the marriage context, but only covers religious discrimination, not sexual minority discrimination.

Finally, objects clauses will now expressly state that all human rights have equal status at international law, and touts the importance of dignity. This emphasises that there is no hierarchy of human rights and that, in the event of conflict, religious freedom should not necessarily give way to equality considerations. This promotes peaceful coexistence by facilitating humility, patience and tolerance in a proportionate and reasonable way, upholding dignity, and explicitly specifying that religion will not be privileged above equality (or vice versa).

VI. Conclusion: The Autonomy of Religious Communities in Australian Law

Australia's legal infrastructure provides only limited protection for the autonomy of religious communities, and this infrastructure promotes peaceful coexistence in accordance with the theological virtues to only a limited degree. Australia has a constitutional freedom of religion provision which provides some protection in principle, but not in effect due to narrow scope and interpretation. Various other aspects of Commonwealth law also enable some protection. Such constitutional and legislative protection, to the extent it is effective, generally promotes peaceful coexistence in accordance with the theological virtues, with some improvements which can be made.

The most significant protections for the autonomy of religious communities in Australia, and simultaneously the protections which require the most change to adhere to the standard of peaceful coexistence, are the religious exemptions in the Sex Discrimination Act. These provide broad abilities for religious bodies and religious educational institutions to discriminate on the basis of sex-related attributes in the process of upholding a religious ethos. However, these exemptions fail to uphold peaceful coexistence because they offensively and unnecessarily target sexual minorities, giving the impression of exceptional powers for religion to maliciously discriminate. This does not adhere to the theological virtues of humility, patience, trust and kindness. However, religious bodies and religious educational institutions do require legal powers to select and regulate their members to cultivate their communal ethos as a function of peaceful coexistence, such as through positive associational rights.

The Religious Discrimination Bills also propose to provide greater protection for the autonomy of religious communities in Australia, allowing them to select and regulate staff in accordance with a religious ethos, and also choose how to manage their facilities, goods and services in accordance with their religious ethos. However, these bills problematically exclude some religious bodies and vendors on the basis of commercial activities, which undermines peaceful coexistence by failing to demonstrate humility and patience for those entities genuinely and consistently engaging in such activities as part of their religion. They also retain the danger of allowing secular courts to impose a view upon a religious community, which does not accord with the virtues of humility and love (as manifested through the golden rule). So, for example, peaceful coexistence would be more effectively implemented by not making distinctions purely on the basis of commercial activities and allowing religious bodies to articulate their own views about what their beliefs and practices entail.

After further theoretical analysis of these legal issues in Part III of the book, Part IV will articulate a broad principled framework for the autonomy of religious communities which promotes peaceful existence through a reasonable, proportionate accommodation of difference. Building on the suggestions alluded to in this chapter, Part IV will entail specific recommendations as to how Australia's legal infrastructure can be amended to better adhere to this framework.

2

United States

I. Introduction

Chapter two evaluates the case law which stems from the First Amendment of the Constitution of the United States of America, focusing on the free exercise and establishment clauses to determine if their content promotes a peaceful coexistence between religious and other communities. It will also consider the federal Religious Freedom Restoration Act ('RFRA'), the federal Religious Land Use and Institutionalised Persons Act ('RLUIPA'), and the religious exemptions in Title VII of the federal Civil Rights Act ('Title VII') in this context. The chapter therefore elucidates the legal infrastructure which governs the autonomy of religious communities in the US, and evaluates this infrastructure to determine the extent to which it promotes a peaceful coexistence of difference in accordance with the theological virtues.

It begins by examining the associational elements of the First Amendment, particularly the free exercise clause and the ministerial exception. Moving to federal legislation, the chapter outlines the legal effect of RFRA, RLUIPA and Title VII on the autonomy of religious communities in the US. The chapter subsequently evaluates the existing legal infrastructure outlined above using peaceful coexistence and the theological virtues as a standard. It argues that the First Amendment provides relatively robust protection for the autonomy of religious communities, but in some specifics undermines peaceful coexistence. For example, the establishment clause is designed to protect religious institutional autonomy by preventing interference from government, but the division regarding the applicable test and the hackneyed 'wall of separation' metaphor results in ambiguities which can undermine the ability of religious communities to meaningfully and equally participate in public life. The spectre of *Smith* still looms over free exercise jurisprudence; the requirement for explicit hostility towards religion or discrimination against religion for free exercise to be enlivened effectively eviscerated religious freedom protections for religious communities impacted by facially neutral laws such as anti-discrimination laws. However, the passing of RFRA to specifically overrule *Smith*, and more recent free exercise jurisprudence which has undermined *Smith* without specifically overruling it, has enabled some protection for religious communities from generally applicable laws. This enables entry into the debate regarding religious freedom and discrimination which was crystallised in but not ultimately decided by *Masterpiece Cakeshop*. By engaging with the harm suffered by those discriminated against and by those seeking religious exemptions, I indicate clearly limited and stringent exemptions may be the best way to preserve peaceful coexistence in accordance with the theological virtues.

Most importantly, in 2012 the Supreme Court recognised a 'ministerial exception' grounded in both the free exercise and establishment clauses which provides significant autonomy for religious communities in the appointment of ministers by barring the application of federal employment discrimination laws to such decisions. Though I argue that the ministerial exception is in principle necessary and correct, I question its broad and comprehensive application. In particular, decisions of institutions to terminate employment on grounds ostensibly unrelated to religion appear to not be in accordance with the theological virtues and undermine peaceful coexistence because they provide an unconstrained licence to discriminate, and so perhaps the ministerial exception should only extend to employment decisions made on religious grounds. The detail of these suggestions relating to the First Amendment will be articulated in Parts III and IV of the book. I broadly conclude that existing federal legislation preserves peaceful coexistence in accordance with the theological virtues, though there is a need for further clarity around the definition and application of central phrases such as 'substantial burden'. Finally, I briefly critique the proposed (at the time of writing) Equality Act, suggesting that it severely undermines the autonomy of religious communities in its current form and is therefore incompatible with peaceful coexistence.

II. The First Amendment of the US Constitution

The religion clauses of the First Amendment state 'Congress shall make no law respecting an establishment of religion, or prohibiting the free exercise thereof …' The 'respecting an establishment of religion' aspect is known as the 'establishment clause', while the 'prohibiting the free exercise [of religion]' aspect is known as the 'free exercise clause'. The First Amendment applies to the national congress, as well as to states and to executive action.[1] Unfortunately, it is practically impossible to give a comprehensive outline of US religion clause jurisprudence in less than one chapter of a book. Entire books have been written on less.[2] So in this chapter I will focus on the landmark cases which transformed establishment (eg *Lemon* and *American Legion*) and free exercise (eg *Smith* and *Trinity Lutheran*),

---

[1] *Cantwell v Connecticut* 20.310 U.S. 296, 303–04, 310 (1940); *Everson v Board of Education* 21.330 U.S. 1, 16 (1947).

[2] See eg K Greenawalt, *Religion and the Constitution Volumes* (Princeton University Press, 2008); D Laycock, *Religious Liberty Volumes* (Eerdmans, 2018); M Breidenbach and O Anderson (ed), *The Cambridge Companion to the First Amendment and Religious Liberty* (Cambridge University Press, 2020); E Chemerinksy and H Gillman, *The Religion Clauses: The Case for Separating Church and State* (Oxford University Press, 2020).

in conjunction with cases which specifically considered religious autonomy and discrimination issues (eg *Masterpiece Cakeshop*). *Hobby Lobby* will be considered in the RFRA context. Finally, I will examine the ministerial exception as a separate category of case with a focus on *Hosanna-Tabor*.

A. The Establishment Clause

The establishment clause is designed to prevent government interference with or support of religion. It is not a protection from religion, but a protection of religion from interference by the state.[3] It therefore has an 'institutional focus, protecting the autonomy of religious institutions from state intrusion into the functions, powers, or identity of a religious organisation'.[4] So it provides some protection for religious institutions but that protection is ambiguous. The first reason for ambiguity is the tenacity of the 'wall of separation' metaphor adopted in *Everson*.[5] This principle was enunciated as a specific legal rule in the seminal case of *Lemon*, which stated that for a law impugned under the establishment clause to be valid, 'first, the statute must have a secular legislative purpose; second, its principal or primary effect must be one that neither advances nor inhibits religion; finally, the statute must not foster an excessive government entanglement with religion'.[6] In this case legislation permitting tax-funded reimbursement to church-affiliated schools for teacher salaries and the cost of texts was struck down. It was found to have a secular purpose, but cause excessive entanglement.

The second reason for ambiguity is the *Lemon* test has been inconsistently applied and there is a lack of clarity regarding how it is to be applied. For example, in *Agostini*, a programme to allow public teachers to teach remedial classes in private schools was upheld as it served a secular purpose. The Court merged the effect and entanglement limbs.[7] More problematically, the Supreme Court has applied other related but distinct tests such as 'endorsement' or 'preferentialism' (whether the government conveys a message that it endorses, favours or prefers one religion over another, or religion over non-religion) and 'neutrality' (whether religion and non-religion are equally treated), incorporating discussions of coercion, historical practice, and the level of controversy.[8] Recently in *American Legion*

---

[3] P Garry, 'Establishment Clause Jurisprudence Still Groping for Clarity: Articulating a New Constitutional Model' (2020) 12(2) *Northeastern University Law Review* 660, 692–93.

[4] ibid 695.

[5] For criticism of the metaphor, see P Garry, 'When Anti-Establishment Becomes Exclusion: The Supreme Court's Opinion in *American Legion v American Humanist Association* and the Flip Side of Endorsement' (2020) 99(3) *Nebraska Law Review* 643.

[6] *Lemon v Kurtzman*, 403 U.S. 602, 612–613 (1971).

[7] *Agostini v Felton* 521 U.S. 203 (1997).

[8] See eg *Lynch v Donnolly*, 465 U.S. 668 (1984); *Wallace v Jaffree*, 472 U.S. 38 (1985); *Zelman v Simmons-Harris*, 536 U.S. 639 (2002). The prohibition against 'an establishment of religion,' of course, precludes preferencing secularism on constitutional grounds. The Free Exercise Clause may provide some protection against governmental preference of non-religion. See *Trinity Lutheran Church of*

the Supreme Court held that crosses erected to honour soldiers killed in World War I did not violate the establishment clause because, though a religious symbol, the cross had acquired a secular meaning through historical tradition. The Court declined to apply the *Lemon* test or the endorsement test in *Lynch v Donnolly*, but did not explicitly overrule them.[9] Barclay contends that as a result the *Lemon* test is no longer viable, and the Court should discard the first two limbs and focus on applying the entanglement limb to its appropriate historical context: preventing religious groups from government interference in their internal affairs, and preventing the government from preferencing religion generally or particular religions.[10]

B. The Free Exercise Clause

The early jurisprudence of the free exercise clause took a strict approach where religious autonomy was protected but this did not prevent the passing of neutral laws which incidentally impacted religious practice.[11] This expanded in *Sherbert v Verner*, where the Supreme Court adopted the 'strict scrutiny' test: religious conduct must be accommodated except where government can show a compelling interest and no less burdensome means to achieve that interest.[12] For example, a member of the Seventh Day Adventist Church could not be denied employment benefits after she was sacked for refusing to work Saturdays against the dictates of her conscience, when the employer could have easily accommodated her religious practice.

However, the Court narrowed this view again in *Employment Division v Smith*, upholding a law against the use of peyote despite its importance as part of a religious ritual. In *Employment Division v Smith*, the Court concluded that a neutral law of general applicability cannot be invalidated by the free exercise clause if there is a rational basis for it (transforming the test from 'strict scrutiny' to the

---

Columbia, Inc. v Comer, 137 S. Ct. 2012 (2017), holding that the exclusion of a church from a generally available government benefit violated the Free Exercise Clause. I discuss further below.

[9] *American Legion v American Humanist Association*, 139 S. Ct. 2067 (2019).

[10] S Barclay, 'Untangling Entanglement' (2020) 97(6) *Washington University Law Review* 1701, 1727–28. The Supreme Court has recently taken a decisive step in precisely this direction, explicitly overruling *Lemon* in *Kennedy v Bremerton School District*, 597 U.S. ___ (2022) and providing that a high school football coach can pray in the public sphere without breaching the establishment clause, as long as that prayer is not within the scope of his duties as a coach such that students are coerced to join. Under this approach, people can participate in a religiously vibrant and diverse public sphere without coercing others in matters of religion. The approach in *Kennedy* consequently contributes to loving our neighbour by exhibiting humility, forgiveness and patience towards different views, a willingness to accept genuine diversity by not excluding any perspectives and enabling the peaceful coexistence of diverse religious communities without government favour of any in particular.

[11] See I Huyett, 'How to Overturn Employment Division v. Smith: A Historical Approach' (2020) 32 *Regent University Law Review* 295, 298–312.

[12] 374 U.S. 398 (1963).

less exacting 'rational basis scrutiny'), though the Court was clear that the government cannot specifically discriminate on the basis of religion or be hostile towards
religion.[13] An individual's religious beliefs do not excuse them from compliance
with such a law. The Court acknowledged that 'leaving accommodation to the
political process will place at a relative disadvantage those religious practices that
are not widely engaged in', but this is the 'unavoidable consequence of democratic
government' and 'must be preferred to a system in which each conscience is a
law unto itself or in which judges weigh the social importance of all laws against
the centrality of all religious beliefs'.[14] The Court went even further, characterising
strict scrutiny of laws which constrain religious freedom as a 'luxury' and refusing
to even consider whether the prohibited conduct was central to the individual's
religion in the context of assessing a compelling interest.[15] Hence, *Smith* 'effectively
announced the complete nullification of substantive free exercise rights' because as
long as a law does not specifically target a religious group the free exercise clause
places no restriction on what the government can do.[16] This demonstrably resulted
in a narrowing of religious freedom for religious communities, most significantly
because the state no longer needed to give reasons or demonstrate a compelling
interest to justify a substantial burden.[17]

The Court has been expanding the doctrine again since *Smith*. In fact, since
2011, the last 12 Supreme Court cases on religious freedom have been wins for
religion, and especially have strengthened protection for the autonomy of religious
communities.[18] For example, in *Trinity Lutheran* the Court held that there must
be a compelling state interest to discriminate on the basis of religious status in the

---

[13] 494 U.S. 872 (1990). The prohibition against religious hostility and discrimination was affirmed in
Church of the Lukumi Babalu Aye v City of Haileah, 508 U.S. 520 (1993), where the Supreme Court held
that even facially neutral laws may breach the free exercise clause under *Smith* if those laws are specifically crafted with hostility to a particular religious group, practice or belief.

[14] 110 S. Ct. at 1600, 1606 (1990). See M McConnell, 'Free Exercise Revisionism and the *Smith*
Decision' (1990) 57 *University of Chicago Law Review* 1109, 1110. Smith refutes the 'law unto itself'
argument in S Smith, *Pagans and Christians in the City* (Eerdmans, 2018) 322–27.

[15] 110 S. Ct. at 1604–06 (1990). This was in the face of strong dissent by O'Conner and Blackmun JJ,
who argued that religious liberty was an essential element of a free and pluralistic society rather than a
'luxury'.

[16] Huyett (n 11) 295–96.

[17] A Carmella, 'A Theological Critique of Free Exercise Jurisprudence' (1992) 60 *George Washington
Law Review* 782, 782–83. Though this was ameliorated by the passing of RFRA: C Corbin, 'US Religion
Clause Jurisprudence' in P Zuckerman and J Shook (eds), *The Oxford Handbook of Secularism* (Oxford
University Press, 2017) 470. And it has been argued that the *Smith* standard actually increased the
rationality of impugned laws by ensuring they are rooted in reason rather than animus, and do not
discriminate between secular and religious circumstances: see J Aimonetti and C Talley, 'Religious
Exemptions as Rational Social Policy (2021) 55 *University of Richmond Law Review*.

[18] J Witte, 'Historical Foundations and Enduring Fundamentals of American Religious Freedom'
(2020) 33 *Journal of the Society of Christian Ethics* 156, 165. Witte counts eight cases at the time of
his writing, and my number includes the most recent decisions (at the time of writing) of *Espinoza
v Montana Department of Revenue*, 140 S. Ct. 2246 (2020), *Our Lady of Guadalupe School v Agnes
Morrissey-Berru*, 140 S. Ct. 2049 (2020), *Fulton v City of Philadelphia*, 593 U.S. ___ (2021), and *Kennedy
v Bremerton School District*, 597 U.S. ___ (2022).

granting of generally available funding. So a state program providing funding for playground resurfacing to secular schools, but not religious schools, violated the clause.[19] The significant case of *Masterpiece Cakeshop*, which will be examined in more depth later in this chapter, also solidified the principle of no government hostility or discrimination towards religion by invalidating 'hostile and unequal enforcement of a facially neutral public accommodation law'.[20] In this context Capps also argues that a central purpose of the free exercise clause is to protect individuals from being compelled by the state to violate their conscience, even if their conscience is wrong.[21] The implication is this protects religious entities in both the 'private' and 'public' sphere, particularly religious vendors.

Similarly, in *Espinoza*, a state scholarship program that provides public funds to allow students to attend private schools cannot discriminate against religious schools and students. States are not required to fund private schools, but once they do they cannot discriminate between the religious and the secular.[22] As Berg and Laycock argue, the religion clauses are ultimately concerned with separating the religious choices and commitments of people from government interference and coercion. Enabling the constitutional support of financial aid to religious schools is part of the process of this protection because it allows people greater choice and diversity to educate their children in accordance with their convictions, in contrast to the strict secularist no-aid separationism which undermines the ability of people to access religious educational institutions because of financial barriers.[23] The decision in *Espinoza* provides significant protection for the autonomy of religious communities such as schools because it constitutionally enables the financial support of religious educational institutions so that they can provide educational options to parents in accordance with a distinct religious ethos. This goes to the heart of a clause to protect the free 'exercise' of religion.[24]

The free exercise clause and establishment clause also work together to protect the autonomy of religious communities as a matter of principle. Both clauses have the objective of preventing government interference with religion, including

---

[19] *Trinity Lutheran Church of Columbia, Inc. v Comer*, 137 S. Ct. 2012 (2017).

[20] T Berg, 'Religious Freedom and Nondiscrimination' (2018) 50 *Loyola University Chicago Law Journal* 181, 188. See *Masterpiece Cakeshop v Colorado Civil Rights Commission* 138 S. Ct. 1719 (2018). *Fulton* was decided on similarly narrow grounds, with the Supreme Court holding that Philadelphia's contractual non-discrimination requirement contained a mechanism of discretionary exemptions which rendered it not generally applicable, meaning its enforcement against Catholic Social Services was hostile and unequal discrimination against religion. More significantly, three justices (Thomas, Alito and Gorsuch) argued *Smith* should be overruled, while another two (Kavanaugh and Barrett) also indicated that it should be overruled but were not sufficiently confident about what could replace it.

[21] C Capps, 'Incidental Burdens on First Amendment Freedoms' (2020) 96 *Notre Dame Law Review* 136.

[22] *Espinoza v Montana Department of Revenue*, 140 S. Ct. 2246 (2020).

[23] See T Berg and D Laycock, 'Espinoza, Government Funding, and Religious Choice' (2020) 35(3) *Journal of Law and Religion* 361–79.

[24] See ibid 365 where Berg and Laycock ground the protection of religious activities (such as education in accordance with religion) in the notion of 'free exercise'.

decisions to associate or not associate with religion.[25] This also occurs through exemptions. Religious exemptions are not a form of religious privilege. Congress may make laws which help religious freedom but do not amount to laws respecting establishment. As Esbeck observes:

> Government supporting religion, on the one hand, and government supporting acts of religious freedom, on the other hand, are two very different things. The former is deemed harmful to liberty and thus prohibited; the latter is good for liberty and so allowed. One long-standing application of this allowable 'good' is the discretionary enactment of religious exemptions.[26]

Hence, the First Amendment provides some protection for religious institutions to operate autonomously in accordance with their religion. However, this protection is significantly enhanced by the 'ministerial exception'.

C. The Ministerial Exception

The ministerial exception is a more religion-friendly (theological) approach which was foreshadowed by Carmella and Laycock; it provides a 'sphere of autonomy' to protect religious decisions relating to ministers, doctrine, and management of institutions.[27] *Hosanna-Tabor* directly addressed the question of whether employment discrimination laws may constitutionally be applied to the employment of ministers.[28] The Supreme Court unanimously held that the First Amendment bars suits brought on behalf of ministers against their churches claiming termination in violation of employment discrimination laws. In other words, federal discrimination laws do not apply to the selection of religious leaders by religious institutions, effectively granting an immunity or exception to ministerial employment:

> We agree that there is such a ministerial exception. The members of a religious group put their faith in the hands of their ministers. Requiring a church to accept or retain an unwanted minister, or punishing a church for failing to do so, intrudes upon more than a mere employment decision. Such action interferes with the internal governance of the church, depriving the church of control over the selection of those who will personify its beliefs.[29]

---

[25] GJ Simson, 'Permissible Accommodation or Impermissible Endorsement? A Proposed Approach to Religious Exemptions and the Establishment Clause' (2018) 106(4) *Kentucky Law Journal* 535, 544.

[26] C Esbeck, 'Do Discretionary Religious Exemptions Violate the Establishment Clause?' (2018) 106(4) *Kentucky Law Journal* 603, 631–32.

[27] Carmella, 'Theological Critique' (n 17) 804. See also D Laycock, 'Towards a General Theory of the Religion Clauses: The Case of Church-Labor Relations and the Right to Church Autonomy' (1981) 81 *Columbia Law Review* 1373. See generally H Alvare, 'Beyond Moralism: A Critique and a Proposal for Catholic Institutional Religious Freedom' (2019) 19(1) *Connecticut Public Interest Law Journal* 149–98.

[28] *Hosanna-Tabor Evangelical Lutheran Church & School v EEOC* 132 S. Ct. 694 (2012). See M McConnell, 'Reflections on Hosanna-Tabor' (2012) 35 *Harvard Journal of Law and Public Policy* 821, 822.

[29] *Hosanna-Tabor* at 705–06.

The establishment clause prevents the Government from appointing ministers, and the free exercise clause prevents Government from interfering with the freedom of religious groups to select their own leaders.[30] In this sense separation of church and state also 'protect[s] the autonomy of organised religion'.[31] Specifically, in *Hosanna-Tabor*, a church fired an employee for pursuing a legal claim against that church in contravention of 1 Corinthians 6, which prohibits Christians from pursuing secular legal action against one another. The church's decision to terminate the employee in turn violated a law against firing an employee for pursuing a legal action. Hence, this law was neutral and generally applicable, and yet the Court held it violated the free exercise clause and so was invalid. '*Hosanna-Tabor* is therefore … direct in its contravention of *Smith*', at least in the unique context of the ministerial exception.[32]

More recently, *Our Lady of Guadalupe* affirmed the exception, grounding it in a general principle of church autonomy which enables religious communities to have freedom over the government of their own institutions.[33] In this case the issue was whether the ministerial exception extends to teachers of religion in religious schools even if they are not technically 'clergy' and also have responsibility for secular subjects. The Supreme Court held that it does, and clarified that the determination of a 'minister' must be based on an evaluation of the religious function the position serves in the organisation ie a question of fact rather than the application of strict rules. According to the Court, religious education is at the core of the mission of a religious school and the selection and supervision of religion teachers is within the sphere of autonomy and must be free from government interference.[34] The ministerial exception therefore provides a broad and significant protection for religious institutional autonomy.

III. Federal Legislation

A. Religious Freedom Restoration Act

In the wake of the controversial decision in *Smith*, Congress disagreed with the removal of the strict scrutiny requirement, and passed RFRA to effectively reverse that decision.[35] The purpose of RFRA was explicitly stated to be to 'restore' the pre-*Smith* compelling interest test and to 'guarantee its application in all cases where free

---

[30] Huyett (n 11) 332.
[31] McConnell, 'Hosanna-Tabor' (n 28) 834.
[32] Huyett (n 11) 329.
[33] *Our Lady of Guadalupe School v Agnes Morrissey-Berru*, 140 S. Ct. 2049 (2020).
[34] ibid 2055–66.
[35] Berg, 'Religious Freedom' (n 20) 193–94.

exercise of religion is substantially burdened'.[36] Thus, it provided that 'Government shall not substantially burden a person's exercise of religion even if the burden results from a rule of general applicability', except if the Government demonstrates the 'application of the burden to the person' is 'in furtherance of a compelling government interest' and 'is the least restrictive means of achieving that interest'.[37] RFRA thus rejected the no exception for neutral laws of general applicability rule in *Smith*, mandating religious accommodation through the exemptions doctrine such that compliance with federal law should be exempted unless the government had a compelling interest which could not be achieved in some less restrictive way. It was adopted with virtually unanimous approval in Congress with the support of liberal and conservative advocacy groups and the enthusiastic approval of the Democrat President Clinton.[38] However, RFRA has since become controversial, a flashpoint for those who reject the idea of giving religious liberty any weight when the religious conduct in question is discriminatory.[39]

In relation to religious communities, the controversial *Hobby Lobby* case decided that closely-held corporations are persons capable of religious exercise, which attracts the protection of RFRA.[40] This means claims under RFRA can be considered as matters of collective religious liberty for two reasons. First, the Supreme Court understood RFRA as not merely a restorative action, but as a law providing very broad protection for religious liberty which extends beyond the pre-*Smith* free exercise jurisprudence. Second, on the basis of this expansive interpretation, the Court held that RFRA could include for-profit corporations which operate not merely as artificial individual persons, but as collective entities.[41] Hence RFRA is capable of providing significant protection for the autonomy of religious communities.

---

[36] *Religious Freedom Restoration Act* 42 U.S.C. § 2000bb (1993).

[37] ibid. The Supreme Court struck the Act down as an unconstitutional overreach as applied to the states, but allowed it to stand when applied to federal action – which is what is relevant for the purposes of this book. See B Martin, 'Ministerial Exception to Title VII (US)' (2010) 59 *Emory Law Journal* 1297, 1313.

[38] Smith, *Pagans and Christians* (n 14) 306, 310. See also D Laycock, 'The Religious Freedom Restoration Act 1993' (1993) *Brigham Young University Law Review* 221, explaining that RFRA effectively enacted a much needed form of a statutory Free Exercise Clause after *Smith*.

[39] Berg, 'Religious Freedom' (n 20) 194.

[40] *Burwell v Hobby Lobby Stores, Inc.* 134 S. Ct. 2751 (2014). This case will be explored more below.

[41] MD McNally, 'Native American Religious Freedom as a Collective Right' (2019) *Brigham Young University Law Review* 205, 275–76. However, as Hardee explores, there are also issues with determining the religious sincerity of a corporation when the members or shareholders of that corporation have diverse religious convictions. She recommends a dual inquiry into the veracity of the shareholders' religious beliefs and an attribution inquiry into whose religious beliefs should be considered in determining the sincerity of the corporation. However, this is a complex question which incorporates corporate law considerations beyond the scope of this book, and requires more careful engagement. See C Hardee, 'Schrodinger's Corporation: The Paradox of Religious Sincerity in Heterogenous Corporations' (2020) 61(5) *Boston College Law Review* 1764, 1764–65.

B. Religious Land Use and Institutionalised Persons Act

RLUIPA was passed by Congress as a supplement to RFRA after the Supreme Court held that RFRA did not apply to the states.[42] Since this book focuses on religious communities I will only consider the Religious Land Use aspect, and leave the institutionalised persons aspect to one side. RLUIPA is intended to prevent religious communities from being unreasonably restricted from using land for religious purposes, reinstating a strict scrutiny analysis (using the same test as in RFRA) for state and local laws which substantially burden religious conduct in the context of land use.[43] In other words, RLUIPA prohibits land-use restrictions that impose a substantial burden on the religious exercise of persons or assemblies, unless the government can demonstrate that the burden furthers a compelling government interest and is the least restrictive means of furthering that interest. It also prohibits the exclusion of religion, discriminatory treatment of religion over non-religion, or the preferencing of particular religions through land use regulations. If a religious community can successfully litigate under RLUIPA, they are exempt from the regulation even though it may be generally applicable.[44] So for example, the overturning of a zoning permit to expand a mosque on the basis of community protests enabled a successful suit for discriminatory treatment under RLUIPA, because the mosque was prevented from religious exercise in a way other faiths were not.[45]

RLUIPA also specifies that the use, building or conversion of real property for the purpose of religious exercise shall also be considered as religious exercise if the entity intends to use the property for that purpose.[46] However, this means not every activity carried out by a religious community will be religious exercise. For example, commercial proceeds from a building's operation controlled by and used to support religious exercise is not religious exercise.[47] The Supreme Court has never considered the land use aspect of RLUIPA, and Willis rejects the lower court approaches of 'effectively impracticable' and 'directly coercive' on the basis that they are too narrow and abstract.[48] Rather, Willis proposes a factor-based test which is clear and flexible to specific circumstances, taking into account the availability of alternative means or locations, improper actions or reasons by the municipality making land use decisions, substantial delay, uncertainty and expense, and unconditional denial of an application.[49]

---

[42] See generally Simson (n 25) 555–56.
[43] A Willis, 'Zoning on Holy Ground: Developing a Coherent Factor-Based Analysis for RLUIPA's Substantial Burden Provision' (2020) 95 *Chicago-Kent Law Review* 425, 430.
[44] RLUIPA 42 U.S.C. § 2000cc (2000).
[45] See Berg, 'Religious Freedom' (n 20) 183–84.
[46] RLUIPA 42 U.S.C. § 2000cc (2000).
[47] Willis (n 43) 432.
[48] ibid 440–41.
[49] See ibid 441–51.

More broadly, the Supreme Court has held that RLUIPA provides the same standard as RFRA for the purposes of free exercise, and like RFRA, this standard provides greater protection than even the pre-*Smith* jurisprudence.[50] Hence, RLUIPA provides significant protection for the autonomy of religious communities by enabling them to use land and property for the exercise of their religion.

C. Civil Rights Act: Title VII Exemptions

The Civil Rights Act of 1964 was enacted to protect the fundamental right of American citizens to be free from discrimination in employment. So for example Title VII prohibits discrimination in employment on the basis of religion for workplaces with 15 employees or more, effectively providing an exemption for many small businesses.[51] Furthermore, to protect First Amendment rights of religious freedom, Congress created specific protections for religious businesses. It is lawful for an employer to hire employees on the basis of religion where religion is a 'bona fide occupational qualification reasonably necessary to the normal operation of that particular business or enterprise'; the term 'religion' is broadly interpreted to mean 'all aspects of religious observance and practice, as well as belief, unless an employer demonstrates that he is unable to reasonably accommodate to an employee's or prospective employee's religious observance or practice without undue hardship on the conduct of the employer's business'.[52] Further protection is provided through a general exception for a 'religious corporation, association, educational institution, or society with respect to the employment of individuals of a particular religion to perform work connected with the carrying on ... of its activities' and a specific exception for religious educational institutions to employ persons of a particular religion.[53] These provisions demonstrate Congressional intent to protect the integrity and autonomy of religious organisations through allowing discrimination against employees performing religious functions, and may also include applying these provisions to 'a religious organization's secular activities because the statute is rationally related to the legitimate purpose of alleviating significant governmental interference with the ability of religious organizations to define and carry out their religious missions'.[54]

So Title VII exempts religious organisations from claims of religious discrimination, possibly even when the employee is performing ostensibly non-religious

---

[50] McNally (n 41) 278–80.

[51] *Civil Rights Act*, Title VII, 42 U.S.C. §§ 2000e (1964).

[52] ibid.

[53] See C Evans and A Hood, 'Religious Autonomy and Labour Law: A Comparison of the Jurisprudence of the United States and the European Court of Human Rights' (2012) 1(1) *Oxford Journal of Law and Religion* 81, 83–94.

[54] J Cappock, 'Meeting the Religious Organisation Exemption to Title VII: Choosing the Proper Test' (2020) 20 *Florida Coastal Law Review* 147, 149–50.

functions (though it does not exempt religious organisations from claims of racial or sex discrimination).[55] For example, in *Amos*, the Supreme Court held that the exemption applied to a worker fired from his engineering job at a gymnasium run by the Mormon Church for not meeting the requirements of church membership.[56] The Court argued that the establishment clause was not violated by such exemptions and suggested they may be required by the free exercise clause: religious employers are 'constitutionally entitled to an exemption from the anti-discrimination laws with respect to those employees who were hired to perform religious functions'.[57] In addition, the Court held that courts should not require religious organisations to hire those who do not share their beliefs and to decide which jobs are religious and non-religious because this could jeopardise the ability of religious organisations to carry out their mission.[58] Hence, it is clear that Title VII provides substantial protection for the autonomy of religious communities by enabling religious employers to internally regulate their employees in accordance with a religious ethos.

IV. Summary: The Legal Infrastructure for the Autonomy of Religious Communities in the US

The First Amendment provides considerable protection for the autonomy of religious communities. The establishment clause protects religious organisations in principle even with the ambiguity of the applicable test, and more expansive interpretations since *Smith* have enabled some protection by the free exercise clause. Of course, the ministerial exception provides explicit, broad and deep protection for the autonomy of religious communities, overcoming the minor deficiencies in the discrete applications of the establishment and free exercise clauses. RFRA also compensates for the narrow interpretation in *Smith* by restoring the more expansive pre-*Smith* jurisprudence; the Supreme Court has even held that the protections in RFRA go beyond that jurisprudence, and in addition apply to closely held corporations. Hence RFRA provides significant protection for the autonomy of religious communities. RLUIPA applies specifically to land use regulations and is framed in similar language to RFRA, and the Supreme Court has held that it provides a similar level of protection. Hence RLUIPA also provides protection for religious

---

[55] Alvare (n 27) 154.

[56] *Corporation of the Presiding Bishop of the Church of Jesus Christ of Latter-Day Saints v Amos*, 483 U.S. 327, 335–36 (1987).

[57] BJ Hill, 'Reconsidering Hostile Takeover of Religious Organisations' (2020) 97 *Washington University Law Review* 1833, 1842–43.

[58] ibid. Cappock (n 54) also advocates for an approach which defers to the claims of the religious organisation that they are religious, as supported by evidence of sincerity and consistency (161–62).

communities to use land as a function of their religious exercise. Finally, Title VII provides significant protection for religious communities to internally regulate their members, specifically by enabling religious employers to discriminate against employees on religious grounds. So the US Constitution and federal legislation provide a detailed and robust infrastructure for the autonomy of religious communities. The pertinent question thus becomes whether that infrastructure and its elements support peaceful coexistence in accordance with the theological virtues.

V. Evaluation of the Law: Peaceful Coexistence and the Theological Virtues

A. First Amendment: Establishment

Establishment clause jurisprudence is unclear and inconsistent. The Supreme Court has applied different tests without any kind of consistent rationale, resulting in outcomes which are difficult to draw principles from. Garry rejects *Lemon* and particularly the endorsement and neutrality tests as problematic.[59] Hence establishment clause jurisprudence and the endorsement test need to be reframed to reject the problematic 'wall of separation' metaphor and to recognise that secularism and humanism are becoming more politically dominant than Christianity.[60] The endorsement test is about remedying social alienation due to religious actions by the government, and 'religious believers have now become the alienated'.[61] The ignorance of and in some cases outright hostility towards religion (as exemplified in cases like Masterpiece Cakeshop) supports this.[62] Garry also rejects the neutrality approach on a similar basis, because facially equal treatment is biased against religion. It denies religion's special role (and special recognition as evidenced in the First Amendment), and erodes religious liberty by using

---

[59] P Garry, 'Establishment Clause Jurisprudence Still Groping for Clarity: Articulating a New Constitutional Model' (2020) 12(2) *Northeastern University Law Review* 660, 660–63.

[60] P Garry, 'When Anti-Establishment Becomes Exclusion: The Supreme Court's Opinion in *American Legion v. American Humanist Association* and the Flip Side of Endorsement' (2020) 99(3) *Nebraska Law Review* 643, 643–45.

[61] Garry, 'Anti-Establishment' (n 60) 651.

[62] ibid 656–60; RT Anderson, 'Disagreement Is Not Always Discrimination: On Masterpiece Cakeshop and the Analogy to Interracial Marriage' (2018) 16 *Georgetown Journal of Law and Public Policy* 123, 127–30. *Masterpiece Cakeshop* illustrated tensions between equality and religious liberty, and demonstrated a rapidly decreasing social acceptance of religious liberty: see A Sorkin, '"Them": Bridging Divides Between Distant Neighbours after *Masterpiece Cakeshop*' (2019) 54(1) *University of San Francisco Law Review* 117, 143–50. For a detailed analysis of how civil rights laws have been enforced disparately against particular disfavoured religious groups and practices, see J Marshall, 'Selective Civil Rights Enforcement and Religious Liberty' (2020) 72 *Stanford Law Review* 1421.

'secular' principles as the comparator for neutral treatment (for example applying general anti-discrimination laws to religious organisations).[63] It favours the secular over the religious by saying that the secular can never offend or alienate, but the religious can.[64] This alienation of the religious is inconsistent with peaceful coexistence in accordance with the theological virtues. It rejects the notions of humility and patience towards diverse and minority views, and fundamentally undermines the law of love because it is not loving our religious neighbours to alienate them or be hostile towards them.

Hence, the establishment clause should be interpreted to enhance the scope of religious liberty rather than to diminish it. If religious believers have become the alienated and the ones suffering hostility, then 'it is the religious believer who should be the beneficiary of the clause'.[65] So Garry argues for an accommodationist view which protects a free and vibrant presence of religion.[66] This view consists of nonpreferentialism as the test.[67] This means the establishment clause keeps government from excluding or marginalising religion or non-religion in the social sphere, and as a result the clause 'protects the opportunity for a vibrantly pluralistic religious presence in society'.[68] Similarly, Barclay argues that since the establishment clause is most plausibly concerned with non-preference of religion or particular religions, it can promote pluralism in the public sphere by enabling non-discriminatory aid of and government cooperation with religious groups. 'Such an interpretation could facilitate an increase in religious pluralism and human flourishing and a decrease in unnecessary cultural fights aimed at excluding religion from the public sphere'.[69] This interpretation would consequently contribute to loving our neighbour by exhibiting humility, forgiveness and patience towards different views, a willingness to accept genuine diversity by not excluding any perspectives and enabling the peaceful coexistence of diverse religious communities without government favour of any in particular.[70]

---

[63] Garry, 'Establishment Clause' (n 59) 661–68. See eg *Zelman v Simmons-Harris*, 536 U.S. 639 (2002); cf *Christian Legal Society Chapter v Martinez*, 558 U.S. 1076 (2009).

[64] Garry, 'Establishment Clause' (n 59) 668.

[65] Garry 'Anti-Establishment' (n 60) 651, 672–73.

[66] Garry 'Establishment Clause' (n 59) 688.

[67] See PM Garry, 'Religious Freedom Deserves More than Neutrality: The Constitutional Argument for Nonpreferential Favoritism of Religion' (2005) 57 *Florida Law Review* 1, 3. Though McConnell has written that nonpreferentialism is not a viable theory, this was prior to the Supreme Court's recent rejection of *Lemon* and the endorsement test: cf MW McConnell, 'Religious Freedom at a Crossroads' (1992) 59 *University of Chicago Law Review* 115, 146–47.

[68] Garry, 'Anti-Establishment' (n 60) 653–54. See also J Wexler, 'Government Disapproval of Religion' (2013) *Brigham Young University Law Review* 119, 121–22.

[69] Barclay (n 10) 1727–28.

[70] See eg A Deagon, 'A Christian Framework for Religious Diversity in Political Discourse' in M Quinlan, I Benson and K Thompson (eds), *Religious Freedom in Australia: A new Terra Nullius?* (Connor Court Publishing, 2019) 130–62.

B. First Amendment: Free Exercise and Smith

Carmella engages in a theological critique of free exercise jurisprudence, espe-cially as enunciated in *Smith*, to demonstrate the broad variety of religious conduct which constitutes 'free exercise' and should attract protection even from generally applicable laws.[71] In particular, religious communities incorporating secular tech-niques and offering secular services, but still operating within a religious context for a primarily religious purpose, should still be considered a protected religious activity.[72] In such determinations, government should 'use theology to the extent that it assists them in identifying what is religious'; this approach will minimise reliance on a secular 'religious minority or cultural liberties paradigm', expanding free exercise protection to religious conduct as distinct from secular conduct.[73] This approach demonstrates an imaginative sympathy with the religious entity in accordance with the law of love and the golden rule, loving neighbour by treating them how you would like to be treated, consistent with the theological virtues.[74]

Carmella observes that the pre-*Smith* cases leading to the *Smith* decision enshrined a narrow, rule-based and ultimately secular notion of religion which defined religion as individual, narrow conscience objections, with the presump-tion that such objections should not often be excused from legal requirements.[75] A more religion-friendly approach would retain the conscience aspect which is of course important for any religious conduct, but also engage with a more sophisticated treatment of ostensibly 'secular' activities such as counselling, rehabilitation, and moral dialogue by recognising that 'these forms of religious conduct are rooted firmly in belief and are motivated by broad obligations to love and serve the neighbour'.[76] These 'secular' or 'cultural' activities are the most effec-tive method of implementing these obligations for many religious organisations, and therefore burdens imposed on these activities by generally applicable laws are substantial burdens on conscience 'in the broadest sense'.[77] Again, this approach involves an imaginative sympathy, in conjunction with the theological virtues of humility, peace and patience displayed by acceptance of distinctive religious and non-religious forms of pursuing the common good.

Hence, free exercise of religion in accordance with peaceful coexistence and the theological virtues includes a capacious understanding of and protection of religious practices, enabling an 'exemption-friendly jurisprudence' which

---

[71] Carmella, 'Theological Critique' (n 17) 784–88.

[72] ibid 789–90.

[73] ibid 793.

[74] See A Deagon, 'The "Religious Questions" Doctrine: Addressing (Secular) Judicial Incompetence' (2021) 47(1) *Monash University Law Review* 60–87.

[75] Carmella, 'Theological Critique' (n 17) 799.

[76] ibid 803–04.

[77] ibid.

'demands respect and equitable treatment for religious practice and identity'.[78] This is also demonstrated in the more recent decision of *Espinoza*, which pursues a 'confident pluralism', or peaceful coexistence in accordance with the theological virtues by graciously welcoming religion to public life and confirming the equal dignity of religious citizens by recognising that government cannot discriminate against religious organisations.[79]

C. First Amendment: Free Exercise, Discrimination and Masterpiece Cakeshop

i. Complicity and Burden

However, exemptions granted to religious communities in a public context can create tension with other laws such as anti-discrimination laws. The obvious example is *Masterpiece Cakeshop*, where a religious vendor refused to create a special cake for a same-sex wedding because of a conscientious objection to same-sex marriage.[80] Though the Court ultimately did not decide the question of whether the First Amendment freedom of religion protection allowed Masterpiece Cakeshop to be exempt from generally applicable anti-discrimination laws (instead deciding in favour of the vendor on more narrow religious animus grounds), the case crystallised the conflict between the freedom of a religious vendor to operate their business in accordance with their convictions, and the equality principle that a person should not be discriminated against for their personal attributes in a public, commercial context. According to leading LGBT activist Chai Feldblum, such conflicts can only be resolved through 'generosity of spirit'.[81] In this book I give substantive content to such calls through applying the theological virtues such as dignity, humility, patience, generosity, kindness, forgiveness and compassion. Particularly relevant to this conflict are dignity and forgiveness, which respectively recognise the inherent worth of all humans as created in the image of God, and a willingness to permit genuine difference, even profound moral disagreement, loving neighbour as self by aiming to persuade to what is true and good as Jesus did, while also accepting freedom to reject and disagree with our most deeply held convictions.

---

[78] A Carmella, 'Progressive Religion and Free Exercise Exemptions' (2020) 68 *Kansas Law Review* 535, 581. Furthermore, lest it be thought that a broad interpretation of the free exercise clause is merely part of a nefarious conservative agenda, it is worth noting that religious freedom crosses party lines, as also seen in this article by Carmella.

[79] See J Inazu, *Confident Pluralism: Surviving and Thriving Through Deep Difference* (University of Chicago Press, 2016).

[80] *Masterpiece Cakeshop v Colorado Civil Rights Commission* 138 S. Ct. 1719 (2018).

[81] C Feldblum, 'Religious Liberty and LGBT Rights: Finding the Right Balance (Ginsburg Lecture)' (2019) 41(2) *Thomas Jefferson Law Review* 163, 164–65.

Of course, what is at stake is not simple discrimination against a person because of a religious rejection of homosexuality. As Anderson notes, the vendor in Masterpiece Cakeshop 'did not discriminate' by refusing to provide services in a commercial context. The vendor 'refused to create an artistic cake to celebrate a same-sex marriage based on his common Christian belief that a same-sex wedding is not marital ... Phillips was simply trying to avoid complicity in what he considers one distortion of marriage among others' – he also refused to create 'divorce cakes'.[82] The request to provide a wedding cake is a request 'directly to facilitate same-sex relationships' in a manner which expresses moral approval.[83]

On the question of burden, Simson notes based on an analysis of free exercise cases that the standard for meeting a 'substantial burden' must be quite high – the burden must be 'severe' and 'inescapable', forcing the claimant to choose between abandoning one of the precepts of their religion or forfeiting benefits/suffering imposition.[84] As they do and should, in the vast majority of cases the courts defer to the claimant's understanding of the burdened belief as 'religious'.[85] The analysis of the extent of burden itself is more complex and requires articulating and balancing the variety of alternatives for their 'practical availability' and 'likelihood of achieving the desired effect'. Simson then argues on this basis that the burden on the baker in *Masterpiece Cakeshop* was not substantial, because he could have removed himself from the wedding cake business and this did not impose as much of a burden as on the merchants in *Braunfeld* where the burden was not viewed as substantial.[86] In *Braunfeld*, the merchants would have had to close for an extra day. But for Phillips, who eventually did decide to remove himself from the industry, the cost was 40 per cent of his business and six of his nine employees.[87] This far exceeds the burden of merely closing one extra day, and following Simson's logic the imposition constitutes a substantial burden given the significant forfeiture of benefits for both Phillips and his employees.

Simson's analysis also fails to account for the devastating effect litigation can have on the religious vendor. The harms suffered by those discriminated against are real and legitimate, but the religious vendor also suffers real, legitimate and arguably more severe harms, facing the impossible choice between supplying a product against their conscience, refusing and receiving the penalty of the law,

---

[82] Anderson, 'Disagreement' (n 62) 129. For further resources explaining how religious communities view themselves as morally complicit in 'sin' if they do not refuse to provide services/venues etc, see A Sorkin, '"Them": Bridging Divides Between Distant Neighbours after *Masterpiece Cakeshop*' (2019) 54(1) *University of San Francisco Law Review* 117, 134–42.

[83] ibid 137–38. See MW McConnell, 'Dressmakers, Bakers, and the Equality of Rights' in WN Eskridge, Jr and R Fretwell Wilson (eds), *Religious Freedom, LGBT Rights, and the Prospects for Common Ground* (Cambridge University Press, 2018) 378–85.

[84] Simson (n 25) 564–68.

[85] ibid 573.

[86] ibid 576–78; see *Braunfeld v Brown* 366 U.S. 599 (1961).

[87] See A Deagon, 'Religious Schools, Religious Vendors and Refusing Services After Ruddock: Diversity or Discrimination? (2019) 93(9) *Australian Law Journal* 766, 773.

or removing themselves from the relevant industry.[88] The vendor in the *Arlene's Flowers* case (a similar situation where a florist who had regularly supplied flowers to a same-sex couple refused to do so for their wedding) is in danger of losing her house, retirement and life savings as a result of the personal case against her.[89] This material and economic harm is in addition to the spiritual harm (as perceived by the vendors) which vendors may suffer if they offend their religious convictions, and the emotional harm which they may suffer from feeling that they are being attacked for their religious beliefs. Conversely, the same-sex couple who is denied a service may suffer a dignity harm if they perceive that they are not being served due to their sexual orientation, but their material and economic harm is minimal. In the vast majority of circumstances an alternative service is easily available and all the vendors who refused service in fact recommended alternative services to the couples.[90] Laycock outlines the issues persuasively:

> the balance of hardships clearly and unambiguously tips in favor of the religious objector. The offended gay couples are referred to another wedding vendor, or readily find one, and they still get to live their own lives by their own values. They will still love each other. They will still be married. They will still have their occupations or professions. But the conscientious objector who is denied exemption does not get to live his own life by his own values. He is forced to repeatedly violate conscience or to abandon his occupation and profession. The harm of regulation on the religious side is permanent loss of identity or permanent loss of occupation, and that far outweighs the one-time dignitary or insult harm on the couple's side.[91]

Furthermore, the claim that (for example) Christian vendors with traditional views on sexuality can simply do something else also undermines the harm and difficulty they may face. There are the sunk costs of investment in a business and the costs of re-educating or re-skilling, the stress of dealing with a potential court case or financial sanction, and the shrinking number of options available to them which are also not impacted by discrimination laws.[92] 'This permanent harm is far greater than the one-time dignitary harm on the couple's side', and therefore the balance of hardship clearly supports exemptions.[93]

Similarly, Berg argues that the harm resulting from a refusal of service is inherently limited. One harm is material, very minor in situations where another

---

[88] A Deagon, 'Defining the Interface of Freedom and Discrimination: Exercising Religion, Democracy and Same-Sex Marriage' (2017) 20 *International Trade and Business Law Review* 239, 283–85.

[89] See www.tri-cityherald.com/opinion/opn-columns-blogs/article222905470.html.

[90] D Laycock, 'The Wedding-Vendor Cases' (2018) 41(1) *Harvard Journal of Law and Public Policy* 49, 63. Furthermore, as Craddock notes, where religious vendors politely and respectfully decline services and recommend an alternative, some customers may not suffer any dignity harm at all; reasonable customers may disagree about whether their dignity has been impugned. See J Craddock, 'The Case for Complicity-Based Religious Accommodations' (2018) 12 *Tennessee Journal of Law and Policy* 233, 248.

[91] Laycock, 'The Wedding-Vendor Cases' (n 90) 65.

[92] Smith, *Pagans and Christians* (n 14) 340–42.

[93] Berg, 'Religious Freedom' (n 20) 207–08.

service is readily available. Another harm is dignitary, but 'cannot be considered in isolation when a claim of liberty of conscience stands on the other side. Religion is also a fundamental identity, so penalizing the objector for her religiously driven conduct also imposes a significant dignitary harm'.[94] The religious vendor believes they are being asked to defy God's will, to do serious wrong that is offensive to the being they worship and value most highly; that will torment their conscience and cause significant emotional distress. Religious liberty is specifically for the purpose of preventing this type of dignitary harm, and therefore the customer's sense of being rejected or disapproved of cannot justify inflicting such harm.[95] As Laycock concludes, the entire First Amendment tradition is settled that offensiveness is not a compelling interest that can justify suppressing liberty. 'Reciprocal moral disapproval is inherent in a pluralistic society; the desire of same-sex couples never to encounter such disapproval is not a sufficient reason to deprive others of religious liberty'.[96]

No doubt there are some people who are simply prejudiced. They hate gays and lesbians and hide behind religious ideas to justify their hate. But the religious vendors generally do not fall into this category. As exemplified by the likes of Phillips in Masterpiece Cakeshop, they have sincere and consistent religious convictions about marriage and are happy to serve gay and lesbian customers in every other context. They are entitled to the presumption that they have a genuine conscience claim, even if the claim is not upheld in the end.[97] As such, the logic of this analysis would not open the floodgates of religious exemption claims. It is a specific, narrowly tailored category where a religious vendor refuses an expressive good or service due to a conscientious objection. And even if this category is established, there may be a compelling interest to deny the exemption if it would 'materially limit' access to goods or services (ie there is no reasonably or readily available alternative) or if the logic of the category is broad enough to lead to 'repeated refusals'.[98] Neither of those limits apply in *Masterpiece Cakeshop* or in most of the wedding-vendor cases.

Hence, dignity and forgiveness are most effectively upheld through limited and carefully defined religious exemptions which promote peaceful coexistence, providing the 'best hope of protecting both sides'.[99] The dignity of those who may be refused services is ensured by enabling access to goods and services without

[94] ibid.
[95] ibid.
[96] D Laycock, 'Liberty and Justice for All' in WN Eskridge, Jr and R Fretwell Wilson (eds), *Religious Freedom, LGBT Rights, and the Prospects for Common Ground* (Cambridge University Press, 2018) 29–30. This also refutes Simson's ((n 25) 593–98) argument that denying an exemption is a compelling interest because of avoiding the ripple effects and stigma associated with endorsing discrimination.
[97] Berg, 'Religious Freedom' (n 20) 187–88.
[98] ibid 207–08; Deagon, 'Defining the Interface' (n 88) 275–83.
[99] Berg, 'Religious Freedom' (n 20) 205–08.

frequent rejection, and rejection will not be allowed if there are no reasonably available alternatives. This can be enhanced by having vendors provide details of readily accessible alternatives.[100] The dignity of the religious vendors is also upheld by allowing them to operate their businesses in accordance with their conscience. Forgiveness and compassion is displayed by having both 'sides' recognise the dignity and rights of the other, enabling them to live authentically and holistically consonant with their identities, even though there may be deep moral disagreement between them.

ii. *Third-Party Harms*

The analysis above has so far only considered parties who suffer direct harm from the presence or absence of religious exemptions. However, other scholars argue religious accommodation is wrong because it imposes third-party harms.[101] For example, NeJaime and Siegel state that where complicity-based religious liberty claims impose third-party harms (such as where the refusal to sell a wedding cake to a same-sex couple imposes a broader dignity and/or material harm by rendering it more socially acceptable to discriminate), these exemptions should be eliminated.[102] However, as already noted above, the discussion of third-party harms does not consider the harms imposed on religious vendors if exemptions are removed.[103] Similarly, material harms imposed on customers are minimal if there are other services readily available as there are in most situations; indeed, many religious vendors with conscientious objections may not refuse services to avoid the legal, social and economic penalties.[104] Smith also saliently points out that in the most well-known and accepted instance of religious accommodation – exemption of religious pacifists from military service – the harm to third parties is real and severe, even if those particular parties are not specifically identifiable. For every person exempted, another will go and fight and perhaps die in their place.[105] The harms to third parties in the controversial accommodation cases (dignity harm, economic harm) pale in comparison, and if the war exemption is accepted in this context of third-party harm, the less harmful accommodation ought to be accepted as a general principle as well.[106]

---

[100] ibid.

[101] See eg F Gedicks and R Van Tassell, 'RFRA Exemptions from the Contraception Mandate: An Unconstitutional Accommodation of Religion' (2014) 49 *Harvard Civil Rights-Civil Liberties Law Review* 343.

[102] D NeJaime and RB Siegel, 'Conscience Wars: Complicity-Based Conscience Claims in Religion and Politics' (2015) 124 *Yale Law Journal* 2516, 2522.

[103] Craddock (n 90) 245, 257–58, 270.

[104] ibid 242, 245, 246.

[105] Smith, *Pagans and Christians* (n 14) 320 fn 75.

[106] See M DeGirolami, 'Free Exercise by Moonlight' (2016) 53 *San Diego Law Review* 105, 131–44. *cf* W Marshall, 'Third-Party Burdens and Conscientious Objection to War' (2018) 106(4) *Kentucky Law Journal* 685 where the author considers this issue in a more sustained (albeit ultimately inconclusive) way.

The third-party harm principle also suffers from overreach. It assumes third-party harm 'is a juridical category that can be both defined and bounded. It cannot. Thus, the logic behind the category risks expanding and overwhelming every religious exemption.'[107] The extension of exemption to some is a loss to all others who do not satisfy the exemptions, however attenuated the harm caused by such differential treatment.[108] 'To abolish exemptions would work primarily to the injury of religious minorities, which would bring about a sea of change in the venerable American practice of extending a welcoming hand to peoples of diverse faiths.'[109] Religious exemptions promote pluralism and enable the participation of religion in public life. Nevertheless, despite these objections to the third-party harm principle, it is entirely proper that consideration of these real and legitimate harms is taken into account.[110] Bearing in mind third-party harms in conjunction with the harms suffered by religious vendors if exemptions are removed affirms the theological virtues of dignity and forgiveness, facilitating peaceful coexistence by acknowledging the intrinsic worth of all stakeholders and recognising diversity.

iii. *The Race Analogy*

Koppelman also dismisses the commonly cited 'racism analogy' (that exemptions for religious vendors to refuse services on the basis of conscientious objections are like exemptions for racists to refuse services on the basis of prejudice, and therefore should not be granted) because religious people are not evil or hateful, and have genuine and rational beliefs about good moral behaviour. This is an essential aspect of religious diversity, and liberal democracies have a long tradition of religious accommodation. Furthermore, where the racists often used violence, the conservative Christians are largely peaceful. It is more conducive to peaceful coexistence to find ways to accommodate the wedding vendors without defeating the point of anti-discrimination, affirming the dignity and worth of all parties, than to intensify conflict by attempting to eradicate diverse views using state coercion.[111] Laycock further distinguishes the wedding-vendor cases from

---

[107] Esbeck (n 26) 608, 628–29.

[108] ibid 628.

[109] ibid 608.

[110] ibid 607. See (2018) 106(4) *Kentucky Law Journal*, containing authors who respond to many of the objections to the third-party harm principle. I do not intend to resolve the debate here. Suffice it to say I agree with Brady that third-party harms should be taken into consideration when determining whether exemptions should be provided, which is a sensible middle ground between ignoring them completely or excluding all religious accommodations which impose third party harms. See K Brady, 'Religious Accommodations and Third-Party Harms: Constitutional Values and Limits' (2018) 106(4) *Kentucky Law Journal* 717, 723; *cf* M Schwartzman, N Tebbe and R Schragger, 'The Costs of Conscience' 106(4) *Kentucky Law Journal* 781.

[111] A Koppelman, *Gay Rights vs Religious Liberty: The Unnecessary Conflict* (Oxford University Press, 2020) 6–8. See also A Koppelman, 'Gay Rights, Religious Liberty, and the Misleading Racism Analogy' (2020)(1) *Brigham Young University Law Review* 1–32. It is worth noting that the conservative Christian objection to same-sex marriage (manifested through service refusal) is centred around two important concepts which further distinguish this objection from the racism analogy. First, where the colour of

the race analogy on the basis that a mere handful of cases indicates that there is no systemic problem; it is therefore in no way equivalent to the systematic oppression of African-Americans in the twentieth century.[112]

To avoid the 'dignity harm' associated with the 'personal rejection' which may be experienced during wedding planning, Koppelman suggests passing laws so that 'vendors are required, as a precondition for exemption, to make their objections to same-sex marriages clear to the public in advance'.[113] Hence, religious freedom can be accommodated by allowing the vendors to adhere to their conscience, while anti-discrimination principles are not undermined through the major source of dignity harm being removed. This is equivalent to the transparency idea discussed in Chapter One. Other 'possible compromises' include 'an exemption for very small businesses, or for religiously oriented businesses, or expressive enterprises such as photographers'.[114]

However, for some this view deeply fails to appreciate the real and substantial harm that results from permitting discrimination – practically, individually and systemically. Practically, it causes a material harm in the sense of the time, effort and expense wasted to find a vendor, only to be told to try one down the road. Individually, it causes a dignity harm in the sense of a personal rejection based on identity. Systemically, it contributes to a culture where discrimination is seen to be legitimate and acceptable, which may cause more instances. Koppelman's proposed solution of making objections clear in advance effectively amounts to a proclamation that 'gays are not welcome here', which in turn contributes to systemic, practical and individual harm.[115] Feldblum too rejects exemptions for religious vendors on the basis that it is in the commercial sphere and would undermine

---

one's skin is an intrinsic attribute which cannot be changed, one's sexual behavior is a choice. This does not require arguing or accepting that sexual orientation is a choice, merely that orientation is distinct from behaviour. So where racists object to an intrinsic attribute, the vendors object to a particular behaviour. This discontinuity is demonstrated by the fact that the wedding vendors are happy to serve members of the LGBT community in general, but a racist would not be happy to serve at all. The second concept is the belief that sex distinction is intrinsic to the concept of marriage. Conservative Christians reject same-sex marriage not because of objection to LGBT people, but because of objection to the idea that marriage can in fact be same-sex. Conversely, the racist rejects the idea of an interracial marriage because of an objection to the people, not because of an intrinsic and principled tradition of what marriage is. See eg Anderson, 'Disagreement' (n 62); G Walsh, 'Same-Sex Marriage and Religious Liberty' (2016) 35(2) *The University of Tasmania Law Review* 106; E Kao and M Burke, '*Masterpiece Cakeshop* and Authentic Pluralism in a Post-*Obergefell* World' (2020) 24(1) *Texas Review of Law and Politics* 97.

[112] D Laycock, 'The Broader Implications of Masterpiece Cakeshop' (2019) *Brigham Young University Law Review* 167, 192–93.

[113] Koppelman, *Gay Rights vs Religious Liberty* (n 111) 10–11.

[114] ibid 11. For a detailed discussion of further criteria see Deagon, 'Refusing Services' (n 87).

[115] See the strident critiques of Koppelman in S Gilreath, 'Anti-Gay Discrimination, "Conscience Exemptions" and the Racism Analogy: A reply to Professor Koppelman' (2020) 1 *Brigham Young University Law Review* 33; J Oleske, 'In the Court of Koppelman: Motion for Reconsideration' (2020) 1 *Brigham Young University Law Review* 51. See also L Melling, 'Religious Refusals to Public Accommodations Laws: Four Reasons to Say No' (2015) 38 *Harvard Journal of Law and Gender* 177, 189–91.

the societal message of equality.[116] This position reflects a broader view expressed by the Chair of the US Commission on Civil Rights that religious liberty in the civil rights context is hypocrisy and a code word for 'discrimination, intolerance, racism, sexism, homophobia, Islamophobia [and] Christian supremacy'; however, as Berg points out, this position is 'wrong and counterproductive'.[117]

It is wrong because as noted above numerous times, the vast majority of religious vendors have genuine conscientious objections to expressing support for particular moral practices. They are not prejudiced or malicious. They are willing to generally serve all customers, and when they cannot, they happily recommend readily available alternatives. It is counterproductive because, as Brownstein and Berg sagely observe:

> If we take religious freedom seriously, not every harm declared by government can suffice to prohibit a religious practice … Rights have costs, and free exercise should be no exception … If religious freedom confers no right to harm others, and modern government can define anything it chooses as a harm, religious freedom will shrink dramatically. That approach can never provide the security for personal rights that will reduce fear and polarization. By the same token, ignoring significant harms can intensify polarization rather than calm it.[118]

As such, narrow and clear exemptions appear to be the best compromise. They are not a perfect solution and will still produce harm to those few customers who are discriminated against, and to the religious vendors who do not satisfy them. But such exemptions affirm the dignity of both parties by seriously considering the respective harms suffered by customers and vendors, and pursue peaceful coexistence by enabling the practice of the theological virtues of forgiveness, patience, humility, kindness and compassion rendered necessary when those who have profound intellectual and moral disagreements share a public space for mutual and common good.

It is also worth noting that it is often objected that religious accommodations violate equality because it treats religious parties differently or privileges them. However, as Smith demonstrates, this is question-begging, for all citizens cannot be treated uniformly. Virtually every law 'discriminates' by treating different classes of people differently. To claim that 'exempting religious believers violates equality because it treats them differently, or because it discriminates, is merely a conclusory form of begging the question'.[119] Equality means like cases should be treated alike, and so the crucial question is whether there is any good reason to treat religious parties differently. This 'good reason' could be because specific constitutional provisions specify special treatment of religion, or because

---

[116] Feldblum (n 81) 172.

[117] Berg, 'Religious Freedom' (n 20) 195.

[118] T Berg and A Brownstein, 'Giving Our Better Angels a Chance: A Dialogue on Religious Liberty and Equality' (2021) 21(2) *Journal of Appellate Practice and Process* 325, 333–34.

[119] Smith, *Pagans and Christians* (n 14) 320–21.

this recognises the possibility of a higher divine authority a religious party may be subject to, or, most importantly, because religious freedom and diversity contributes to the common good.[120]

iv. Religious Communities and the Common Good

Finke and Mataic show that facilitating the autonomy of religious communities is important for the common good by empirically demonstrating how repression of religion is associated with violence and social conflict. 'Although government restrictions on religion are often justified in an effort to reduce tensions and conflict, research suggests that the opposite occurs; government restrictions are associated with higher levels of tension and conflict' and, in a vicious cycle, 'social restrictions lead to higher levels of government restrictions, which in turn lead to persecution that is more violent. Following the heightened violent persecution, religious groups respond with heightened social restrictions'.[121] One of the 'strongest predictors' for social restrictions are 'government favouritism for a single religion', which entails government discrimination against religion.[122]

Similarly, Carlson-Thies argues that an 'extensive freedom for religious institutions to be distinctive – to depart from generally accepted practices and standards – is necessary to achieving the common good'.[123] Providing autonomy for religious communities to govern themselves enables the creation of diverse facilities and services which develop in accordance with different moral and religious convictions. These diverse convictions do not imply disrespect or harm towards groups that do not believe or act in accordance with such convictions, but rather contribute towards a rich tapestry of understandings which seek to promote public good using different methods.[124] Diverse institutions provide a safe haven for diverse individuals with varying self-understandings and convictions, as opposed to policies which flatten or eliminate religious diversity in pursuit of the admittedly important goal of eliminating wrongful discrimination.[125] For example, it is

---

[120] ibid 321–22. See eg T Berg, 'Religious Freedom and the Common Good: A Summary of Arguments and Issues' (2019) 15(3) *University of St Thomas Law Journal* 517; T Berg, 'Freedom to Serve: Religious Organizational Freedom, LGBT Rights, and the Common Good' in WN Eskridge, Jr and R Fretwell Wilson (eds), *Religious Freedom, LGBT Rights, and the Prospects for Common Ground* (Cambridge University Press, 2018).

[121] R Finke and DR Mataic, 'Promises, Practices and Consequences of Religious Freedom: A Global Overview' (2019) 15(3) *University of St Thomas Law Journal* 587, 601.

[122] ibid 595–600.

[123] S Carlson-Thies, 'The Common Good Requires Robust Institutional Religious Freedom' (2019) 15(3) *University of St Thomas Law Journal* 529, 529.

[124] ibid 532–33. See J Harrison, *Post-Liberal Religious Liberty* (Cambridge University Press, 2020).

[125] Carlson-Thies (n 123) 533. See Also RW Garnett, 'Religious Freedom And The Nondiscrimination Norm' in A Sarat (ed), *Legal Responses To Religious Practices In The United States: Accommodation And Its Limits* (Cambridge University Press, 2012) 194, 194–227. See also NA Berkeley, 'Religious Freedom And LGBT Rights: Trading Zero Sum Approaches For Careful Distinctions And Genuine Pluralism' (2015) 50 *Gonzalez Law Review* 1, 1–28.

a common view that religious vendors should not discriminate against customers. However, allowing diverse establishments will appeal to diverse employees and customers.[126]

For a genuine reconciliation of these tensions, Brownstein observes that the fears, concerns and harms on both sides need to be taken seriously. For both gay couples and religious individuals, their commitments are not mere lifestyle choices but life-defining and identity-constituting. Unfortunately both sides can view each other as evil.[127] So Brownstein advocates empathy as a solution, which strongly correlates to theological virtues such as humility and patience. Practically, this empathy can be demonstrated by gay rights advocates supporting protections of religious liberty (where LGBT or other core rights are not at risk) and religious liberty advocates accepting the outcome of the same-sex marriage debate and supporting civil rights laws protecting the LGBT community in areas where religious liberty is not an issue. In harder issues where LGBT and religious liberty rights conflict, Brownstein indicates compromise may be possible in a limited number of professional services where the religious beliefs of the provider cannot be separated from the delivery of quality services, such as religious marriage counsellors.[128] But this is also the case for situations like *Masterpiece Cakeshop*, as Laycock argues – the job of the creative wedding vendor is to make the marriage the best it can be, to promote their product with specific reference to the nature of the couple's relationship as informed by their beliefs. In principle then, limited exemptions could be granted to religious vendors as outlined above.[129]

As Brady explains, what is needed is a 'more nuanced balancing approach that gives greater weight to the value of religious liberty' and takes into account the full range of relevant factors that affect the seriousness of any harm, including the 'type and magnitude of the religious burden' and the 'nature, degree and likelihood' of harm.[130] For example, where government rules threaten religious conduct perceived as critical to the faith or interfere with the autonomy of a religious community, religious believers are more likely to seek exemptions. The goal should always be to seek solutions which minimise burdens on both sides, rather than focus on one at the expense of the other. 'Mutually acceptable compromises' are possible but require listening and working together 'in good faith'.[131]

---

[126] Carlson-Thies (n 123) 532. For a penetrating discussion of Religious Freedom and Commercial Entities, see RJ Colombo, *The First Amendment and the Business Corporation* (Oxford University Press, 2014). See also SV Monsma and S Carlson-Thies, *Free To Serve: Protecting The Religious Freedom Of Faith-Based Organizations* (Brazos Press, 2015) 101–04.

[127] A Brownstein: 'Choosing Among Non-Negotiated Surrender, Negotiated Protection Of Liberty And Equality, Or Learning And Earning Empathy' in WN Eskridge, Jr. and R Fretwell Wilson (eds), *Religious Freedom, LGBT Rights, and the Prospects for Common Ground* (Cambridge University Press, 2018) 12–15, 19–20. See also Laycock, 'Liberty and Justice' (n 96) 26–27.

[128] Brownstein (n 127) 20–22.

[129] Laycock, 'Liberty and Justice' (n 96) 29; Deagon, 'Refusing Services' (n 87).

[130] Brady, 'Third party harms' (n 110) 723.

[131] ibid 727, 730.

Brady endorses the solution proposed in this chapter, which involves narrow and clear exemptions.[132] Specifically, genuinely religious vendors would be exempt from providing marriage-related services if they give notice of their policy and provide access to reasonably available alternative services. Brady aptly characterises this compromise as follows:

> The most serious burdens on each side will be addressed while reducing harms to the other side. The overall message of such a compromise will not be second-class citisenship for either conservative religious believers or same-sex couples. It will be respect for those on both sides of the culture wars and recognition of their place within the larger community. Without a solution that accounts for the interests of both sides, our divisions will deepen and further undermine larger social and political values we have in common. When James Madison repeated the call in Virginia's Declaration of Rights for all to practice mutual forbearance, love, and charity, he linked these virtues with civic harmony. We need to keep this lesson in mind today.[133]

In other words, this compromise therefore preserves peaceful coexistence in accordance with the theological virtues, as explicitly referenced by Brady. It encourages respect for both sides (dignity), recognition of their place in the broader community (forgiveness), and accounts for the interests of both sides while reducing harms (love of neighbour).

D. First Amendment: Ministerial Exception

Shah argues that 'institutional religious freedom' (or the autonomy of religious communities) is an 'essential service to the common good'.[134] This conception is consistent with the outcome in *Hosanna-Tabor*, arguing that institutional religious freedom is not merely a freedom to be left alone (negative liberty), but a positive freedom to disseminate and publish religious doctrine and practice to build the common good. This entails legal rights to personality or entity status for the religious organisation, to rent or own property as a meeting space for religious activities, to propagate its teachings publicly on matters of public and private interest, to choose its own leaders, members and authority structures, to secure funding sources, to use sub-entities to carry out educational and charitable activities, and to educate the children of adherents in its teachings, and recruit new members. This is essentially 'the right of religious institutions and religious communities to be self-organizing', a 'right to self-determination', to 'decide upon and administer their own affairs without government interference'.[135] It is an 'effective power'

---

[132] ibid 731–32.
[133] ibid.
[134] T Shah, 'Institutional Religious Freedom in Full' (2020) 10(2) *Journal of Christian Legal Thought* 29, 29.
[135] ibid 30.

to be 'free from coercive interference' from individuals, groups or government in 'the conduct of internal affairs' and 'external affairs or engagement with wider society'.[136] The vertical dimension of autonomy (leadership structure, hierarchy, membership and discipline) is subject only to criminal sanction, for example where violence is authorised and carried out. The horizontal dimension (to act and express core convictions in society and public life) is only limited where it authorises or engages in violence, or unjustifiably infringes the fundamental rights and freedoms of others.[137]

So through the ministerial exception in *Hosanna-Tabor*, which focused on the vertical dimension, the Supreme Court referred to the principle of the autonomy of religious communities as a basis for giving religious organisations broad scope to determine the employment of employees who perform religious duties – and this is grounded in the First Amendment.[138] Michael McConnell has argued that the free exercise clause in particular was always intended to protect the public exercise of religion by communities as well as individuals.[139] Very recently, McConnell has also grounded the same principle in freedom of association. 'The freedom of association necessarily includes the freedom to limit your association to persons who share your values and beliefs … Freedom of association therefore plainly presupposes a freedom not to associate.'[140] The Supreme Court, in the ministerial exception cases and other First Amendment cases, has explained that there is no clearer example of interference with the autonomy of religious communities than compulsion to accept members the community does not desire; such compulsion impairs the ability of the original members to express the views that caused them to associate in the first place.[141]

The ministerial exception therefore in principle contributes to peaceful coexistence by building the common good. It enables religious communities to cultivate and articulate their own versions of the good, loving neighbour and enhancing the virtues of honesty, patience and forgiveness by allowing religious citizens the dignity of their own autonomous groups, and motivating considered debate

---

[136] ibid.

[137] ibid 29–30, see also W Cole Durham, Jr, 'The Right to Autonomy in Religious Affairs: A Comparative View' in G Robbers (ed), *Church Autonomy: A Comparative Survey* (Peter Lang, 2001).

[138] Shah (n 134) 33. The ministerial exception is an application of a much broader 'autonomy of the church' doctrine of deference to the internal decisions of religious associations which had its origins in the foundational First Amendment cases of *Watson v Jones*, 80 U.S. 679 (1871) and *Kedroff v Saint Nicholas Cathedral*, 344 U.S. 94 (1952).

[139] M McConnell, 'The Origins and Historical Understanding of Free Exercise of Religion' (1989) 103 *Harvard Law Review* 1409, 1488–91.

[140] M McConnell, 'Freedom of Association: Campus Religious Groups' (2020) 97(6) *Washington University Law Review* 1641, 1644–45.

[141] ibid 1645. See also M Helfand: 'Implied-Consent Religious Institutionalism: Applications and Limits' in WN Eskridge, Jr and R Fretwell Wilson (eds), *Religious Freedom, LGBT Rights, and the Prospects for Common Ground* (Cambridge University Press, 2018). Helfand argues that when a profit or non-profit business is organised around a core religious mission, special accommodation ought to follow because employees have at least impliedly consented to the ethos of the organisation.

outside of those groups in areas of profound disagreement with the mutual aim of good for all. However, there are at least two issues concerned with the breadth of the ministerial exception and the possibility that its broad scope may actually undermine peaceful coexistence. The first issue is the definition of 'minister'. Obviously, defining minister to only be official clergy will make the exception too narrow to be effective (because many employees of religious organisations undertake indisputably ministerial roles without necessarily being employed as clergy), but defining minister too broadly may allow a religious group to discriminate against any employee with impunity.

Hill observes that the category of ministerial employee is 'ill-defined, but assumes some religious functions and some measure of leadership within the organisation'.[142] However, courts are secular institutions which are not sufficiently qualified to make determinations regarding who is a minister. Goodman therefore suggests that the use of religion experts to assist with determining who is a minister will remove some of the ambiguity surrounding who qualifies as a minister.[143] While it is true that expert evidence would assist in this manner and the suggestion should not be dismissed out of hand, using experts raises the problem of meta-expertise: how do the courts decide between experts who disagree? Just as courts are not qualified to decide who is a minister, a court is not competent to decide which religion expert should be accepted, and the choice to choose one necessarily involves preferencing one view of religion over another. Hence, at a point of dispute, another solution is to accept the testimony of the religious organisation (which must be supported by evidence).[144]

Pope argues that minister should be defined as an employee who plays a role of 'substantial religious importance' in furthering the religious group's mission.[145] However, as this question is fundamentally religious in character and requires an understanding of the religious group's doctrine and practices, courts must 'defer to the religious group's determination of which of its employees play a role of substantial religious importance and are therefore ministers'.[146] The religious group is clearly in the best position to determine and articulate this, as is part of their First Amendment rights.[147] The alternative is to substitute the judgment of the secular court to determine the religious importance and function of a particular role within a group, and this is an inappropriate entanglement of government

---

[142] B Jessie Hill, 'Reconsidering Hostile Takeover of Religious Organisations' (2020) 97 *Washington University Law Review* 1833, 1841.

[143] M Goodman, 'Courts' Failure to Use Religion Experts to Decide Difficult Fact Questions Concerning Who is a Minister for the Ministerial Exception: A Holy Mess' (2020) 72 *Baylor Law Review* 1.

[144] See Deagon, 'Religious Questions' (n 74).

[145] A Pope, 'Of Substantial Religious Importance: A Case for a Deferential Approach to the Ministerial Exception' (2020) 95 *Notre Dame Law Review* 2145, 2162.

[146] ibid 2162.

[147] ibid 2167.

in religious affairs.[148] It would fundamentally interfere with the autonomy of religious communities by undermining 'the religious autonomy contemplated by the Religion Clauses'.[149]

It could be objected that if this deferential approach is accepted, it would allow religious organisations to strategically adopt expansive definitions of 'minister' to successfully avoid scrutiny of discriminatory practices. However, Hill notes that the Supreme Court has also suggested courts should defer to a religious entity's articulation of its own hierarchy and structure, even if that articulation has been adopted for the purposes of litigation.[150] And of course, the determination and articulation of the definition must be supported by evidence, as noted above. Nevertheless, this exposes the second issue with the ministerial exception, which is that it is far too broad and allows employment discrimination which is completely unrelated to religion.

Prior to *Hosanna-Tabor*, Martin argued against a blanket ministerial exception to Title VII discrimination rights on the basis that there was no clear foundation for it. Though that discussion is now rendered obsolete, it is worth mentioning Martin's policy reasons for limiting the ministerial exception.[151] In particular, he argues that where there is no religious justification for discriminatory conduct, the courts should balance church and government interests rather than simply deferring to religious organisations, at least applying strict scrutiny review.[152] After all, in *Hosanna-Tabor*, the discrimination was related to disability, with no obvious connection to the religious aspect of the role. It is not impossible to imagine that disability could be relevant for religious service.[153] But let us put that aside as an unrealistic prospect for enlivening the exception on a purely religious basis today.

A blanket ministerial exception which insulates discrimination for any reason is probably too broad. It undermines peaceful coexistence by providing an unconstrained licence to discriminate. This is contrary to the theological virtues of love and patience, because such a power goes too far in undermining the dignity of those who may be discriminated against without a relevant religious reason (such a religious reason would be a function of the autonomy of religious communities). However, it is also too limiting to only accept explicitly or overtly religious discrimination as within the exception. There may be cases (such as where a minister engages in sex outside of heterosexual marriage) involving conduct viewed as ostensibly 'non-religious'. In turn, a religious organisation may argue employment discrimination on the basis of such conduct (eg termination) is religious

---

[148] ibid 2170.

[149] ibid 2146.

[150] Hill (n 142) 1850–51. See eg *Serbian E. Orthodox Diocese for the U.S. & Can. v Milivojevich*, 426 U.S. 696, 718–20 (1976).

[151] Martin (n 37).

[152] ibid 1301–02.

[153] For example, in Leviticus 21:16–24, the *Torah* specifies that only priests without deformities or disabilities can serve at the altar.

because the conduct is contrary to the religious ethos of the organisation. So the standard should be a presumption of deferral to the religious organisation, but with an opportunity for the party discriminated against to present evidence that the discrimination was not related to the religious ethos (beliefs and behavioural standards) of the organisation. The organisation may then have an opportunity to demonstrate the religious link. For example, termination for 'immoral sexual conduct' is not actionable according to the ministerial exception where rules for sexual conduct are part of the religious ethos of the organisation, but termination on the basis of disability (where this does not impact employee competence, and where that disability is not relevant to religious ethos) is actionable. Martin recommends a similar procedure for Title VII claims, though he says the religious organisation should have the initial burden of proof.[154]

In any case, a more sensibly limited ministerial exception facilitates peaceful coexistence by advancing the autonomy of religious communities to construct their own distinctive contributions to the common good. In accordance with the theological virtues, the ministerial exception recognises forgiveness between citizens by enabling individuals of equal dignity and worth to participate in communities that are part of the democratic fabric of society despite profound moral disagreement.

E. Religious Freedom Restoration Act

In the context of whether it is consistent with peaceful coexistence for commercial entities to attract the protection of RFRA, the scope of the ratio of the *Hobby Lobby* case is pertinent as mentioned above.[155] The *Hobby Lobby* case concerned a private company which wanted an exemption from obligations under the healthcare mandate because they did not want to be morally complicit in abortions by funding reproductive healthcare insurance for their employees.[156] The Supreme Court held 5:4 that this exemption should be granted because a private company can exercise the right to religious freedom and belief.[157]

As the Supreme Court noted, the corporation (at least in this case) is a legal person who can raise religious freedom claims under the Religious Freedom Restoration Act.[158] The corporations may pay the penalty, but 'the humans who own and control these companies' are subject to the burden on religion.[159]

---

[154] Martin (n 37) 1334–1335.
[155] See Deagon, 'Refusing Services' (n 87).
[156] *Burwell v Hobby Lobby Stores, Inc.* 134 S. Ct. 2751 (2014).
[157] For a detailed analysis, see M Schwartzman, C Flanders and Z Robinson (eds), *The Rise of Corporate Religious Liberty* (Oxford University Press, 2016).
[158] *Hobby Lobby* (n 156) 2768–70.
[159] ibid 2768.

This case involved 'closely held corporations, each owned and controlled by members of a single family'.[160] Conversely, in her impassioned dissent, Ginsburg J argued that the right to religious exercise should not extend to 'for-profit corporations'.[161] Horwitz observes that two fundamental, related assumptions undergird this view that religious freedom should not be used to discriminate in commercial contexts. The first is that religion is private in nature and should be 'zoned out' of market relations, and the second is that commerce in the market-place should be reciprocal, detached and unaffected by private views.[162] However, as Horwitz goes on to note, many religious traditions agree that dividing faith from work is a 'fundamental error', and an increasing number of corporations and other businesses are bearing in mind 'moral considerations' as they interact in the marketplace, including investing funds in morally and socially conscious aims, and recognising that their role involves something beyond simply the pursuit of profit.[163]

Rex Ahdar too has persuasively argued that 'there are some companies who pursue moral and religious objectives in tandem with profit-making', and this is 'hardly a novel observation'; the idea originates with John Paul II.[164] Owners of such 'faith-based companies' 'firmly eschew a rigid dualism between the sacred and the secular spheres in favour of a holistic view of life' where work and faith are not separated, but faith is expressed through work.[165] Nicholas Aroney also observes the autonomy of religious communities more generally extends to worship, teaching, propagation, identifying conditions of membership and standards of conduct, and appointing officers, leaders and employees. Such practices are all protected, even if the organisations are formed in broader social or commercial contexts.[166] Like Ahdar, Aroney argues that for many religious people, religious convictions are pervasively relevant to all areas of life:

> some people who regard themselves as religious nonetheless tend to regard their religion as one aspect of their lives among many; others see their religion as definitive of their whole lives, so that even the most mundane activities are seen in religious terms. Such people frequently gather together, not only for narrowly 'religious' activities such as prayer or scriptural study, but also for what might be described as social and cultural activities, such participation in games and sports, or the provision of educational, medical or charitable services. For many such people, such activities are deeply religious.[167]

---

[160] ibid 2774.

[161] ibid 2796.

[162] P Horwitz, 'The Hobby Lobby Moment' (2014) 128 *Harvard Law Review* 154, 177–78.

[163] ibid 180–81.

[164] R Ahdar, 'Companies as Religious Liberty Claimants' (2016) 5(1) *Oxford Journal of Law and Religion* 1, 4.

[165] ibid.

[166] N Aroney, 'Freedom of Religion as an Associational Right' (2014) 33(1) *University of Queensland Law Journal* 153, 157–58.

[167] ibid 161 at fn 46.

Small businesses (or closely held corporations) are often the embodiment of their owners, and to imply that religious vendors should bracket their beliefs in social and commercial contexts is a severe imposition on their religious identity and religious freedom.[168] In principle then, granting religious vendors of these types religious freedom protections under RFRA is in accordance with peaceful existence and the theological virtues, because it recognises the intrinsic dignity of the religious person in terms of their holistic identity. It does not undermine their dignity or reject their position as neighbour by refusing to allow them to live out their identities authentically and publicly. It expresses forgiveness by allowing religious vendors full participation in society despite what may be profound moral disagreement with their beliefs or conduct. Nevertheless, as I articulate elsewhere, this ability is not unlimited. Such vendors must be truly and consistently religious in nature, and must be engaging in the provision of goods and services which can reasonably enliven conscience issues from the perspective of the vendor; this is roughly equivalent to the need to establish a 'substantial burden' on religious exercise under RFRA.[169]

One limitation of *Hobby Lobby* which could affect its ability to facilitate peaceful coexistence is the ambiguity surrounding the concept of substantial burden. *Hobby Lobby* certainly supports the conclusion that generally applicable civil rights laws can substantially burden religious liberty rights under RFRA (even if that issue arises in a commercial context, for RFRA can and should protect businesses), but it does not provide much guidance as to how a substantial burden is to be determined and therefore how future cases should be adjudicated.[170] In *Hobby Lobby* the Supreme Court indicated that they would be 'deferential to a religious institution's claim of a burden on free exercise'; the Court's 'narrow function … is to determine whether the plaintiffs' asserted religious belief reflects an honest conviction'.[171] The Court was clear that the rule required the plaintiffs to engage in conduct they found objectionable, and the cost resulting from a failure to comply created a substantial burden. The Court rejected the argument that the complicity was too attenuated to be cognizable on the basis that it could not engage in a theological analysis of whether the burden was true and substantial; 'a sincerely held belief that results in severe penalties is sufficient to establish a substantial burden under RFRA'.[172]

Though deference to the beliefs of the religious claimant is an essential aspect of any analysis of substantial burden, deference may be subject to understandable objections that it casts the net of substantial burden too broadly, undermining

---

[168] See T Berg, 'What Same-Sex Marriage Claims and Religious Liberty Claims Have in Common' (2010) 5(2) *Northwestern Journal of Law and Social Policy* 206.

[169] See Deagon, 'Refusing Services' (n 87).

[170] Brownstein (n 127) 16; Laycock, 'Liberty and Justice' (n 96) 34–35.

[171] Alvare (n 27) 158.

[172] Carmella, 'Progressive Religion' (n 78) 581–82.

the pursuit of neutral and worthy government interests such as anti-discrimination. This perceived or real lack of balance would undermine peaceful coexistence by failing to love one's neighbour. Hence, Girgis usefully explores the meaning of 'substantial burden' in more detail, proposing a more objective framework for determining substantial burden which does not simply defer to religious belief, but nevertheless properly takes the realities of religious belief into account.[173] Girgis proposes two types of religious exercise (performance of religious obligations and substantial religious autonomy) and four types of cognizable burden (forego religious exercise, to exercise and forego public benefit, to exercise and suffer legal penalty, or to be prevented from religious exercise). Only laws that affect at least one of the two categories of exercise and that create at least one of the four types of burden will create a substantial burden. Hence, the court's analysis can be simplified to asking what type of religious exercise does the law burden, and what type of impact does the law have on that exercise.[174]

Girgis observes that substantial religious autonomy entails a person's religion motivating, directing and organising their other spheres of life in order to achieve harmony with their notion of the highest or ultimate source of reality. A wide range of actions on the part of a believer can be construed as efforts to preserve or advance that harmony. It is therefore the case that religious exercise often pervades the boundaries of conventional religious practices (such as prayer or worship): 'it shapes choices about where to live, whom to befriend and to marry, how to raise children and where to send them to school, and which profession to pursue' – all these are exercises of religious autonomy.[175] Applied to *Hobby Lobby*, a Christian family's ability to operate their retail arts and crafts business according to their religious convictions (offering health insurance plans that do not cover the cost of certain abortifacent contraceptives) is an example of religious autonomy exercise. That exercise was burdened by the fact they needed to pay a fine of hundreds of millions of dollars a year to continue it (a burden of exercising and suffering legal penalty). Hence, the creation of one of the types of burdens with respect to one of the types of religious exercise means a substantial burden was created.[176]

That purely legal analysis aside, the situation giving rise to the *Hobby Lobby* litigation was fraught with failure to pursue peaceful coexistence in accordance with the theological virtues, particularly forgiveness, patience, love of neighbour, and acknowledgement of the dignity of both parties. Free contraceptive coverage is an important interest for women, providing a health entitlement and economic opportunity. Yet religious freedom through the autonomy of religious communities is also a centrally important interest. There are options which allow

---

[173] See GM Girgis, 'What is a "Substantial Burden" on Religion Under RFRA and the First Amendment?' (2020) 97 *Washington University Law Review* 1755, 1781.
[174] ibid 1755–56.
[175] ibid 1767–68.
[176] ibid 1780–81.

employees of objecting groups to receive free contraception without imposing on the conscience of those groups, but the government simply ignored the religious freedom of the groups while the groups put little effort into suggesting alternatives. Employees of overtly religion-affiliated organisations work in that environment on the understanding that the religious orientation will significantly influence the workplace, employment relationships and processes. The evangelical Christian objection to abortion is well known, as was the evangelical Christian orientation of Hobby Lobby stores. So, for example, given only some contraceptives function as abortifacents, Hobby Lobby could only object to those kinds of contraceptives. Only some employees would need those kinds of contraceptives, and for many the costs will be manageable.[177] Finding reasonable compromises which uphold the dignity and worth of all concerned parties in accordance with theological virtues, such as forgiveness and patience, will better contribute to peaceful coexistence.

F. RLUIPA and Title VII Exemptions

In regard to RLUIPA, as discussed above this provides the same standard of protection as RFRA, so many of the same principles apply. As Girgis outlines, a religious community would need to show that a land zoning requirement imposes a substantial burden upon their religious exercise.[178] Allowing religious communities to meet together and conduct religious exercise is central to their autonomy, and this protection upholds peaceful coexistence in accordance with the theological virtues by respecting the dignity of these communities to actively engage in their religious lives.

In regard to the Title VII exemptions, more clarity is required for the application of the relevant tests. The layers of questions include the nature of the accommodation requested and whether it is reasonable, whether that accommodation would be a hardship for the employers or the employee's coworkers, and whether any such hardship would be undue. Undue hardship has been interpreted to require no more than a minimal impact on the employer's operations or other coworkers.[179] However, membership in a religious organisation differs from membership in other voluntary associations because individual identity is often constituted by membership with the religious community; religious identity is experienced by many as something more akin to an immutable characteristic such as ethnic identity.[180] Emphasising this point, in conjunction with Alvare's suggestion to more clearly articulate the role of (say) an employee in a religious community or institution in the context of dismissal, will strengthen a religious

---

[177] Brady, 'Third Party Harms' (n 110) 731, 747.
[178] Girgis (n 173) 1782.
[179] Alvare (n 27) 154.
[180] Hill (n 142) 1846.

institution's reliance on Title VII to prefer co-believers, especially where ostensibly non-religious activities are a factor. 'Were a religious institution to explain how the community sustains and transmits the faith, and how an opposing witness distorts understanding of sexual teachings, there would be far less room for judges' speculating about hidden status-based discrimination'.[181] Hence, the Title VII exemptions generally facilitate peaceful coexistence in accordance with the theological virtues by enabling religious employers (particularly small businesses which more substantively reflect the religious identity of the owners) to maintain a religious ethos by preferring employees who believe and act in accordance with the ethos, upholding the dignity of the religious party and promoting forgiveness through allowing the religious group to exist and participate in society. Love of neighbour and the dignity of those who may be discriminated against are also taken into account by ensuring that any discrimination is on the grounds of religion only rather than sex or race, and by implementing a relatively narrow reasonable accommodation standard.

VI. Conclusion: The Autonomy of Religious Communities in US Law

US legal infrastructure provides significant protection for the autonomy of religious communities, and this protection mostly promotes peaceful coexistence in accordance with the theological virtues. The free exercise and establishment clauses of the First Amendment provide the majority of this protection. The establishment clause can be interpreted to prevent government interference with religious communities, but ambiguities in interpretation based on secularist 'separation' approaches can restrict the ability of religious communities to participate in public life, which undermines peaceful coexistence. Similarly, the *Smith* interpretation of the free exercise clause undermined peaceful coexistence by preventing only overt and explicit discrimination against religious exercise. However, more recent decisions have started to recognise that generally applicable laws such as anti-discrimination laws can undermine peaceful coexistence by placing substantial burdens on religion, which damages the dignity of religious entities.

This raises the fraught question of how to resolve conflict between religious freedom and anti-discrimination in a way which promotes peaceful coexistence by upholding the dignity of religious parties and those discriminated against, and encouraging forgiveness by tolerating the equal public participation of those with deep moral disagreements. Unfortunately, both sides are affected by a lack of vision to see the longer term effects of intransigence, and to see each other as

---

[181] Alvare (n 27) 189.

humans of equal dignity and worth rather than an opponent to be defeated.[182] Douglas Laycock warns against this 'Puritan mistake, in which each faction sought liberty for itself and its allies, but oppose[d] liberty for those with whom it deeply disagreed'.[183] This chapter suggests narrow and clear religious anti-discrimination exemptions for religious vendors as best upholding the dignity of both parties and promoting a society where people of deep moral difference can peacefully coexist by recognising their respective right to meaningfully participate in and contribute to public life.

The most significant protection for the autonomy of religious communities in US law is the ministerial exception grounded in the free exercise and establishment clauses of the First Amendment, where the employment decisions of religious organisations are immune from prosecution through employment discrimination laws. The ministerial exception in principle upholds peaceful coexistence because it allows a religious community to select and regulate staff in accordance with a religious ethos, upholding the dignity of the members of that organisation and enabling them to distinctively contribute to public good. However, the exception is arguably too broad as it stands because it allows discrimination on the basis of attributes unrelated to religion. This undermines the theological virtues of trust, kindness and love of neighbour by potentially allowing malicious discrimination unrelated to upholding an ethos. A more limited exception on the basis of religion or religion-related conduct would better uphold peaceful coexistence in more practical terms.

Existing federal legislation such as RFRA, RLUIPA and the Title VII exemptions also provide some protection for the autonomy of religious communities by preventing the government from imposing substantial burdens on religious exercise, and enabling religious employers to select and regulate staff on limited religious grounds. In general these uphold peaceful coexistence, though there is a need for further clarity around central terms such as substantial burden, and more generally, for affected parties to cultivate the theological virtues to facilitate reasonable compromises. However, the proposed Equality Act, which at the time of writing has passed the House of Representatives and is on the Senate Calendar, amends Title VII to extend protection against discrimination on the basis of sex to also include sexual orientation and gender identity. This amendment also effectively removes the Title VII exemption for small businesses (less than 15 employees). Most significantly, in section 1107 it specifically excludes the application of RFRA, which means that any person with a substantial burden imposed on them as a result of the Act is prevented from making a claim under RFRA.

This legislation is, unfortunately, an example of opposing religious liberty without compromise. It could consequently be used to severely damage the religious

---

[182] See generally A Sorkin, '"Them": Bridging Divides Between Distant Neighbours after *Masterpiece Cakeshop*' (2019) 54(1) *University of San Francisco Law Review* 117.

[183] D Laycock, 'The Campaign Against Religious Liberty' in M Schwartzman, C Flanders and Z Robinson (eds), *The Rise of Corporate Religious Liberty* (Oxford University Press, 2016) 231.

freedom of communities including churches, schools, charities and businesses. While expanding anti-discrimination protection is a laudable goal consistent with the theological virtues of compassion and dignity, the almost complete removal of religious freedom protection is not consistent with the theological virtues of love of neighbour, patience and tolerance. It fails to uphold the dignity of religious persons and organisations by ignoring their participation and contribution to public good, and therefore severely damages peaceful coexistence. Conversely, some congressional representatives have introduced the Fairness for All Act, which expands LGBT protections while simultaneously enabling religious communities to operate according to their religious ethos through strengthening accommodations and not excluding Title VII and RFRA. This proposal seems to more effectively underscore that all people, religious and/or LGBT, are created in the image of God and therefore possess intrinsic dignity and worth. It appears to promote peaceful coexistence in accordance with the theological virtues such as love of neighbour and forgiveness, contributing to a society where people with profound moral differences can live together with greater respect and understanding.

After further theoretical analysis of these legal issues in Part III of the book, Part IV will articulate a broad principled framework for the autonomy of religious communities which promotes peaceful existence through a reasonable, proportionate accommodation of difference. Building on the suggestions alluded to in this chapter, Part IV will entail specific recommendations as to how the US legal infrastructure can be amended to better adhere to this framework.

3

England

I. Introduction

Chapter three considers the UK with a focus on English law. In the context of England's unique position as a unitary state with an established religion, this chapter evaluates the legislation and case law relating to the autonomy of religious communities and potential tensions with equality under the Human Rights Act and the Equality Act to determine if their content promotes a peaceful coexistence of difference in accordance with the theological virtues, including analysis of relevant European Court of Human Rights jurisprudence. The chapter therefore elucidates the legal infrastructure which governs the autonomy of religious communities in England, and evaluates this infrastructure to determine the extent to which it promotes a peaceful coexistence of difference in accordance with the theological virtues.

Unlike the US and Australia, there is no codified UK Constitution; it is embodied in a range of written and unwritten sources. It has developed in a pragmatic and principled way through statutes and cases. This is in accordance with the principle of parliamentary sovereignty, where the UK Parliament has the authority to make or unmake any law and there is no entity which can override or set aside such law. There are no constitutional limitations enforceable through judicial review. However, British citizens still formally have significant civil rights and liberties almost equivalent to that of the US, including in the area of religious freedom.[1] This chapter will focus on the most pertinent issues raised by the general regime and specific illustrative cases rather than being a comprehensive overview.

The chapter first examines the associational elements of Article 9 of the European Convention of Human Rights ('the Convention') and its associated jurisprudence, which has been incorporated into English law by virtue of the Human Rights Act ('the HRA'). It then outlines the legal effect of the Equality Act

---

[1] R Reyes, '*Masterpiece Cakeshop and Ashers Baking Company*: A Comparative Analysis of Constitutional Confections' (2020) 16(1) *Stanford Journal of Civil Rights & Civil Liberties* 113, 125–26. For a comprehensive overview of the UK legal regime see S Knights, *Law, Rights, and Religion*, 2nd edn (Oxford University Press, 2020). For overviews of various aspects of Article 9 and UK education and employment law, see eg K Alidadi, *Religion, Equality and Employment in Europe: The Case for Reasonable Accommodation* (Hart Publishing, 2017), which considers comparative cases on Article 9 (including the UK), but focuses on individual employees rather than the autonomy of religious communities. See also generally M Hunter-Henin (ed), *Law, Religious Freedoms and Education in Europe* (Ashgate, 2011).

('the EA') on the autonomy of religious communities in England. The chapter subsequently evaluates the existing legal infrastructure using peaceful coexistence and the theological virtues as a standard. It first argues that despite explicit protection for the group manifestation of religious belief in the Convention, and an explicit requirement in the HRA for English courts to have regard to the rights of religious organisations under the Convention where they are relevant, the autonomy of religious communities in England is not sufficiently protected in terms of practical effect. The jurisprudence surrounding interpretation of Article 9 on this issue is inconsistent and confused, and in any case, it has not had a significant impact on English law because English courts have not properly taken it into account. Hence, to preserve peaceful coexistence in accordance with the theological virtues, the European Court of Human Rights ('the ECtHR') must provide a clear rationale for religious liberty and a substantive jurisprudence for protecting the autonomy of religious communities by building on the scattered points which already exist. Furthermore, English courts must then incorporate this jurisprudence in their decision-making to facilitate the autonomy of religious communities, in accordance with the HRA.

Second, and similarly in regard to the EA, the chapter argues that although there are protections for the autonomy of religious communities through anti-discrimination protection for religion and exemptions to other aspects of anti-discrimination law, the scope and application of these are contentious and unclear, and cases which have arisen often unreasonably and disproportionately privilege equality over religious freedom. The cases and scholarship frame the autonomy of religious communities as necessarily and intrinsically in conflict with equality considerations, and since equality is prioritised over religious freedom, accommodations which acknowledge the dignity and virtue of both parties are sometimes avoided. This detracts from the autonomy of religious communities and therefore undermines peaceful coexistence in accordance with the theological virtues. The chapter analyses these tensions with respect to overlapping areas which have already received attention in previous chapters (the autonomy of religious communities in education, employment, and provision of goods and services), ultimately concluding that peaceful coexistence and upholding the theological virtues will only be possible if there are genuine attempts at reconciliation, understanding and compromise where disputes exist, and thus reasonable and proportionate accommodations of difference can occur for the good of the community as a whole.

II. European Convention of Human Rights

A. Article 9: Freedom of thought, Conscience and Religion

Article 9 in the Convention is partly an absolute right and partly a qualified right. It is an absolute right in the sense that the internal dimension, freedom to believe or change belief, is inviolable and not subject to limitation. It is a qualified right in the sense that the external dimension, manifestation of that belief, is subject to the limitations indicated in Article 9 itself. Any limitation must be 'necessary in a democratic society', which requires a test of 'proportionality': the Court considers whether the purpose of the limitation of the right is 'legitimate', whether the limitation is 'necessary for attaining that purpose', and whether the measure strikes the proper balance between that purpose and the right being restricted.[2] Article 9 states:

1. Everyone has the right to freedom of thought, conscience and religion; this right includes freedom to change his religion or belief and freedom, either alone or in community with others and in public or private, to manifest his religion or belief, in worship, teaching, practice and observance.

2. Freedom to manifest one's religion or beliefs shall be subject only to such limitations as are prescribed by law and are necessary in a democratic society in the interests of public safety, for the protection of public order, health or morals, or for the protection of the rights and freedoms of others.

Applicants must establish that the complaint falls within the scope of Article 9 by demonstrating that it concerns the manifestation of a religion or belief, and then demonstrating there has been an 'interference' with that manifestation through the State restricting or prohibiting religiously motivated conduct.[3] As intimated above, an interference may be justified if the restriction or prohibition is prescribed by law and necessary to achieve one of the legitimate aims in Article 9(2). In practice, the Court's analysis of legitimacy is superficial and a State's argument is generally accepted, especially where the purpose is said to be protecting the rights and freedoms of others.[4] The term 'necessity' does not have its dictionary meaning of 'indispensable', but it is a higher threshold than 'reasonable' or 'desirable'; it is concerned with addressing a 'pressing social need' in a democracy aiming to reconcile and facilitate the freedom of a plurality of beliefs.[5] However, the ECHR has often avoided this more sophisticated analysis by applying the 'margin of appreciation' doctrine.[6] The margin of appreciation is where the Court defers to the actions of states and gives them a wide ambit to balance competing rights, and a discretion to weigh competing religious and other values according to their own criteria. The idea is that individual States are better situated to evaluate what is necessary, proportional and legitimate in their domestic context, especially in the application of Article 9. However, the margin of appreciation is not unlimited, and it can both assist and undermine religious freedom.[7]

---

[2] C McCrudden, *Litigating Religions: An Essay on Human Rights, Courts, and Beliefs* (Oxford University Press, 2018) 64–65.

[3] M Hill, 'The Qualified Right to Freedom of Religion: An Examination of the Limitations Contained in Article 9 of the European Convention on Human Rights' (2020) 23 *Studies in Religious Law* 73, 74–76.

[4] ibid 83, 89.

[5] ibid 89–91.

[6] ibid 93–94.

[7] ibid 93–95; McCrudden, *Litigating Religions* (n 2) 88.

In regard to the autonomy of religious communities specifically, there are some emerging themes in Article 9 jurisprudence. These recognise that associations can themselves bear rights, including the right to structure themselves in accordance with religious precepts. Religious communities have the autonomy to determine their own leadership and membership structure, and standards for those leaders and members to follow, as long as those members of the community also have the freedom to leave the organisation.[8] Hence the ECHR is 'clearly willing to protect associational activity within the "private" sphere of religious worship. However, the rights of religious associations also include a certain public presence, as well as an area of overlap with State activity. Restrictions on activities in these areas are much easier for States to justify'.[9] In conjunction with a broader margin of appreciation, this can often mean religious communities engaging in public activities which may be restricted by States are not necessarily well protected by Article 9.

III. UK Legislation

A. Human Rights Act 1998 (UK)

The Human Rights Act gives effect to those rights contained in the European Convention of Human Rights through section 1, including Article 9. Section 2 states a court deciding a question in connection with a Convention right must take into account the jurisprudence of the European Court of Human Rights. Section 3 states all legislation must be read in a way which is compatible with Convention rights as much as possible, though this does not affect the validity of such legislation. Section 6 states that it is unlawful for any public authority to act in a way which is inconsistent with a Convention right. This includes both government and private actors discharging public functions. Sections 12 and 13 state that a court must have 'particular regard to the importance' of the corresponding Convention rights of freedom of expression and freedom of thought, conscience and religion where an action is brought; section 13 specifies that the particular regard must occur where a determination 'might affect the exercise by a religious organisation (itself or its members collectively) of the Convention right to freedom of thought, conscience and religion'.[10] Hence, the HRA obliges English courts to have particular regard to the importance of the Article 9 right where a law affects the operation of religious communities, which offers some formal protection for the autonomy of religious communities. However, though the incorporation of Article 9 has

---

[8] J Rivers, *The Law of Organised Religions: Between Establishment and Secularism* (Oxford University Press, 2010) 57–58, 70–71.

[9] ibid 70–71.

[10] See generally P Weller, K Purdam, N Ghanea and S Cheruvallil-Contractor, *Religion or Belief, Discrimination and Equality: Britain in Global Contexts* (Bloomsbury, 2013) 41–65.

led to the emergence of a number of cases, domestic laws are applying Article 9 restrictively. For example, in *Begum* the Court held that interference is not easily established, and as a consequence courts have generally held there is no interference with the right to manifest religion, and in the rare cases where they hold there is interference, they have held the interference is justified under Article 9(2).[11] Sandberg observes that this 'restrictive' interpretation means litigants tend to 'argue anything *but* Article 9'.[12]

B. Equality Act 2010 (UK)

The Equality Act is an anti-discrimination act which protects, among other attributes, persons from discrimination on the basis of religion or belief (section 10) and sexual orientation (section 12). It prohibits direct and indirect discrimination in the provision of services (Part 3), employment (Part 5), education (Part 6), and in membership of associations (Part 7). Schedules 3, 9, 11, 16 and 23 provide a number of general and specific exemptions for religious communities (schools and associations). Commercial (religious) vendors are in effect excluded from exemption under Schedule 23. The EA consolidates the equality and human rights agendas of the UK government into a single comprehensive document which, in conjunction with the Human Rights Act, regulates human rights matters including the balance between religious freedom and anti-discrimination in the UK.[13] Similar to the Human Rights Act, the Equality Act extends these to public authorities and private actors exercising public functions, mandating regard to the elimination of discrimination and the advancement of equality.[14] However, it is a general practice under English law to provide exceptions to discrimination law for religious groups so they can 'follow their own beliefs regarding human sexuality', religion and other matters.[15] Hence, the Equality Act provides a number of exceptions for religious groups, including from sex, sexual orientation and religious discrimination law, allowing religious groups to discriminate with respect to employment and the provision of goods and services.[16] For example, section 202 of the Equality Act provides that religious organisations are under no obligation to host civil partnerships for registration purposes, effectively enhancing the rights of religious communities. This section was inserted at the behest of religious organisations and their supporters on the basis that the religious organisations did not want to be

---

[11] See *R (on the application of Begum) v Headteacher and Governors of Denbigh High School* [2006] UKHL 15.

[12] R Sandberg, 'The Right to Discriminate' (2011) 13(2) *Ecclesiastical Law Journal* 157, 162.

[13] Weller et al (n 10) 51, 55–56. See generally A McColgan, *Discrimination, Equality and the Law* (Hart Publishing, 2014).

[14] Weller et al (n 10) 55.

[15] Sandberg, 'The Right to Discriminate' (n 12) 159–60.

[16] See eg Sch 9, para 2; Sch 23, para 2.

compelled to host civil partnership ceremonies contrary to their religious convictions about marriage.[17] These developments have produced tensions, especially the 'existence and scope of exceptions allowing religious groups and employers to discriminate on grounds of sexual orientation'.[18]

The EA provides exceptions for indirect religious discrimination where there is a proportionate application of genuine and determining occupational requirements, and the proportionate application of a genuine occupational requirement for a religious ethos employer. For the latter, regard must be had to the ethos of the employer and nature of the role, but the requirement is not determining. There are similar provisions for indirect sexual orientation discrimination. Employment for the 'purposes of an organised religion' is not unlawful if the discriminating requirement is applied to comply with the doctrine of the religion or to avoid conflicting with the strongly held religious convictions of a significant number of adherents. These are known as the 'compliance' and 'non-conflict' principles.[19] The scope of 'organised religion' is contentious and unclear. The phrase seems intended to limit the ambit of the exception to a narrow range of employment; ministers of religion and a small number of lay roles that exist to promote and represent religion.[20] In particular, 'organised religion' is narrower than 'religious organisation', potentially excluding religious schools or welfare organisations, and also excluding sundry posts such as administrative staff.[21] Hunt further notes that the Catholic and Anglican Churches were concerned that the 2010 Equality Act retain the exemptions for the purposes of organised religion, keeping the exemption as it was in previous legislation so it could not be even more narrowly interpreted to exclude employment decisions not relating to explicit 'ministers'.[22] For example, it is likely that the exception would include the employment of a Diocesan Youth Officer, consistent with earlier case law.[23]

In regard to the compliance and non-conflict principles, their scope is also unclear and problematic. Determining whether a 'significant number' of followers may be offended is not easy, and the only guidance suggests reference to the national rather than local membership of the religion. In addition, the reference to doctrine is vexed, as there is a general principle that courts ought not to rule upon doctrinal issues or intervene in the governance of religious organisations.[24]

---

[17] S Hunt, 'Negotiating Equality in the Equality Act 2010 (United Kingdom): Church-State Relations in a Post-Christian Society' (2012) 55(4) *Journal of Church and State* 690, 700–03.

[18] Sandberg, 'The Right to Discriminate' (n 12) 171.

[19] Rivers, *The Law of Organised Religions* (n 8) 125–28.

[20] Sandberg, 'The Right to Discriminate' (n 12) 174–76.

[21] Rivers, *The Law of Organised Religions* (n 8) 128.

[22] Hunt (n 17) 697–700.

[23] Sandberg, 'The Right to Discriminate' (n 12) 174–76. See eg *Reaney v Hereford Diocesan Board of Finance* [2007] Employment Tribunal, judgment 17 July 2007 (Case No 1602844/2006); *R (Amicus MSF Section) v Secretary of State for Trade and Industry* [2004] EWHC 860.

[24] Sandberg, 'The Right to Discriminate' (n 12) 176–78. See A Deagon, 'The "Religious Questions" Doctrine': Addressing (Secular) Judicial Incompetence' (2021) 47(1) *Monash University Law Review* 60–87 where I address this principle.

Finally, the employer can only discriminate where the employee does not meet the imposed requirement or the employer is not satisfied it is met and it is reasonable to be not satisfied. This is emphasised in *Reaney*, where the Bishop rejected the gay Diocesan Youth Officer's assurance that he would remain celibate after being in a same-sex relationship. The Employment Tribunal found that Reaney did meet the requirement and it was not reasonable for the Bishop to conclude otherwise, so the Bishop could not rely on the exception.[25]

Under the EA, churches also cannot regulate terms of membership with respect to religion unless they have more than 25 members and a selection process, and they cannot discriminate on the basis of religion in employment, provision of services, use of facilities, or in public functions.[26] However, there is an exception for religious organisations (which would include churches) which have the purpose of enabling persons of a religion to receive a benefit or engage in an activity within the framework of that religion. This allows the organisation to impose restrictions on membership, participation in activities, and access to goods, services and facilities on the grounds of the purpose of the organisation or to avoid causing offence to persons of that religion associated with the organisation. The exception does not apply if the main purpose of the organisation is commercial, and a similar exception also applies for charitable organisations. For example, section 60 of the EA states that it is 'not unlawful for a charity to require members, or persons wishing to become members, to make a statement which asserts or implies membership or acceptance of a religion or belief', and the context makes clear that this was intended to apply to organisations with a faith ethos which require some kind of pledge.[27] However, faith-based providers are 'under increasing constraints' from the 'public sector equality duty', which requires public authorities (including private bodies exercising public functions) to have due regard to removing disadvantage, discrimination and other prohibited conduct between groups sharing protected characteristics in order to foster good relations and understanding between those groups.[28]

IV. Summary: The Legal Infrastructure for the Autonomy of Religious Communities in England

There is considerable formal protection for the autonomy of religious communities in England. The HRA explicitly incorporates Article 9 jurisprudence into English law, including religious associational freedom in the private sphere. The HRA further explicitly enjoins English courts to have particular regard to this

---

[25] Sandberg, 'The Right to Discriminate' (n 12) 178.
[26] Hunt (n 17) 704.
[27] Rivers, *The Law of Organised Religions* (n 8) 278.
[28] ibid 282–83.

jurisprudence in cases which affect the freedom of religious groups. The EA protects against discrimination on religious grounds, and provides exceptions for religious organisations to discriminate on the grounds of religion and sexual orientation as part of regulating their internal membership and leadership. However, there are some deficiencies in the substantive or practical effect of these laws, especially in public contexts. Both the Article 9 jurisprudence applied through the HRA and the application of the EA are inconsistent and unclear, and have been applied restrictively where religious groups are engaging in public activities or providing public services such as education and welfare. As a result, the autonomy of religious communities in social engagement is receiving some pressure. The following will evaluate whether the substantive protection that does exist supports peaceful coexistence in accordance with the theological virtues.

V. Evaluation of the Law: Peaceful Coexistence and the Theological Virtues

A. Article 9 of the Convention and Human Rights Act

There is a consistent view that Article 9 jurisprudence, even when incorporated into English law, has not provided sufficient protection for the autonomy of religious communities. For example, John Finnis has argued that courts have enforced disproportionate equality restrictions against religious freedom, resulting in wrongful discrimination against religious persons. They have essentially endorsed the position that 'refusal to accommodate discriminatory religious beliefs would always be proportionate'; the right to equality is given a weight and claim that is superior to that of religious freedom, and very strong justifications are required to interfere with equality on the ground of religious freedom. This is part of a more general process minimising the impact of Article 9 by courts and correspondingly by the British legislature.[29] Similarly, Christopher McCrudden observes that though Article 9 formally safeguards the freedom of religions to operate in their collective dimension, the ECHR has protected the collective dimension of religion 'in some confusion' and 'in a multiplicity of voices'.[30] ECHR jurisprudence has been 'chequered and inconsistent', with the result that it is often unclear whether particular manifestations of religious belief will be protected.[31] Some cases indicate that it is only where religious duty has been infringed; others argue that religious liberty is also diminished where a practice is preferred or permitted by a religion,

---

[29] J Finnis, 'Equality and Religious Liberty: Oppressing Conscientious Diversity in England' in T Shah, T Farr and J Friedman (eds), *Religious Freedom and Gay Rights: Emerging Conflicts in the United States and Europe* (Oxford University Press, 2016) 24–26.
[30] McCrudden, *Litigating Religions* (n 2) 68.
[31] Weller et al (n 10) 59.

but legally prohibited. The 'explicit collapse' of religion into equality under the Equality Act also does not allow for these nuances to be properly explored.[32] There is no clear guidance on how to resolve conflicts between religion and equality, and cases are often approached in a manner partial to the claimant, resulting in a failure to coherently and effectively enforce Article 9 rights.[33] Hence, 'there is little legal evidence to suggest that Article 9 has delivered more robust legal protection for the manifestation of religion or belief'.[34] Indeed, Ahdar and Leigh note that the incorporation of Article 9 in the HRA was intended to bolster the right of religious bodies to maintain a distinctive ethos and engage in self-government. However, subsequent court decisions have indicated the provision has not had a significant impact and has actually coincided with erosion in the freedom of religious communities.[35]

Subordination of religion to the interests of the state is the antithesis of true freedom. Where there is tension between religious freedom and equality, both rights should be accommodated as much as possible.[36] However, the limitations in Article 9 mean that religious freedom is unduly constrained when there is a clash with another human right such as equality, because 'there is nothing here to safeguard a right to religious freedom when other rights are brought into play'.[37] For example, Article 9 and the HRA failed to protect a religious adoption agency from refusing to offer children against its religious ethos.[38] In this sense the religious freedom of a religious association was 'disregarded', and accommodations were ruled out even though it was possible for impugned couples to adopt through other agencies, and the necessary withdrawal of general services meant many children were not provided for.[39]

Another example is where the ECtHR found against a church who dismissed an organist for having an extramarital affair.[40] The Court held the right to privacy trumped the right of the religious organisation to demand its employees (even one in an overtly religious role) adhere to their principles. 'The result is there is no respect for the particular ethos of a church or other religious institution, and

---

[32] ibid 59–60.

[33] H Keller and C Heri, 'The Role of the European Court of Human Rights in Adjudicating Religious Exception Claims' in S Mancini (ed), *The Conscience Wars: Rethinking the Balance between Religion, Identity, and Equality* (Cambridge University Press, 2018) 314–15.

[34] Weller et al (n 10) 61.

[35] R Ahdar and I Leigh, *Religious Freedom in the Liberal State*, 2nd edn (Oxford University Press, 2013) 378–80. There is a further risk under s 6 of the HRA because that provision requires public authorities (including private authorities undertaking public functions) to pursue equality and non-discrimination. This leads to potential liability for religious organisations, even private associations, due to their discrimination to maintain a religious ethos. The respect that the Convention shows for the right of religious bodies to govern themselves would be undermined domestically by a wide interpretation of public authorities (191).

[36] R Trigg, *Equality, Freedom and Religion* (Oxford University Press, 2012) 37–38.

[37] ibid 99.

[38] ibid 39.

[39] ibid 118.

[40] See *Schuth v Germany*, ECHR 1620/03, 23 September 2010.

indifference as to whether a religion can continue to uphold its principles through example and teaching. The institution, the court believes, has no claim on someone's private life … [but] the harm of imposing our views of equality on a group contrary to its religion is discounted completely by those who would prevent the harm of sexual inequality'.[41] This severely undermines the autonomy of religious communities and is inconsistent with the theological virtues of dignity, forgiveness and love of neighbour in the sense that it prevents the group manifestation of distinct religious beliefs which can pursue the good in an autonomous community within the broader society. This approach substitutes the idiosyncratic beliefs of the individual for the orthodox beliefs of the group, and enforces those beliefs against the group such that they cannot have their own defining ethos.[42]

Furthermore, the application of the margin of appreciation doctrine has only exacerbated this lack of clear protection. As mentioned earlier, the ECHR is increasingly engaging in subjective judgements which rely on the 'amorphous and unpredictable', 'capricious' margin of appreciation.[43] This also renders any decision effectively non-justiciable because it simply defers to the decision of the impugned state rather than actually engaging with whether there has been a breach of Article 9.[44] More substantively, the margin of appreciation doctrine is also starting to undercut the autonomy of religious communities because the ECtHR is more frequently relying on a growing public consensus which supports equality and LGBT rights as characteristic of tolerant European democratic societies. This means the genuine religious convictions of individuals and groups are given little weight and dismissed.[45]

Harrison surmises that the rise of a liberal 'dominant state-individual paradigm' has caused the 'surprising' result that Article 9 is not having any 'discernible impact' on religious liberty in England despite formal incorporation through the HRA.[46] As Ahdar and Leigh note, 'the failure of the European Courts to develop an adequate jurisprudence on religious freedom under Article 9 of the ECHR is … due in no small measure to their failure to understand and provide a coherent rationale for religious liberty'.[47] The failure to properly account for religious liberty significantly detracts from peaceful coexistence, undermining the theological virtues of dignity, patience, forgiveness and love of neighbour which entail recognising and facilitating different approaches to the pursuit of good, just as we would desire our approach to be respected. Along these lines, there are substantive principles of the common good and pluralist themes the ECtHR could draw on to more clearly and substantially articulate a framework for the autonomy of religious communities in Article 9.

---

[41] Trigg (n 36) 119–20.
[42] J Harrison, *Post-Liberal Religious Liberty* (Cambridge University Press, 2020) 49–52.
[43] Hill (n 3) 97–98.
[44] ibid 98.
[45] Keller and Heri (n 33) 311, 315.
[46] Harrison, *Post-Liberal Religious Liberty* (n 42) 177–78.
[47] Ahdar and Leigh, *Religious Freedom in the Liberal State* (n 35) 23.

The ECtHR has recognised that religious organisations have legal personality and distinct rights. 'The importance of the collective dimension to religious freedom has emerged as an important theme in Convention jurisprudence'.[48] Harrison notes that the autonomy of these groups is linked with their ability to privately maintain their traditions and publicly express their beliefs. There is a 'distinct line of jurisprudence that emphasises the importance of religious associations to a vital civil society'.[49] For example, in the foundational case of *Kokkinakis v Greece*, the Court states:

> As enshrined in Article 9, freedom of thought, conscience and religion is one of the foundations of a democratic society ... it is, in its religious dimension, one of the most vital elements that go to make up the identity of believers and their conceptions of life ... The pluralism indissociable from a democratic society ... depends on it.[50]

The collective dimension of Article 9, the freedom to manifest in community with others, contributes to the common good, pluralism and peaceful coexistence of different communities in a democratic society. Protecting 'the autonomy of the religious institution' in this way is essential for preserving 'the pluralism indissociable from a democratic society'.[51] As McCrudden emphasises, 'the autonomous existence of religious communities is indispensable for pluralism in a democratic society and is thus an issue at the very heart of the protection which Article 9 affords ... Were the organisational life of the community not protected by Article 9 ... all other aspects of ... freedom of religion would become vulnerable'.[52] The most powerful cases demonstrate this principle through protecting the autonomy of religious organisations in selecting their leaders.[53] In addition, Article 9 has limited horizontal effect in disputes between members of a religious organisation and the organisation itself, for 'religious group autonomy requires clear limits to the freedom of individuals. The freedom that an individual has to leave a religious organisation in the event of a dispute is fatal to bringing a religious liberty claim against it under the Convention'.[54] Manifesting religious belief through joining with others in a corporate or associational aspect involves a 'necessary exclusion of people of a different or no religion'; if such exclusion is not legally protected 'the perverse effect will be to undermine religious liberty'.[55]

Hence religious communities have the right to determine their own structure, membership, policy, objectives and so on. 'Selection of leaders is one of the very core aspects of religious association autonomy ... religious bodies have the right to reject candidates for ministry or discipline or expel an existing pastoral minister even if the grounds for doing so appear to liberals (and others) to be archaic,

---

[48] ibid 138.
[49] Harrison, *Post-Liberal Religious Liberty* (n 42) 174–75.
[50] *Kokkinakis v Greece* (1993) 17 EHRR397 [31].
[51] McCrudden, *Litigating Religions* (n 2) 68–70.
[52] ibid 139; Ahdar and Leigh, *Religious Freedom in the Liberal State* (n 35) 376–77.
[53] McCrudden, *Litigating Religions* (n 2) 68–70.
[54] Ahdar and Leigh, *Religious Freedom in the Liberal State* (n 35) 138–39.
[55] ibid 350.

illiberal or bigoted. The grounds for selection and dismissal are matters within the province of the religious community, and it alone, to decide', including on the basis of race (for example a Jewish community), sex (ordination of men and not women), and sexual orientation (not appointing a gay man to a leadership position).[56] Any state remedies would be invasive and destructive to religious freedom and, indeed, the separation of church and state and democracy itself; state-determined appointment or dismissal of religious leaders, and/or penalties for non-compliance, are hallmarks of authoritarian and religiously repressive regimes.[57] In short, 'the right of religious communities to select their own religious leaders is borne out by the European Convention case law. The European Court of Human Rights has made it abundantly clear that attempts by a state to interfere in the selection of leaders will not be tolerated'.[58]

Similarly, the margin of appreciation can be more wisely used. The ECHR 'should encourage solutions that make practical concordance of the rights in question possible and accommodate religious objections where doing so is reasonable and does not excessively impact the rights of others, especially vulnerable minorities'.[59] This approach would entail an attempt to find 'mutually acceptable solutions to the equality-religion conflict' that encourage democratic deliberation which listens and understands rather than adversarial litigation which intensifies tensions.[60] As Harrison intimates, Article 9 jurisprudence demonstrates the importance of the group as a justification for and determining feature of the religious liberty which undergirds the pluralism of a democratic society. And the group as such has authority because it is 'grounded in its direction towards some kind of higher good … that civil authority should be responsive towards'.[61] Hence, the mutual though distinctive pursuit of the good is characteristic of the theological virtues of patience, forgiveness and love of neighbour in the sense of enabling each person to associate and practise their beliefs as part of this process, even though others may have different approaches. It preserves the peaceful coexistence of communities with different beliefs and practices by enabling them to pursue the good in its distinctive forms and emphases without imposing uniformity and conflict.

B. Equality Act

The EA protects against both direct and indirect discrimination on grounds such as religion and sexual orientation.[62] However, due to the need for a comparator in

---

[56] ibid 395.
[57] ibid.
[58] ibid 396–99.
[59] Keller and Heri (n 33) 316.
[60] ibid 326.
[61] Harrison, *Post-Liberal Religious Liberty* (n 42) 165, 173.
[62] For an overview of how the Equality Act prohibits direct and indirect discrimination on the ground of religion in employment and the provision of goods and services, see Ahdar and Leigh, *Religious Freedom in the Liberal State* (n 35) 353–55.

establishing a disadvantage for the purposes of indirect discrimination, it is generally easier to accommodate religious claims based on collective practice. Indeed, as noted above, there are some protections for collective religious practice through anti-discrimination exemptions. These enable religious groups to maintain a distinctive ethos and identity through preserving autonomy to regulate internal affairs without necessarily being subject to 'secular' standards. 'These exceptions clearly enhance religious liberty at the institutional level'.[63] In this sense, 'equality could be understood as requiring accommodating religious beliefs, either because majoritarian norms affect different groups disparately or else because a neutral law affects the differently situated religious person differently'.[64]

However, accommodating religion through exceptions to equality law has resulted in the emergence of an 'image of conflict'; equality advocates argue that accommodating religious groups which treat people less favourably on the basis of sexual orientation (for example) would be unacceptable if linked to some other ground such as race.[65] Religious freedom advocates similarly point to a perception that the protected characteristics and associated rights are set up against each other so that there has been increased conflict between social groups and that the adversarial nature of law has become dominant in the attempt to resolve these tensions, and conversely claim that equality has become a 'trump' right.[66] Religious communities do not see their fundamental beliefs as discriminatory in nature, but the subordination of religious freedom to equality in discrimination law has excessively curtailed religious freedom and could even generate new forms of oppression.[67] As Trigg notes, the courts 'consistently refuse to accommodate religious belief, in the face of the demands of equality,' and so, as Ahdar and Leigh put it, seem 'in effect to prioritise one stream of equality law (sexual orientation) over another (religion or belief) rather than to hold the two in balance'.[68]

Rivers considers that this debate often misses the fact that liberty and equality are overlapping and complementary. It is a restriction on liberty when a religious vendor cannot exercise discretion over their business, but it is also a restriction on liberty when a purchaser cannot obtain a good or service from that business. Similarly, it is a restriction on equality when a same-sex couple cannot openly celebrate their relationship, and it is also a restriction on equality 'when I cannot live openly with my religion because of legal restrictions on the contexts in which I can live consistently with its precepts'.[69] One would hope that equality and liberty

---

[63] M Gibson, 'The God "Dilution": Religion, Discrimination and the Case for Reasonable Accommodation' (2013) 72 *Cambridge Law Journal* 578, 581–83.

[64] Harrison, *Post-Liberal Religious Liberty* (n 42) 28; See eg J Maclure and C Taylor, *Secularism and Freedom of Conscience* (Harvard University Press, 2011) 68–75.

[65] M Bell, 'Bridging a Divide: A Faith-Based Perspective on Anti-Discrimination Law' (2020) 9(1) *Oxford Journal of Law and Religion* 56, 60–61.

[66] Weller et al (n 10) 57.

[67] Bell (n 65) 60–61.

[68] Trigg (n 36) 154; Ahdar and Leigh, *Religious Freedom in the Liberal State* (n 35) 356.

[69] J Rivers, 'Is Religious Freedom under Threat from British Equality Laws?' (2020) 33 *Studies in Christian Ethics* 179, 185.

perspectives would be legally balanced, and though European human rights law and British equality law ostensibly seeks to do this, the scope for taking into account liberty perspectives in equality law is 'limited', the law is 'too rigid', and the way equality and religious freedom rights have been legally implemented creates a 'structural imbalance' in favour of equality.[70] Religious liberty is effectively limited by equality law because religious liberty must be limited where necessary to protect the rights of others, and equality is a right.[71]

It is also significant that many religions take the view that 'all of life is inspired by or generated by faith and belief'; the most mundane behaviours such as eating, drinking and gardening can be a manifestation of belief just as much as prayer and worship.[72] Consequently, 'countless schools, hospitals, orphanages, soup kitchens and shelters have been run by religious organisations as part of their religious mission. Running a café, gymnasium, medical centre or bookshop could equally be part of one's religious calling'.[73] The effect of the social, political and legal dominance of equality, in conjunction with the comprehensive nature of religious belief and practice, means that is 'inevitable and unsurprising that there should be tensions between religious liberty and equality law'.[74] Rivers identifies that there are then only three conditions according to which equality law would not excessively constrain religious liberty. First, religious liberty never entails discrimination. This is obviously false. Religious communities must discriminate as to religion at least, and other characteristics as well – for example male-only priesthood, or sexual practices. As Rivers explains:

> A religious group cannot sustain its distinctive identity unless it [discriminates]. Such distinctions may be unjust in a public context but entirely necessary in a religious context. To reject a potential employee on account of their theological heterodoxy would be intolerable behaviour on the part of a public administrator but an essential part of the role of a church ministerial selection board. This is simply social pluralism in practice, and equality law recognises it in exemplary form when it excludes 'single characteristic associations' (ie those whose main purpose is to bring together people who share a certain characteristic) from the non-discrimination obligations applying to membership in associations generally.[75]

The second condition is that the religious activities in question are not legally relevant. This must also be discounted, for denying 'the overlap between religions and private right is radically to disempower, and we might even say outlaw religious groups. That is not religious liberty'.[76] This leaves the third condition as the only option: 'the law makes sufficient provision for religious individuals and groups

---

[70] ibid 185–87.
[71] ibid.
[72] Ahdar and Leigh, *Religious Freedom in the Liberal State* (n 35) 157.
[73] ibid.
[74] Rivers, 'Is Religious Freedom under Threat?' (n 69) 182–83.
[75] ibid.
[76] ibid.

to comply with the precepts of their religion'.[77] Attempts have been made to do this through the equality exemptions outlined above.[78] However, as mentioned, there are difficulties in simply limiting religious conduct which apparently harms others or infringes their rights. For example, 'many aspects of religious liberty are recognised to be communal and, consequently, to uphold the individual's rights may be to restrict the group's rights'.[79] There are questions of whether limitations are reasonable or proportionate: 'the harm to the other person, or society, may in some cases be a minor inconvenience when weighed against an acute crisis of conscience for the religious claimant. Might not the state sometimes be asked to accommodate religious belief where the cost to itself, or another person, is relatively minor?'[80] Hence reasonable limitations are a better approach.

Ahdar and Leigh articulate a broad systematic approach to religious liberty claims which entails reasonable, proportionate accommodations. These involve establishing and assessing the extent of burden, establishing the necessity of denying the religious exemption or maintaining the restriction, and demonstrating the unavailability of a less restrictive means of accommodation.[81] A 'flexible, contextual, casuistical approach is the way forward' which entails a nuanced and sensitive analysis of the context, and a fair and deep consideration of the competing goods and principles.[82] Such an approach is in accordance with the theological virtues of dignity (respecting the intrinsic value of all concerned parties), patience (respecting that different perspectives and communities have distinct but equally valuable contributions to the common good), and the golden rule (loving neighbour as self by genuinely and empathetically engaging with their perspective, just as we would want others to engage with ours). As already intimated, these issues arise most starkly in three distinct but sometimes overlapping areas: education, employment, and provision of goods and services. The following sections will critique the dominance of equality principles in these areas and suggest mechanisms for reconciling religion and equality by reasonably accommodating religion to facilitate peaceful coexistence in accordance with the theological virtues.

C. Education

The Equality Act contains specific religious exceptions for the autonomy of religious schools. The Act's requirements to not discriminate in relation to the provision of services do not apply to schools with a religious ethos in the context of

---

[77] ibid.
[78] See also Rivers, *The Law of Organised Religions* (n 8) 251–67 for a comprehensive review of the framework outlined above.
[79] Ahdar and Leigh, *Religious Freedom in the Liberal State* (n 35) 165.
[80] ibid 166.
[81] ibid 192–97.
[82] ibid 197.

the school curriculum, admission to the school, acts of worship or other religious activities organised by the school, or to the responsible body of such a school, and so on. That is, religious schools can effectively discriminate on the basis of religion.[83] Reasonable religious criteria can also be used to determine admissions to a faith school if these criteria are clearly determined and agreed to by the relevant religious authority.[84] However, these rules have been problematically applied. For example, in *R v JFS*,[85] the Jews' Free School refused to admit a child who was not recognised as Jewish according to Orthodox Judaism by the Office of the Chief Rabbi. The Supreme Court held that a religious ethos school can rely on religious criteria to allocate places because they are exempted from the prohibition of discrimination on the grounds of religion under the Equality Act. However, the exemption does not extend to racial grounds, and the Court found that the refusal relied on racial rather than religious grounds, so the pupil had to be admitted.[86] Though the Court was correct to hold that a religious ethos school can rely on EA exemptions to discriminate on religious grounds, and this supports the autonomy of religious communities, the specific application of this principle to JFS actually undermines the autonomy of religious communities and damages peaceful coexistence by not adhering to the theological virtues of dignity, patience, forgiveness and love of neighbour. Fundamentally, the Court failed to appreciate that ethnicity contains a religious component for certain religions such as Judaism, and so a religious exemption ought to extend to ethnicity in those unique circumstances.[87] More broadly, and more insidiously, 'the law as interpreted by the majority requires a non-Jewish definition of who is Jewish'.[88]

Rather than the Court deciding that the criteria were racial contrary to the school's self-understanding, the Court should have deferred to the school and recognised that the availability of conversion meant it was a religious requirement.[89] To say that a person is or is not really part of a religious community 'comes perilously close to making determinations about what really lies at the core of different religions'.[90] Similarly, Trigg critiques the 'interference of courts in theological issues' in the JFS case, arguing that an apparent reluctance to allow discrimination for religious reasons 'itself produces a form of discrimination against religious people, in this case Jews, who are not being allowed to practise the faith they have held for thousands of years … It is ironic that, in this case, this is being done in the

---

[83] Weller et al (n 10) 52.

[84] Rivers, *The Law of Organised Religions* (n 8) 255–57.

[85] *R (on the application of E) v Governing Body of JFS and the Admissions Appeal Panel of JFS* [2009] UKSC 15.

[86] Weller et al (n 10) 52.

[87] J Rivers, 'Promoting Religious Equality' (2012) 1 *Oxford Journal of Law and Religion* 386, 396.

[88] Rivers, *The Law of Organised Religions* (n 8) 255–57.

[89] McCrudden, *Litigating Religions* (n 2) 89–91. For a more detailed critique see C McCrudden, 'Multiculturalism, freedom of religion, equality and the British Constitution: The JFS case considered' (2011) 9 *International Journal of Constitutional Law* 200. See also Deagon, 'The "Religious Questions" Doctrine' (n 24).

[90] McCrudden, *Litigating Religions* (n 2) 96.

name of avoiding racial discrimination'.[91] As one of the dissenting judges noted, the decision of the majority means there can be no Jewish faith schools which give preference to children because they are Jewish according to Jewish religious law and belief. 'One thing that has certainly gone wrong has been the court's willingness to wade into a theological dispute without any willingness to appreciate its nuances'.[92] Hence, in the JFS case, the school's religious ethos and their autonomy more broadly was diluted because the Court effectively imposed a definition of Jewish upon the Jewish school. This was 'an inflexible application of the law' which produced an 'obvious interference with religious autonomy'; there is 'little controversy over the freedom of private religious schools to discriminate on grounds of admission where religion is concerned'.[93]

This undermines peaceful coexistence in accordance with the theological virtues because the Court was 'disrespectful' in its failure 'to engage with the group's self-understanding, its reasons for existing or its purpose'.[94] This meant the Court undermined the dignity of the group and damaged its ability to pursue its distinctive understanding of the good, and also did not love neighbour as self by refusing to allow the group to internally maintain its identity. Harrison suggests an alternative approach which better facilitates peaceful coexistence in accordance with the theological virtues by engaging with the 'tradition' and 'shared way of life' which ultimately constitutes religious communities.[95] This 'ecclesiological account' allows, for example, greater respect for the Jewish community's self-understanding by recognising that the Jewish people are constituted by a living tradition and practice which is both racial and religious, a 'shared heritage'.[96] This properly acknowledges 'the good of forming a people committed to the spiritual, moral, and cultural heritage of Judaism'.[97]

More broadly for religious communities, the 'crucial challenge' is to 'reconcile State requirements flowing from the participation of religious institutions in public services with the preservation of their own religious ethos. Cooperation with or absorption into the state system does not entail giving up the religious ethos which characterises a particular school'.[98] As mentioned, religious schools are 'allowed to discriminate in the appointment and management of their staff', with some given greater discretion based on the extent of connection to a religion.[99] But given this

---

[91] Trigg (n 36) 115–16.

[92] ibid 117.

[93] Ahdar and Leigh, *Religious Freedom in the Liberal State* (n 35) 251.

[94] Harrison, *Post-Liberal Religious Liberty* (n 42) 201–02.

[95] ibid 193–94, 196.

[96] ibid 201–02.

[97] ibid.

[98] M Hunter-Henin, 'Religious Freedoms in European Schools: Contrasts and Convergence' in M Hunter-Henin (ed), *Law, Religious Freedoms and Education in Europe* (Ashgate, 2011) 18.

[99] ibid 18. Rivers, *The Law of Organised Religions* (n 8) 247, 265 outlines the principles. Essentially, private religious schools have more rights to select and regulate membership of their community than State religious schools as a function of the pluralism that private education offers to service specific religious communities.

distinction is not relevant for the religious ethos of a religious school (that is, a school may equally wish to uphold a religious ethos regardless of the extent of their formal links with a religious body), the distinction is not relevant for the purposes of a power to select and regulate staff.[100] Any religious schools should have the ability to select and regulate (discriminate) in accordance with the religious ethos of the school. However, the state is arguably justified in monitoring religious schools to ensure basic education standards and equality of social and economic opportunity.[101] As Ahdar and Leigh contend, 'plainly, the state has an interest in well-educated citizens who share a commitment to democratic values. Beyond this minimum, however, we contend the state ought to respect the paramount religious liberty and duty of parents to nurture the education of their children in a way that does not damage the children's spiritual potential'.[102] This upholds the dignity of religious citizens and demonstrates patience and forgiveness through acknowledging distinct contributions to the common good. Fundamentally then, allowing religious schools supervised discretion to select and regulate their community in accordance with their religious ethos, and deferring to their understanding of that ethos rather than imposing a secular view upon them, are essential components of protecting the autonomy of religious communities in England, which in turn preserves peaceful coexistence in accordance with the theological virtues.

D. Employment

The autonomy of religious communities can be manifested through schools, colleges, charities, welfare groups and adoption agencies, in conjunction with churches. These religious groups may want to employ ministry workers, or 'may run a social or commercial enterprise in order to raise funds or as an element of their mission. They may want to keep themselves separate from non-members and may discriminate against others in order to do so'.[103] Such employers may manifest their liberty by requiring that the behaviour and lifestyle of employees be consistent with the employer or community's beliefs and practices. In the context of anti-discrimination law this effectively becomes a question of whether such employment practices are protected.[104]

As a matter of general principle, Vickers observes that protection of religious liberty 'is justified on the basis that it helps to uphold fundamental interests in equality, autonomy and human dignity', but that protection may be limited where

---

[100] Hunter-Henin, 'Religious Freedoms in European Schools' (n 98) 18.
[101] Ahdar and Leigh, *Religious Freedom in the Liberal State* (n 35) 252–53.
[102] ibid 297.
[103] L Vickers, *Religious Freedom, Religious Discrimination and the Workplace* (Hart Publishing, 2016) 2.
[104] Ahdar and Leigh, *Religious Freedom in the Liberal State* (n 35) 358–59.

it disproportionately affects others on the same basis.[105] The importance in this context of religion as identity also provides justification for religious group rights, because being part of a religious group is critical to the formation of religious identity.[106] As Vickers explains, religious beliefs ought to be protected because, among other reasons, it is not a simple matter of choice. The question of whether religion is a chosen characteristic is 'highly contested'; there is little mobility between religious groups, there are costs to individuals from renouncing religious affiliation, and many religious people and groups do not understand their religion as a choice, but rather as a duty or obligation to the truth. Choice is also not accepted as a reason to deny protection for other attributes, such as pregnancy.[107] Vickers notes there are difficulties in defining the precise content of dignity, but correctly concludes that it is a value which should be upheld. It is likely her difficulty is because she is operating within liberal political theory which views dignity as an axiomatic good but eschews the theological justifications that originally produced the concept.[108] However, as explained in the Introduction, this book more coherently gives substantive content to the concept of dignity by placing it within a theological framework. Hence, pursuing dignity as a theological virtue through upholding the genuine nature of religious belief and manifestation contributes to peaceful coexistence.

However, the EA 'has substantially increased the regulatory reach of the State and raised a new set of problems for religious organizations', and 'the arguments of religious organizations for accommodation have not always been well received'.[109] For example, on the issue of potential sexual orientation discrimination, many religions such as Christianity, Judaism and Islam oppose homosexual activity on religious grounds, and therefore may refuse to employ people engaging in such activities. Such a refusal may also be on the ground of religion if the group believes 'the individual cannot be in good standing with the religion if they live in a homosexual relationship'.[110] Rivers observes that it is 'hardly surprising' if a religious organisation takes views about who can hold certain offices or be employed with them. Adherence to the beliefs in question is really an obvious requirement, but also, certain positions may only be filled by men, or require racial alignment in the case of ethnic religions such as Judaism, and certain beliefs may also extend to appropriate sexual behaviour.[111] Finnis is even more explicit:

> The negative impact of the UK equality law on freedom of religion and conscience here overlaps with its negative impact on other established common law constitutional rights

---

[105] Vickers, *Religious Freedom* (n 103) 9. See ch 3 for a more detailed justification.

[106] ibid ch 3.

[107] ibid.

[108] See A Deagon, 'The Name of God in a Constitution: Meaning, Democracy and Political Solidarity' (2019) 8(3) *Oxford Journal of Law and Religion* 473; S Smith, 'Equality, Religion and Nihilism' in R Ahdar (ed), *Research Handbook on Law and Religion* (Edward Elgar, 2018) 41–44.

[109] Rivers, *The Law of Organised Religions* (n 8) 124–25.

[110] Vickers, *Religious Freedom* (n 103) 9.

[111] Rivers, *The Law of Organised Religions* (n 8) 122–23.

such as freedom of association, and/or on recognised human rights such as freedom of parents to educate their children toward good forms of life. In each case, the negative impact involves also a substantial shrinking of private life, or invasion of it, by coercive law. The legal requirement that parents who wish to band together to employ professional teachers for their children must, against their wishes, be fully willing and ready to employ as teachers qualified applicants who live openly unchaste lives (according to the conception of chastity accepted by those parents and desired for their children's education) is plainly an interference with their legitimate interest in associational freedom. And it is generally a quite disproportionate interference, given that the only kind of unchastity protected by equality law is one indulged in by persons sufficiently few that they can find readily desirable employment in schools that are uninterested in promoting chastity, or that conception of chastity.[112]

The complexities are enhanced by the fact that there are different types of workplace; what is appropriate for a small religious employer may not be appropriate for a larger secular workplace, and some public services are delivered through religious bodies, such as charities and schools.[113] Many religious groups are concerned that they cannot 'staff their organisations with fellow believers', and the 'genuine occupational requirement' exception is too narrow; others are concerned that the preference of religious bodies for fellow believers may result in other forms of discrimination such as sexual orientation discrimination.[114] If the exception is too broad, and any employer can require staff to be of a particular religion because they deem the employment to be religious, this could significantly reduce employment prospects for non-adherents of that religion. However, if it is too narrow, religious groups may need to employ those who do not share their beliefs, undermining the ethos of the group and restricting the freedom of religious groups to employ fellow believers.

As outlined above, the Equality Act 'does allow for religious requirements to be imposed in order to maintain the religious ethos of a religious employer' as long as this is 'proportionate', which leaves the determination to a tribunal as to whether the requirement is appropriate, taking into account the specific features of the job and organisation.[115] This allows an employer of a particular religion to only hire a person of that religion where it is a genuine occupational requirement, having regard to the employer's religious ethos, the nature and context of the role, and whether it is proportionate to apply that requirement in the case. So for example the role of finance administrator in a particular Christian charity was restricted because of the employer's emphasis on Christian prayer in undertaking the role.[116] The EA also contains a second exception applicable to employment in an organised religion which allows an employer to impose a requirement related to sex,

---

[112] Finnis (n 29) 26.
[113] Vickers, *Religious Freedom* (n 103) 2.
[114] ibid 8.
[115] ibid 8–9. See EA, Sch 9, paras 2 and 3.
[116] Ahdar and Leigh, *Religious Freedom in the Liberal State* (n 35) 370–71.

marriage and sexual orientation if this complies with the doctrine of the religion or to avoid conflict with the convictions of a significant number of adherents.

However, as already noted, the employment exceptions in the EA are relatively narrow and unclear. The 'organised religion' exception likely excludes schools, charities and businesses, but would clearly apply to churches with discriminatory ordination practices. On sexual orientation discrimination, 'these provisions give very little space to employers with religious objections to act on their own moral judgements about homosexual conduct. They may only do so in the narrow confines of the 'organised religion' exception … [this] may result in a substantial narrowing of the right to manifest one's religious beliefs'.[117] There is no legal articulation of the difference (if any) between an organisation relating to religion or belief, and an organised religion; consequently, 'the exemptions are widely misunderstood, and … the law is inconsistent'.[118] The general indication is the exceptions are narrow, but 'the complexity of the provisions and the ambiguity of the language are likely to increase the likelihood of concern, tension and litigation'.[119] Furthermore, the fact that it is left to a tribunal to determine whether any requirement of a religious organisation is appropriate raises the spectre of secular courts imposing their views in relation to religious questions. Questions raised may include whether beliefs are core to the religion, and whether particular requirements or practices are manifestations of belief or merely actions motivated by belief. A court potentially deciding issues outside their competence in this way could have grave implications for religious freedom.[120]

In short, the EA exemptions are narrow and the scope of them is unclear. They entail 'considerable restrictions' on the ability of religious communities to select and regulate employees; in addition, 'whilst legal interference with their autonomy has not been completely restrictive, it has been vaguely so'.[121] Furthermore, the fact that a secular court is enabled to pronounce a theological judgement on what is a proportional or appropriate employment requirement for a religious body 'denies the free association of the body'.[122] As alluded to above, narrow, unclear exemptions which enable the imposition of secular conditions on religious bodies

---

[117] ibid 372–73.

[118] R Sandberg and N Doe, 'Religious Exemptions in Discrimination Law' (2007) 66(2) *Cambridge Law Journal* 302, 311–12.

[119] Sandberg, 'The Right to Discriminate' (n 12) 178.

[120] See L Vickers, 'Promoting Equality or Fostering Resentment? The Public Sector Equality Duty and Religion and Belief' (2011) 31 *Legal Studies* 135, 141–45. There may also be a need to identify those who authentically speak for a religious group whose practices are impugned, especially if there is disagreement within the group. Great care would need to be taken to not foster further resentment among communities by actually or apparently favouring some religious views or groups above others. See Deagon, 'The "Religious Questions" Doctrine' (n 24); N Foster, 'Respecting the Dignity of Religious Organisations: When Is It Appropriate for Courts to Decide Religious Doctrine?' (2020) 47(1) *University of Western Australia Law Review* 175.

[121] Rivers, *The Law of Organised Religions* (n 8) 137–38.

[122] Ahdar and Leigh, *Religious Freedom in the Liberal State* (n 35) 360–61.

increase conflict and litigation, and therefore undermine peaceful coexistence by damaging the theological virtues of dignity and patience.

As Rivers states, 'these defects need remedying'.[123] One option is to 'simply insist on applying general non-discrimination standards to churches and religious associations; this would be … oppressive depending on the degree to which the religious body diverges from the new legal norm'.[124] Another would be to exempt religious bodies completely from the operation of discrimination law. Both of these extremes would not love neighbour as self or uphold the dignity of citizens, and would undermine peaceful coexistence by amplifying tensions. An accommodation is where 'the law is applicable, but some freedom is carved out for the religious body'.[125] This could be done in different ways, including making the preservation of religious ethos a legitimate aim in employment practices, 'reasonable deference' to the views of the body as to how it seeks to preserve that ethos and allowing them to demonstrate those views, seeing the 'organised religion' exception as a 'genuine exemption' in relation to core ministry posts, and 'building the religious perspective into the structure of judgments of appropriateness, such that requiring a priest to be a man, for example, does not even count as discrimination in the first place'.[126] Ahdar and Leigh further note that this approach has the advantage of providing clarity to both employer and employee by stating the position in advance rather than requiring a factually specific justification.[127] These kinds of clear and generous exemptions which genuinely listen to and engage with the perspective of religious bodies would contribute to upholding peaceful coexistence in accordance with the theological virtues.

Though anti-discrimination advocates may object to this apparent special privilege for religion (religious employers can discriminate in a way that secular employers cannot), this fails to recognise what religious freedom really entails:

> Freedom to associate with others of like mind necessarily involves freedom to exclude people who do not share the beliefs in question … those so excluded are free to join other religious groups (or form their own group) and so this should not be seen as harmful. On the contrary: if the state were to prevent exclusivity through its non-discrimination laws, this would amount to denial of a basic aspect of religious liberty. Paradoxically, perhaps, exclusive societies add to the diversity of society.[128]

It may be further objected that this also follows for secular employment organisations who may wish to exclude religious people; that would be true for organisations which are avowedly 'secular' and explicitly adhere to atheistic and humanistic doctrines. They would then be treated as a 'belief' organisation akin to

---

[123] Rivers, *The Law of Organised Religions* (n 8) 137–38.
[124] ibid 124–25.
[125] ibid.
[126] ibid 124–25, 137–38.
[127] Ahdar and Leigh, *Religious Freedom in the Liberal State* (n 35) 359.
[128] ibid 360.

a religion. However, regular non-religious organisations have a 'thin' ethos in the sense that there is no belief aspect to the employee role, and therefore the above logic does not apply.

Though 'a religious body should be free to constitute its membership and leadership according to its beliefs, even if those conflict with general non-discrimination norms', the claim for exemption is arguably weaker when a religious body is performing public or secular functions generally available to the public.[129] However, this again raises the issue of who determines what functions are secular; a religious body may offer public services in accordance with God's will, commit business decisions to prayer, only provide material consistent with the religion, and so on. This applies for businesses, schools, hospitals, and the like.[130] So Rivers contends:

> In relation to core liturgical, ritual, and doctrinal teaching posts, organized religions should be completely exempt from the requirements of secular non-discrimination law. Secular bodies, including legislatures and courts, have no competence to assess any supposed 'balance' between religious factors and requirements of non-discrimination operating outside the religious sphere.[131]

Therefore, the most 'straightforward' and 'correct' approach is 'for the court to defer to the interpretation rendered by the church's internal governing structure' in such matters.[132] As argued above, this fulfils peaceful coexistence by loving our religious neighbours as ourselves, upholding their dignity to govern themselves, and patiently recognising their distinctive contribution to the common good.

E. Provision of Goods and Services

As discussed above, the EA provides an exception for 'an organisation relating to religion or belief' discriminating on the basis of sexual orientation in relation to providing goods and services; however, this does not apply to an organisation 'whose sole or main purpose is commercial, or to any action done 'on behalf of a public authority' and 'under the terms of a contract between the organisation and a public authority'.[133] In effect, this means that a religious vendor operating a business cannot refuse to provide goods and services, and a religious organisation which has a contract with the state to provide goods and services also cannot refuse to provide them (even where the provision of such for both kinds of organisations conflicts with their religious ethos). Using peaceful coexistence and the theological

---

[129] ibid 361.
[130] ibid 362–63.
[131] Rivers, *The Law of Organised Religions* (n 8) 136–37.
[132] Ahdar and Leigh, *Religious Freedom in the Liberal State* (n 35) 384.
[133] Equality Act, Sch 2.

virtues, I will analyse the tensions and conflict produced by these provisions with respect to three illustrative cases: *Catholic Care, Bull v Hall*, and *Asher's Baking*.[134]

In *Catholic Care*, the religious adoption agency had a contract with the State to provide adoption services. However, they refused to provide adoptions for same-sex couples because of their religious beliefs regarding the nature of right relationships. The Tribunal held that under the EA provisions, Catholic Care could not discriminate on the basis of sexual orientation because they were providing an adoption service on behalf of a public authority under a contract with that authority.[135] The provisions undergirding this decision have received significant critique which is justified by the ultimate consequences of the case. One Catholic adoption agency became embroiled in litigation, two closed down, and faced with this 'plight' the remaining nine agencies changed their ethos to operate consistently with the law, and inconsistently with the obligations required by the church.[136] So Rivers concludes:

> Thus while there is clear scope for *religious* pluralism in education and welfare services, there is no scope for *sexual-ethical* pluralism. Or rather, what it means to be religious is partly defined by excluding sexual ethics from its scope. Catholic adoption agencies can be Catholic in some sense of the word, but they cannot act on the basis of a Catholic sexual ethic.[137]

As Finnis argues, people 'wrongly' call religious exemptions to discrimination law 'an arbitrary license to discriminate. In Britain … the disproportionality or needlessness of the refusal to accommodate associational and religious liberties in the new laws against sexual-orientation discrimination in the employment practices of schools was even more vividly manifested by the law prohibiting adoption agencies from continuing' to place children with families consistent with their convictions.[138] This 'coercion', which resulted in some adoption agencies withdrawing from the service, was imposed by British law even though same-sex adopters had other competent and numerous adoption agencies willing to cater for them.[139] Indeed, the Catholic adoption agencies were small in number but successful, particularly for Catholics. There were many other agencies that would place children with homosexual couples. However, the Charity Commission 'forced these adoption agencies to abandon their faith principles or lose government funding and thereby be forced to close', and furthermore, the Catholic agencies were 'refused a right of discrimination which is given to same-sex groups'.[140]

---

[134] See *Catholic Care (Diocese of Leeds) v Charity Commission for England and Wales* CA/ 2010/0007 26 April 2011 (Charity Tribunal); *Catholic Care v Charity Commission* [2012] UKUT 395; *Bull & Bull v Hall & Preddy* [2013] UKSC 73; *Lee v Asher's Baking Company Ltd* [2018] UKSC 49.

[135] Sandberg, 'The Right to Discriminate' (n 12) 178–79.

[136] Hunt (n 17) 706.

[137] Rivers, *The Law of Organised Religions* (n 8) 285 (emphasis in original).

[138] Finnis (n 29) 26.

[139] ibid 26–27.

[140] N Kerton-Johnson, 'Governing the Faithful: A Discussion of religious freedom and liberal democracies with particular focus on the UK' (2011) 4(2) *International Journal for Religious Freedom* 77, 84–85.

The Regulations allow sexual orientation discrimination by a charity if that charity was established for the provision of services to a particular sexual orientation. As Kerton-Johnson outlines:

> Catholic adoption agencies seeking permission to discriminate on sexual grounds in order to only place children with heterosexual couples were refused in what can only be deemed a double standard – in other words one can discriminate on a sexual basis if one is a sexual group, but not if one is a religious group.[141]

This is a 'strong example of the failure' of the equality legislation; the state 'is essentially empowering a system of conflict'.[142] This inconsistency clearly undermines the dignity of the religious charity and does not love them as a neighbour, and damages peaceful coexistence by facilitating tension.

The refusal of State funding for particular religious ethos charities also produces a discrimination issue which runs parallel to autonomy for religious communities. A religious charity has Article 9 rights to promote a traditional sexual ethic grounded in its beliefs. There is no convention right to receive a charitable service.[143] Similarly, religious charities are not constrained in their ethos and activities by the receipt of State funds, except by the terms of any contract they may enter into with the public funding body. But the terms of that contract may themselves breach convention rights by constraining religious beliefs and manifestation, and by directly discriminating against a religious body. The question will ultimately be whether such constraints and discrimination is appropriate given the availability of readily accessible alternative welfare providers (which, incidentally, there usually are).[144] However, both legislation and case law indicate the aim may be the 'imposition of ideological conformity in the sphere of public welfare services', which is obviously problematic for religious charities with distinct moral perspectives.[145] Thus, the EA has fundamental flaws. Though there is some acknowledgement of the need to balance equality considerations with religious freedom, the trend appears to be that equality will trump religion in the event of conflict; 'it is likely that the narrowness of the exceptions will be continued to be stressed until the exceptions narrow to the extent that they cease to exist'.[146]

A similar outcome occurred in *Bull v Hall*, where the Christian owners of a bed and breakfast who had consistently refused to provide accommodation to those engaged in 'sinful lifestyles' (including unmarried heterosexual couples) refused to provide accommodation to a gay couple. In that case they were found guilty of direct discrimination on the basis of sexual orientation. The Christian hotel owners were viewed to be undertaking a public function, and ultimately it was held that their discrimination under what became the 2010 Equality Act could

---

[141] ibid.
[142] ibid.
[143] Rivers, *The Law of Organised Religions* (n 8) 286–87.
[144] ibid 281–82.
[145] ibid.
[146] Sandberg, 'The Right to Discriminate' (n 12) 179–81.

not be justified under Article 9. The Supreme Court conceded that religious beliefs had been interfered with, but concluded religious freedom must be appropriately limited to protect the rights of others (in this case a right not to be discriminated against).[147] Specifically, Lady Hale for a majority of the Court held that since their general policy extended to unmarried couples (based on the religious convictions of the owners about only having sexual relations within the sanctity of marriage), and at the time gay couples could not get married, it was effectively direct sexual orientation discrimination because 'the criterion of marriage or civil partnership' is 'indissociable from the sexual orientation of those who qualify to enter it'.[148] There is an exception for religious organisations in the relevant Regulations, but Lady Hale held the owners did not qualify because they are individuals.[149] Lady Hale then considered the impact of Article 9, which includes the right to hold and manifest religious beliefs, and Lady Hale accepted that the policy was a manifestation of the religious beliefs of the owners.[150] However, though the owners had the right 'to manifest their religion by conducting their business in accordance with their religious beliefs', this manifestation also interfered with the Convention rights (Articles 8 and 14) of the gay couple to enjoy respect for their private lives without discrimination on the basis of sexual orientation.[151]

Any limitation of the rights of the owners is therefore consistent with one of the legitimate aims in Article 9(2) (fundamental rights and freedoms of others) and the limitation is in accordance with law. This begs the question of whether the limitation is necessary in a democratic society; that is, whether there is proportionality between the means employed and the aim sought to be achieved.[152] Lady Hale held that the limitation would be proportionate. Though the owners have the right to run their business in accordance with their religious convictions, they have many other ways of doing this. And though the owners had a clear policy and were not demeaning, and refunded the money with extra for the inconvenience, there is no less restrictive means of achieving the legitimate aim of equality law. According to Lady Hale, denying same-sex couples the equivalent accommodation to married couples denies the equal rights of same-sex couples and the public interest in recognising and encouraging stable, committed, long-term relationships, and would simultaneously create a class of people who are exempt from discrimination law. In short, though the religious freedom rights of the owners under Article 9 were limited, this limitation was a proportionate means of achieving a legitimate aim according to law (to protect the right to not be discriminated against under English anti-discrimination law).[153]

---

[147] Weller et al (n 10) 50–51.
[148] *Bull & Bull v Hall & Preddy* [2013] UKSC 73 [3], [17], [20], [22], [29].
[149] ibid [8].
[150] ibid [41].
[151] ibid [43].
[152] ibid [44]–[45].
[153] ibid [34]–[39], [45]–[55].

Some commentators saw this case as another example of the marginalisation of Christians in liberal democracies where equality principles reign. Kerton-Johnson asserts:

> Christians in Western states, or at least Christians who adhere to traditional understanding of their faith, are facing increasing hostility within Western democracies … the right to religious freedom was subordinated to those of homosexual clients … Mr. and Mrs. Bull's case again represented a hierarchy of rights in which religious belief is subordinated to the right to receive services.[154]

Finnis similarly claims that the UK and European courts have failed to develop a reasonable doctrine of accommodation for individuals who make conscientious religious objections to generally applicable (typically, anti-discrimination) laws. Instead, they have tended to levy disproportionate restrictions against religious freedoms, such as when the UK Supreme Court held that the owners and operators of a hotel could not, for religious reasons, deny a double room to a homosexual couple, even when this rule applied to all unmarried couples.[155] However, this is a more difficult case than education, employment, or even *Catholic Care* in terms of the balancing required.

Keller and Heri observe that the cancellation occurred in a friendly way, and that a refund or alternative lodging was offered. However, in their view, this attempted 'reasonable accommodation' (acceptance of adjustments or exceptions for one group in the interests of the other) fails because 'it confuses the ability to participate in society at all with the ability to participate fully and equally'.[156] Even if genuine alternatives are offered, and the policy is clearly articulated to avoid surprise, the end result is still differential treatment on the basis of a protected attribute. It produces a 'deep, intense and tangible hurt' to the refused persons, an 'assault' on 'dignity'.[157] Brems similarly argues that the harm is of a 'brutal' nature (informing a person that a refusal of service is because they do not approve of their relationship), and even if any material harm is mitigated by providing alternative accommodation, 'it keeps the expressive harm, which is arguably the crucial matter in this case, intact. It can therefore not be considered a balanced solution', and would obviously in this sense damage peaceful coexistence and be inconsistent with theological virtues such as dignity.[158] Fredman goes even further, arguing at a general level that the notions of tolerance and neutrality are themselves value commitments within a broader hierarchy of values. As such, she proposes substantive equality as occupying the apex of this hierarchy of values, and applies this framework to complicity claims involving third party harms to argue that religious

---

[154] Kerton-Johnson (n 140) 79–80.

[155] See generally Finnis (n 29).

[156] Keller and Heri (n 33) 322–24.

[157] ibid.

[158] E Brems, 'A Conflicting Rights Approach' in S Mancini and M Rosenfeld (eds), *The Conscience Wars: Rethinking the Balance between Religion, Identity and Equality* (Cambridge University Press, 2018) 292.

freedom should be limited where it exacerbates disadvantage and demeans through discrimination.[159]

With respect to *Bull v Hall* and similar scenarios of refusal, Fredman notes that it is possible to uphold freedom of religion through accommodations which are also compatible with redressing disadvantage and are not demeaning to those refused a service, such as offering alternatives or referrals. However, she argues that this position 'assumes that such an alternative exists. It is conceivable that all marriage registrars, bed-and-breakfasts and bakeries could take a similar stand'.[160] However, this is really beyond the pale. It is conceivable but not a realistic situation that all service providers would refuse services on the basis of sexual orientation. Implausible hypotheticals do not provide a sound basis for law. The only justification Fredman provides for this frankly outlandish claim is 'this is not a far-fetched possibility ... refusal to provide contraception or abortion can be so widespread so as to significantly impede access'.[161] This justification is insufficient for at least three reasons. First, while this may be true, the fact that a conscientious refusal is so widespread should provide pause. If so many people apparently object to being part of the action, it actually strengthens the argument that an accommodation is necessary because it implies the conviction has greater weight and significance. Second, and correlatively, abortion involves questions of life and death, and so is naturally more susceptible to issues of conscience. Refusals to provide marriage, retail or hospitality services are not at that level so it is a non sequitur to reason that widespread refusal in an abortion context justifies denying accommodations in other less urgent contexts – the analogy is false. Finally, as I have argued elsewhere and earlier, accommodations should not be extended where alternatives are not reasonably available – but on a factual basis rather than spurious claims about how theoretically widespread refusal could be.[162]

Bull v Hall also suggests it is more difficult to justify discrimination on the ground of sexual orientation than it is to justify discrimination on the ground of religion. In other cases, employer concerns about sexual orientation trumped an employee's right not to discriminated against on the ground of religion. But in *Bull*, when the service provider's concern about religious freedom clashed with sexual orientation discrimination, the customer won. This is a 'staggeringly different' approach which reveals the law provides 'very little, if any' accommodation for religious service providers.[163] As such, Wintemute advocates for a harm

---

[159] S Fredman, 'Tolerating the Intolerant: Religious Freedom, Complicity, and the Right to Equality' (2020) 9(2) *Oxford Journal of Law and Religion* 305, 306.

[160] ibid 316–17.

[161] ibid 317.

[162] See eg the discussion in ch 2; A Deagon, 'Defining the Interface of Freedom and Discrimination: Exercising Religion, Democracy and Same-Sex Marriage' (2017) 20 *International Trade and Business Law Review* 239.

[163] Sandberg, 'The Right to Discriminate' (n 12) 173. At the time of writing for Sandberg the case had only been heard at county level, but his analysis applies equally to the Supreme Court judgment, which by majority came to a similar conclusion.

framework which also bears in mind the extent of harm imposed on the accommodating party (dignity, cost, disruption or inconvenience) to guide a case-by-case assessment of whether exemptions should be granted.[164] So Adenitire claims that conscientious exemptions should not be granted to religious vendors because doing so would cause 'unjustifiable dignitary harm' to members of the LGBT community; protection from harm is a 'compelling reason' for equality to prevail in the 'context of providers of commercial services'.[165] Religious freedom rights are still protected under various mechanisms and religionists 'can associate in institutions whose constitutive belief is that homosexuality is sinful or immoral and which exclude those in the LGB community'.[166] However, Adenitire admits that a 'limited class of service-providers (such as photographers who have to physically attend pro-homosexuality events) have a legitimate claim to be exempted from sexual orientation anti-discrimination norms' so they are not compelled to participate in such events; according to Adenitire this is a more balanced position.[167] Adenitire is on the right track here, with two minor points. First, as I analysed in depth in chapter two, dignitary harm is also a relevant consideration for religious vendors, so the imposition of dignity harm is not a determining factor in favour of the refused members of the LGBT community. It is incorporated into the overall balance. Second, elsewhere I have articulated a more consistent approach to the question of which service providers should be exempt: the vendor is a genuinely religious entity providing a marriage-related service, and an equivalent service is not reasonably available elsewhere.[168] Creating products or messages which endorse pro-homosexuality events like same-sex marriage is not qualitatively different from physically attending such events in terms of endorsement, and so a reasonable accommodation would provide clear and narrow exemptions for photographers, videographers, bakeries and the like as well. As articulated in chapter two, this would preserve peaceful coexistence in accordance with the theological virtues by upholding the dignity of both parties and facilitating forgiveness and patience, the existence of distinctive methods of contributing to the good.

Returning to *Bull v Hall*, Brems claims that an exemption should not be given in such scenarios because the burden of conscience is more limited than in situations involving the endorsement of a marriage; it is merely 'indirect involvement in the lifestyle of others' – though Brems does admit that the burden would be more serious for the owner who receives guests into their own home and treats them as family, as opposed to one who lives elsewhere and leaves most of the

---

[164] R Wintemute, 'Accommodating Religious Beliefs: Harm, Clothing or Symbols, and Refusals to Serve Others' (2014) 77(2) *Modern Law Review* 223, 223–24.

[165] J Adenitire, *A General Right to Conscientious Exemption* (Cambridge University Press, 2020) 9. See also the edited collection J Adenitire (ed), *Religious Beliefs and Conscientious Exemptions in a Liberal State* (Hart Publishing, 2019).

[166] Adenitire, *A General Right to Conscientious Exemption* (n 165) 9.

[167] ibid.

[168] See my arguments in A Deagon, 'Religious Schools, Religious Vendors and Refusing Services After Ruddock: Diversity or Discrimination? (2019) 93(9) *Australian Law Journal* 766.

interaction to other staff.[169] Yet even here the peripheral harm imposed on the owner is outweighed by the harm imposed on the refused couple, which goes to the core of their rights.[170] One problem is this position does not properly consider the fact that for religious service providers like those in *Bull v Hall*, their very vision, purpose and execution of their service is infused with religion. They see every aspect of their provision as part of their service to God, a religious call-ing, as demonstrated by their consistent policy applying to any guests who were not in a heterosexual marriage.[171] So if they are forced to accept guests in a way which conflicts with their conscience, this does actually go to the core of their belief and practice, and it does impose a dignity harm upon them.[172] Nevertheless, it does seem to be the case that the circumstances are only indirectly connected to marriage-related services compared to vendors providing marriage-related services, so in that sense it is arguable that on balance an exemption ought not to be provided. Using the elements of my approach, the service provided is not a marriage-related service. But we should be clear about the implications of this. If the logic of proximity to marriage is accepted as an important determining factor or element of whether exemptions should be provided, it follows (as I have explained above) that exemptions should be provided to religious vendors offering marriage-related services such as registrars, ministers and celebrants, photogra-phers/videographers, bakers, and so on.

As such, in the famous case of *Asher's Baking*, the Supreme Court sided with the religious vendor. In *Asher's Baking*, the owners of a bakery who consistently oper-ated the bakery in accordance with Christian principles were asked to bake a cake proclaiming a message supporting same-sex marriage.[173] They refused to do so because of a religious objection to the message, and were sued for discrimination. Lady Hale for the Court held that there was no direct or indirect sexual orienta-tion discrimination under the Northern Ireland Sexual Orientation Regulations (issued under the 2006 English Equality Act, the precursor to the 2010 Act) because the bakers refused service on the basis of objection to expressing a politi-cal message, not on the basis of the sexual orientation of the customer.[174] However, Lady Hale further held that the bakers may have discriminated on the basis of political opinion (protected under the law of Northern Ireland but not under the English Equality Act) by refusing to supply a cake because of the political beliefs of the customer (supporting gay marriage).[175] Lady Hale proceeded to consider

---

[169] Brems (n 158) 292–94.
[170] ibid.
[171] Ahdar and Leigh, *Religious Freedom in the Liberal State* (n 35) 157.
[172] As I discuss with regard to religious vendors more broadly in ch 2.
[173] *Lee v Asher's Baking Company Ltd* [2018] UKSC 49.
[174] ibid [20]–[36]. See R Reyes, '*Masterpiece Cakeshop and Asher's Baking Company*: A Comparative Analysis of Constitutional Confections' (2020) 16(1) *Stanford Journal of Civil Rights & Civil Liberties* 113, 121–28 for an overview of the applicable legal regime.
[175] *Asher's Baking* [37]–[48].

the impact of the Convention Rights on this question, especially Articles 9 and 10 on freedom of religion and freedom of expression respectively. Both these Articles protect the right to not be obliged to hold and manifest beliefs that one does not hold.[176] Hence, Lady Hale subsequently concluded that since the bakers were required to produce the cake, 'they were being required to express a message with which they deeply disagreed', and as a function of section 3 of the Human Rights Act, domestic laws 'should not be read or given effect in such a way as to compel providers of goods, facilities and services to express a message with which they disagree'.[177]

Asher's Baking, even as a company, could avail itself of the protection of Article 9 because the company was viewed as indissoluble from the owners. So the UK Supreme Court did not hold that the company has rights under Article 9, but rather that the owners had rights under Article 9 (and consequently so did the company).[178] This is a similar principle to that held by the US Supreme Court in *Hobby Lobby* which contributes to the autonomy of religious communities, as discussed in the previous chapter.[179] And similarly to the US context, the owners of Asher's Baking believed that by fulfilling the cake order they were doing something deeply wrong and sinful, and in that sense the dignity harm imposed upon them by compelling them to undertake an activity or express a message contrary to their conscience is significant.[180] So the decision was correct in the sense that it supported peaceful coexistence by upholding the theological virtue of dignity. However, as a general principle, it should be noted that the HRA and Article 9 do not limit the UK government in the same way the US First Amendment limits the US government; Parliament retains its power to legislate inconsistently with the ECHR, and a judicial declaration of incompatibility does not affect the validity or operation of impugned domestic legislation. It merely puts political pressure on the government to revise the law.[181]

In the context of balancing, the weight courts place on the importance of religion and religious belief with respect to dignity will also affect the proportionality analysis. 'The more importance the court places on religion, the more weight it has; the more weight it has, the more those limiting religious practices and beliefs must show that that limitation is justified, despite the effect of those limitations on those practices and beliefs'.[182] So in *Asher's Baking*, the Court of Appeal (before being overturned by the Supreme Court) did not give significant weight to religious

---

[176] See ibid [49]–[52].

[177] ibid [54], [56].

[178] See R Ahdar and J Giles, 'The Supreme Courts' Icing on the Trans-Atlantic Cakes' (2020) 9(1) *Oxford Journal of Law and Religion* 212, 219.

[179] See generally R Ahdar, 'Companies as Religious Liberty Claimants' (2016) 5(1) *Oxford Journal of Law and Religion* 1.

[180] Ahdar and Giles (n 178) 221.

[181] Reyes (n 174) 127–28.

[182] McCrudden, *Litigating Religions* (n 2) 120.

conscience and its importance to human dignity in order to find that the need to eradicate discrimination in the public sphere outweighed the conscience objection of the bakers.[183] In other words, pursuing peaceful coexistence in accordance with the theological virtues such as human dignity, which provides a high weight to religious conscience, may tip the balance towards religious vendors.[184]

Conversely, Adenitire relies on dignity to elaborate a general principle that LGBT persons should not be denied commercial services. Adenitire considers the objection that forcing religious vendors to provide services contrary to their conscience would undermine their dignity by designating them as social outcasts, but dismisses that charge because in a liberal society which supports a diversity of beliefs, religious vendors who disagree with homosexuality have their social standing protected by law in other ways. 'Hence, safeguarding LGB people from the dignitary harm they would suffer if the law allowed them to be turned away by providers of commercial services is a legitimate balancing of conflicting rights: this is because the social standing of both those that oppose and those that support homosexuality is protected by liberal law.'[185] Adenitire also accepts some specific exemptions on the basis of the 'no religious rites principle', which states that a person should not be compelled to participate in rites which have a significant religious or moral character; this would exonerate vendors like photographers from being compelled to provide their services to a same-sex marriage because it entails their presence at the ceremony.[186] Adenitire emphasises that 'the principle would be inapplicable to other service-providers (such as bakers or printers) to the extent that their presence at the ceremony is not needed to fulfil their services'.[187]

However, as already indicated above, this principle proves too much for Adenitire. Applying the elements of the principle to religious vendors such as bakers, for many religious vendors marriage itself is a religious rite, and providing their services for a same-sex marriage would constitute, for them, participation in that rite – even if they are not physically present at the ceremony.[188] One should of course accept the general rule that a person should not be denied goods and services on the basis of their sexual orientation as a matter of dignity. But this is not what clear and narrow religious vendor exemptions entail. These are exemptions to the general rule for the purpose of preserving the dignity of religious vendors and promoting a pluralistic society committed to pursuing the good in diverse ways.[189] So even following Adenitire's logic religious vendors should be entitled to exemptions in the way I have already outlined above. Adenitire himself seems to

---

[183] ibid 121.

[184] See generally C McCrudden (ed), *Understanding Human Dignity* (Oxford University Press, 2014).

[185] J Adenitire, 'Conscientious Exemptions in a Liberal State' in J Adenitire (ed), *Religious Beliefs and Conscientious Exemptions in a Liberal State* (Hart Publishing, 2019) 282–83.

[186] ibid 283–84.

[187] ibid.

[188] See my arguments in Deagon, 'Refusing Services' (n 168) 770–76; Ahdar and Leigh, *Religious Freedom in the Liberal State* (n 35) 157. See the similar discussion above with respect to *Bull v Hall*.

[189] See Deagon, 'Refusing Services' (n 168), and the discussion above.

arrive at a view consistent with this proposition, arguing that involvement in the religious ceremony of marriage 'can be reasonably construed as taking part in the ceremony', which is conduct protected under the 'freedom not to practice' religion aspect of Article 9.[190]

Rivers observes that 'this new sense that equality is a matter of fundamental public policy gives it something of the character of a state-sanctioned ideology'.[191] Though courts have started to restrain this movement (as in *Asher's Baking*, where the Court held that a religious vendor should not be compelled to express support for messages with which they disagree), it demonstrates the 'potential that equality policy has for infringing rights ... the over-zealous implementation of blunt equality policies can be detrimental to the protection of rights and is in practice a more significant threat to religious liberty than the law it claims to serve'.[192] Ahdar and Giles go further, contending there is 'a distinct air of unreality, if not farce' to these cases; they involve almost 'entirely trivial' matters where very few consumers would be denied services, and where these rare cases exist, there is very little direct material or economic injury to complainants.[193] It is true that there is some dignitary harm suffered, but 'to be offended by the moral stance of another is surely part of the hurly-burly of living in a liberal democracy. It is well established that speech is not subject to be curtailed by the state simply because it offends or hurts the feelings of some group'.[194]

Therefore, Ahdar and Giles argue, religious vendors 'ought not to be bludgeoned into providing goods or services when their consciences would genuinely be violated'.[195] Of course, there must be limits around this principle, and the specific circumstances and nuances of each case should be considered, including the type and nature of the good or service, the creative input of the vendor and the extent of their conscience burden, whether an equivalent good or service is reasonably available, the nature of the harm suffered by the complainants who are refused the good or service, and so on.[196] In prior work and in previous chapters of this book, I have suggested a clear and narrow exemption for genuinely religious vendors providing marriage-related goods or services where such goods or services are not reasonably available elsewhere.[197] This upholds the dignity of both the religious

---

[190] Adenitire, 'Conscientious Exemptions in a Liberal State' (n 185) 284. Adenitire refers to 'physically being present', but there is no reason to think mere physical presence at the ceremony implies more or less endorsement than creating a special product specifically for that ceremony. In both situations the service provider is directly supporting the ceremony by providing a good or service essential to the performance of that ceremony.

[191] Rivers, 'Is Religious Freedom under Threat?' (n 69) 188–89.

[192] ibid.

[193] Ahdar and Giles (n 178) 221–22, assuming the absence of a local monopoly or a rural area where there are actually no other options.

[194] ibid.

[195] ibid 227.

[196] ibid. See also C Stychin, 'Faith in the Future: Sexuality, Religion and the Public Sphere' (2009) 29(4) *Oxford Journal of Legal Studies* 729, 752.

[197] See Deagon, 'Defining the Interface of Freedom and Discrimination' (n 162); Deagon, 'Refusing Services' (n 168).

vendors and those seeking marriage services, while also recognising and promoting distinctive pursuits of the common good. In the final section of this chapter, I further consider such accommodationist approaches in the context of service provision, with the aim of more effectively pursuing the peaceful coexistence of the religious and LGBT communities in particular.

F. Accommodation and Peaceful Coexistence

The concern for dignity specifically applies to the status harms which may be caused by the religious belief that same-sex sexual conduct is not appropriate. On this view, legal permission (even as an exception) for discriminatory conduct effectively states that same-sex persons are of less worth or dignity, and that permission should be removed. Logically, this could extend to all contexts, including individuals, vendors, associations, schools and churches, leading to the uniform application of discrimination norms. 'Put another way, human dignity, in the sense of cultivating respect for each person's unique identity, is paradoxically achieved by eliminating religious difference'.[198] However, the requirement of governance 'does not mean that some accommodation cannot often be made to respect people's consciences. A government can be gracious while still able to administer the law in the interests of everyone … a failure to accommodate can itself help to build up serious resentment and discord within a country'.[199] Ignoring accommodations 'displays an unacceptable use of coercion by the state' and 'ignores the source of a flourishing democracy'.[200] A government seeking to graciously incorporate and balance diverse interests through promoting compassion rather than coercion upholds peaceful coexistence in accordance with the theological virtues. Hence, for clarity and accord it is wiser to have these exemptions recognised by the legislature from the start rather than having them be created (or denied) as a result of litigation.[201] The alternative to reasonable accommodation is 'to see society as simply the ground of warring factions with competing interests, who have all to be bought off', and this would obviously damage peaceful coexistence – 'there must be some vision of what makes a just society and what constitutes human good and harm'.[202] In regard to dignity, reasonable accommodation of difference also recognises that religious vendors have a relevant harm imposed upon them if compelled to violate their conscience. In this sense exceptions to anti-discrimination law may be justified on equality grounds to remove the imposition of rules which uniquely

---

[198] Harrison, *Post-Liberal Religious Liberty* (n 42) 47–48.
[199] Trigg (n 36) 92.
[200] ibid.
[201] ibid 92–93, 116.
[202] ibid 124.

and severely burden religious believers.[203] So Ahdar and Giles advise a 'collaborative approach' which 'abandon[s] a … winner-takes-all mindset'.[204]

Wintemute suggests that accommodation may be possible if three cumulative conditions are satisfied: 'the particular manifestation of religious beliefs itself causes no direct harm to others', 'the requested accommodation involves minimal cost, disruption or inconvenience to the accommodating party', and the requested accommodation will 'cause no indirect harm to others'.[205] This provides a practical test for evaluating whether the direct or indirect harm caused to others is too great to accept the proposed accommodation. Wintemute consequently argues that religiously motivated refusals to serve ought not to be accommodated because they impose harm by refusing service to a customer for a prohibited reason either directly (to their face) or indirectly (through a general exclusion sign or some such indication of 'segregation'), even if the accommodation involves minimal cost or inconvenience due to a readily accessible alternative.[206] 'It is insulting for the employee to tell the customer, orally or using a sign, that the employee does not serve persons of the customer's sex, race, religion or sexual orientation', and it is not relevant that an equivalent good or service is available 'across the street'.[207] So Wintemute concludes:

> If a religious individual could exceptionally claim that providing a particular service to a same-sex couple, or a lesbian and gay non-governmental organisation, would force them to disseminate to the public a clear message with which they disagreed (not the case when renting rooms or venues, taking photographs, providing flowers, or baking cakes), they might be able to claim an exemption based on their right to freedom of expression, assembly or association. Otherwise, the religious individual must serve all couples, regardless of sexual orientation (as they must serve all individuals and couples regardless of race or religion), or shut down the particular service or their business.[208]

Wintemute admits that exemptions 'must be granted to religious organisations', but exemptions for religious individuals or vendors 'would allow them to impose their beliefs on others'.[209] This admission in regard to religious organisations is significant, for religious vendors too are religious bodies engaging in religious conduct which has the effect of expressing beliefs. If exemptions for religious organisations are acceptable, they could in principle be acceptable for religious vendors as well, for the same reasons.[210] Furthermore, the disqualifying condition for religious vendor exemptions cited by Wintemute (the imposition of belief on others) is problematic, for it is equally arguable that beliefs are being imposed on the conscientious objector when they are compelled to provide goods and services

---

[203] ibid 124, 131.
[204] Ahdar and Giles (n 178) 228.
[205] Wintemute (n 164) 228–29.
[206] ibid 228–29, 240, 242.
[207] ibid 241, 242.
[208] ibid 252.
[209] ibid 250.
[210] I build this argument in Deagon, 'Refusing Services' (n 168).

contrary to their belief. As such, a reasonable accommodation which allows people to be served and religious vendors to exist consistent with their beliefs is a solution which recognises the dignity and good of all parties, contributing to peaceful coexistence.

Turning to specifically consider Wintemute's proposed conditions for accommodation, the direct harm (as so characterised by Wintemute) resulting from an explicit refusal to serve by a religious vendor may be avoided through clear and transparent messaging that the refusal is about not endorsing a particular view about marriage, not about the sexual orientation or otherwise of the customer. As I indicate in previous chapters and other work, if proposed exemptions are limited to genuinely religious vendors providing marriage-related goods and services, and those vendors have clear policies about circumstances where they do not provide such goods and services, this mitigates direct harm.[211] This naturally raises the issue of indirect harm suffered as a result of generally communicated refusals, but this is basically the third-party harm objection. I have addressed this extensively in the previous chapter by suggesting that it is a factor to be considered rather than a criterion to be satisfied. Indeed, rather than framing accommodation as cumulative conditions which are rigid and not nuanced or contextual, all of Wintemute's conditions would be better framed as factors to be considered. This recognises that the wedding-vendor cases are primarily about endorsement of a view rather than discrimination against a person. The implied exclusion of religious vendors from communicating messages is also problematic in principle. As discussed above and elsewhere, the assumption that the goods and services provided by religious vendors are non-religious is incorrect. Many vendors are essentially religious bodies and provide these goods and services as a function of their religion. Similarly, the provision of a good or service can itself communicate a message about an idea.[212] The Supreme Court acknowledged both these points with respect to Asher's Baking. Hence, Wintemute's ultimatum to simply shut down the service or business is callous and inconsistent with the theological virtues of forgiveness and patience.

However, Fredman also considers that Asher's Baking were not compelled to express support for same-sex marriage, and were not even a religious organisation because they operated commercially. She claims that Asher's 'did not present itself as protecting the religious interests of its owners' and has 'no express religious purpose or affiliation', 'nor were they being compelled to support gay marriage'.[213] These claims are just factually incorrect at a number of levels. Asher's Baking demonstrably operates in accordance with religious convictions. The owners, Daniel and Amy McArthur, state:

> as Christians … our beliefs affect every part of our lives, including running our business, and the decisions that we make in our business … Contrary to popular opinion

---

[211] See ibid; ch 1 and ch 2 of this book.
[212] See Deagon, 'Refusing Services' (n 168).
[213] Fredman (n 159) 326.

we are not called Mr & Mrs Asher. Our name comes from the Bible. Asher was a tribe of Israel who had many skilled bakers and created bread fit for a king.

Consequently they do not accept content or images for cakes which contain any 'threatening, defamatory, blasphemous or pornographic material'.[214] Hence Asher's Baking has an express religious purpose and affiliation, and recognising commercial corporations as religious entities is entirely consistent with established religious freedom principles.[215] Bell, for example, also acknowledges Asher's Bakery as an organisation 'which seeks to uphold certain religious values in its activities'.[216] Furthermore, the McArthurs were demonstrably being compelled to express support for gay marriage by being told to bake a cake with the message 'support gay marriage'. Even Fredman implicitly acknowledges this when she notes that 'it is arguable that the McArthurs themselves should not be compelled to bake cakes with messages they disapproved of', indicating that this is in fact what they were being asked to do.[217]

In short, the decision in *Asher's Baking* indicates it is possible to reach accommodations which protect religious vendors from expressing messages which violate their conscience (preserving the autonomy of religious communities) without such accommodations preventing persons from accessing goods and services in the marketplace (which would undermine equality norms).[218] The Court distinguished between literally expressing a message of support and merely providing a good or service. Reyes observes that while in *Asher's* the cake actually stated a written message, in similar US cases such as *Masterpiece Cakeshop* the perceived message was just the created cake itself. In the latter case the vendor was not required to literally express a message contrary to their conscience, and not providing an exemption for such refusals would 'respect both religious liberty and LGBTQ equality'.[219] Reyes is likely right that this distinction clarifies the issue in some way. But this position dismisses too lightly the religious objection to supporting particular causes through artistic creations. It could be conceded that an exemption for religious vendors would not extend to goods or services provided for general use (for example, a generic cake selected by a same-sex couple for their wedding, as opposed to a cake specially created for a same-sex wedding). This would not be the provision of a marriage-related service. However, for many religious vendors, it is simply the case that their specific creations for special events are indissolubly linked to their religious convictions.[220] 'The fact that there is a real

---

[214] See www.christianpost.com/news/christian-couple-who-lost-gay-marriage-cake-case-sees-profits-soar-to-millions-despite-controversy.html.

[215] See Deagon, Refusing Services (n 168) 775–76 and the discussion regarding *Hobby Lobby* in ch 2.

[216] Bell (n 65) 59.

[217] See Fredman (n 159) 326.

[218] Reyes (n 174) 139.

[219] ibid 140–41.

[220] See Deagon, 'Refusing Services' (n 168), and the previous discussion stating that for many religious persons, all activities, including their business decisions and product creations, are a manifestation of their religious convictions.

and deeply felt interference with religious freedom where the law obliges individuals to act contrary to their religious convictions certainly deserves emphasis'.[221] Part of a better approach which upholds the dignity of religious vendors would be to properly take the relevant convictions into account through the vendor providing evidence about the nature, sincerity and consistency of their beliefs.

Ultimately then, where there is tension between religious freedom and anti-discrimination, and there is 'no principled basis for deciding between them', the 'appropriate solution' is an 'accommodationist approach' which seeks to preserve both to the maximum extent possible.[222] This facilitates peaceful coexistence by upholding the dignity of both parties and pursuing forgiveness and patience with a diversity of views contributing to the common good. For example, a conscientious objection from a religious vendor or organisation can be accommodated with limited adverse effects if there is a genuine engagement with practical solutions which protect both religious freedom and equality, rather than simply allowing equality concerns to override and marginalise religious convictions – creating another form of discrimination.[223]

Keller and Heri describe a need to create a 'culture of compromise that emphasises openness, reciprocity', and a 'mutual respect' from the common ground of belief in living publicly in a way that is authentic to 'one's sense of self'.[224] This creates a 'real pluralism' which is about 'the reality of the irreconcilable existing side by side, civilly, in the public sphere, and of finding ways of living together'.[225] Stychin also refers to the need for 'contextual analysis', 'compromises', and the 'goal of civility and the hope that areas of common ground might be found' with reliance on 'solidarity and shared values'.[226] Stychin goes on to outline these 'ethical rules of engagement':

> openness to the Other, reciprocity, mutual respect, the ability to listen, good faith, the ability to reach compromises, and a willingness to rely on discussion to resolve stalemates. The institution of a culture of compromise largely centres on all of these factors that foster the coordination of action and the peaceful, concerted resolution of disputes.[227]

Stychin characterises these as 'ultimately grounded in the principles of liberalism', but as I have outlined extensively in the Introduction, these are more robustly and coherently conceived as theological virtues including love, patience, forgiveness and dignity, which form a principled framework for peaceful coexistence in a liberal democracy.[228]

---

[221] Keller and Heri (n 33) 325–26.
[222] McCrudden, *Litigating Religions* (n 2) 147.
[223] J Rivers, 'Promoting Religious Equality' (2012) 1 *Oxford Journal of Law and Religion* 386, 399.
[224] Keller and Heri (n 33) 325.
[225] Stychin (n 196) 753.
[226] ibid 749–50.
[227] ibid 754.
[228] ibid. I specifically elucidate the connection between the liberal principles of civility and the theological virtue of love in A Deagon, 'The Law of Love as Principles of Civility: Secular Translation or

Cumper and Lewis propose a holistic approach which entails 'meaningful engagement' and emphasises 'areas of common ground' to 'build bridges' and find accommodations of difference on divisive issues at the policy level rather than through the acrimonious and adversarial method of litigation.[229] Such engagement will defuse tension and remove suspicion. They suggest focus on three 'interrelated criteria': 'compromise and dialogue …; and perhaps most crucially, empathy'.[230] Compromise is difficult because it does not address the issue of who should compromise, and disputes are usually characterised by 'intransigence'.[231] Dialogue has the advantages of breaking down barriers and pursuing resolutions through listening, but in practice dialogue is imprecise and unclear.[232] An ideal scenario would be where potential adversaries can learn to respect each other's positions through reasonable discussion, and perhaps even alter those views through compromise, but the debate is often characterised by inflexible attitudes. However, Cumper and Lewis argue that 'common human values (and in particular the universal principle of empathy)' will facilitate dialogue and compromise.[233]

Empathy entails genuine imagination of the situation from the other side, how the other feels. It asks if you had my sexuality, or believe what I believe, how would you feel in my position?[234] This sounds similar to a solution McCrudden proposes with respect to understanding religious perspectives. It involves an 'imaginative sympathy with the religious internal point of view' to produce a genuine dialogue which is mutually beneficial.[235] This 'internal approach' engages 'seriously the belief systems of religious believers themselves, and the significance of those beliefs, from their own (internal) perspective. This involves an attempt to understand rather than simply observe'.[236] It requires the appreciation and understanding of the guiding standards authoritative for that religion, religious body/organisation, or individual religious believer.[237] However, as already intimated above and discussed in the Introduction, the notion of universal human principles such as empathy are really reducible to the universally applicable theological virtues such as love, patience and kindness, which entail the type of imaginative sympathy/empathy articulated by other scholars in secular terms. Examples of common ground which may be used as a foundation for building dialogue and compromise include the respective position of many religious believers and members of the

---

Religious Contribution?' in J Neoh, K Thompson and Z Calo (eds), *Christianity, Ethics and the Law: The Concept of Love in Christian Legal Thought* (Routledge, forthcoming 2022).

[229] P Cumper and T Lewis, 'Human Rights and Religious Litigation – Faith in the Law?' (2019) 8 *Oxford Journal of Law and Religion* 121, 122.

[230] ibid 135–36.

[231] ibid 136.

[232] ibid 137.

[233] ibid 138.

[234] ibid 140.

[235] McCrudden, *Litigating Religions* (n 2) xii. See 138–50 for details.

[236] ibid 92–93.

[237] ibid.

LGBT community as vulnerable minorities, the importance of identity and what authentic living in a public space means (that it is not a simple matter of choice but underpins ways of being), and the fact that many people of faith are also members of the LGBT community.[238]

Obviously, greater engagement between religious and LGBT communities will not eliminate all differences, but it will provide a greater appreciation for the intrinsic dignity of diverse perspectives and approaches to pursuing the common good, which upholds the theological virtues and facilitates peaceful coexistence of difference.[239] In particular, as Gibson observes, 'the link between human dignity and equality particularly affords accommodation of ... difference'.[240] Rather than 'inflexible' responses which unnecessarily privilege equality above religious freedom, reasonable accommodations are possible which enable religious communities not to compromise their convictions (upholding their dignity), and remain 'cognisant of the competing legitimate equality imperative and the need not to compromise service users' dignity'.[241]

Harrison applies a similar deep theological lens to the issue of service provision, articulating a framework which in effect facilitates peaceful coexistence in accordance with the theological virtues by accommodating diverse perspectives of and approaches to pursuing the common good. He suggests that we can understand the acceptance of same-sex marriage and sexual orientation equality from within the Christian framework of seeking 'true human ends', which then 'affords a basis for accommodating dissenting traditionalist claims'; the *Catholic Care* case 'illustrates ... the possibility of a more complex understanding of groups participating in shared goods (here, adoption services) despite differences'.[242] Under the EA, Catholic Care could only discriminate if this was a proportionate means of achieving a legitimate aim. Rather than articulating their aim and means in terms of Catholic teaching regarding the nature of marriage and family, Catholic Care accepted that something more than a 'mere' religious claim was required and adopted an instrumental argument that the loss of their services would result in reduced child placements and a loss of support from Catholic parishioners. The Charity Tribunal rejected both these arguments: the former because this would depend on the willingness of local authorities to engage, and the latter because they asserted there is a wide range of views amongst donating Catholics. The discriminatory policy was 'particularly demeaning' to same-sex couples, implying that such couples were of 'less worth', undermining their dignity.[243] Putting aside the problem that the Charity Tribunal effectively imposed its view about acceptable adoption provision from a Catholic perspective by referring to internal differences

---

[238] Cumper and Lewis (n 229) 142–44.
[239] See Bell (n 65) 77–78.
[240] Gibson (n 63) 584.
[241] ibid 606.
[242] Harrison, *Post-Liberal Religious Liberty* (n 42) 208–09.
[243] ibid 209–11.

within Catholicism,[244] Harrison argues that Catholic Care were effectively forced to rely on an instrumental secular argument because of an account of religious liberty which excludes religion from application in the public sphere, rather than developing a rich and substantive argument that, for example, 'its desire to serve the community was shaped by a Catholic understanding that the family was to mirror an ideal, in which gender difference participates in God's natural order', and doing so is 'part of God's desire for restoration, here restoring children to a loving family'.[245]

Harrison therefore aims to essentially reframe the debate in terms of pursuing peaceful coexistence in accordance with the theological virtues, 'an account of religious liberty rooted in the claim that there can be a plural search for shared ends, that different groups can contribute to goods in common in order to form a community, and that this entails and acknowledges as a good a religious quest and orientation'.[246] For Harrison, these claims 'only make sense within a stance of trust' (which is a theological virtue) that there is a created order, 'love' which is personal and permanent (as in the law of love), and dignity ('we each bear God's image' and 'equally matter').[247] So claims for sexual orientation equality pursue the common goods of relationship and dignity, just as claims for exemptions pursue the common goods of sharing gifts and talents for rightly ordered relationship, all within a theological framework of trust, love and dignity.[248]

As such, exemptions to promote autonomy for religious organisations such as Catholic Care should exist as part of diverse aspirations to pursuing the common good through a shared life. Such religious communities are not merely entering a secular domain, but contributing to the peaceful coexistence of different religious and non-religious perspectives on the good, in accordance with theological virtues such as patience and forgiveness.[249] This applies equally to other religious communities such as schools. 'A church does not enter into the already defined public domain of the state when it engages in educational activities. Rather, a religious school is one component making up or determining' a communal life in pursuit of the good.[250] A similar principle applies for vendors:

> A cake-baker or a florist who objects to supplying services for a same-sex wedding … is informed or compelled by moral and conscientious judgement regardless of the setting. Markets and morality are not separated; religion is not confined to the church or school … Importantly, the claim is limited. The baker or florist is not claiming, and could not claim, a general right not to serve sexual minorities; rather, he or she seeks a

---

[244] See (n 120) and surrounding text.
[245] Harrison, *Post-Liberal Religious Liberty* (n 42) 209–11.
[246] ibid 212–13.
[247] ibid 217–18.
[248] ibid 218–20.
[249] ibid 222–23.
[250] ibid 223.

right not to exercise his or her creative talents in the context of what everyone agrees is a deeply significant moral act. As with the adoption agency, we can again recognise that such bakers and florists continue to contribute to our common good; they participate in celebrating marriages, albeit with a difference.[251]

VI. Conclusion: The Autonomy of Religious Communities in English Law

English law provides significant formal protection for the autonomy of religious communities. Article 9 of the Convention, which protects the associational freedom of religious groups as a function of persons manifesting their beliefs in a community, is incorporated into English law through the HRA. Courts must pay special attention to this protection where a law impacts the manifestation of religious belief by a group. The EA also has protections for religious organisations through protection against religious discrimination and exemptions for religious organisations which allow them to discriminate in employment and the provision of goods and services for the purposes of maintaining a community ethos.

However, these formal protections are ultimately deficient in their substance and practical effect. Article 9 jurisprudence is inconsistent and unclear, and often sets up a conflict between religion and equality where equality generally prevails. This detracts from peaceful coexistence and undermines the theological virtues of love, patience and forgiveness. I suggest a more principled and robust articulation of religious liberty that takes into account the autonomy of religious communities to construct an ethos through membership standards, facilitating a balance which reasonably accommodates difference and pursues peaceful coexistence that English courts can help implement.

Similarly, the exemptions in the EA are narrow and unclear, constructing a tension between equality and religion where the religious perspective is often minimised and marginalised when there is conflict with equality principles in key areas such as education, employment, and the provision of goods and services. Rather than an adversarial approach which rejects the dignity of one or both parties, and undermines peaceful coexistence by refusing to countenance the theological virtues of love, forgiveness and patience expressed through facilitating diverse understandings and pursuits of the good, I suggest an approach which embraces mutual respect and understanding. Authentic and imaginative sympathy and engagement with other people and perspectives which recognises the distinctive contributions to the common good provided by sexual orientation equality and religiously inspired communities will facilitate more reasonable and

---

[251] ibid 222.

effective accommodations so we can peacefully coexist even in the face of deep and profound moral difference. This sort of engagement ought to occur at the level of civil society, but is also important in the policy process to extend and clarify the exemptions which do exist.

After further theoretical analysis of these legal issues in Part III of the book, Part IV will articulate a broad principled framework for the autonomy of religious communities which promotes peaceful existence through a reasonable, proportionate accommodation of difference. Building on the suggestions made in this chapter, Part IV will entail specific recommendations as to how England's legal infrastructure can be amended and more effectively applied to better adhere to this framework.

PART III

Theoretical Frameworks

4

Australia: Pragmatic Pluralism or Mild Establishment?

I. Introduction

Part II of this book outlined the legal infrastructure pertaining to the autonomy of religious communities in Australia, the US, and England, and evaluated the legal framework for each jurisdiction with respect to the extent they preserved peaceful coexistence in accordance with the theological virtues. Part III of the book explores the theoretical approach to the autonomy of religious communities in each jurisdiction with respect to promoting a peaceful coexistence of difference. It will identify the underlying theoretical perspectives which undergird the legal infrastructure of each jurisdiction, drawing on the established theoretical models of church and state. The book will then evaluate each theoretical approach by determining whether and how they promote peaceful coexistence in each jurisdiction. This evaluation will involve consideration of how they reconcile freedom and equality through producing a proportionate, reasonable accommodation of difference in accordance with the theological virtues.

In regard to Australia, chapter one suggests Australia's legal framework promotes peaceful coexistence in only a limited way. Specifically, the exemptions in the Sex Discrimination Act ('SDA') unfairly and unnecessarily target sexual minorities, giving the impression of a special privilege to maliciously discriminate. Chapter one further suggests protection for the autonomy of religious communities ought to reframed in the form of positive associational rights, maintaining the ability for religious communities to select and regulate their members in accordance with their religious ethos while simultaneously addressing equality concerns by removing specific targeting of sexual minorities. This promotes a peaceful coexistence of difference in accordance with the theological virtues. In this chapter, the book will identify two theoretical models which potentially capture Australia's legal framework for the autonomy of religious communities with a particular focus on the acknowledgement of God in the preamble of the Constitution and the freedom of religion provision in section 116, in conjunction with the relationship between religion and education expressed through, for example, the religious exemptions in the SDA. I will evaluate these models as to the extent they provide peaceful coexistence of difference in accordance with the theological virtues by facilitating a proportional, reasonable accommodation of difference, and discuss more precisely how Australia's legal infrastructure should be reframed in this context.

Part II of the chapter considers Australia's constitutional position and the perennial connection between religion and education to demonstrate that Australia can be categorised as pragmatically pluralist. However, part III argues that though a pragmatically pluralist approach has provided a considerable level of autonomy for religious communities, without a principled basis grounded in shared premises this autonomy has decreased over time; equality has been slowly dominating religious freedom as the scope of anti-discrimination laws increase. Part IV proposes a new approach: mild establishment in the form of 'Christian democracy'. Though this may seem counter-intuitive for the purpose of reconciling religious freedom with equality to create a peaceful coexistence, I argue that (at least my version of) mild establishment or Christian democracy is compatible with Australia's constitutional and legal infrastructure, and preserves peaceful coexistence of difference on a more robust basis by appealing to universal virtues such as love, dignity, forgiveness and patience – which in turn ground religious freedom and equality. As Hunter-Henin observes, all countries 'in search of harmonious social cohesion therefore have to ensure that the recognition of difference ... does not erect an impossible hurdle in the way of the unity of all believers and non-believers ... The concept of religious freedom offers the key to reconciling diversity within unity and unity within diversity'.[1] Since Christian democracy is ultimately grounded in virtues shared by all (regardless of belief or non-belief), I argue that it provides a more principled and effective framework for accommodation of difference. In Part V I discuss implications for how to reframe legal protection for the autonomy of religious communities in Australia through positive associational rights bearing in mind this model of Christian democracy, before concluding in Part VI that application of this model cannot be standard and must be contextual, varying depending on the diverse religious, political, social and cultural aspects of different jurisdictions, and within particular jurisdictions.

II. Australia as Pragmatically Pluralist

Pluralism recognises and embraces the 'public dimension of religion' by attempting 'even-handed cooperation'.[2] Pragmatic pluralism observes that such cooperation is 'expedient' in a religiously diverse society to promote 'harmony' between religions where 'religious pluralism is a fact of life'.[3] Religious life 'is not confined to

---

[1] M Hunter-Henin, 'Introduction: Religious Freedoms in European Schools: Contrasts and Convergence' in M Hunter-Henin (ed), *Law, Religious Freedoms and Education in Europe* (Ashgate, 2012) 19.

[2] R Ahdar and I Leigh, *Religious Freedom in the Liberal State,* 2nd edn (Oxford University Press, 2013) 109.

[3] ibid 111–12.

the private sphere; the state recognises and accommodates a variety of religious groups and is, for example, prepared to fund social programmes run by faith communities.[4] Chavura, Gascoigne and Tregenza note in their extensive study that Australia's position is particularly difficult to categorise given Australia's institutional separation of church and state which sits in tension with explicit acknowledgement of God in its Constitution, the mixing of religion and politics through parliamentary prayers and government funding of religious schools, and a historically strong (but declining) Christian population grappling with an increase in other religions and those who profess no religion. Australia's historical religious settlement was a 'Christian secularity', where 'secular' means non-sectarian in the sense of not favouring any particular Christian denomination.[5] This eventually shifted to a 'secular Christianity', where the confessional nature of politics withered away but the emphasis on Christian morality remained, until the current situation where religion is largely seen as archaic and irrelevant, at least in a public context.[6] Hence, Australia as a secular state can mean a non-sectarian Christianity.[7] 'The relationship between secular and religion' in Australia 'is better thought of as an ongoing dialogue'.[8]

Monsma and Soper observe that Australia has been through four different models of State–religion relationship: establishment, plural establishment, liberal separationism and pragmatic pluralism.[9] They suggest Australia best fits the pragmatic pluralism model through, for example, the government funding of religious schools or tax exemption for religious bodies.[10] Furthermore, the reason for this funding is to facilitate the existence of religious bodies assisting with governmental functions, rather than some principled articulation of pluralism. The rationale is, in other words, pragmatic. Renae Barker therefore agrees that the relationship between religion and the State today would best be described as 'pragmatic pluralism'.[11] Australia is a multi-cultural and multi-faith democracy with a large number of people professing no religion. Australians enjoy a relatively high level of religious freedom despite the narrow scope and interpretation of section 116 and the lack of a charter of rights.[12] There is a close relationship between the state and religion, and religion continues to play an important part in Australian life.[13]

---

[4] ibid 112.

[5] S Chavura, J Gascoigne and I Tregenza, *Reason, Religion and the Australian Polity: A Secular State?* (Routledge, 2019) 10.

[6] ibid 12–14.

[7] ibid 254–55.

[8] ibid 256.

[9] S Monsma and JC Soper, *The Challenge of Pluralism: Church and State in Five Democracies*, 2nd edn (Rowman & Littlefield Publishing Group, 2009) 93.

[10] ibid 107–15.

[11] R Barker, *State and Religion: The Australian Story* (Routledge, 2019) 34–35, 325, 328.

[12] Barker, *State and Religion* (n 11) 325–26; N Aroney and BB Saunders, 'Freedom of Religion' in M Groves, J Boughey and D Meagher (eds), *The Legal Protection of Rights in Australia* (Hart Publishing, 2019) 285–311.

[13] Barker, *State and Religion* (n 11) 42.

These factors are relevant in examining where section 116 fits in the context of Australia as a pragmatically pluralist nation.

A. The Preamble and Section 116 of the Constitution

Section 116 is sometimes appealed to in order to support an argument that Australia is a secular nation which structurally separates religion and state, although commentators have conflicting views on what 'secular' means.[14] Some features of Australia's history may appear to support a secular or separationist understanding of section 116. State funding for religious schools was removed by all the Australian colonies by Federation,[15] and in the late nineteenth century there was also a belief in the separation of church and state, namely that the institutions of church and state should be kept separate.[16] Another key principle was that of non-establishment, namely that no religion or denomination should be established as the official religion of the state, which was directly included in one of the clauses of section 116.[17] In theory, section 116 could form the foundation of a secular/structural separation model. However, in effect, section 116 has not been interpreted as requiring a US-style 'wall of separation', and the 'level of interaction between the State and religion is too high to fit this model'.[18] As Nicholas Aroney has observed:

> The High Court has very explicitly affirmed that the non-establishment clause does not prohibit governmental assistance being given to religious bodies, and it certainly has never held that s. 116 somehow prohibits the enactment of federal laws or the execution of government policies that are supported, either in whole or in part, on the basis of religious considerations or reasons … To suggest that the non-establishment principle makes religious considerations entirely irrelevant to federal law-making and policy-formation is simply beyond the pale – particularly in Australia.[19]

[14] See Barker, *State and Religion* (n 11) 41; A Deagon, 'Secularism as a Religion: Questioning the Future of the 'Secular' State' (2017) 8 *The Western Australian Jurist* 31, 53–60. Examples include R Mortensen, 'Blasphemy in a Secular State: A Pardonable Sin?' (1994) 17(2) *UNSW Law Journal* 409, 426–27 (s 116 is 'one of our most important institutions of liberal secularism'); *Hoxton Park Residents Action Group Inc v Liverpool Council* [2016] NSWCA 157 [249] (Basten JA) (s 116 'establishes Australia as a secular polity'); M Thornton and T Luker, 'The Spectral Ground: Religious Belief Discrimination' (2009) 9 *Macquarie Law Journal* 71, 72 (Australia is committed to 'the philosophy of state secularism'); L Beck, 'Clear and emphatic: the separation of church and state under the Australian Constitution' (2008) 27(2) *University of Tasmania Law Review* 161, 182, 187, 195 ('Australia's system of government is secular', Australia is a 'secular state' with 'secular institutions of government'); W Sadurski, 'Neutrality of Law Towards Religion' (1990) 12 *Sydney Law Review* 421.

[15] R Barker, 'Under Most Peculiar Circumstances: The Church Acts in the Australian Colonies as a Study of Plural Establishment' (2016) 3(3) *Law & History* 28, 50.

[16] Chavura, Gascoigne and Tregenza (n 5) 77–125.

[17] ibid.

[18] Barker, *State and Religion* (n 11) 36.

[19] N Aroney, 'The Constitutional (In)Validity of Religious Vilification Laws: Implications for their Interpretation' (2006) 34 *Federal Law Review* 287, 302.

Furthermore, a secular or separationist account of section 116 cannot be maintained. An explicit acknowledgement of the Christian God was inserted into the Constitution at the insistence of many religious leaders and church groups during the Federation Convention debates, who represented the broader wishes of the people. The institutional separation of church and state and the principle of non-establishment did not mean a belief in the removal of religion from public life. At Federation, there was a widespread belief that Australia should not be irreligious but should be underpinned by Christian values and that religion should be widely suffused throughout society.[20] 'The federation settlement included an acknowledgement of God and yet guaranteed national piety would not result in religious coercion by the federal government'.[21] Today, the number of religious adherents and the influence of religion in Australian society has declined, but many remnants of the enmeshing of religion and the government survive.[22] Since section 116 only restricts Commonwealth laws, its actual and intended effect is to facilitate the autonomy of individual states with respect to religious matters. As a result of facilitating state autonomy with respect to religion there is significant, legitimate interaction between religion and government in such important policy areas as education and welfare, which reside within the plenary powers of individual states.[23] The drafters of section 116, for example, 'were prepared to allow Sunday observance laws as long as it was the States and not the Commonwealth who legislated for it'.[24]

Section 116 is therefore not designed to enshrine the separation of church and state, is not intended to separate religion from society or government, and allows for positive interactions between religion and the Commonwealth. These matters can be accounted for by understanding section 116 as a pluralist provision which supports all religions in a non-discriminatory way and supports all kinds of religion in the public sphere, as a pragmatic response to a pluralist society where many different religions exist.[25] The 'singular concern' of section 116 is 'freedom from the state forcing or prohibiting religious observances'.[26] The importance of religious liberty to the constitutional drafters and the overall spirit of the debates indicates a robust concern for the flourishing of religion. Both the acknowledgement of God in the preamble and the corresponding freedom of religion provision 'came about through religious engagement with the federation movement, not in

---

[20] See A Deagon and BB Saunders, 'Principles, Pragmatism and Power: Another Look at the Historical Context of Section 116' (2020) 43(3) *Melbourne University Law Review* 1033; BB Saunders and A Deagon, 'Religion and the Constitution: A Response to Luke Beck's Safeguard Against Religious Intolerance Theory of Section 116' (2021) 44(4) *University of New South Wales Law Journal* 1558.

[21] Chavura, Gascoigne and Tregenza (n 5) 12.

[22] ibid 10. For example, the Commonwealth continues to financially support religious schools, and Parliament still opens with the Lord's Prayer.

[23] Barker, *State and Religion* (n 11) 98.

[24] ibid 84.

[25] ibid.

[26] Chavura, Gascoigne and Tregenza (n 5) 136.

spite of or in opposition to it ... [it] was not the result of any ardent secularist impulse seeking to banish religion from public affairs'.[27] The institutional relations provided by section 116 do not at all imply that Australia is or should be a secular nation where religion has no public place. As Chavura, Gascoigne and Tregenza observe:

> Judgments about the secular nature of Australian democracy have often been obscured by a tendency to focus on institutional relations between church and state ... often those most emphatic about separating church and state through the nineteenth century were driven by religious motivations and were concerned to protect the church from the incursions of the state and the impositions of an official religion. This is a reversal of most contemporary 'secular' arguments that invoke church–state separation as a means of 'cleansing' the public sphere from religious influences. When this conception is read back into the past, it not only distorts the intentions of the actors themselves but also prevents an appreciation of the way that religion influenced state institutions and the broader public sphere.[28]

Similarly, Zimmermann and Weinberger argue that section 116 'never intended' a true separation between religion and state.[29] The acknowledgement of God in the preamble, in conjunction with the desire of the framers to promote and protect the flourishing of religion without discriminating against any particular religion, 'dispel[s] any claims that the Australian Constitution established secularism by virtue of section 116'.[30] Interpretation of the establishment clause has left the boundary line between religion and state much less sharply demarcated than in the US, a difference which reflects 'greater ideological pragmatism' on the part of Australia.[31] Since section 116 allows cooperation between religion and government, the contours of that relationship have been determined by the political process – and for largely pragmatic reasons, Australia has chosen to provide funding to religious schools and effective funding to religious organisations through tax exemptions.[32]

B. Religion and Education

The substantive historical interaction between religion and government in the colonial period has continued into the twentieth and twenty-first century, especially in the education sector. Australia has more significant church and religious

---

[27] ibid 136–37.
[28] ibid 157.
[29] A Zimmermann and LD Weinberger, 'Secularization by law? The establishment clauses and religion in the public square in Australia and the United States' (2012) 10(1) *International Journal of Constitutional Law* 208, 221.
[30] ibid 223–24.
[31] Chavura, Gascoigne and Tregenza (n 5) 225–26.
[32] Barker, *State and Religion* (n 11) 25, 34–35, 279.

involvement in education than the US, and has implemented initiatives such as the return of state aid and the introduction of school chaplaincy programmes. This could 'be seen as an indication of vestigial religious attachment and perhaps a lingering sense … that religion remains an important element in character formation and continues to have social utility'.[33] It could simultaneously be explained by 'contingent political dynamics' in the sense that the government recognises this perception of the importance of religion among the population and so beneficially engages with religion as a function of pragmatism.[34] Indeed:

> Part of the nature of the Australian political settlement hammered out in the century leading up to federation in 1901 was a willingness on the part of the state to work with other institutions to achieve what were regarded as the goals of good government. Utility, rather than ideological purity, had been the dominant tenor of the political process which allowed, for example, temporary state aid to the churches … [and] funding for schools.[35]

The most compelling argument for funding religious schools was a pragmatic one: it saved government funds provided for education generally because the funding for religious schools was also subsidised by parents and religious institutions.[36] For example, in the early twenty-first century the conservative Howard government outsourced many social services to churches and faith-based service providers, and initially funded and implemented the religious school chaplaincy programme. However, this did not have (at least solely) a religious motive; it was more likely 'a result of the influence of economic rationalism and its imperative to privatise and outsource as many public services as possible for the sake of efficiency' – or, in other words, a pragmatic decision.[37] This is supported by the fact that the more progressive subsequent Labor government continued this process, and today education remains an important interface of the Australian State-religion relationship, including the funding of religious schools (not only Christian, but also a small number of Jewish and Islamic schools). Barker concludes that this has 'come about as a result of political expediency, rather than as a deliberate decision to alter the relationship between the State and religion'.[38]

As such, Australia's polity is secular only in the sense of not being identified with any particular church. More substantively, the relationship between religion and state is 'porous' enough to enable cooperation in the provision of public services such as education and social welfare.[39] Barker categorises this balance, as we have seen, as 'pragmatic pluralism'; 'pluralism is not a matter of principle in Australia, but rather a pragmatic response to a multi-cultural and therefore

---

[33] Chavura, Gascoigne and Tregenza (n 5) 3–4.
[34] ibid 208–09.
[35] ibid 222.
[36] ibid 223.
[37] ibid 242–43.
[38] Barker, *State and Religion* (n 11) 277.
[39] Chavura, Gascoigne and Tregenza (n 5) 226.

multi-faith society in which multiple faiths exist alongside a significant propor-tion of the population who identify as having no religion'.[40] The Commonwealth has also granted religious schools some exemptions from anti-discrimination law. This, too, could be seen as pragmatically pluralist in the sense that it enables religious schools to functionally exist autonomously and implement their unique religious ethos, providing efficiency and savings to the government so the state does not need to shoulder the entire burden of education funding and provision. A wholly secular state can severely limit religious freedom by positively exclud-ing, marginalising or eliminating religion.[41] A pragmatically pluralist approach facilitates the existence and positive contribution of religious communities for public good.

III. Evaluation of Australia's Pragmatic Pluralism

And yet, while Australia's pragmatic pluralism has worked well in the past, increas-ing diversity has led to decreasing common ground on significant moral and religious issues. Parkinson observes in particular that the religious freedom and anti-discrimination debate has been 'polarised', 'divisive', 'alienating' and 'unhelp-ful'; it undermines the dignity of Christians and the LGBT community by creating a 'paradigm of conflict' which fails to acknowledge the intrinsic good of both sides and the common ground they have.[42] The locus of this conflict is centered around the religious exemptions in the Sex Discrimination Act ('SDA') which enable reli-gious schools to discriminate on the basis of sex-related attributes for the purposes of upholding a religious ethos. However, as noted in chapter one, these exemptions fail to uphold peaceful coexistence because they offensively and unnecessarily target sexual minorities, giving the impression of exceptional powers for religion to maliciously discriminate. However, religious bodies nevertheless require legal ability to select and regulate their members to cultivate their communal ethos as a function of peaceful coexistence. For example, as also mentioned in chapter one, Hilkemeijer and Maguire argue the SDA exemptions are inconsistent with European human rights law for two fundamental reasons: the law is imprecise because injury to religious susceptibilities is a vague basis to exercise the exemp-tion, and the law is overly broad because it does not take into account whether the person is engaged in secular or religious activities and the grounds of dismissal

---

[40] Barker, *State and Religion* (n 11) 329. Most recently, Barker has called this a 'non-establishment pluralism', in the sense that Australia prohibits the establishment of a state religion or church, but simultaneously permits cooperation between religion and government in the public sphere. See R Barker, 'Pluralism versus Separation: Tension in the Australian Church-State Relationship' (2021) 16 *Religion and Human Rights* 1–40.

[41] Barker, *State and Religion* (n 11) 328.

[42] P Parkinson, 'The Future of Religious Freedom' (2019) 93(9) *Australian Law Journal* 699, 700.

could be unrelated to religion.[43] They propose a better option for reform is either a law requiring the school to demonstrate that it is necessary to employ staff who adhere to the school's religious faith (the narrowest option), or a law allowing schools to discriminate if they can demonstrate that the discriminatory action is a genuine occupational requirement and it satisfies a reasonableness test.[44]

There are a number of problematic assumptions in and consequences of these arguments and proposals by Hilkemeijer and Maguire. First, as demonstrated in the previous chapter of this book, ECtHR jurisprudence is mixed on the matter of religious institutional autonomy. There are no clear principles and so one can also point to cases and themes which support robust institutional autonomy (as I do in the previous chapter). Parkinson states 'there are cases that could be cited on either side'.[45] In one seminal case, the ECtHR observed that religious communities exist in organised structures and the 'autonomous existence of religious communities is indispensable for pluralism in a democratic society and is an issue at the very heart of the protection which Article 9 affords'.[46] The EU Directive acknowledges the right of religious organisations to require employees to adhere to the ethos of the organisation.[47] Thus, Aroney and Taylor note that in a number of cases the ECtHR has found in favour of the religious institution when an employee has breached the institution's ethos, 'even when the ethos requirements of the employer organisation impinge on the employee's fundamental human rights'.[48] For example, dismissals of teachers of religious doctrine and educators in religious educational facilities were not found to breach the ECHR:

> In some, perhaps most, religious schools loyalty might not be expected from those employees who are not engaged in representing the ethos of the organisation by functions such as chaplaincy or religious education. In some other schools, however a wider range of employees (perhaps even all of them) may be commissioned to promote the religious calling of the school. Their terms and conditions of employment would presumably reflect this in some way. The faith-based calling of a school, and the degree to which there is an expectation that the staff in question share that faith and will be actively engaged in promoting its mission, become the distinguishing features justifying them being contractually bound to remain loyal to the ethos of the organisation. This is not that far removed from the political allegiance expected of those employed by political parties and lobbyists.[49]

---

[43] A Hilkemeijer and A Maguire, 'Religious Schools and Discrimination against Staff on the Basis of Sexual Orientation: Lessons from European Human Rights Jurisprudence' (2019) 93(9) *Australian Law Journal* 752, 756–61.

[44] ibid 763–65.

[45] Parkinson, 'Future of Religious Freedom' (n 42) 702.

[46] *Sindicatul 'Pastorul Cel Bun' v Romania*, App. No. 2330/09, Judgment of 9 July 2013 [136].

[47] European Council Directive 2000/78/EC of 27 November 2000, establishing a general framework for equal treatment in employment and occupation.

[48] N Aroney and P Taylor, 'The Politics of Freedom of Religion in Australia: Can International Human Rights Standards point the way forward?' (2020) 47(1) *University of Western Australia Law Review* 42, 56–58.

[49] ibid 58–60.

Second, the assumption that there is a relevant distinction between 'religious' and 'secular' activities is incorrect. Moulds also makes this mistake when she considers that the fact that religious bodies are significantly involved in providing a range of essential public services such as education, healthcare, adoption, aged care, and other commercial activities raises the question whether the exemptions which exist in relation to 'core' religious activities should be extended to the provision of these public services.[50] As discussed at length in previous chapters, for many religious communities, all activities are religious. There are no purely secular activities and for many religious associations the provision of public services in accordance with the ethos of the religion is a core activity of the religion. The mathematics teacher can be a religious mentoring and guidance position which acknowledges the beauty and precision in the understanding of God's creation, and the groundsman can be a religious mentoring and guidance position in the cultivation and care of God's creation, just as much as the religious studies teacher is a mentor and guide in understanding religion.[51] Religion 'embraces a broad number of activities including freedom to choose leaders, establish seminaries and schools, prepare and distribute religious texts, and serve the community through daycare centres and soup kitchens'.[52] As Ahdar and Leigh observe, 'opponents in the debates about the application of equality norms to religious ethos employers have been to a very large degree talking past each other because of their fundamentally incompatible starting points about the nature of employment'; in particular, the secular or 'instrumental' view that is about outcomes and functions, as opposed to the religious 'organic' approach which sees work as a vocation in the context of service to God and fulfilling the religious mission of an organisation; 'A liberal, pluralist, society can only flourish by permitting diverse groups within civil society, and that includes, we suggest, organisations that are religiously exclusive'.[53]

This is because religion is a communal and social matter which ought to be passed on to future generations through institutions which shield religion from overly regulatory states. Efforts should be made to accommodate both democratic priorities and the autonomy of religious communities.[54] Refusing accommodation of difference involves several 'dangerous' assumptions, including courts determining what are and are not 'core beliefs' of the religion (eg the nature of marriage), that religion should be irrelevant in the context of public services, and concordantly, that religion is irrelevant in the public sphere.[55] 'The idea that religious

---

[50] S Moulds, 'Drawing the Boundaries: The Scope of the Religious Bodies Exemptions in Australian Anti-Discrimination Law and Implications for Reform' (2020) 47(1) *University of Western Australia Law Review* 112, 119.

[51] See eg R Ahdar and I Leigh, *Religious Freedom in the Liberal State,* 2nd edn (Oxford University Press, 2013) 157; N Aroney, 'Freedom of Religion as an Associational Right' (2014) 33(1) *University of Queensland Law Journal* 153, 161 fn 46.

[52] Ahdar and Leigh, *Religious Freedom in the Liberal State* (n 51) 375–77.

[53] ibid 374.

[54] R Trigg, *Equality, Freedom and Religion* (Oxford University Press, 2012) 157.

[55] ibid 119.

organisations should be wholly subject to the demand of the civil law reflects the increasing indifference of many to religion ... If the institutions of any religion are, without hesitation or any weighing of the effects made, subject to the demands of the law, whatever their own doctrines, secular interests are bound to come to dominate those of a religious nature'.[56]

So Parkinson argues that simply removing exemptions and replacing them with genuine occupational requirements grounded in secular understandings of religion would 'greatly reduce the freedom of religious organisations to have staffing policies consistent with their identity and ethos'.[57] Many schools see their religious ethos as central to the educational mission of the school and believe this requires staff to believe and act consistently with that ethos.[58] Rather than exemptions, as alluded to in chapter one, the law should be expressed as a positive associational right, which would also be consistent with international law.[59] In chapter three I have also suggested a reframing (or more accurately, a clarification) of Article 9 jurisprudence which emphasises the freedom of religious organisations to select and regulate their membership in the form of a positive right for manifestation of religion in a community.

Third, and following from this, an exemption or right which places the decision in the hands of a secular tribunal to decide whether an activity is 'religious', an occupational requirement is 'genuine', or a discriminatory action is 'reasonable', runs significant risk of imposing a secular perspective on a theological question, which would severely undermine the autonomy of religious communities.[60] It is true that the imprecision of the current exemptions in terms of injury to religious susceptibilities is vague and unhelpful.[61] However, as I have noted elsewhere, religious 'convictions' or 'beliefs' may be more clear terms than sensibilities or susceptibilities, at least insofar as religious beliefs of organisations can be ascertained to see if these convictions are injured.[62] That will be a question of fact in any given situation and courts should accept the testimony of the religious communities on this rather than acting as a secular arbiter of a theological dispute, which would damage peaceful coexistence by undermining the virtues of dignity and the golden rule.[63]

---

[56] ibid.

[57] Parkinson, 'Future of Religious Freedom' (n 42) 702.

[58] ibid.

[59] ibid; Aroney and Taylor (n 48) 56–62. This proposition is explored further later in the chapter.

[60] N Foster, 'Respecting the Dignity of Religious Organisations: When Is It Appropriate for Courts to Decide Religious Doctrine?' (2020) 47(1) *University of Western Australia Law Review* 175; A Deagon, 'The "Religious Questions" Doctrine': Addressing (Secular) Judicial Incompetence' (2021) 47(1) *Monash University Law Review* 60–87.

[61] See eg C Evans and L Ujvari, 'Non-Discrimination Laws and Religious Schools in Australia' (2009) 30 *Adelaide Law Review* 31, 53.

[62] A Deagon, 'Defining the Interface of Freedom and Discrimination: Exercising Religion, Democracy and Same-Sex Marriage' (2017) 20 *International Trade and Business Law Review* 239, 282.

[63] See Foster, 'Respecting the Dignity of Religious Organisations' (n 60); Deagon, 'The "Religious Questions" Doctrine' (n 60).

Religious group autonomy is also not merely an aggregation of individual rights, which is a 'secular liberal and deficiently atomistic approach which undermines religious freedom' by allowing government interference in the group to satisfy individual rights.[64] Robust autonomy for religious communities better upholds peaceful coexistence in accordance with the theological virtues because it acknowledges 'the group itself as possessing legal identity and rights' as a result of the 'intrinsically collective dimension to religious freedom and the centrally communal component of manifesting religion'.[65] Consequently, 'religious group association may [and must] sometimes trammel individual rights' because that is intrinsic to the definition of association itself; the ability to associate necessarily entails the ability to exclude, and it is up to the association to put standards in place to make these decisions in relation to leadership, membership, employment, and external activities.[66] As a reasonable accommodation, individuals have a right to leave the group if they wish and, if they like, form a new association with others of similar mind. 'As a general principle, and putting aside situations where no meaningful right of exit exists, it is not for the state to force a religious body to change its ethos to suit belligerent or disgruntled individuals'.[67]

Thus, freedom of religion is not merely individual; when exercising this right humans usually do so in community, which means they require an appropriate infrastructure to practise their religion. As a function of a proportionate, reasonable accommodation of difference in a democracy, education requires strong legal protection of associational freedoms and associational autonomy through positive rights for religious educational institutions. Reasonable accommodations of difference are part of a flourishing diverse community which coexists peacefully in accordance with the theological virtues.

Conversely, a secular separationist or even 'neutral' approach is 'potentially anti-religious ... [s]eparating the religious from the sphere of government action privileges the non-religious or the antireligious in the public square'.[68] The idea of state neutrality (as, for example, advanced by Patrick) embeds a distinct state preference for particular types of religion and religious expression, and is therefore 'not one of neutral evenhandedness', not to mention that true neutrality itself is problematic in an arena of moral pluralism.[69] Indeed, where the state is expanding in regulatory power, religions which do not adhere to state policies face further restriction. An expanding regulatory state seeking to implement its vision of the good (for example through equality norms), and assuming religion is private or

---

[64] Ahdar and Leigh, *Religious Freedom in the Liberal State* (n 51) 375–77.
[65] ibid.
[66] ibid 392.
[67] ibid 392–94.
[68] R Mortensen, 'The Establishment Clause: A Search for Meaning' (2014) 33(1) *University of Queensland Law Journal* 109, 124.
[69] ibid 124–25; *cf* J Patrick, 'Religion, Secularism, and the National School Chaplaincy and Student Welfare Program' (2014) 33(1) *University of Queensland Law Journal* 187.

at least subservient to state interests, will lead to increasing state interference with religious belief or practice that conflicts with the state vision.[70]

This also exposes the fundamental weakness of pragmatic pluralism. A pragmatically pluralist approach provides a considerable level of autonomy for religious communities, but without a principled basis this may decrease for pragmatic reasons as the scope of anti-discrimination laws increases, especially without a principled and robust defence of what religious liberty truly entails as public and communal.[71] This would undermine the dignity of religious communities. Australians are becoming religiously illiterate, with more Australians identifying with no religion and the diversity of minority religions growing. This de-Christianisation poses 'significant challenges'.[72] The decline of Christian ethos and an associated culture of ethical responsibility to the community has transformed into 'hollow' appeals and 'ideological rallying cries' in a 'society of self-interested individuals lacking a common ethic of service'.[73] This has naturally progressed to our current situation of polarised dispute where there is a lack of understanding of the intrinsic good and common ground shared by all sides, damaging peaceful coexistence by eschewing the virtues of patience and forgiveness. Hence, the pragmatic pluralism approach is no longer sufficient, and a more principled, conceptually substantive theoretical framework is needed. The framework will need to be based in shared premises which explicitly reconcile religious freedom and equality to facilitate peaceful coexistence.

IV. Proposing an Alternative: Mild Establishment?

In this part I propose 'mild establishment' as such a framework, which means recognising Australia as a 'Christian Democracy' through institutionally facilitating the general support of religion to produce peaceful coexistence of diverse perspectives in accordance with the universal theological/Christian virtues. As I explain in more detail below, this would be constitutionally permissible because mild establishment as I define it does not amount to formal or substantive state identification with a religion or legally preferring one religion to another. Mild establishment is also conceptually consistent with the acknowledgement of God in the preamble of the Constitution and the understanding of section 116 as a pluralist freedom of religion provision, because mild establishment has a similar effect to pluralism in the sense of beneficial interaction between religion and government.[74] It may seem counter-intuitive to propose mild establishment as

---

[70] Ahdar and Leigh, *Religious Freedom in the Liberal State* (n 51) 17–18.

[71] Even a more principled pluralism would also have the same weakness as a matter of simply prioritising equality over religion in the event of conflict because states cannot be neutral on the question, though perhaps to a lesser extent. See ibid 110–11.

[72] Barker, *State and Religion* (n 11) 329.

[73] Chavura, Gascoigne and Tregenza (n 5) 201.

[74] Barker, *State and Religion* (n 11) 49.

an alternative to pragmatic pluralism when the weakness of pragmatic pluralism is due to increasing religious diversity and decreasing religiousity. But this criticism of mild establishment assumes a secular neutral approach which, as intimated above, does not exist – and since no state is neutral, even a principled pluralism would not succeed in preserving the autonomy of religious communities where there is conflict with equality. Thus, mild establishment actually gives principled space for religious diversity, which augments peaceful coexistence because it will not undermine the autonomy of religious communities if supporting them is no longer consistent with equality norms enforced by the state. In this sense, as I argue further below, mild establishment improves democracy (especially for religion) by promoting inclusion, compassion and responsibility in accordance with the theological virtues such as love, kindness, forgiveness and patience. Even for those who are not Christian or even religious, these virtues are universal and consequently facilitate peaceful coexistence for the entire political community.

A.   Mild Establishment and Constitutional Consistency

Whether mild establishment is an appropriate model generally will depend on the historical relationship between state and religion, the legal and political system of that state, and the religious demographics of the state. There is no model which is 'truly neutral'.[75] Strong establishments (such as theocracy and erastianism, as opposed to the mild establishment proposed here) fuse the state and religion and usually preference a particular religion for special treatment and support. This can actually undermine freedom of religion by disadvantaging minority religions; 'optimum' freedom of religion generally lies somewhere near the middle of theocracy and strict secular separation, depending on the individual context of a state.[76] States may also have weaker, symbolic kinds of establishment which do not have a legally substantive effect and do not impose religion. Barker puts the preamble of the Constitution which contains 'humbly relying on the blessing of Almighty God' into this category, while Ahdar and Leigh characterise nations such as Australia who invoke dependence upon a deity as having 'formal establishments of a symbolic kind'.[77] Barker also considers Australia's financial support of religion through tax exemptions and education funding for religious schools and chaplains as a kind of establishment.[78]

---

[75] Barker, *State and Religion* (n 11) 22; Ahdar and Leigh, *Religious Freedom in the Liberal State* (n 51) 87.

[76] Barker, *State and Religion* (n 11) 23–24, 29, 45; Ahdar and Leigh, *Religious Freedom in the Liberal State* (n 51) 90.

[77] Barker, *State and Religion* (n 11) 47; Ahdar and Leigh, *Religious Freedom in the Liberal State* (n 51) 104.

[78] See Barker, *State and Religion* (n 11) 45 fn 13, 49, and chs 8–9. See also Ahdar and Leigh, *Religious Freedom in the Liberal State* (n 51) 116. However, Saunders and Meagher argue that this is not establishment in the s 116 sense because it is not the creation of a state church which identifies a religion with the body politic. Establishment is an either/or proposition. See BB Saunders and D Meagher,

None of this kind of mild establishment in the Australian context is incompatible with section 116. Analysis of the historical and theological context for the acknowledgement of God in the preamble and the subsequent inclusion of section 116 demonstrates that it was driven by the theological conviction that religion plays an important role in public life. People at the time of federation did not believe in a separation of religion and state and were not, for the most part, suspicious of the influence of religion. Section 116 therefore cannot be plausibly understood as intended to establish a separation between religion and the state, or as being intended to guard against the influence of religion.[79] It 'protects religious bodies in Australia against unwanted intrusions of the federal government', and 'does not inhibit the federal government from identifying itself with the religious impulse, as such, or from authorizing religious practices where all could agree on their desirability' (including permitting the promotion of Christianity), and allows laws to facilitate the practice and funding of religion; section 116 merely prevents the strong establishment of a state religion to the detriment of other religions.[80] Section 116 therefore cannot be a secularist separation provision. It does not separate religion and government or prevent the government from fostering diverse religious beliefs in a non-discriminatory way, and does not 'prevent religion contributing to politics and public policy, or prevent the election of religious ministers as politicians, and it does not contain an absolute prohibition on the Commonwealth passing laws that relate to religion'.[81] Hence, section 116 permits mild establishment because it enables positive interactions between religion and the Commonwealth by permitting the Commonwealth to support religion and permitting religion to influence the Commonwealth. Section 116 is not opposed to giving official imprimatur to religions and religious principles, but only with preventing a religion from being established as the officially endorsed state religion.[82]

The mild establishment proposed here therefore does not impose religious beliefs or coerce religious actions. It merely recognises a shared heritage and tradition and respects the importance of religion to the community, while simultaneously producing a political solidarity between citizens by motivating virtuous

---

'Taking Seriously the Free Exercise of Religion under the Australian Constitution' (2021) 43(3) *Sydney Law Review* 287, 297–98. This is perhaps too simplistic. As seen above there are different kinds of establishment: mild, strong, formal, symbolic, substantive and so on. Saunders and Meagher are correct that the kind of establishment the High Court considered in *DOGS* (a state church, which would be strong/substantive establishment) is an either/or proposition. But it is also possible for a mild/symbolic establishment to be consistent with s 116, such as through the acknowledgement of God in the Preamble. In any case, the fundamental point on which there is consensus is that such interaction between state and religion does not amount to a constitutionally prohibited kind of establishment.

[79] Deagon and Saunders (n 20); See also Chavura, Gascoigne and Tregenza (n 5) ch 6 for another detailed account of the religious motivations for and influence on s 116.

[80] Zimmermann and Weinberger (n 29) 223–24.

[81] Deagon and Saunders (n 20) 1065; *cf* L Beck, *Religious Freedom and the Australian Constitution: Origins and Future* (Routledge, 2018) 77, 119.

[82] See Saunders and Deagon (n 20).

conduct and opening the political to the transcendent, enhancing democracy.[83] As Chavura, Gascoigne and Tregenza identify, our public 'doctrine' of human rights, human dignity and moral equality 'is established on deep layers of Christian sediment.'[84] These ideas are 'not only in large part the product of the Christian moral revolution that helped make the West, but are philosophically incoherent without the kind of metaphysical grounding provided by something like Christian natural law theory.'[85] Mild establishment as a theoretical framework makes more sense of our fundamental understanding of the human seeking to live in a community which pursues the good.

This kind of mild establishment is further supported by Australia's historical establishment as a Christian nation, and a possible continuing form of establishment. Australia's Constitution was 'infused with religiosity from the outset' and the nation was created as a 'Christian Commonwealth.'[86] The overwhelming public support for an explicit acknowledgement of God reflected the widespread belief that the constitution of a new nation fundamentally relied on God's providence. The recognition in the preamble 'exemplifies Australia's religious, and specifically Christian, heritage.'[87] There is a dominant view that Australia historically had the Church of England as an established religion, though this is not a universally held view.[88] Whether Australia did or does have an established religion depends upon the definition used. Australia has a symbolic establishment through the acknowledgement of God in the preamble, but it has had little substantive effect. A wide view of establishment implies Australia still establishes religion by financially supporting religion through tax exemptions and education funding. Chavura, Gascoigne and Tregenza argue the Church of England was certainly established in Australia at colonisation, if only for a short period.[89] There existed 'the natural assumption that the Australian colony should follow the practice of its mother country, including in the position of the established church. This did not preclude toleration for – and even some support of – churches other than the established church.'[90] Ultimately, Barker too concludes that even if the Church of England was not formally established in the colonial period, it was treated as if it was. After the dismissal of alternatives such as pluralism and neutrality as

---

[83] See A Deagon, 'The Name of God in a Constitution: Meaning, Democracy, and Political Solidarity' (2019) 8(3) *Oxford Journal of Law and Religion* 473, 473, 486.

[84] Chavura, Gascoigne and Tregenza (n 5) 208–09.

[85] ibid 255–56.

[86] Zimmermann and Weinberger (n 29) 215. See also A Zimmermann, *Christian Foundations of the Common Law: Vol III Australia* (Connor Court, 2018) for a comprehensive discussion of Australia's legal foundation as a 'Christian' nation and enduring aspects of this foundation, including the acknowledgement of God in the preamble of the Constitution, protection of freedom of religion in s 116 of the Constitution, and the beneficial interaction between religion and government in politics, education, health and welfare.

[87] Zimmermann and Weinberger (n 29) 216.

[88] See Barker, *State and Religion* (n 11) 43–68.

[89] See Chavura, Gascoigne and Tregenza (n 5) chs 2–3, 224.

[90] ibid 40.

descriptively inaccurate, 'this leaves only establishment as a viable description for the State–religion relationship during this period'.[91]

Even accepting the broader view of establishment, symbolic establishment and financial support are not inconsistent with section 116 and not incompatible with pluralism and religious diversity.[92] Hence, section 116 was not designed to undermine the Christian heritage of Australia – only to prevent the creation of a national church and the imposition of religious beliefs and practices by the Commonwealth. Section 116 is 'actually theistic in its heritage' because it reflects a 'theological conception of society' which emphasises that the state should not control the church, and the church should not control the state – in other words, it emphasises the autonomy of religious communities.[93] One of the primary concerns facing Australia in the late 1890s was ensuring that religious difference did not devolve into religious conflict. The claim that Australia was a secular state is an 'illusion, brought on by an inadequate understanding of what religion, and the religious condition, mean, together with a dash of wishful thinking'.[94] Rather, similar to the American situation, though it was felt that the community should have a religious character, the Commonwealth should avoid promoting any one religion (or denomination, as Australia at the time was almost universally Christian) over any other, and avoid hindering religious liberty. It was a climate which endorsed religion and aimed to advance religion, reflected through 'the avoidance of religious preference and the protection of individual and group autonomy in matters of religion as participants in the wider community'.[95] Australia is secular merely in the sense that there is no State church, and 'it is religious, even arguably Christian, in that religion and faith continue to play an important part in the lives of many of its citizens including its political leaders'.[96] As Chavura, Gascoigne and Tregenza aptly put it, Australia is both anti-strong establishment and 'non-secular': 'the state should not be godless, and yet … it should not privilege one Christian church over others'.[97] Categorising Australia as a 'Christian Democracy' through mild establishment means supporting religion to facilitate a peaceful coexistence of difference. It does not entail the creation of a national church and the imposition of religious beliefs and practices, and therefore this theoretical framework is entirely compatible and consistent with section 116 of the Constitution and the constitutional context more broadly.

---

[91] Barker, *State and Religion* (n 11) 66–67.
[92] Barker, *State and Religion* (n 11) 49; Chavura, Gascoigne and Tregenza (n 5) 224.
[93] Zimmermann and Weinberger (n 29) 228, 232–33.
[94] G Melleuish and S Chavura, 'Utilitarianism contra Sectarianism' in W Coleman (ed), *Only in Australia: The History, Politics, and Economics of Australian Exceptionalism* (Oxford University Press, 2016) 63.
[95] A Deagon, 'Secularism as a Religion: Questioning the Future of the 'Secular' State' (2017) 8 *The Western Australian Jurist* 31, 57–59. See also Chavura, Gascoigne and Tregenza (n 5) 126.
[96] Barker, *State and Religion* (n 11) 42.
[97] Chavura, Gascoigne and Tregenza (n 5) 126.

B.   Mild Establishment and Peaceful Coexistence

Ahdar and Leigh argue that establishment is 'worthwhile' because 'establishment is a reminder that God, rather than the state, is the ultimate source of authority and, conversely, that "secular" institutions such as the monarchy draw legitimacy and strength from religious underpinnings. A pluralist version of the same argument is that the spiritual sphere cannot simply be ignored: hence, it is appropriate for religious representatives to take part in the legislative process ... alongside many other groups'.[98] Establishment also recognises that the 'state is not a secular one where religion is legally privatized ... [this] attracts support for the continuation of establishment from other, non-Christian religions on the basis that establishment is a visible reminder of the spiritual sphere to life ... establishment is more anti-secularist than it is religious'.[99] In the Australian context, religion's metaphysical support for morality and its ability to produce harmonious community supported 'notions of religion's indispensability for civil society in Australia well into the twentieth century and, to some extent, even to the present'.[100]

Early colonial thought held that the secular was built on the sacred, religion is both the metaphysical and motivational foundation of morality, and there-fore religion is necessary for an orderly and harmonious society. As such public policy should assist in the promotion of religion in general, even if not a particular denomination. These assumptions were to shape much of the subsequent debates about church and state in Australia and their influence still remains with us today.[101] It is the role of the state to facilitate autonomy for religious associations to develop their own versions of the good, rather than impose the state's own version of morality on the religious association; to do so would 'endanger virtue in democracy itself by rendering such associations impotent to contribute to the common good'.[102] Chavura, Gascoigne and Tregenza summarise this perspective as follows:

> a political union based merely on a modus vivendi of individual self-interest is inher-ently unstable. Each individual is civil only until it is in his interest to be uncivil ... this utilitarianism, which ... is mere rational self-interest, cannot provide the normative conditions for social harmony. It is common Christianity that generates civic fraternity, that furnishes citizens with a conception of justice, enjoining citizens to see one another as more than mere vectors of utility ... Not rational egoism but religious sense (charity) was the surest basis for perpetual social happiness. The secular state could not be truly secular, that is, successful in securing temporal happiness and well-being, without an interest in the flourishing of religion, that is, general Christianity.[103]

---

[98] Ahdar and Leigh, *Religious Freedom in the Liberal State* (n 51) 108.
[99] ibid 109.
[100] Chavura, Gascoigne and Tregenza (n 5) 28.
[101] ibid 32, 80–81.
[102] Ahdar and Leigh, *Religious Freedom in the Liberal State* (n 51) 390–91.
[103] Chavura, Gascoigne and Tregenza (n 5) 88–89.

Mild establishment is therefore consistent with the argument that 'Australia's Christian heritage still has normative significance' for the purpose of facilitating a society of peaceful coexistence.[104]

This kind of 'weak' or 'mild' establishment is also 'compatible with pluralism' and consistent with traditional liberal democracy – and can be termed a Christian democracy.[105] It is justified on the basis that it is 'the working out of a transcendent reality', and a recognition that it is not possible to separate the spiritual from the secular.[106] It involves a theoretical framework which entails several overlapping ideas: the moral purpose and divine calling of the state, that God rather than the state is the ultimate source of authority and 'secular' institutions draw their legitimacy from religious concepts, that the spiritual sphere is part of the lives of many and cannot be ignored by the state, and associatively, that the state has a responsibility to ensure the spiritual welfare of its citizens.[107] According to this view, pure secular autonomous reason is not sufficient to ground liberal institutions which rely on concepts of intrinsic human dignity (and it is doubtful such reason even exists).[108] A transcendent source such as the recognition of God is required to acknowledge a shared heritage and tradition, bind citizens together as a community to produce political solidarity, and to illuminate the eternal foundations of citizenship which provides for a beneficial relationship between religion and the state and gives political engagement a deeper meaning.[109] However, this recognition of God does not have any substantive legal effect, and so it does not involve the imposition of religion.[110] Indeed, there are persuasive arguments that religion, and Christianity in particular, is the best mechanism to guarantee the democratic institutions which support equality and religious freedom.[111]

---

[104] ibid 240.

[105] Barker, *State and Religion* (n 11) 47. See generally Deagon, 'Name of God' (n 83).

[106] Ahdar and Leigh, *Religious Freedom in the Liberal State* (n 51) 107.

[107] ibid 108.

[108] See EW Böckenförde, *State, Society, and Liberty: Studies in Political Theory and Constitutional Law* (Oxford, 1991); B Berger, 'Liberal constitutionalism and the unsettling of the secular' in R Ahdar (ed), *Research Handbook on Law and Religion* (Edward Elgar, 2018). See generally A Deagon, *From Violence to Peace: Theology, Law and Community* (Hart Publishing, 2017).

[109] M Schulz, 'The Existential and Semantic Truth of Religion in Jurgen Habermas's Political Philosophy and the Possibility of a Philosophy of Religion' (2017) 31(3) *Journal of Speculative Philosophy* 457–67. See generally Deagon, 'Name of God' (n 83).

[110] See R Domingo, *God and the Secular Legal System* (Cambridge University Press, 2016).

[111] H-M Ten Napel, *Constitutionalism, Democracy and Religious Freedom* (Routledge, 2017) 106. Ten Napel indicates Christianity in particular facilitates democratic, pluralistic liberal order and tolerant decision-making, and speculates that the decline of Christianity in the West is likely to detrimentally affect how democracy functions. John Milbank and Adrian Pabst go even further and argue Christianity is the source of democracy. See J Milbank and An Pabst, *The Politics of Virtue: Post-Liberalism and the Human Future* (Rowman & Littlefield, 2016) 6–7; J Milbank, *Beyond Secular Order: The Representation of Being and the Representation of the People* (Blackwell, 2013) 10, 164. See also the important empirical article by Woodberry which incontrovertibly demonstrates the link between Protestant mission, democracy and religious liberty: R Woodberry, 'The Missionary Roots of Liberal Democracy' (2012) 106(2) *American Political Science Review* 244–74. Finally, Francis Oakley has provided a compelling thesis that the origins of modern constitutionalism derive from Christian thought: see eg F Oakley, *The Watershed of Modern Politics: Law, Virtue, Kingship, and Consent* (Yale University Press, 2015). See generally also Ahdar and Leigh, *Religious Freedom in the Liberal State* (n 51) 24–50.

Hence, mild establishment (or Christian democracy) provides a framework for peaceful coexistence of difference that transcends and fulfils the liberal democratic ideals of equality and freedom which secular liberalism proclaims but can never attain. It is not the theocratic imposition of the Christian religion on society, but the consequence of recognising first that there is no neutral model of religion-state relations, and second, that Christian ontology and the theological virtues provide a uniquely robust and principled framework for harmonious community, the peaceful coexistence of difference.[112] The mild establishment of Christianity does not alienate or discriminate against those who are not Christian or religious. As noted earlier, the Christian theological virtues are truly democratic because they are universally open to and practised by all. Indeed, coerced religion is antithetical to Christianity which advocates belief as persuasion through revelation. Christian democracy therefore has the effect of promoting the harmonious existence and interaction of diverse religious and non-religious perspectives.[113]

Christian democracy further benefits both religious and non-religious citizens by providing a uniting political symbol that points to transcendent meaning and deeper conceptions of the good. This in turn enhances democracy by producing political solidarity between citizens where it is recognised that each citizen, religious or non-religious, is an essential and valuable part of the community. Recognising the tradition and heritage of religion in a community, and the value of religion in contemporary society, creates social cohesion and political solidarity as part of the democratic mechanisms of the state. Solidarity here takes its classical meaning of 'deeper relationality and mutual love as a bond between citizens of a community through a cooperative order. This entails understanding mutual dependence and responsibility, culminating in communities of mercy, grace, and generosity'.[114]

Finally, Christian democracy also motivates virtuous thought and conduct towards each citizen as an intrinsically dignified member of the community with a higher meaning and destiny. It strengthens the intrinsic dignity, equality and freedom of every human because of their creation in the image and likeness of God, providing a transcendental ground for the ontological status of the human as a pre-political bearer of rights and responsibilities protected and enforced by law. Mild establishment reminds the community that immanent political structures point to transcendent realities and are informed by eternal virtues.[115] This accordingly has the effect of motivating people to treat others as valuable and dignified members of the community, which enhances the democratic process by providing political participation with a deeper and substantive aspiration for the relations between citizens as members of a community with mutual rights and responsibilities in a cooperative order.[116]

---

[112] See A Deagon, 'Reconciling John Milbank and Religious Freedom: "Liberalism" through Love' (2019) 34(2) *Journal of Law and Religion* 183 for a detailed discussion.

[113] See ibid 204–09.

[114] See Deagon, 'Name of God' (n 83) 483–84.

[115] ibid 487–88.

[116] See ibid 487–88, 491–92.

In short, the idea of state neutrality is impossible and secularism is not neutral.[117] This means the state must take a position on religion.[118] My proposition is that mild establishment through Christian democracy is the position which best facilitates peaceful coexistence and a reasonable accommodation of difference in a principled way. As Trigg argues:

> The public recognition of one religion or one particular Christian denomination by a state, in preference to others, does not of itself imply the existence of a monopoly, or lack of freedom for others. It depends on what form the recognition takes, and how much toleration there is of those of different faiths ... the whole point of democracy is to provide a way in which those of many differing viewpoints can live together.[119]

This is precisely what Christian democracy entails. In contrast to the view that the state endorsement of a religion is exclusive and discriminatory, 'the single-minded pursuit of equality and an urge to root out all forms of discrimination and preference to some sections of the population can involve a major assault on the heritage, and even the identity of a country'.[120] Given Australia's Christian heritage, the effect of unbridled equality norms 'can lead to a strongly secular public sphere'.[121] And as noted previously, a secular separationist public sphere is not neutral and does not facilitate peaceful coexistence or accommodation of difference because a secular equality approach 'prevent[s] people from expressing their religion in a public manner'.[122] Hence, 'democracy is not just founded on religious principles, but needs religion to teach its citizens how to act in the wider interest, as well as for their own good'.[123] A false dichotomy is often drawn between a democratic and pluralistic society (a secular state where religion is privatised) and a theocracy where there is no religious freedom and one religion dominates.[124] However, I propose the option of a Christian democracy, a polity where Christianity informs democracy and pluralism while simultaneously supporting religious freedom and equality.

V. Implications for Australia's Legal Framework

A. The Principle of Accommodation

Since Christian democracy is ultimately grounded in virtues shared by all, it provides a principled framework for peaceful coexistence which entails a

---

[117] See A Deagon, 'State (non-)Neutrality and Conceptions of Religious Freedom' in J Doomen and M van Schaik (eds.), *Religious Ideas in Liberal Democratic States* (Rowman & Littlefield, 2021).
[118] See R Trigg, *Equality, Freedom and Religion* (Oxford University Press, 2012) 4–5.
[119] ibid 30.
[120] ibid 32. *cf* eg M Nussbaum, *Liberty of Conscience* (Basic Books, 2008).
[121] Trigg (n 118) 32.
[122] ibid 33.
[123] ibid 141.
[124] ibid 154–55.

reasonable, proportionate accommodation of difference, and reconciles freedom with equality. Given the important role of religion in human life and community, legislatures and courts should be ready and willing to respect religion by considering exemptions or positive rights.[125] Of course, all parties affirm the importance of religious liberty; what matters are the perceived limits of religious liberty. It has always been the case that religious liberty is limited by what is conducive to public good, but today notions of the public good are strongly informed by equality, inclusion and mental health, especially applied to the LGBT community. As Chavura, Gascoigne and Tregenza observe:

> These ideals are operating to constrict religious liberty, particularly as it applies to religious associations and institutions, whose historic right to discriminate in order to preserve institutional authenticity conflicts with the demands of individualistic authenticity that animates so much moral discourse today.[126]

However, 'interfering with the beliefs and practices' of religious communities 'carries its own dangers'.[127] Though secular liberalism is focused on individuals, religion is strongly communal. Religious associations and institutions (communities) have an existence and distinctive character apart from their members; 'without criteria of membership, and distinctive activities, they would cease to exist'.[128] This character matters because they not only reflect the beliefs of members, but help to mould them for the good of the broader community.[129] Though some challenge the autonomy of religious communities to set their own standards as undermining individual rights, 'it is usually recognised that religious freedom is safeguarded as long as any individual has a right of exit'.[130] Rather than simply restricting religious freedom because it may undermine equality norms, a proposal which more effectively upholds peaceful coexistence by accommodating difference is to consider how competing interests may be reconciled. For example, exemptions could be granted where the inconvenience is relatively minor and equivalent secular services are available.[131]

Evans and Gaze also warn that 'individuals are entitled to develop and live out their own conceptions of the good life and that this entitlement is an important bulwark against deadening social conformity and, at the extreme, totalitarianism'.[132] Similarly, Trigg observes that the 'liberal ideal of ... equality' can itself 'take on the status of an orthodoxy, which can be potentially oppressive'.[133] In effect, 'a concern

---

[125] ibid 151.
[126] Chavura, Gascoigne and Tregenza (n 5) 48.
[127] Trigg (n 118) 39.
[128] ibid 43.
[129] ibid 44.
[130] ibid 99.
[131] See C Baines, 'A Delicate Balance: Religious Autonomy Rights and LGBTI Rights in Australia' (2015) 10(1) *Religion & Human Rights* 45, 48; C Evans and B Gaze, 'Between Religious Freedom and Equality: Complexity and Context' (2008) 49 *Harvard International Law Journal Online* 46–48.
[132] Evans and Gaze (n 131) 45.
[133] Trigg (n 118) 83.

for equality can visibly diminish religious freedom.[134] Hence, the autonomy of religious communities should be accommodated to protect Australian democracy and freedom.[135] Australia as a Christian democracy 'should recognise its dependence on Christianity, rather than be opposed to it.'[136] A supposedly neutral or uniform approach which is religion-blind and treats all religions equally makes it 'impossible to accommodate laws to the sensibilities of different religions', which creates a 'particular burden' which is unique to believers.[137]

This does not mean equality norms are to be abandoned or ignored. 'Acknowledgement of equality need not imply uniform treatment.'[138] Reasonable accommodation involving differential treatment can be made to maintain equality and preserve freedom. It is important to note the associational freedom to 'discriminate' in this context is not only a function of religious freedom, but also preserves equality between religious and non-religious educational institutions. As I have argued previously:

> Generally applicable laws, such as anti-discrimination legislation, fall disproportionately or unequally on those whose religious practices conflict with them. Those who do not engage in religious belief or practice are not subject to the same practical restrictions resulting from the laws ... the exemptions are necessary in order to preserve equality ... specific exemptions are required to address this specific situation where there is an unequal or disproportionate application of law.[139]

In other words, such exemptions are a proportionate, reasonable accommodation of difference because they mitigate the effect of anti-discrimination laws that apply unequally to religious communities.[140] The need to accommodate religion can be traced to equality itself. Thus, upholding the dignity and diversity of all parties through patience and forgiveness, and facilitating peaceful coexistence of difference, requires respecting religion through accommodation, either with exemptions or positive associational rights.[141]

B. Exemptions or Positive Rights?

Professor Reid Mortensen articulates the foundational principles:

> [O]ne inherent paradox in *all* discrimination laws is that, although they aim to protect social pluralism, the principles of equality they usually promote also present a threat to

---

[134] ibid 32, 116, 119–20, 128–32.
[135] Baines (n 131) 49. See also A Deagon, 'Equal Voice Liberalism and Free Public Religion: Some Legal Implications' in M Quinlan, I Benson and K Thompson (eds), *Religious Liberty in Australia: A new* Terra Nullius? (Connor Court Publishing, 2019) 314–17, 325–26.
[136] Trigg (n 118) 83.
[137] ibid 88.
[138] ibid 139–40.
[139] Deagon, 'Defining the Interface' (n 62) 276–78.
[140] See Trigg (n 118) 3–4, 31–32, 87–88, 114.
[141] ibid 124, 151–52.

the protection of religious pluralism in the political sphere. This occurs when, despite the traditional recognition of rights of religious liberty, the discrimination laws apply to religious groups that deny the moral imperatives of, say, racial, gender or sexual orientation equality. In this respect, Caesar has generally been prepared to render something to God through the complex exemptions granted in the discrimination laws to religious groups and religious educational or health institutions.[142]

Mortensen therefore claims that to 'honour rights of religious liberty, religious groups are probably entitled to broad exemptions from the operation of sexual orientation discrimination laws'.[143] More emphatically, the right to free exercise in the Constitution 'does not suggest a "balance" to be struck between anti-discrimination standards and rights of religious liberty, but a constitutionally required preference for religious liberty'.[144] While accepting these contentions in principle, as noted at the beginning of the chapter, the current exemptions do not uphold peaceful coexistence. They are 'irrelevantly' and 'offensively' targeted at sexual minorities, and do not provide what is really needed, which is 'the ability of such organisations to maintain their religious ethos generally, in terms of both the committed beliefs and conscientious practices of their employees'.[145]

Similarly, Neil Foster argues that framing religious freedom protection as 'exemptions' from anti-discrimination laws might give the impression that powerful religious lobby groups are simply bullying politicians into giving them a special privilege to engage in otherwise unlawful conduct (which is not an unfounded concern), and give the impression that in general equality is more important than religious freedom. A better approach is to 'see the limits drawn around discrimination laws as an integral part of a structure designed to reflect the relevant human rights as a whole'.[146] In other words, since equality and religious freedom are both positive rights under international law, and there is no hierarchy of human rights, it is more accurate to provide positive protection for religious freedom which reflects its status as a human right alongside and not inferior to the right of equality. So rather than framing religious freedom protections as exemptions to anti-discrimination laws which intuitively subordinates religious freedom to equality, Aroney advocates for positive rights to select staff who adhere to the beliefs and observe the practices of the religious group in question.[147] He concludes:

> Given that international human rights law recognises that religious freedom extends to the establishment and maintenance of religious, charitable, humanitarian and educational institutions, and the right to establish associations with like-minded people

---

[142] R Mortensen, 'Rendering to God and Caesar: Religion in Australian Discrimination Law' (1995) 18 *University of Queensland Law Journal* 208, 231.

[143] ibid 228–29.

[144] ibid 231.

[145] Aroney and Taylor (n 48) 61–62.

[146] N Foster, 'Freedom of Religion and Balancing Clauses in Discrimination Legislation' (2016) 5 *Oxford Journal of Law and Religion* 385, 389.

[147] N Aroney, 'Can Australian Law Better Protect Freedom of Religion' (2019) 93(9) *Australian Law Journal* 708, 716, 719.

includes the right to determine conditions of membership and participation within such organisations, consideration should be given to protecting freedom of religion in the context of anti-discrimination laws through the enactment of statutory affirmations of the positive right of religious bodies to select staff who share their religious beliefs so as to maintain the religious ethos of the organisation ... that is a consequence of living in a diverse society which respects religious freedom.[148]

For these reasons I have proposed positive associational rights as an alternative to exemptions. As Wolterstorff contends, natural human rights are grounded in the intrinsic dignity of God loving all human persons 'equally and permanently' as persons of worth, and so this is a more robust framework for reconciling religious freedom and equality grounded in the theological virtues.[149] But the form of positive associational rights for the autonomy of religious communities is contentious, particularly whether such rights should be recognised through separate legislation, or through some kind of human rights charter.[150] Hobbs and Williams argue that the solution for the weak protection of religious freedom in Australia is a Human Rights Act or Charter of Rights which places freedom of religion in the context of limitations and balances required by considering other human rights such as equality.[151] Freedom of religion should be 'positively protected' rather than conceived through exceptions.[152] They reject a Religious Discrimination Act on the basis that this is a narrow lens to view religious freedom which will provide a limited scope for religious freedom. Such a mechanism is unable to resolve complex issues of balancing between different anti-discrimination protections (for example religious freedom and equality) as they arise.[153] A comprehensive Human Rights Act will equally protect fundamental democratic rights and freedoms and include a mechanism for balancing competing rights. This approach will best 'accommodate' the perspectives of the religious and the non-religious in a way that 'respects religious belief, while creating a space for robust and open debate about faith-based practices'.[154] Only protecting religious freedom 'tilts the balance one way' which will increase tensions and undermine peaceful coexistence.[155]

However, Nicholas Aroney critiques existing state human rights charters as offering protection that is 'limited and selective' for four reasons.[156] First, they do not adopt the strict limitations which appear in Article 18 of the International Covenant on Civil and Political Rights ('ICCPR'). They say religious freedom may

---

[148] ibid 720.

[149] N Wolterstorff, *Justice: Rights and Wrongs* (Princeton University Press, 2008) 360.

[150] For various perspectives on a charter of rights, see generally P Babie and N Rochow (eds), *Freedom of Religion under Bills of Rights* (University of Adelaide Press, 2012).

[151] H Hobbs and G Williams, 'Protecting Religious Freedom in a Human Rights Act' (2019) 93(9) *Australian Law Journal* 721, 722.

[152] ibid 731.

[153] ibid 732.

[154] ibid.

[155] ibid.

[156] Aroney, 'Freedom of Religion' (n 147) 715. See also Aroney and Taylor (n 48) 46–48.

be subject to reasonable limits that are for a legitimate purpose, which is a 'vaguer and lower' threshold than the necessary limits for the particular purposes in the ICCPR.[157] Second, the charters indicate that all aspects of freedom of religion are potentially subject to limitation, which contradicts a clear principle of international law that freedom of belief is inviolable and cannot be limited. Third, the charters contain very little protection for the liberty of parents to educate their children in conformity with their convictions as required by Article 18(4). The Australian Capital Territory charter merely protects the religious freedom of parents to educate their children in non-government schools (effectively excluding the majority of parents unable to afford the cost of private education from the international law protection), while the other charters (Victoria and Queensland) provide no protection at all.[158] Finally, the protections in the state charters are 'at a high level of generality' which fails to provide sufficient protection in the many specific ways law and religion may interact; indeed, 'there is no evidence to suggest that religious freedom has been more adequately protected [by human rights charters] … in fact, at times, religious freedom has received weaker protection in such jurisdictions'.[159] Aroney demonstrates this by comparing the outcomes in a Victorian case where religious freedom was not protected despite the presence of a human rights charter to a similar case in New South Wales where religious freedom was protected without a human rights charter.[160]

In addition, protections for religious freedom in Victoria separate from the existing human rights charter are generally strong, apart from allowing the possibility that certain religious beliefs could be unlawful (contravening a clear principle of international law) and the fact that the protections are framed as exceptions. The existing protection seems to be due to nothing more than democratic activity and the parliamentary process.[161] The critique of state human rights charters is relevant because a federal charter would likely fail to protect freedom of religion in similar ways. 'Perversely, the charters fail to provide the guarantees required by the ICCPR, and at the same time invite an interpretation of them that fundamentally detracts from the protection they purport to afford'.[162]

---

[157] Aroney, 'Freedom of Religion' (n 147) 715.
[158] ibid.
[159] ibid.
[160] ibid 716–18. For further analysis, see Deagon, 'The "Religious Questions" Doctrine' (n 60), where I suggest the major determining factor was the extent to which the judges adhered to the golden rule and engaged in imaginative sympathy as part of their judgement process, especially in deferring to the religious parties' articulation of their own beliefs and practices. This indicates adherence to the theological virtues will better protect religious freedom and preserve peaceful coexistence.
[161] Aroney, 'Freedom of Religion' (n 147) 715–16. See also N Aroney, J Harrison and P Babie, 'Religious Freedom under the Victorian Charter of Rights' in C Campbell and M Groves (eds), *Australian Charters of Rights a Decade On* (Federation Press, 2017) 120. It must be said the democratic process in Victoria allowed the passing of the Change or Suppression (Conversion) Practices Prohibition Act 2021 (Vic) and the recent passing of amendments to the Equal Opportunity Act 2010 (Vic) which significantly undermine religious freedom. However, this merely underscores the point that the Victorian Human Rights Charter provides limited protection.
[162] Aroney and Taylor (n 48) 47–48.

Since the existing charters fail to properly give effect to Australia's international obligations, 'there is a lack of confidence … that a [national] charter will do much to protect [religious] freedoms'.[163] Zimmermann further notes that bills of rights are unnecessary in a federal system with checks and balances, and may even reduce individual rights (depending on socio-political context) because many nations with bills of rights engage in significant levels of human rights abuse while paradoxically pointing to their entrenched protection of rights to deny such abuse occurs.[164] Constitutional luminaries such as Jeremy Waldron, Jeffrey Goldsworthy and James Allan also express typical concerns that a charter of rights undermines democracy by providing too much power to unelected and incompetent judges, and simultaneously politicises the judiciary – undermining the separation of powers and the rule of law.[165]

The point is that the ideological dominance of equality norms in rights discourse may well cause a charter to result in the undermining of religious freedom rather than reconciliation and peaceful coexistence. This is another aspect of the weakness of pragmatic pluralism as discussed above. Parkinson summarises:

> The problem is when absolutist claims about the moral requirements of a charter are used to mask and provide some special authority for the policy positions of people with particular agendas. At the heart of Christian concerns about the development of a charter is that secular liberal interpretations of human rights charters will tend to relegate religious freedom to the lowest place in an implicit hierarchy of rights established not by international law but by the intellectual fashions of the day.[166]

Parliamentary processes informed by Christian democracy are therefore a more appropriate forum for resolving competing moral claims between religious freedom and equality, because this will facilitate nuanced consideration of all perspectives in accordance with the theological virtues, supporting peaceful coexistence.

Finally, in a similar vein, Harrison critiques the kind of proportionality and balancing analysis characteristic of what is required by human rights instruments on the basis that such processes are structured by a contestable secular narrative which fails to truly understand and engage with the claims of religious parties. Harrison criticises 'monolingual adjudication' which is 'inattentive to the actual arguments of religious groups, or else potentially fails to comprehend the

---

[163] P Parkinson, 'Christian Concerns about an Australian Charter of Rights' in P Babie and N Rochow (eds), *Freedom of Religion under Bills of Rights* (University of Adelaide Press, 2012) 132.

[164] A Zimmermann, 'The Wrongs of a Bill of Rights for Australia: A Rights-Based Appraisal' in A Zimmermann (ed), *A Commitment to Excellence: Essays in Honour of Emeritus Professor Gabriel A. Moens* (Connor Court, 2018) 33–34.

[165] See eg J Waldron, 'A Rights-Based Critique of Constitutional Rights' (1993) 13 *Oxford Journal of Legal Studies* 18; J Goldsworthy, 'Legislative Sovereignty and the Rule of Law' in T Campbell, K Ewing and A Tomkins (eds), *Sceptical Essays on Human Rights* (Oxford University Press, 2001); J Allan, 'Why Australia does not have, and does not need, a National Bill of Rights' (2012) 24 *Journal of Constitutional History* 35.

[166] Parkinson, 'Christian Concerns' (n 163) 120–21. See also P Parkinson, 'Christian Concerns about an Australian Charter of Rights' (2010) 15 *Australian Journal of Human Rights* 83.

seriousness of what is at stake'.[167] Rather than considering 'the diversity of arguments presented by claimants', they are subsumed into the same 'abstract language' of secular reasons.[168] This means the 'real nature of the community's argument may be lost'.[169] The very religion-based reasons why a tension is experienced by a religious claimant is eliminated at the outset, and 'there is something deeply unsatisfying or else anaemic in this framing'.[170] To resolve this Harrison suggests bypassing the courts as much as possible and having a richer debate through the democratic process with enacted changes better reflecting religious perspectives, which is precisely what I advocate through a Christian democracy conducted in accordance with the theological virtues for a peaceful coexistence of difference.[171] However, even if more religiously inclusive legislation is passed, it will need to be interpreted by courts, so when judicial interpretation is necessary an approach in accordance with the theological virtues is to apply the golden rule and an imaginative sympathy which genuinely engages with the views of religious parties and defers to their own understanding of those views rather than imposing a secular perspective.[172]

Even Hobbs and Williams admit that the state Human Rights Acts 'fal[l] short of the standard required under international law' because freedom to believe (as opposed to manifesting belief) is subject to limitation under the relevant Acts, and the limitation provisions themselves are also a 'problem' because they permit 'reasonable' limitations while the international instruments permit only 'necessary' limitations.[173] Despite the enduring criticisms, Hobbs and Williams maintain that at the very least, a human rights charter will have the symbolic effect of demonstrating the value of human rights by explicitly protecting them, and providing a framework for resolving competing rights.[174] Perhaps it is possible to protect the autonomy of religious communities with a human rights charter, but all these concerns would need to be addressed and implemented. It seems more likely that separate laws providing positive associational rights would more effectively preserve the autonomy of religious communities without undermining equality.

Schools desire 'freedom to conduct their educational functions through a curriculum and in a manner which is consistent with their religious ethos, delivered by and within a community of like-minded others', and 'make suitable appointments based on the alignment of fundamental beliefs and practices';

---

[167] J Harrison, 'Towards Re-thinking "Balancing" in the Courts and the Legislature's Role in Protecting Religious Liberty' (2019) 93(9) *Australian Law Journal* 734, 738.
[168] ibid 738–39.
[169] ibid 739.
[170] ibid.
[171] ibid 742–46.
[172] See Deagon, 'The "Religious Questions" Doctrine' (n 60); Foster, 'Respecting the Dignity of Religious Organisations' (n 60).
[173] Hobbs and Williams (n 151) 728–29.
[174] ibid 732–33.

this desire is consistent with international law under the ECHR and ICCPR.[175] Positive associational rights would enable schools to select staff consistent with their religious and institutional ethos and to enforce generally applicable procedures and rules with regard to student advocacy, conduct, dress and so forth. Such legislation would ameliorate hostility, reconciling both religious freedom (by enabling religious schools to require employees to believe and act consistently with an ethos) and equality (by removing the targeted sexuality-based religious exemptions). An example might be amending the Fair Work Act 2009 (Cth) to provide employment rights to organisations established for a particular religious purpose or social cause, which would legally affirm the autonomy of religious communities to choose or prefer members who adhere to the ethos of the organisation in their beliefs and conduct.[176]

This framing would address the perception that schools are engaging in 'unloving' behaviour by seeking special privileges to discriminate based simply on prejudice. The 'positive rights' framework recognises that schools are creating a community with a distinct ethos which will contribute to public good, and that ultimately seeks the good of the neighbour, facilitating peaceful coexistence in accordance with the theological virtues. This proposition might well sit awkwardly with those who do not adhere to the doctrines of the particular religious institution. Nevertheless, if we desire a healthy democracy which coexists peacefully and accommodates difference for the pursuit of mutual and public good, we must allow religious communities the freedom to publicly conduct themselves in such a way as to maintain their unique identity on their terms so they can contribute to this diversity.[177] Ultimately, though pragmatic pluralism facilitates a peaceful coexistence of difference by allowing mutually beneficial interaction between religion and government, mild establishment through Christian democracy provides a more robust theological framework which supports the autonomy of religious communities while consistently upholding and strengthening the foundations of equality law through theological virtues such as dignity, love, forgiveness and patience. This approach forms the foundation undergirding a principled framework for the autonomy of religious communities which reconciles religious freedom and equality.

VI. Conclusion

In this chapter I have argued that mild establishment in the form of Christian democracy (rather than pragmatic pluralism) is a principled framework which

---

[175] Aroney and Taylor (n 48) 61–62.

[176] Parkinson, 'Future of Religious Freedom' (n 42) 702–03.

[177] In regard to religious vendors, I will discuss the issues more in the following US and UK chapters. In short, similar principles apply to Australia. In ch 1 I noted Australia has no protection for religious vendors, in ch 2 I proposed narrow and clear exemptions for religious vendors, and in ch 3 I framed these as rights for religious vendors. So for Australia, I would recommend narrow and clear positive

best preserves peaceful coexistence and accommodation of difference in Australia, reconciling the autonomy of religious communities with equality. Though mild establishment is in accordance with Christian theological virtues, it does not exclude or alienate those who are not Christian or not religious because the theological virtues are democratic, universally available to be practised by all. In particular, the virtues of dignity and love undergird equality by providing a transcendent foundation for the intrinsic value of the human and the corresponding love for neighbour which follows from that value. As Cecile Laborde observes, 'a state of modest establishment that takes seriously the principle of equality between citizens … can … meet liberal desiderata'.[178] Both pragmatic pluralism and mild establishment are consistent with religious freedom and 'score highly in that they recognise a measure of interaction and cooperation between government and religious communities is useful'.[179] However, pragmatic pluralism has the weakness of potentially undermining religious freedom when faced with the ideological dominance of equality because it lacks a robust and principled articulation of the transcendent and immanent good of religious freedom in accordance with the theological virtues. Hence, mild establishment is the preferred framework. It acknowledges the transcendent foundations of the state and citizenship and 'the public dimension of religion while refuting the liberal claim that privatisation is neutral'; it concordantly provides a robust basis for the autonomy of religious communities while simultaneously reconciling religious freedom with equality by pointing to the intrinsic dignity of all humans.[180]

Nevertheless, as Ahdar and Leigh warily point out, 'it is difficult to single out one model of religion-state relationship as indisputably the best in terms of religious freedom'.[181] I have argued that mild establishment is best for Australia, but that may not be the case with respect to the US and England. Development of a principled framework is necessarily contextual, and the specifics of the framework may vary depending on the diverse religious, political, social and cultural aspects of different jurisdictions. In the following two chapters I consider theoretical frameworks with respect to the US and England, before concluding in the final part of the book by using the principled framework(s) to articulate general principles for engaging with the tensions between religious freedom and equality identified in the Introduction, and providing specific recommendations for legal and policy changes in each jurisdiction to more effectively preserve a peaceful coexistence which accommodates difference for the good of the community.

---

rights for religious vendors not to creatively participate in significant moral acts (such as same-sex marriage).

[178] C Laborde, 'Political Liberalism and Religion: On Separation and Establishment' (2013) 21(1) *Journal of Political Philosophy* 67, 76.

[179] Ahdar and Leigh, *Religious Freedom in the Liberal State* (n 51) 124.

[180] ibid 123.

[181] ibid 124.

5

United States: Secularism or Pluralism?

I. Introduction

Chapter two suggests the First Amendment of the US Constitution provides relatively robust protection for the autonomy of religious communities, largely preserving the peaceful coexistence of difference in accordance with the theological virtues. However, the First Amendment can more effectively promote the peaceful coexistence of difference in three specific ways. First, establishment clause jurisprudence must be clarified in a way that properly protects the autonomy of religious communities and their ability to meaningfully and equally participate in public life by rejecting the 'wall of separation' metaphor. Second, free exercise jurisprudence should facilitate the autonomy of religious communities to meaningfully and equally participate in public life by explicitly overruling the *Smith* requirement that such communities are necessarily subject to generally applicable laws which may have the incidental effect of targeting religion. As such, clearly limited and stringent religious exemptions protect the dignity and life of both religious communities and those who may be discriminated against. Third, though the ministerial exception is in principle necessary and correct, an extremely broad approach may provide an unconstrained licence to discriminate, and therefore application of the ministerial exception should be limited to employment decisions regarding religion or religion-related conduct. In this chapter, and with these three principles in mind, the book will identify two theoretical models which potentially capture the US legal framework for the autonomy of religious communities with a particular focus on the First Amendment. I will evaluate these models as to the extent they provide peaceful coexistence of difference in accordance with the theological virtues by facilitating a proportional, reasonable accommodation of difference, and discuss more precisely how the US legal infrastructure should be reframed in this context.

Part II briefly considers the First Amendment and associated characterisations of the US as a secular state which separates not only church and state, but also religion and government. However, Part III argues this kind of secular separationism actually detracts from the peaceful coexistence of difference, damaging the autonomy of religious communities and marginalising religion from the public sphere. Part IV proposes pluralism as an alternative. I argue that pluralism is compatible with the structure of the First Amendment, and indeed is a more historically and jurisprudentially accurate model to make sense of the free exercise and establishment clauses. Furthermore, pluralism is a more robust basis for peaceful coexistence of difference in accordance with the theological virtues because it engages with religion as a public and communal good and reconciles equally the diversity of perspectives which exist in a democracy. In Part V I discuss implications for how to reframe legal protection for the autonomy of religious communities in the US under the First Amendment with an emphasis on upholding the theological virtues of dignity, love, patience and kindness, and bearing in mind a pluralist approach. I conclude in Part VI that pluralism is the model which best conceptualises and facilitates the legal and social religious diversity of the US.

II. United States as Secular Separationist

Jonathan Fox argues that the US is a 'prime model' of secular separationism, where any government involvement in religion is a threat to religious freedom. The state should neither support nor hinder religion, but there is debate about to what extent government and religion should be functionally separated and what this actually means.[1] Bejan notes that 'separationism is the defining characteristic' of 'American secular liberalism'.[2] This 'secular separationist' model is implemented by the 'Establishment and the Free Exercise Clauses of the First Amendment'.[3] Zimmermann and Weinberger observe that the establishment clause concept of a 'wall of separation' undergirded this notion of a 'strict separation' of religion and government, where religion is privatised.[4] Fundamentally then, from the separationist perspective, the state should be secular in the sense that religion should not influence, support, or control public state power because religion is intrinsically private.[5]

---

[1] J Fox, *Thou Shalt Have No Other Gods Before Me: Why Governments Discriminate Against Religious Minorities* (Cambridge University Press, 2020) 25. I have explored the different nuances of 'secular' in multiple publications and do not repeat the analysis here. See eg A Deagon, *From Violence to Peace: Theology, Law and Community* (Hart Publishing, 2017); A Deagon, 'Secularism as a Religion: Questioning the Future of the Secular State' (2017) 8 *Western Australian Jurist* 31; A Deagon, 'Towards a Constitutional Definition of Religion: Challenges and Prospects' in P Babie, N Rochow and B Scharffs (eds), *Freedom of Religion or Belief: Creating the Constitutional Space for Fundamental Freedoms* (Edward Elgar, 2020). I adopt the standard use as specifically defined in this chapter.

[2] T Bejan, 'In Search of an Established Church' (2021) 26(2) *Roger Williams Law Review* 284, 287.

[3] G Halmai, 'Varieties of State-Church Relations and Religious Freedom through Three Case Studies' 2017(2) *Michigan State Law Review* 175, 180.

[4] See A Zimmermann and D Weinberger, 'Secularization by Law? The Establishment Clauses and Religion in the Public Square in Australia and the United States' (2012) 10 *International Journal of Constitutional Law* 208, 209.

[5] For a more detailed philosophical articulation of this perspective and a response, see A Deagon, 'Liberal Secularism and Religious Freedom in the Public Space: Reforming Political Discourse' (2018) 41(3) *Harvard Journal of Law and Public Policy* 901.

This kind of secularist separationism is expressed in the *Lemon* non-establishment test: 'First, the statute must have a secular legislative purpose; second, its principal or primary effect must be one that neither advances nor inhibits religion, finally, the statute must not foster an excessive government entanglement with religion'.[6] The test has been used to reach 'separationist' outcomes in a number of cases, including prohibiting equal government funding of private religious schools.[7] Application of this secularist test has had the practical effect of privatising religion protection under the First Amendment.[8] For example, Bradley has argued that the Supreme Court was committed to articulating and enforcing a 'normative scheme' which uses secularism to privatise religion, assuming that religious beliefs have no 'political relevance'.[9] Gedicks has also affirmed that 'The privileging of secular knowledge in public life as objective and the marginalizing of religious belief in private life as subjective has been a foundational premise of American jurisprudence under the Religion Clause of the First Amendment. Most of the Supreme Court's Religion Clause decisions reflect this elevation of the objective/secular over the subjective/religious'.[10]

Despite a common assumption that non-establishment is equivalent to secular separationism, the American non-establishment principle does not necessarily mean 'the state must refrain from regulating religion or that religion must be relegated to the private sphere'.[11] In this chapter I defend a pluralist approach which facilitates beneficial interactions between the state and religion in public contexts without undermining the non-establishment principle. However, a secularist approach does effectively dictate that religious communities, while having a limited level of private autonomy, are 'ultimately subject to the overarching values of the liberal state'.[12] This is a major weakness of separationism and can result in the imposition of secular values on religious communities.

---

[6] *Lemon v Kurtzman*, 403 U.S. 602, 612–13 (1971). See F Venter, 'The justiciability and adjudication of religious disputes' in R Ahdar (ed), *Research Handbook on Law and Religion* (Edward Elgar, 2018) 291.

[7] B Scharffs, 'Protecting Religious Freedom: Two Counterintuitve Dialectics in US Free Exercise Jurisprudence' in P Babie and N Rochow (eds), *Freedom of Religion under Bills of Rights* (University of Adelaide Press, 2012) 285, 294–95.

[8] See RS Myers, 'The Supreme Court and the Privatization of Religion' (1991) 41 *Catholic University Law Review* 19.

[9] GV Bradley, 'Dogmatomachy: A "Privatization" Theory of the Religion Clause Cases' (1986) 30 *St Louis University Law Journal* 275, 276–77. More recently, Bradley has continued to affirm that the public and private realms in the US are converging toward the privatization of religion. See G Bradley, 'Emerging Challenges to Religious Freedom in America and Other English-Speaking Countries' in AD Hertzke (ed), *The Future of Religious Freedom: Global Challenges* (Oxford University Press, 2013) 216.

[10] FM Gedicks, 'Public Life and Hostility to Religion' (1992) 78 *Virginia Law Review* 671, 681–82.

[11] J Cohen, 'Rethinking Political Secularism' in J Cohen and C Laborde (eds), *Religion, Secularism, and Constitutional Democracy* (Columbia University Press, 2016) 113, 115.

[12] J Neo, 'Regulation of Religious Communities in a Multicultural Polity' in R Ahdar (ed), *Research Handbook on Law and Religion* (Edward Elgar, 2018) 193.

III. Evaluation of Secular Separationism in the US

The idea of 'church-state separation and the derivative commitment to freedom of conscience' had its genesis in a 'Christian worldview' where persons owed allegiance to both the state and God, but ultimately to God as the transcendent jurisdiction; in a 'secular framework', the 'inherited commitments of church-state separation and to free exercise of religion lose their grounding'.[13] This is evident through the wall of separation metaphor employed in the *Lemon* test, which only protects government action not influenced or motivated by religious considerations, excluding the possibility of the transcendent. 'From this position, it is not a far leap to the concept that religion is, in fact, better when it is kept private'.[14] However, as Zimmermann and Weinberger observe:

> The privatization of religion … has troubling implications for society. The … principle that leads to the privatization of religion is only workable if religion is an isolated component of life. It is not. Religion has broad, holistic implications for the lives of its adherents, as a world and life view that shapes the way one thinks and acts … It is thus impossible to truly implement a religion-neutral public square. To the contrary, the pursuit of such a religion-free zone is, in fact, highly intolerant. The strong form of secularism … constitutes a radical attempt to redefine what it means to live in a democratic society.[15]

Privatising religion entails the 'suffocation' of religious beliefs by assigning them zero political relevance.[16] This ignorance or rejection of the 'value of religious experience, the importance of faith to identity formation, the principle of religious freedom, or anything else that captures the unique value of religion within the context of clashes between religion and equality' is characteristic of secularist approaches which are ultimately unfriendly to religion.[17] In this sense, secular separationism damages peaceful coexistence in accordance with the theological virtues by failing to exercise patience, kindness and love towards religion, undermining the autonomy of religious communities and their contribution to the good of neighbour. In particular, religious institutions are vital because they contribute to the vibrant interrelationships of civil society which form a bastion against excessive state enforcement hostile to isolated individuals. The paradox of privileging individual liberty and equality is state-enforced equality actually undermines the freedom of individuals and consequently their equality. This is illustrated in situations where religious groups are compelled to accept members who do not adhere to the ethos of the organisation. Application of a rule against

---

[13] SD Smith, 'Discourse in the Dusk: The Twilight of Religious Freedom?' (2009) 122 *Harvard Law Review* 1869, 1887.

[14] Zimmermann and Weinberger (n 4) 236.

[15] ibid 238.

[16] Bradley, 'Dogmatomachy' (n 9) 276–77.

[17] M Helfand, 'Reasoning Through Clashes Between Religion and Equality: Case Law, Skeptics and Social Coherence' (2018) 33 *Constitutional Commentary* 27, 34.

religious discrimination to a religious group is fundamentally confused because maintenance of standards of belief is essential to the meaningful existence of a religious organisation.[18] 'The bottom line is that it is impossible to create a religiously neutral public square unless religion is defined in such a way as to exclude certain groups'.[19]

More significantly, as Ledewitz argues, the First Amendment and particularly the free exercise clause demonstrates that 'America is not neutral towards religion', 'but favours it'; it takes a position of 'pro-religious practice' and advocates the need for a 'high public regard of religion'.[20] Thus the appellation of the US as a 'secular' state 'must be understood in a very restricted sense'.[21] Institutional separation, of course, safeguards religious and political freedom. However, as Garnett points out, 'the maintenance of an appropriately secular government does not require the blanket exclusion of churches from generally available (and secular) public benefits or rule out cooperation between governments and religious institutions in advancing the common (and secular) good'.[22] Indeed, Ledewitz objects to categorising the US as a 'secular democracy' because it 'does not seem an apt description of the American constitutional system' which 'reserves a place for God in American public life' and arranges public life to allow 'religious denominations to create their own institutional structures'.[23] America has consequently 'never been a genuinely secular democracy' and 'religion is a necessary aspect of liberal constitutionalism in America' because it is an essential 'source of meaning to build a sustainable public life'.[24] As I indicate below, the US should be considered secular only in the sense that there is an institutional separation of church and state. Religion is very much part of the public sphere and there is, and should be, beneficial interactions between religion and government. And this restricted sense of secular is more accurately described as accommodationist or pluralist.

Therefore, the establishment clause 'was not the statement of a principle of secularism, separation, disestablishment, or anything else' – it was simply the rejection of a national church.[25] In any case, accommodation is distinct from the advance of religion and is to be 'encouraged' under pluralist establishment doctrine.[26] 'The fact that the First Amendment explicitly singles out religion as a special legal category suggests that differential treatment does not in itself violate constitutional equality requirements'.[27] In a free exercise context discussing the

---

[18] R Trigg, *Equality, Freedom and Religion* (Oxford University Press, 2012) 51–52.
[19] Zimmermann and Weinberger (n 4) 240.
[20] B Ledewitz, 'Is Religion a Non-Negotiable Aspect of Liberal Constitutionalism?' 2017(2) *Michigan State Law Review* 209, 220–22.
[21] ibid 223.
[22] R Garnett and J Blais, 'Religious Freedom and Recycled Tires: The Meaning and Implications of Trinity Lutheran' (2016) *Cato Supreme Court Review* 105, 122.
[23] Ledewitz (n 20) 225–27.
[24] ibid 230, 251–52.
[25] D Drakeman, *Church, State and Original Intent* (Cambridge University Press, 2010) 330.
[26] S Smith, *Pagans and Christians in the City* (Eerdmans, 2018) 319.
[27] ibid 321.

Smith decision, Steven Smith points out that granting accommodations through religious exemptions does not mean a person is 'a law unto himself'; rather they are subject to a specific higher authority (and it is not for the secular court to question a religion or individual's interpretation of that authority) – and, furthermore, if an accommodation is granted under the *law* of the First Amendment, a person is not a law unto themselves by definition.[28] Any objection to this implicitly rejects the possibility of a transcendent authority because the state cannot countenance submission to an authority in conflict with its own. Hence, the 'law unto themselves' argument which formed the foundation for *Smith* is ultimately based in a secularist approach which rejects the possibility of a transcendent authority.[29] Concordantly, *Smith* also imposes a 'formal and defective' secularist distinction between religious belief and conduct motivated by that belief, protecting the former but not the latter. This ignores the fact that religious believers must necessarily implement their beliefs 'in the charitable works of their religious organisations, in their daily lives, and in their professions and occupations.[30]

DeLoach crystallises these thoughts in his incisive critique of secularism, which he describes as 'the rigid separation and strictly neutral relationship of state and religion', which 'in reality aims to neutralize religion' and 'shield citizens from competing religious values.[31] It entails treating 'religion to be a personal affair, distinct and separate from public affairs' and driving 'religion out of the sphere reserved for politics in the city: that is to say, the public sphere.[32] The call for neutrality (which entails the marginalisation of religion) has been renewed in concert with an equality paradigm which seeks to limit perceived discrimination by religion. The same secularist ideology which espouses the privatisation of religion effectively pursues radically uniform equality by limiting the ability of religion to 'discriminate.[33] DeLoach concludes by rejecting secularism and advocating a pluralist 'religious freedom' approach:

> Ideological secularism tends to prioritize repressing religious belief and practice, rather than protecting freedom for a plurality of beliefs. It is not meant to keep worshipers from discriminating; it is meant to keep worshipers from worshiping … At bottom, the difference between religious freedom and secularism is that religious freedom is meant primarily to protect religion, whereas secularism is meant primarily to protect the state. Religious freedom consists of several interdependent principles meant to help religion, society, and individuals flourish. It recognizes the good of religion and values

---

[28] ibid 323–25.

[29] ibid 325–27.

[30] D Laycock, 'Liberty and Justice for All' in WN Eskridge, Jr and R Fretwell Wilson (eds), *Religious Freedom, LGBT Rights, and the Prospects for Common Ground* (Cambridge University Press, 2018) 27; Scharffs (n 7) 310–11.

[31] A DeLoach, 'What's the Use of Religious Freedom?' (2020) 10(2) *Journal of Christian Legal Thought* 1, 3–4.

[32] ibid.

[33] ibid 6, 8.

the freedom to believe (or disbelieve) and to exercise that belief in public. Secularism prioritizes a civil religion of the State and values superficial concord. To achieve national cohesion, therefore, secularism must quarantine religion.[34]

Ahdar and Leigh arrive at a similar position in their analysis of secular states. A secular state has a separation between religion and government, entailing (but not necessarily equivalent to) a structural separation of church and state. Though this structural or institutional separation is in principle achievable, a complete substantive separation between religion and government is not.[35] Nevertheless, some secular states contend for an ideological separation which views religion as a private matter that is irrelevant and inappropriate for the public sphere, politics and policy.[36] The aim of secularism is often to preserve neutrality between religion and non-religion, but in practice this can 'unerringly and alarmingly slide into a hostile secularism' which ideologically marginalises religion and establishes a polity of unbelief.[37] Ultimately, secularism is not neutral, for it takes a particular position on religion (negative or at least indifferent) in the public sphere on the basis of ideological assumptions about the nature of religion and politics.[38] Secularism entails that God is irrelevant and inappropriate for the political sphere, and in that sense 'is tantamount to practical atheism'.[39] 'Separationism interprets state neutrality to mean that religion and state are structurally separate and … all religious influence is to be expunged from public life. Religion is to be privatised'.[40] Secularism consequently carries certain dangers if it manifests in its ideological form, which adopts the philosophy of separation, and therefore excludes religion and religious influences from politics and public life:

> Whilst it is conceivable that secularism can take benign, even-handed forms which welcome religious contributions to the public sphere, the more prevalent tendency, in practice, is for secularism to be hostile to religion. Secularism seldom remains for long as a straightforward state refusal to align itself with, or establish, a particular faith: rather, experience suggests it inexorably develops a commitment to actively pursue a policy of established unbelief. A thoroughgoing privatisation of religion by the state, compounded by official endorsement of secular beliefs, denies many faiths the public witness they desire, and indeed are obliged, to make'.[41]

As such the 'secularist philosophy' of separationism 'can in practice produce a climate of hostility to religion and its free exercise'.[42] This undermines the peaceful coexistence of difference by excluding religion, and fails to adhere to the

---

[34] ibid 8.
[35] R Ahdar and I Leigh, *Religious Freedom in the Liberal State,* 2nd edn (Oxford University Press, 2013) 92.
[36] ibid 94.
[37] ibid 95–96.
[38] ibid 98–99.
[39] ibid 99.
[40] ibid 109.
[41] ibid 122.
[42] ibid 124.

theological virtues of loving neighbour as self by allowing religious citizens to fully participate in society.

Despite the clear weaknesses of secularist separationism, Chermerinsky continues to argue for separation 'to the greatest extent possible'.[43] Somewhat ominously, he does not elaborate on the question of 'possible for what?' Later, he claims that 'separation is not hostile to religion' while simultaneously assuming a 'religious presence in government' is not 'permissible' and articulating his interpretation of the First Amendment as 'requiring separation of church and state', which for him means 'excluding religion' and 'enforcing the view that the place of religion should be in the private realm'.[44] However, as I have explained above and demonstrated elsewhere, this strict separationist approach, at least in its effect if not in its exclusionary and marginalising terms, discriminates against and is hostile to religion.[45] Strict secular separation only produces a 'less turbulent political system' (so claimed by Chermerinsky) by oppressing, coercing, and marginalising religion.[46] It is similarly arguable that authoritarian regimes have less turbulent political systems by simply excluding alternatives by force, but this is not a persuasive reason to adopt them.

Chermerinsky contends separation is necessary to prevent coercion, to prevent people of non-mainstream beliefs from feeling like or being treated as outsiders, that it is wrong to tax people to support religions they do not believe, and that separation best protects religion.[47] However, as I have already intimated and will articulate in more detail below, not only is pluralism more effective at fulfilling these laudable aims, strict separationism actually undercuts them. Pluralism prevents coercion by providing freedom for religious and non-religious communities to operate; separationism coerces non-religion in the public and political sphere. Pluralism ensures all beliefs are respected and encouraged in political discourse; secularism makes religious believers feel like outsiders and enforces their expression in only a private context. Pluralism facilitates the financial support of diversity as part of living in a democracy with different perspectives; separationism compels financial support of non-religion. Finally, separationism is not friendly to religion; pluralism encourages the flourishing of religion.

Alternatively, it is sometimes argued that the US should be neutral, which means that the state should be religion-blind in the sense that religion is to be treated no differently than anything else, and religious citizens should be treated no differently to non-religious citizens.[48] However, such an approach has a practically secularising effect by ignoring the unique claims of religious communities. 'Such

---

[43] E Chermerinsky, 'No, It is Not a Christian Nation, and It Never Has Been and Should Not Be One' (2021) 26(2) *Roger Williams Law Review* 404, 414. See generally E Chermerinsky and H Gillman, *The Religion Clauses: The Case for Separating Church and State* (Oxford University Press, 2020).

[44] Chermerinsky (n 43) 417.

[45] See eg Deagon, 'Liberal Secularism' (n 5).

[46] Chermerinsky (n 43) 417; *cf* Deagon, 'Liberal Secularism' (n 5).

[47] Chermerinsky (n 43) 414–17.

[48] See eg C Eisgruber and L Sager, *Religious Freedom and the Constitution* (Harvard University Press, 2007) 52.

a religion-blind approach imposes heavy costs upon believers in certain circumstances where their faith requires conduct which the general law proscribes', as in the case of *Smith* where religious communities cannot be exempt from neutral laws of general applicability, despite the unique burden on certain believers imposed by such laws.[49] This problem is exacerbated by the fact that there are often no secular analogues to religious conduct, which can undermine the perceived validity and weight of the impugned religious conduct.[50] In this sense 'formal' neutrality is not too different in effect from a secular state and is equally unable to preserve peaceful coexistence in accordance with the theological virtues. It can descend into secularism by ignoring or downplaying genuine and significant religious claims in the guise of being religion-blind. Though neutral laws do not specifically target religion, they have the effect of inhibiting religious freedom.

Conversely, a substantive neutrality which essentially prevents government interference with religion, sometimes by actively accommodating and providing exemptions, is an approach which better preserves peaceful coexistence by taking into account religious considerations in accordance with the theological virtues. Substantive neutrality explicitly considers religious perspectives and aims to leave religion as far as possible to co-exist, and may require government support to ensure even-handedness.[51] 'So, for example, exemptions from laws of general application may be required for affected believers. This is not so much special treatment but more a recognition that limited corrective action may be required to ensure that existing government policies that unwittingly discourage religious practice are ameliorated'.[52] This is pluralism in effect and, with Ahdar and Leigh, I support a 'baseline that favours maximum religious choice and religious practice'.[53] The approach of pluralism therefore adopts and augments these positive aspects of substantive neutrality, facilitating the flourishing of religion (and non-religion) and beneficial interaction between state and religion (or non-religion).

IV. Proposing an Alternative: Pluralism

A. Pluralism and Constitutional Consistency

As alluded to above and in previous chapters, pluralism is 'compatible with religious freedom', for it recognises 'the public dimension of religion while refuting the liberal claim that privatisation is neutral', and accepts that 'religious institutions have a role to play in social programmes'.[54] Therefore, pluralism 'scores highly'

---

[49] Ahdar and Leigh (n 35) 113–14.
[50] ibid.
[51] ibid 115–19.
[52] ibid 123–24.
[53] ibid 124.
[54] ibid 122.

with respect to upholding the autonomy of religious communities because it recognises that 'interactions and cooperation between government and religious communities is useful'.[55] Though it might be said that the US was founded as a 'Christian' nation, this was not in the formal sense of Anglicanism as in the established religion of England, but in the more cultural sense that Christian assumptions were pervasive in public and political discourse.[56] Constitutionally, the framers did not see the document as endorsing Christianity. Rather, it is a framework for governance which facilitates the pursuit of whatever policies and principles the people may embrace. The First Amendment 'might reflect Christian or biblical assumptions' but the constitutional framework is 'compatible' with any religion or demographic and in this sense may be described as truly 'pluralist'.[57] Chermerinsky in particular persuasively argues that America is not a Christian nation as a matter of law through demonstrating that American establishment means government cannot prefer one religion over another.[58] This means mild establishment is not a plausible model for religion-state relations in the US, which is why I have focused on pluralism and secularism. However, for the reasons articulated in the previous part, secularism should be rejected because it does not uphold peaceful coexistence. In this section, I explain why pluralism should be preferred as a framework for understanding the US First Amendment; in the subsequent section, I explain why pluralism more effectively preserves the peaceful coexistence of difference.

As Steven Smith observes:

> The First Amendment does not actually *say* (either explicitly or by persuasive implication) that government must be 'secular' ... the Americans who drafted and enacted that amendment almost certainly did not understand it to have any such implication. Moreover, the modern secularist conception of the community goes strongly against the grain of a great deal in [US] political tradition.[59]

Green is also clear that the Supreme Court has maintained 'that the paradigm of pluralism more accurately reflected the correct understanding of church-state relations ... That conscious use of terminology supported the idea of religious pluralism as an alternative paradigm to secularism ... The implication was that the government should not impose a regime of secularism, but one ... that fostered religious pluralism' as demonstrated by granting exemptions to religious communities.[60]

---

[55] ibid 124.

[56] Smith, *Pagans and Christians* (n 26) 260–62.

[57] ibid 266–67, 295–97.

[58] Chermerinsky (n 43); See also Chermerinsky and Gillman (n 43).

[59] Smith, *Pagans and Christians* (n 26) 274–75; see also S Smith, *The Rise and Decline of American Religious Freedom* (Harvard University Press, 2014).

[60] S Green, 'The Legal Ramifications of Christian Nationalism' (2021) 26(2) *Roger Williams Law Review* 430, 469–71. Berlinerblau agrees US separationist secularism is not in the Constitution and the US is more accommodationist (pluralist) than secularist: see J Berlinerblau, *Secularism: The Basics* (Routledge, 2022).

Those who are opposed to robust institutional autonomy and exemptions for religious vendors have an anaemic (secular) conception of religious freedom which seeks to exclude transcendent religion from the public square.[61] In contrast, the 'accommodationist' (or what I call pluralist) strategy involves the government respecting 'people's religious commitments', and government 'should make an affirmative effort to avoid burdening or interfering with these commitments'; 'government should affirmatively try to leave space for people to live in accordance with their diverse understandings of the sacred'.[62] 'So if a particular law would require a person or group to violate a sincerely held religious commitment, then a just and humane government will, if reasonably possible, find ways to excuse compliance by those people whose religion would be burdened'.[63] The accommodationist position has been the typical American approach to religious diversity and recognises 'religion as something valuable that government should affirmatively respect and, if reasonably possible, look for ways to avoid interfering with it'.[64] Steven Smith explains that accommodationism is consequently an approach with a discernibly 'Christian or transcendently religious character' both historically and substantively because it is 'oriented toward recognition of a transcendent authority'.[65] Historically, accommodation has its roots in the Christian idea of dual jurisdictions, that deference to 'God' or 'conscience' must take precedence over the separate sphere of government.[66] Substantively, accommodation recognises that we have obligations to a temporal authority (the state) and a higher eternal authority (God); where these obligations conflict a person must be allowed obedience to the higher authority.[67]

As an example of the anaemic view, Schragger and Schwartzman view such accommodations as religious preferentialism and therefore anti-liberal. Unfortunately, the pejorative epithet of 'anti-liberalism' creates the mistaken impression that critics of secular liberalism are categorically anti-liberal.[68] In actual fact, for example, the kind of political community I advocate in this book and other work is supportive of liberal virtues such as freedom, equality and tolerance – while placing these in a religious tradition which brings them to a fulfilment that a secular approach can never provide.[69] To the extent Schragger and Schwartzman reject the possibility that a political community infused with religion in this way is 'liberal', they have unwittingly adopted the idiosyncratic

---

[61] Smith, *Pagans and Christians* (n 26) 303.
[62] ibid 304–05.
[63] ibid 305.
[64] ibid 306–08.
[65] ibid 310.
[66] ibid 310–13; Smith, *Rise and Decline* (n 59) 17–43.
[67] Smith, *Pagans and Christians* (n 26) 313–15.
[68] R Schragger and M Schwartzman, 'Religious Antiliberalism and the First Amendment' (2020) 104 *Minnesota Law Review* 1341.
[69] See my discussion in the Introduction, and in particular see A Deagon, 'Reconciling John Milbank and Religious Freedom: "Liberalism" through Love' (2019) 34(2) *Journal of Law and Religion* 183.

assumption that liberalism is secular by definition.[70] Indeed, Schragger and Schwartzman characterise liberalism as 'private', 'the domain of individual conscience', in contrast to secular law as 'public'.[71] This is essentially secular liberalism or secularism. They support a secularist separation of 'state and religion' which they uncritically equate to 'the separation of church and state'.[72] They reject accommodation of religion expressed through recent First Amendment cases like *Hosanna-Tabor* and *Trinity Lutheran* as 'religious preferentialism' and anti-liberal, instead advocating the secularist *Smith* approach to free exercise and a separationist approach to establishment.[73]

However, as Brownstein points out, 'a broad range of religion-state doctrinal choices are consistent with liberal constitutionalism'.[74] Even Schragger and Schwartzman similarly admit that 'a liberal political order is compatible with a range of permissible church-state relations, including regimes that provide legal exemptions for conscientious objectors and funding on equal terms for religious groups'.[75] This implies a pluralist framework which accepts the accommodationist strategy of religious exemptions and equal funding is not anti-liberal, even under their approach which is hostile to religion. They do proceed to imply pluralism may be responsible for 'the aggressive assertion of Christian nationalism in the United States', and thereby insinuate pluralism should be rejected in favour of secular separationism.[76] I disagree for the reasons that I outline in this chapter: secular separationism has the effect of discriminating against religion and undermines social peace, and is a questionable interpretation of the First Amendment. Conversely, pluralism accommodates religion (and non-religion), facilitating social peace, and is a better interpretation of First Amendment jurisprudence. Steven Smith confirms with respect to Christianity specifically:

> Christianity has proven to be compatible with – and at the same time in tension with – a whole variety of political and cultural regimes … The common feature has been that Christian societies have embraced as an aspiration and critical standard a transcendent ideal … A central feature of any contemporary Christian society under conditions of modern pluralism is that it is unlikely to sponsor any official account of what transcendence is and requires – any official orthodoxy. The modern Christian society would be open to transcendence, and it would attempt to accommodate its citizens in their efforts to live in accordance with their understandings of transcendence.[77]

As such, government support of religion in general does not undermine religious liberty or threaten equality. Political life entails exposure to perspectives one may

---

[70] See eg Schragger and Schwartzman (n 68) 1350–55.

[71] ibid 1350.

[72] ibid 1351.

[73] ibid 1381–1410.

[74] A Brownstein, 'The Multiple Sources and Dimensions of Religion-State Frameworks in Liberal Constitutions' 2017(2) *Michigan State Law Review* 163, 167.

[75] Schragger and Schwartzman (n 68) 1345–46.

[76] ibid 1412.

[77] Smith, *Pagans and Christians* (n 26) 378.

not share, and the fact one may be in a minority is a simple function of democratic politics in action. One still retains the same fundamental rights and citizenship status as someone in the majority, all else being equal.[78]

In addition, the US has a significant heritage of public religion, and the First Amendment does not repudiate this.[79] The establishment clause was simply a limit on the federal government's power to coerce religion by establishing a national religion or disestablishing the religion a state had adopted.[80] It was primarily concerned with preserving 'the freedom, or autonomy, of … churches'.[81] It was not concerned with separating religion from government or preventing the public expression of religion, and there was no intention to 'undermine the religious, and specifically Christian, heritage of' the US.[82] The 'supreme irony' of arguing for secular separationism is 'the clause so often viewed as separating religion from civil government was itself a consequence of religion's influence on government'; the First Amendment is 'theistic' in its heritage and reflects a 'theological conception of society'.[83] A pluralist or accommodationist approach which encourages beneficial interaction and cooperation between religion and government is therefore appropriate.

In regard to the establishment clause specifically, Adside argues that it only forbids coercion and actually facilitates cooperation between church and state. Adside notes that it seems unlikely the constitutional framers would freely and frequently invoke the presence of God and call for national days of prayer and thanksgiving while simultaneously designing a clause to prohibit such conduct. The early American government 'frequently engaged with religious institutions' and 'Jefferson's references to a wall of separation referred to preventing coercion, not permitting beneficial interaction. The founders never believed and never practiced a strict secularist separation'.[84] The First Amendment 'did not forbid cooperation between church and state' and the state 'may favour or accommodate religious practice' without coercion, such as through public prayer, references to Deity, and acknowledgement of religious holidays.[85] For these reasons, Adside contends, the *Lemon* test should be abandoned. 'It prevents the constitutional coexistence between free speech and religious liberty' and 'insulates religious minorities from the marketplace of ideas'.[86] Rather, a 'direct coercion' test should be implemented, which provides that 'the government cannot implement or mandate a religion,

---

[78] ibid 272–73.

[79] Zimmermann and Weinberger (n 4) 210–11, 217–18.

[80] ibid 222, 226.

[81] Scharffs (n 7) 290–91.

[82] Zimmermann and Weinberger (n 4) 228.

[83] ibid 232–33.

[84] C Adside, 'The Establishment Clause Forbids Coercion, Not Cooperation, between Church and State: How the Direct Coercion Test Should Replace the Lemon Test' (2020) 95 *North Dakota Law Review* 533, 559, 560–62.

[85] ibid 533, 536.

[86] ibid 538.

nor can it coerce its citizens into either supporting or participating in a faith. This impermissible coercion requires "religious orthodoxy [or] financial support by force of law and threat of penalty".[87] The direct coercion test properly and clearly maintains the balance between establishment, free exercise and free speech, and 'offers clear, repeatable answers to controversies in this area'.[88] The Supreme Court 'has avoided an absolute or literal separation between Church and State' because it simply does not reflect America's constitution and cultural history; 'the reality in our country [is] that there is no strict wall between Church and State'.[89]

Furthermore, the implementation of accommodationist religious exemptions as a reflection of pluralism are entirely consistent with the establishment clause. As Garry notes, the establishment clause simply 'allows government accommodation and interaction with religion as long as that interaction does not discriminate between religions ... government can accommodate religion's role and presence in society'.[90] Such accommodation has provided greater flexibility for court decisions to allow equal funding and access to religious communities providing public services, enabling a de facto shift in the *Lemon* test.[91] In this way, accommodation and pluralism is about equality as well, enabling religious communities to freely exist equally alongside other kinds of communities, reconciling freedom and equality. So Esbeck observes that 'the establishment clause is not violated' when 'such accommodations ... have as their purpose to ameliorate hardships borne by religious minorities and other dissenters who find themselves out of step with the prevailing social or legal culture. Statutory religious exemptions are commonplace in this nation where there is a long and venerable tradition of religious tolerance toward our neighbours, as well as those who have made their way to America to escape persecution'.[92] Where provisions remove 'government imposed burdens on religious exercise' this is 'a permissible accommodation of religion', and thus 'a narrow legislatively crafted religious exemption can withstand Establishment Clause scrutiny'.[93] This is essential as a 'safeguard to protect religious minorities'.[94] It is therefore worth noting that religious exemptions provided as part of a pluralist framework are not only consistent with the First Amendment, but also effectively preserve the peaceful coexistence of different minority perspectives.

In regard to the free exercise clause, by stating in *Trinity Lutheran* that the denial of generally available benefits to religious entities on the basis of their

---

[87] ibid 535–36. See *Lee v Weisman*, 505 U.S. 577, 587, 640 (1992).

[88] Adside (n 84) 540, 556–57, 563–64.

[89] ibid 548.

[90] P Garry, 'Establishment Clause Jurisprudence Still Groping for Clarity: Articulating a New Constitutional Model' (2020) 12(2) *Northeastern University Law Review* 660, 698.

[91] Scharffs (n 7) 296–97.

[92] C Esbeck, 'Do Discretionary Religious Exemptions Violate the Establishment Clause' (2017) 106(4) *Kentucky Law Journal* 603, 604.

[93] Scharffs (n 7) 317.

[94] Esbeck, 'Religious Exemptions' (n 92) 633.

religious character violates the free exercise clause, the Supreme Court has 'eroded the liberal strict separation of church and state … and replaced it with greater tolerance for church-state cooperation'.[95] This was a movement from the secularist 'wall of separation' doctrine to a more accommodationist and pluralist 'equal treatment' doctrine.[96] Similarly, *Hosanna-Tabor* demonstrates pluralist assumptions that are contrary to the secular separationist assumptions in *Smith* in two senses. First, the Court considered the internal actions of churches to be not merely acts, but decisions essential to the faith and mission of the church, and thus part of free exercise and beyond challenge by 'neutral laws' such as employment discrimination. Second, in doing so, the Court engaged deeply with the theological implications of church governance, resulting in a broad interpretation of actions which are essential to the free exercise of religion for religious institutions.[97] McConnell suggests this indicates a shift in free exercise jurisprudence from a focus on individual believers to a focus on the autonomy of organized religious institutions. Rather than a restrictive secularist (private) view of religion where it 'is essentially a matter between individuals and their God', *Hosanna-Tabor* endorsed 'the idea that religious exercise must be rooted in the teachings of a faith community'.[98] It is a move which adopts a broad community-focused and associational view of religion which is more characteristic of religion itself, accepting the substantive theological view that it is for the religion, and not the state, to determine who is a minister and the scope of that role.[99] Hence, the most recent decision on the ministerial exception affirmed the doctrine and clarified that the determination of a 'minister' must be based on an evaluation of the religious function the position serves in the organisation, ie a question of fact rather than the application of strict rules.[100] As a result of this free exercise jurisprudence endorsing a pluralist framework, the Court was therefore prepared to support more robust protections for the autonomy of religious communities.

Steven Green provides further support for the view that pluralism is a more plausible framework for the First Amendment than secularism. The Supreme Court has shifted away from the separation paradigm, and scholars have argued that the 'principle is ahistorical, anti-Catholic in origin, or simply hostile to

---

[95] A Carmella, 'Progressive Religion and Free Exercise Exemptions' (2020) 68 *Kansas Law Review* 535, 565–66.

[96] R Garnett and J Blais, 'Religious Freedom and Recycled Tires: The Meaning and Implications of *Trinity Lutheran*' (2016) *Cato Supreme Court Review* 105, 107.

[97] See I Huyett, 'How to Overturn Employment Division v. Smith: A Historical Approach' (2020) 32 *Regent University Law Review* 295, 332–33, 340; M McConnell, 'Reflections on *Hosanna-Tabor*' (2012) 35 *Harvard Journal of Law and Public Policy* 821, 834; H Alvare, 'Beyond Moralism: A Critique and a Proposal for Catholic Institutional Religious Freedom' (2019) 19(1) *Connecticut Public Interest Law Journal* 149, 192. See also generally D Laycock, 'Hosanna-Tabor and the Ministerial Exception' (2012) 35 *Harvard Journal of Law and Public Policy* 839.

[98] McConnell, 'Reflections' (n 97) 836–37.

[99] See Alvare, 'Beyond Moralism' (n 97).

[100] *Our Lady of Guadalupe School v Agnes Morrissey-Berru*, 140 S. Ct. 2049 (2020).

religion.[101] Disestablishment was designed to ensure 'religious peace and pluralism'.[102] This has been demonstrated recently by cases such as *Trinity Lutheran*, where the adoption of a pluralist model resulted in the non-discriminatory government funding of religious communities. Hence, 'separationism is no longer necessary for the correct ordering of church-state relations'.[103] A paradigm of separation simply does not reflect the reality of equal funding for religious and secular entities and cooperative social welfare ventures between government and religious communities. This is not coercing support for religion in a First Amendment sense because 'taxpayers today are compelled to support a host of policies to which they hold ideological disagreements'.[104] This is simply pluralism in action, where a state supports and engages with a variety of diverse perspectives to achieve social and public good. Fundamentally then, the First Amendment protects the autonomy of religious communities in a pluralist framework.

In his extended essay on church autonomy, Esbeck observes that the Supreme Court's doctrine is broad and deep in its protections for religious communities, including in the formation and interpretation of religious doctrine, the appointment and removal of leaders and members (and in the development and application of regulative standards of belief and conduct in this respect), and in public communication and interaction with outsiders. The First Amendment grants 'freedom' for religious communities, an 'independence from secular control or manipulation' which is characteristic of pluralism rather than secularism.[105] Hence, Esbeck argues that in relation to the ministerial exception cases of *Hosanna-Tabor* and *Our Lady of Guadalupe*, the claim that the employees were not dismissed for religious reasons is irrelevant. 'The purpose of church autonomy is to set aside … internal governance and keep [it] autonomous from civil government'.[106] In chapter two I took a different view, arguing that this position is too broad. The ministerial exception ought only to apply for employer conduct that occurs for religious reasons. Regardless, here Esbeck probably draws too stark a distinction between religious and secular reasons. In both cases the critical reasons for dismissal were religious – launching a suit in contradiction of 1 Corinthians in the former, and failure to be certified in the provision of catechism in the latter. In *Our Lady*, the stated reasons for dismissal of the classroom teachers in Catholic schools (who were categorised as ministers) were poor performance and not acquiring new skills, or what might be characterised as 'secular' reasons.[107] But this is actually understated by the schools, because the

---

[101] S Green, 'The "Irrelevance" of Church-State Separation in the Twenty-First Century' (2019) 69(1) *Syracuse Law Review* 27, 29.

[102] ibid 40.

[103] ibid 29–31, 62.

[104] ibid 66–67.

[105] CH Esbeck, 'An Extended Essay on Church Autonomy' (2021) 22 *Federalist Society Review* 244, 247.

[106] ibid 251.

[107] ibid 253.

relevant performance and skill requirements were obtaining catechism certifi-
cates to more effectively teach the faith. In other words, the dismissals were for
a failure to meet the religious requirements of the schools. Hence, my slightly
narrower ministerial exception still provides a broad protection with respect
to Esbeck's identified areas of autonomy if employer conduct occurs for genuinely religious reasons, while simultaneously preserving equality by removing
protection if the claimed religious reasons are not actually determinative for the
employer conduct.

So Esbeck concludes that the 'separation' envisioned by the establishment
clause is merely a separation of institutions for pluralist purposes:

> The separation should not be exaggerated. This is a separation of the institutions of
> religion from the institutions of the republic. While the institutions of church and
> government can be separated, religion and politics cannot. Such a disjunction would rob
> believers and the organizations they form of the right enjoyed by all others. Churches
> and other houses of worship appropriately speak to how their teachings bear on social
> and political issues, all consistent with their right to freedom of speech.[108]

Adopting the coercion test advocated by Adside would then concordantly allow
more explicit freedom for government to 'support or accommodate religion'.[109]
The direct coercion test is more consistent with the original purpose of the First
Amendment, which is to avoid religious persecution through government power
and the imposition of religion on dissenting groups.[110] It appropriately 'permits
ample space for the government to interact with institutions of faith and thus
fosters a hospitable environment for religious exercise'.[111]

The autonomy of religious communities therefore protects religious entities as
'ontological beings' which 'exist in their own right' under the First Amendment;
indeed, they 'preexisted the state' and 'transcend the state'.[112] So Zimmermann and
Weinberger conclude that it is 'erroneous' to assert that the First Amendment was
'aimed at ensuring a secular public square. Both the context behind the drafting of
the clauses, and the Christian roots of the concept of a separation of church and
state, combine to negate [that] proposition'.[113] Viewing the establishment clause as
preventing coercion 'strikes the balance' by forbidding government interference in
religion while also allowing religion to freely flourish under the free exercise clause

---

[108] ibid 268.
[109] Adside (n 84) 554.
[110] ibid 558–59. In personal correspondence, Gerard V Bradley suggests that actual coercion is not
an essential aspect of establishment because a legal arrangement which privileges a particular religion
may not directly coerce belief or financial support, but would still be establishment. However, this is to
assume American establishment merely entails legal privilege of religion by definition, and in that sense
is to beg the question. Here I argue, following Adside, that a coercion test is historically more consistent with the purpose of the First Amendment, clarifies establishment doctrine, and more effectively
facilitates a pluralist approach to the autonomy of religious communities.
[111] ibid 563–64. *cf* J Ragosta, 'A Wall Between a Secular Government and a Religious People' (2021)
26(2) *Roger Williams University Law Review* 545.
[112] Esbeck, 'Church Autonomy' (n 105) 272.
[113] Zimmermann and Weinberger (n 4) 241.

through 'debate and compromise'.[114] Adside poignantly references the theological virtues in articulating this balance: 'To borrow from one religious tradition, you have heard it said that the two greatest commandments are to love God and to love one's neighbor. Our Constitution protects that divine law by making sure that following the former never means breaking the latter'.[115] A pluralist approach is therefore not only entirely consistent with the First Amendment, it is the most plausible framework for the First Amendment because it facilitates religious freedom and diversity, and beneficial interaction between the state and religion, while preventing the state from coercing religion. It thus also most effectively preserves peaceful coexistence of difference in accordance with the theological virtues because it supports the law of love: freedom to love God, and dignity and compassion to love neighbour.

B. Pluralism and Peaceful Coexistence

Chai Feldblum, a noted advocate for LGBT rights, acknowledges the link between pluralism and religious freedom and emphasises the importance of protecting both. She suggests productive discussions that are respectful and genuinely consider both sides.[116] With regard to religious freedom, she concedes that protecting pluralism entails robustly protecting the autonomy of religious communities:

> It ... means protecting their ability to constitute religious associations through which they can practice their religious beliefs and can transmit their beliefs to the next generation ... Safeguarding religious pluralism means safeguarding the ability of religious people to gather in protected associations and communities ... A commitment to religious pluralism must include a commitment to allowing such associations to survive and indeed, to thrive–even if the views they hold may be out of step with current societal values and mores.[117]

Fundamentally then, this section argues pluralism promotes the peaceful coexistence of difference by facilitating the flourishing of autonomous religious communities which develop and implement the theological virtues such as love, dignity, patience and kindness in private and public spaces, contributing to the common good and benefiting society more broadly. Conversely, coercion of conscience and oppression of public religion increases tensions and social conflict, undermining peaceful coexistence. For example, as Rosenfeld puts it, 'pluralism prescribes peaceful accommodation of as many diverse and competing

---

[114] Adside (n 84) 567.

[115] ibid.

[116] C Feldblum, 'Moral Conflict and Liberty: Gay Rights and Religion' (2006) 72 *Brook Law Review* 61, 63.

[117] C Feldblum, 'Religious Liberty and LGBT Rights: Finding the Right Balance (Ginsburg Lecture)' (2019) 41(2) *Thomas Jefferson Law Review* 163, 164, 172.

conceptions of the good as possible'.[118] Separationist approaches privilege secularism and marginalise religion, while pluralist approaches accommodate all perspectives which see citizens as 'equal in worth and dignity', and 'mediates' between a diversity of perspectives with the 'aim of achieving … the greatest possible peaceful coexistence'.[119] Pluralism consequently upholds peaceful coexistence of difference in the theological sense considered in this book, and does so in accordance with theological virtues such as dignity. Even Wexler, who is an atheist and whose work is not particularly friendly to Christian religion, agrees and prefers pluralism over separationism. A pluralist public square filled with all kinds of religious and nonreligious voices 'can be experienced as empowering for religious minorities' and may result in citizens 'being better educated with respect to religion and religious diversity'. Hence, it is possible that a 'religiously diverse public square might result in more toleration and mutual respect among those who hold different beliefs and create the conditions for a more stable social peace than pure separationism'.[120]

Protecting the autonomy of religious communities is a central feature of a pluralism which preserves peaceful coexistence because they are 'independent centres of value formation and inculcation that is beneficial to society' and therefore 'perform a valuable social function'.[121] For example, Berg has argued that protecting the autonomy of religious communities substantively contributes to public good. Religious freedom does not simply benefit its adherents, but 'also preserves space for religion and religious communities to benefit the broader society (including by benefiting individuals)'.[122] The economic, social and cultural impact of faith-based organisations significantly enhances the common good.[123] Violations of religious freedom rights through, for example, compelling religious organisations to adhere to majority norms on sexuality, would cause many such organisations to either fold or reduce their services, which would undermine the common good.[124]

---

[118] M Rosenfeld, 'The Conscience Wars in Historical and Philosophical Perspective: The Clash between Religious Absolutes and Democratic Pluralism' in S Mancini and M Rosenfeld (eds), *The Conscience Wars: Rethinking the Balance between Religion, Identity and Equality* (Cambridge University Press, 2018) 59.

[119] ibid 66–67.

[120] J Wexler, 'Secular Invocations, the First Amendment, and the Promise of Religious Pluralism' (2021) 26(2) *Roger Williams Law Review* 620, 622–23.

[121] B Jessie Hill, 'Reconsidering Hostile Takeover of Religious Organisations' (2020) 97 *Washington University Law Review* 1833, 1855–56. See also RW Garnett, 'Assimilation, Toleration, and the State's Interest in the Development of Religious Doctrine' (2003) 51 *University of California Los Angeles Law Review* 1645.

[122] See generally T Berg, 'Religious Freedom and the Common Good: A Summary of Arguments and Issues' (2019) 15(3) *University of St Thomas Law Journal* 517, 518.

[123] ibid 520–21.

[124] See eg SV Monsma, *Pluralism and Freedom: Faith-Based Organizations in a Democratic Society* (Rowman and Littlefield, 2011) 15–44; SV Monsma and SW Carlson-Thies, *Free to Serve: Protecting the Religious Freedom of Faith-Based Organizations* (Brazos Press, 2015); T Berg, 'Freedom to Serve: Religious Organizational Freedom, LGBT Rights, and the Common Good' in WN Eskridge, Jr and R Fretwell Wilson (eds), *Religious Freedom, LGBT Rights, and the Prospects for Common Ground* (Cambridge University Press, 2018).

Furthermore, as Brady observes, forcing violations of conscience 'undermines the vitality of America's religious traditions and the moral resources they contribute'.[125] 'Religious diversity has been a central aspect of American pluralism, and it has been integral to the processes through which we have continuously challenged, deepened, and renewed our public values'.[126] In addition, forcing violations of conscience 'risks provoking resistance, resentment and strife', as well as 'palpable anger' and 'bitterness'.[127] Though some have argued that accommodations will intensify conflict, Craddock explains why 'total war tactics are deleterious to social cohesion' and a pluralism which 'requires ... accommodation of religious believers' is necessary:

> Subjecting sympathetic religious objectors to severe penalties and jail time may alienate those who would otherwise support socially liberal policies on abortion and LGBT issues. Court rulings which are perceived to crush religious dissenters may unintentionally revive the spectre of persecution (perhaps plausibly), leading disfavoured religious objectors to cling more intensely to their beliefs. A hard line approach would socially exclude and marginalize religious objectors, driving many people of faith out of entire industries and segments of society. Indeed, activists demanding the withdrawal of religious liberty protections may themselves be engaged in a form of social hostility toward religious groups that adhere to traditional moral beliefs.[128]

Kao and Burke provide extensive empirical support to justify these claims, drawing from the comprehensive study of global religious freedom by Brian Grim and Roger Finke.[129] Cultural hostility towards religion can drive a government towards restricting peaceful religious practice and even excluding certain beliefs from the public square. Grim and Finke 'debunk the myth that religious diversity or religiosity are the drivers of social conflict'; rather, 'the more a government restricts religion, the more social hostilities tend to increase'.[130] Such restriction and hostility has an exacerbating effect, leading to the further decline of religious freedom, starting with social marginalisation and progressing to economic and legal penalties, and finally vigilante or state-sanctioned violence.[131] Kao and Burke outline the converse findings which demonstrate a positive correlation between religious

---

[125] K Brady, 'Religious Accommodations and Third-Party Harms: Constitutional Values and Limits' (2018) 106(4) *Kentucky Law Journal* 717, 725.

[126] ibid.

[127] ibid 726.

[128] J Craddock, 'The Case for Complicity-Based Religious Accommodations' (2018) 12 *Tennessee Journal of Law and Policy* 233, 275–77, 278. *cf* D NeJaime and RB Siegel, 'Conscience Wars: Complicity-Based Conscience Claims in Religion and Politics' (2015) 124 *Yale Law Journal* 2516, 2553–63.

[129] See E Kao and M Burke, '*Masterpiece Cakeshop* and Authentic Pluralism in a Post-*Obergefell* World' (2020) 24(1) *Texas Review of Law and Politics* 97; B Grim and R Finke, *The Price of Freedom Denied: Religious Persecution and Conflict in the Twenty-First Century* (Cambridge University Press, 2010).

[130] Kao and Burke (n 129) 99.

[131] ibid.

freedom and pluralism, and the consequent creation of conditions which facilitate peaceful coexistence and social flourishing:

> Strong religious freedom creates the conditions for authentic religious pluralism to flourish. First, religious freedom affirms the idea that individuals and institutions that hold different beliefs have equal rights under the law to live according to those beliefs in thought, speech, and action in both the public sphere and in private. It creates a level playing field for the competition of ideas … Freedom has a pacifying effect on social conflict … frictions dissipate, creating a virtuous cycle.[132]

Thus, robust protection for the autonomy of religious communities within a pluralist framework is more likely to promote peaceful coexistence in accordance with the theological virtues. Where separationism and the undermining of religious freedom builds anger, bitterness and social hostility, pluralism and religious freedom creates compassion, kindness and social peace.

However, this general principle does not account for the perceptions of hostility experienced by those who may be inadvertently discriminated against. One way forward is suggested by Alvare, who observes that the refusal of Catholic institutions to cooperate with the sexual expression of others (eg through adhering to federal contraception or abortion mandates, or hiring a same-sex married minister) can seem disingenuous and unkind, as affronts to the dignity of those discriminated against. She proposes that a way to address this is for Catholic institutions to provide a 'clear statement about the character of the Church as a believing community whose members are called to witness the living Christ to one another and to onlookers … this communal witness is theologically and practically constitutive of Catholicism … the Church's communal character grounds the necessity of its institutions' maintaining final authority over membership in the community – including not only leadership and employees, but in some cases also students and clients'.[133] In making this statement the Church can also articulate how Catholic teachings on sex, marriage and parenting are central to demonstrating who Christ is and 'how he loves the human race, and how he wants human beings to love one another'.[134] This has significant value to wider society as a contribution to the common good because 'the sexual mores advanced by Catholics and others in fact better serve human flourishing, as well as human equality, dignity, freedom and happiness'.[135] It will also have more appeal to outsiders to help them make

---

[132] ibid 98–100. See generally M McConnell, 'Accommodation of Religion: An Update and a Response to the Critics (1992) 60(3) *George Washington Law Review* 685. Vance also suggests following the example of German religious liberty jurisprudence which promotes pluralism by requiring the state to cooperate with religion and religious groups, substantively acknowledging the religious life of citizens: K Vance, 'German Religious Liberty Jurisprudence: A Proposed Solution for the U.S. Supreme Court's Double-Barreled Dilemma' (2020) 63(2) *Journal of Church and State* 300.

[133] H Alvare, 'Beyond Moralism: Catholic Institutional Religious Freedom' (2019) 19(1) *Connecticut Public Interest Law Journal* 149, 149–50.

[134] ibid 150.

[135] ibid 196. Alvare provides substantial evidence to support this in her article.

sense of why Catholic institutions engage in 'discriminatory' conduct, and how this is consistent with (or more accurately, the proper fulfilment of) the injunction to 'love your neighbour as yourself'.[136] Though this book takes a broader Christian perspective, the principles are the same. Preserving the autonomy of religious communities ensures these communities are able to build an internal community in accordance with their theological principles. Even though this freedom may entail the ability to discriminate, it can be reconciled with equality on the basis that the internal theological principles of the community can be applied and deployed more broadly to enhance the common good (including notions of dignity expressed through the theological virtues such as compassion, generosity, forgiveness and patience), thus improving equality overall.[137]

For example, a religious community could more effectively demonstrate substantial burden by articulating how their communal life is based around the intrinsic value of every human, and demonstrating the profound connection between marriage, sex and children – and as such compelling them to engage in conduct which effectively separates these aspects of family life constitutes a substantial burden on them.[138] Without deference to the religious community as to what constitutes religious activities, it is likely a judge will not understand the religious tenets and mission of an organisation and impose a secular norm upon the religious community. 'Fear of potential liability might affect the way an organisation carried out what it understood to be its religious mission', undermining the peaceful coexistence of difference by effectively preventing religious communities from functionally existing.[139] Hence, Alvare's proposal benefits any ministerial exception defence by describing what a religious institution is actually doing when it staffs and manages its organisations: it is building a community of faith designed to teach and model a particular ethos.[140] It is not tenable, in this context, for an institution to continue employing a person who does not adhere to that ethos in their beliefs and/or behaviour. It would undermine the very religious purpose and nature of that community. This is the precise *ratio* for the development of the ministerial exception in *Hosanna-Tabor*.[141] Those who object to protecting the autonomy of religious communities in this way 'are ignoring the theological and practical communal dynamics by which … faith is articulated and transmitted', and such extensive state interference would ultimately result in state control of the church, destroying pluralism and religious freedom.[142]

Sorkin suggests 'meaningful compromise' and 'dialogue' is essential for reconciling these tensions.[143] Adopting the theological virtues, for the LGBT community

---

[136] ibid 150–51.
[137] See Alvare's illustrations at ibid 186–89.
[138] ibid 184–86.
[139] ibid 193.
[140] ibid 190–91.
[141] As Alvare shows: see ibid 190–95.
[142] ibid 196.
[143] A Sorkin, '"Them": Bridging Divides Between Distant Neighbours after *Masterpiece Cakeshop* (2019) 54(1) *University of San Francisco Law Review* 117, 150.

this involves upholding dignity by valuing the autonomy of religious communities and the dignity of the individuals who constitute those communities, and engaging in patience and forgiveness by refusing to treat every perceived slight as a litigious matter, and 'forgiving the faith community for wrongs committed in the past'.[144] For faith communities, this involves upholding dignity by seeing members of the LGBT community as worthy and valuable, and demonstrating humility by 'extending themselves to members of the LGBT community', 'embracing the humanity and identity of the LGBT community' and seeking 'friendship' and 'complementary relationships between the communities'.[145] Such gestures 'cultivate a willingness from both communities toward meaningful reconciliation'.[146] This does not require an approval of specific conduct, merely that each group sees the other as a human being of equal dignity pursuing a diverse range of good human purposes in order to allow mutual fellowship in the understanding of difference. Thus, directly applying (in effect if not in explicit terms) the theological virtues of humility, patience, kindness and compassion to preserve peaceful coexistence, Sorkin argues 'we should strive to mediate between distant neighbors by extending oneself through gestures of repair – acts of contrition rooted in a true personal conviction for the well-being of the other. We should no longer seek selfish ambition, but seek mutual profit'.[147] Sorkin concludes:

> What a moment it will be if the Christian community begins to advocate for laws that protect against sexual orientation discrimination in employment, while the LGBT community willingly concedes to exempt religious convictions from those same laws.[148]

Sorkin's proposals therefore seek to implement the framework of facilitating peaceful coexistence in accordance with the theological virtues, endorsing the creation of a community of communities in the sense of trying to strengthen ties and compromise without sacrificing the essentials of faith.[149] However, there are some issues with his specific applications. For example, to say that religious communities must ask serious questions about where 'conscience and complicity are able to adapt and bend to the changes of a secular world' perhaps concedes too much, given many religious communities will have different and entrenched views on many matters, compared to the secular world.[150] It may lead to the situation Smith describes, where both sides offer terms of mutual accommodation which seem fair to them but could never actually be accepted by the other. This could drive religious communities 'to practice their faith in secret or in silence'.[151]

---

[144] ibid 165–66.
[145] ibid 150, 177, 184.
[146] ibid 179.
[147] ibid 186–87.
[148] ibid 179.
[149] ibid 151, 153.
[150] ibid 154.
[151] See Smith, *Pagans and Christians* (n 26) 131–57.

Indeed, Sorkin's argument about the vendor's refusal in *Masterpiece Cakeshop* because of the purpose the cake will be used for is misconceived. Sorkin claims: 'Phillips approaches the absurdity of those in Augustine's time who precluded themselves from the use of the sun because some men worship that luminary. Phillips cannot make a cake if that cake is being used toward a sinful activity because, in his mind, his artistic expression vicariously joins him to the activity therein'.[152] But this is a false analogy. 'Men' did not make the sun. The sun is already in existence to benefit humanity generally. The equivalent analogy would be if Phillips refused to eat cake because cakes could be used for same-sex weddings. Rather, Phillips is refusing to create a particular cake for the specific purpose of celebrating a same-sex wedding. Moreover, he was always happy to provide pre-made cakes to LGBT people for general reasons. The complicity link which creates a substantial burden on Phillips' religion remains. Putting aside such quibbles though, as a matter of general principle, Sorkin's approach is valuable because it helps us to re-examine how we engage with those who we disagree with, enabling us to see them as dignified individuals pursuing the good in diverse ways. This will certainly help decrease tensions and provide the groundwork for a peaceful coexistence, and compromise wherever possible for the believer or community.

This general principle can be specifically applied to the issue of religious exemptions under the First Amendment arising from factual scenarios such as *Masterpiece Cakeshop*. For example, as Minow outlines:

> Exemptions of some sort can be justified out of respect for the liberty of conscience at the core of the free exercise clause, acknowledgment of the contributions religious organizations have brought to individuals and society over time, and prudential avoidance of direct confrontation between the government and influential religious groups over controversial issues.[153]

Hornby suggests that the lack of consensus over a simple proposition such as this has resulted from a failure to cultivate and practise the theological virtues. Secularist separation fails to take account of religion generally and religious difference specifically, and 'toxic political dialogue … denigrates our ability to co-exist'.[154] An 'inclusive pluralism' requires mutual effort and compromise, a productive dialogue and embracing collective, a patience and kindness which acknowledges the dignity of those seeking services alongside the dignity of those who cannot provide certain services for religious reasons.[155]

Spindelman takes an explicitly devotional and theological approach to *Masterpiece Cakeshop*, imploring each 'side' to recognise that we are all part of

---

[152] Sorkin, 'Bridging Divides' (n 143) 162.

[153] M Minow, 'Should Religious Groups be Exempt from Civil Rights Laws?' (2007) 48 *Boston College Law Review* 781, 782.

[154] G Hornby, 'Let Them Eat Cake: A Comparative Analysis of Recent British and American Law on Religious Liberty' (2020) 58 *Duquesne Law Review* 377, 401–02.

[155] ibid 407.

a broader community which implies 'friendship' rather than mere tolerance.[156] This is modelled by the Court's engagement with and treatment of the parties, which is a 'robust' and 'generous' demonstration of creativity and sensitivity akin to the 'imaginative sympathy' I have discussed in other work; this imaginative sympathy is part of applying the golden rule, linked to the theological virtue of love.[157] So if there is to be an 'escape' from the 'constant warfare' into 'freedom to live their respective ways of life the ways they wish', the political community must 'recall their equality to one another and their shared relation' through 'a political morality of … love'.[158] This will produce a public space of 'friendship … and love … a political space of mutual understanding in which they might will to work together, lovingly, toward a shared future of equal concern and respect for all that is of their own collective making'.[159] However, to teach these 'enemies' to become true 'neighbours', to become 'friends' and 'political family', requires a transcendent source of 'grace'.[160]

Thus, as DeLoach observes, a pluralism which acknowledges the possibility of the transcendent ensures the peaceful coexistence of difference and the cultivation of the theological virtues. 'It is precisely the nature of a pluralistic society' to 'encourage' 'a diversity of beliefs … A society without religious viewpoints is less pluralistic, not more'.[161] Love of neighbour means 'concern for the good of every person', and 'promotion of the common good is an outgrowth of religion, particularly Christianity'.[162] Conversely, secularism 'promises only private individual good', an 'atomistic individualism' which excludes the transcendent, and undermines an 'emphasis on neighbour' and the common good.[163] Thus, the autonomy of religious communities is protected for the benefit of all religions, not Christians only. Indeed, it benefits society more broadly by reconciling virtue with difference in the sense of cultivating a space of peaceful coexistence of difference where the theological virtues can be practised.[164] DeLoach concludes:

> Religious freedom in full enlivens public compassion, charity, and love toward neighbors in ways that break down bigotry and discrimination. This is not simply tolerance, but also a recognition of fundamental human dignity and worth … Religious freedom is essential to human flourishing and the common good, and these depend on religion's necessarily public dimension.[165]

---

[156] M Spindelman, 'Masterpiece Cakeshop's Homiletics' (2020) 68 *Cleveland State Law Review* 347, 408.

[157] ibid 409. See also A Deagon, 'The "Religious Questions" Doctrine': Addressing (Secular) Judicial Incompetence' (2021) 47(1) *Monash University Law Review* 60–87.

[158] Spindelman (n 156) 410.

[159] ibid 419.

[160] ibid.

[161] DeLoach (n 31) 9.

[162] ibid.

[163] ibid.

[164] ibid 10–11. See also A Deagon, *From Violence to Peace: Theology, Law and Community* (Hart Publishing, 2017).

[165] DeLoach (n 31) 10–11.

A principled framework for protecting the autonomy of religious communities therefore does not sacrifice equality. Rather, by pursuing peaceful coexistence in accordance with theological virtues, the principled framework upholds freedom and equality as matters of love and dignity for all persons, thus reconciling freedom and equality.

V. Implications for the United States Legal Framework

A pluralist approach which reconciles freedom and equality in this way has particular implications for the three areas of improvement identified at the beginning of this chapter. The establishment clause has been considered in detail in the previous part. This part focuses on the ministerial exception and religious exemptions under the First Amendment. Regarding religious exemptions, part of a pluralist approach which preserves peaceful coexistence in accordance with the theological virtues is upholding the dignity of religious persons by paying respect and deference to their religious beliefs, and not passing judgement on whether the belief is reasonable, correct or important. It is a humble openness to the possibility of the transcendent and an understanding of the implications for those who believe in it, as the Court modelled in *Masterpiece Cakeshop*.[166] Conversely, a secularist approach 'sidelines' and 'subordinates' the perspective of the religious objector, and narrowly assumes religious beliefs are irrelevant in the public and commercial sphere.[167] As Bauges acknowledges:

> Many religious citizens cannot divorce the practice of their religion from their daily tasks, including their vocations. Those with sincerely held religious beliefs may view their religion as ingrained in their personhood such that their work lives are integral to their religious identities, and therefore central to their religious practice. In the employment context, therefore, the choice might be between a person's religious beliefs and their livelihood.[168]

Laycock further argues that a general protection for conscientious objectors along these pluralist lines is a logical application of *Masterpiece Cakeshop*. Applying the principle from *Masterpiece* that unequal treatment of religion is hostility to religion which is prohibited by the First Amendment, where a law has no religious exception but an equivalent secular exception, the law is not neutral and generally applicable because it discriminates against religion. And if a law discriminates against religion, it breaches the free exercise clause. Therefore, any secular exception for a conscientious objector, even an implied one, must have

---

[166] B Bauges, 'Balancing Religious Liberties and Antidiscrimination Interests in the Public Employment Context: The Impact of Masterpiece Cakeshop and American Legion' (2020) 54(4) *Richland Law Review* 943, 950–52, 958.

[167] ibid 953–55.

[168] ibid 966. See also T Bradley, 'Religious Liberty, Discrimination, and Same-Sex Marriage: Escaping the Obergefell Catch-22' (2020) 95(3) *Notre Dame Law Review* 1339.

a religious counterpart for it to not fall foul of the free exercise clause. 'And the state's willingness to grant secular exemptions seriously undermines any claim to a compelling interest in enforcing the law without exemptions'.[169] Laycock therefore concludes that *Masterpiece* is an important aspect of protecting the autonomy of religious communities, and this contributes to the common good and peaceful coexistence because religious liberty 'reduces human suffering' and 'reduces social conflict'.[170]

Masterpiece Cakeshop involves a collision of the dignity of equal citizenship and the dignity of religious conscience. The gay couple 'suffered serious dignitary harm in the form of personal insult' and 'humiliation' by being refused service.[171] Yet Phillips as well is entitled to the dignity of religious conscience, which is evident in the protection for religion in the First Amendment.[172] However, Gedicks argues that the free exercise of religion is an 'equality' right rather than a 'liberty' right, and is strongest in the private sphere – whereas the dignity of equal citizenship is strongest in the public sphere.[173] So, Gedicks claims, 'personal dignity of conscience cannot override the dignity of citizenship' in a public space, and even if the conscience claim can be accommodated, 'it ought not to' be: for example, government officials who cannot issue marriage licences to same-sex couple should 'resign'.[174] Gedicks acknowledges that commercial businesses and religious nonprofits are closer to the private sphere, but then states 'it is difficult to argue that an activity is private when it harms other people'.[175] The implication is where a person is harmed by being discriminated against, this is sufficiently 'public' for a conscience accommodation to be refused. However, there are two problems with this argument. First, as discussed above and in previous chapters, it assumes a public/private divide which is not sustainable for religious communities who view their public activities as a necessary aspect and outworking of their faith – nor, indeed, is it sustainable for LGBT persons who seek public recognition and approval of their relationships, not merely the freedom to practise them privately in their bedrooms.[176] Second, as discussed in chapter two, adopting that same harm logic entails considering the harm suffered by religious people by refusing the public accommodation of their beliefs, and it is plausible that there is

---

[169] D Laycock, 'The Broader Implications of Masterpiece Cakeshop' (2019) *Brigham Young University Law Review* 167, 168–69, 182–83, 187.

[170] ibid 204. See also D Laycock, 'The Wedding-Vendor Cases' (2018) 41(1) *Harvard Journal of Law and Public Policy* 49; T Berg, G Bradley and L Melling, 'Masterpiece Cakeshop and its Implications' (2020) 45 *University of Dayton Law Review* 289.

[171] F Gedicks, 'Dignity and Discrimination' (2021) *Brigham Young University Law Review* 101, 105–06.

[172] ibid 109–10.

[173] ibid 111.

[174] ibid 113–14.

[175] ibid 114, 116.

[176] See eg T Berg, 'What Same-Sex Marriage Claims and Religious Liberty Claims Have in Common' (2010) 5(2) *Northwestern Journal of Law and Social Policy* 206. Gedicks, 'Dignity and Discrimination' (n 171) 114 himself notes the questionable nature of the public/private divide.

less harm in simply providing an accommodation than there is in compelling the person against their conscience or compelling them to shift professions.[177]

In a series of recent articles, Netta Barak Corren argues, with empirical evidence, that religious exemptions increase the risk of discrimination (and therefore harm) against same-sex couples by providing a greater licence to discriminate and even emboldening those who would not normally discriminate to discriminate.[178] Apart from demonstrating the harm that such exemptions cause to imply that they should not be granted in principle, Barak Corren's analysis also challenges the view that allowing religious exemptions will not cause greater harm or discrimination to those who are refused services than not allowing them.[179] While accepting the force of Barak Corren's contentions, they are based on a purely consequentialist (arguably utilitarian) analysis, and consequences are not the only relevant consideration. Religious freedom and equality are important imperatives because pursuing them is right and good, not merely because the failure to pursue them will cause harm.[180]

Turning then to the substance of Barak Corren's arguments, it is worth emphasising that her research does not distinguish between refusal on the basis of a person's status (impermissible attribute discrimination) and refusal on the basis of a message the vendor is asked to express through providing the good or service (potentially permissible product discrimination). Even leaving that aside and taking the findings at face value, at one level the conclusions are not particularly radical or unexpected. It is obvious that allowing exemptions will entail greater discrimination and harm to those discriminated against than not allowing exemptions, and supporters of religious liberty have never denied that. The more important question is whether denying exemptions will cause less harm overall, taking into account the harm suffered by religious communities (and the general community) if exemptions are not provided. In the wedding-vendor cases, the balance of harm lies upon the vendors if they are denied exemptions, especially if they are merely refusing to supply a product which expresses a message. More broadly, religious communities contribute significantly to society, culture and the economy – and if religious communities are not allowed to be distinctively religious by virtue of autonomy through exemptions or positive rights, then

---

[177] See eg D Laycock, 'The Wedding-Vendor Cases' (2018) 41(1) *Harvard Journal of Law and Public Policy* 49, 63–65; T Berg, 'Religious Freedom and Nondiscrimination' (2018) 50 *Loyola University Chicago Law Journal* 181, 207–08.

[178] N Barak Corren, 'A License to Discriminate? The Empirical Consequences and Normative Implications of Religious Exemptions' (2021) 56(2) *Harvard Civil Rights-Civil Liberties Law Review* 315; N Barak Corren, 'Religious Exemptions Increase Discrimination Towards Same-Sex Couples: Evidence from Masterpiece Cakeshop' (2021) 50(1) *The Journal of Legal Studies* 75.

[179] *cf* eg A Koppelman, 'Gay Rights, Religious Accommodations, and the Purposes of Antidiscrimination Law' (2015) 88 *Southern California Law Review* 619, 627–29; Laycock, 'Broader Implications' (n 169) 192–93.

[180] See eg A Koppelman, *Defending American Religious Neutrality* (Harvard University Press, 2013) 120–65; J Neoh, 'The Good of Religion' (2019) 93(9) *Australian Law Journal* 791; J Finnis, 'Freedom of Religion: Special, Valuable and Qualified' in M Breidenbach and O Anderson (eds), *The Cambridge*

the negative impact will be significant. Enabling religious freedom is a compelling interest as well.[181] Therefore, it is not at all clear that exemptions should be denied on the basis of a purely empirical and consequentialist analysis. The best way to reconcile religious freedom and equality is to allow narrow exemptions with clear limits which will minimise harm to both sides and maximise freedom for all, in accordance with a pluralist framework which seeks peaceful coexistence in accordance with the theological virtues. This approach is also consistent with Barak Corren's research which engages with religious communities.[182]

A number of authors have suggested this kind of balanced approach which gives appropriate weight to the autonomy of religious communities. Brady proposes a multifaceted and nuanced approach which takes into account the nature and size of any burdens and harms and whether there are secular exemptions which impose similar costs.[183] Bauges also advocates a factually specific, circumstantial multi-factorial test which takes into account both harm to those discriminated against and the weight of the religious interest which, when neutrally administered, is a balanced approach that reconciles freedom and equality: 'the decision maker should immediately be looking for strong justification that would prohibit free exercise accommodation ... dignitary harm would not be enough to overcome an interest in protecting religious liberties'.[184] Sorkin argues religious vendors can justify an exemption by showing a 'sincerely held belief', that the 'requested service is part of those expressive acts protected by the First Amendment', and that 'readily alternative means exist for acquiring the sought after services'.[185] These principles can be applied where the refused party faces minimal hardship in finding equivalent services elsewhere, and this reflects the fact that in the wedding-vendor cases virtually all the refused parties have easily found alternative services, often recommended by the vendor. A requirement of 'substantial hardship' is needed to remove the exemption, balancing the rights of members of the LGBT community and religious vendors.[186]

Companion to the First Amendment and Religious Liberty (Cambridge University Press, 2020) 74–98. See generally the articles in (2019) 15(3) *University of St Thomas Law Journal* on Religious Freedom and Common Good.

[181] See, for example, the articles in (2012) 51(2) *Journal for the Scientific Study of Religion*; M Marty and J Moore, *Politics, Religion and the Common Good: Advancing a Distinctly American Conversation About Religion's Role in our Shared Lives* (Wiley, 2000). For a general response to the claim that religion is not special and should not enable exemptions because these privilege religion, undermine other rights, and harm others, see J Witte and J Nichols, '"Come Now Let Us Reason Together": Restoring Religious Freedom in America and Abroad' (2016) 92 *Notre Dame Law Review* 427–50. See also the discussion and references above and in ch 2 of this book which argue that religious diversity (enabled by the autonomy of religious communities) promotes the common good, and conversely the restriction of religion through refusing exemptions, rights or accommodations will merely intensify social conflict and fracture.

[182] See N Barak Corren, 'Taking Conflicting Rights Seriously' (2020) 65(2) *Villanova Law Review* 259.

[183] Brady (n 125) 739.

[184] Bauges (n 166) 986–88.

[185] A Sorkin, 'Make Law, Not War: Solving the Faith/Equality Cultural Crisis' (2018) 12 *Liberty University Law Review* 663, 663–64.

[186] ibid 732–33.

These solutions are consistent with my proposal in chapter two, which is that genuinely religious vendors should be exempt from providing marriage-related services if they give notice of their policy and provide access to reasonably available alternative services.[187] It incorporates tests of transparency, whether the vendor is genuinely and consistently religious, that the service is expressive in the sense of being marriage-related, and that alternative services are provided. This test provides a narrow and clear religious exemption which gives weight to the nature of the belief and service provided, in conjunction with taking into account equality considerations by ensuring that members of the LGBT community are not prevented from accessing such services. The issue of transparency (the extent to and method by which a religious vendor may inform the public of their conscientious objection in advance) which was canvassed earlier in the book raises the difficult problem of balancing individual dignity harm (if the customer is spontaneously refused) against potentially greater and broader systemic harm (if customers are informed that certain services are not provided through a public notice which all can see). There are no perfect outcomes which will remove all harm for all parties, but perhaps a notice in website terms and conditions rather than a public proclamation would best serve to minimise harm, and promote the virtues of patience, kindness and respect for religion and equality which is a 'constitutional imperative'.[188]

In the context of the ministerial exception, Feldblum acknowledges the commitment to pluralism means the autonomy of religious communities 'should prevail' over the commitment to non-discrimination.[189] Feldblum also agrees that religious associations should have 'discretion' to hire people for positions that are important for that entity's religious character in accordance with an ethos, 'however the entity want to define that' – such discrimination should be 'permitted'.[190] Where they hire some people not of their faith, they should be 'able to establish rules for conduct' for those jobs, because they primarily serve people of their own faith and a significant purpose is to pass on the ethos of the faith.[191] Feldblum consequently contends:

> For many religious associations, those who participate in gatherings or groups are the ones that constitute the religious character of the enterprise. Therefore ... a religious entity ... should be permitted to set the rules of conduct for participation that will

---

[187] To develop this proposal I drew on my previous work in A Deagon, 'Defining the Interface of Freedom and Discrimination: Exercising Religion, Democracy and Same-Sex Marriage' (2017) 20 *International Trade and Business Law Review* 239 and A Deagon, 'Religious Schools, Religious Vendors and Refusing Services After Ruddock: Diversity or Discrimination? (2019) 93(9) *Australian Law Journal* 766.

[188] SA Marcosson, 'Masterpiece Cakeshop and Tolerance as a Constitutional Mandate: Strategic Compromise in the Enactment of Civil Rights Laws' (2020) 15 *Duke Journal of Constitutional Law & Public Policy* 139, 167.

[189] Feldblum, 'Religious Liberty' (n 117) 173.

[190] ibid 175.

[191] ibid.

ensure the religious character of the enterprise will be maintained, even if some of those rules (e.g., no transgender people and no practicing homosexuals) will also preclude LGBT people from participating.[192]

But Feldblum says the calculus should be different if the entity receives public funds or serves the public generally.[193] However, this condition once again assumes the questionable public/private divide already refuted above and in previous chapters. As Shah emphasises, a pluralism which robustly protects the autonomy of religious communities also protects their right to operate entities which offer public services 'that reflect their religious values', and their 'freedom to seek and secure the financial resources necessary to operate and sustain these entities'.[194] Without the freedom to operate publicly for the common good, and the freedom to fund and support those operations, then the 'right to institutional religious freedom is merely formal and empty'.[195]

The ministerial exception under the First Amendment reflects this broad and robust protection for the autonomy of religious communities, and in this sense *Hosanna-Tabor* is a 'resounding vindication of religious group autonomy'.[196] The Court took a broad (and correct) interpretation of minister by including a person who was involved in modelling and teaching religious doctrine, even though they were not an official minister and undertook both secular and religious tasks.[197] Ahdar and Leigh note the Court held that the purpose of the exception is not to safeguard the ability to fire a minister for religious reasons, but to provide a sphere of autonomy where the decision of who will minister to the faithful is purely ecclesiastical. To inquire into the allegedly non-religious reasons for the decision is to entangle the secular court into making a theological decision on what is a religious or non-religious reason, which poses 'grave problems for religious autonomy'.[198] However, as I have indicated above and in a previous chapter, the ministerial exception should not be used as a pretext to dismiss a person for any reason at all. This is not a pluralist accommodation of difference and undermines peaceful coexistence. There should be protection for dismissals for religious and religion-related reasons, and there is an evidential process by which a religious group can establish and prove these reasons, and the court must defer to the testimony of the religious group rather than theologically evaluating it, in accordance with imaginative sympathy and the golden rule as I have discussed above and elsewhere.[199] This reconciles freedom and equality by protecting the equal dignity

---

[192] ibid 175–76.
[193] ibid.
[194] T Shah, 'Institutional Religious Freedom in Full' (2020) 10(2) *Journal of Christian Legal Thought* 29, 35.
[195] ibid.
[196] Ahdar and Leigh (n 35) 401.
[197] ibid 401–02.
[198] ibid 402.
[199] See A Deagon, 'The "Religious Questions" Doctrine': Addressing (Secular) Judicial Incompetence' (2021) 47(1) *Monash University Law Review* 60–87.

of ministers dismissed for non-religious reason, and protecting the autonomy of religious communities to select and regulate staff according to the doctrines and standards required by the relevant religion.

As Casper notes, there are occasions where otherwise illegal conduct is not related to religion, and the ministerial exception should not apply to exclude remedies addressing such illegal conduct. However, care needs to be taken to ensure mere disagreement or enforcement of religious doctrine and behavioural standards is not perceived or characterised as 'hostile'; rather, this regulation of belief and conduct is the essence of church autonomy and enlivens the ministerial exception. Casper's suggested case-by-case analysis allows this to be considered.[200] Similarly, Alvare (correctly in my view) advocates for the broad approach to the autonomy of religious communities facilitated by the ministerial exception as articulated in *Our Lady of Guadalupe*. She argues that this broad approach, which is characterised by the flexibility and deference the Court showed to religious perspectives on whether employees are ministers, is constitutionally necessary under the First Amendment given religious doctrine about how the personnel and ethos of religious communities are essential to the effective teaching and propagation of faith, the execution of mission, and the preservation of religious beliefs, norms and behaviour.[201]

Alvare also notes that the broad approach is not without limits. It does not grant religious institutions general immunity from secular laws, or endorse a blanket deference to a religious group's opinion about the role of its employees. Rather, the religious group's opinion is an important factor to be considered within a factual evaluation of whether the employee undertakes a ministerial function.[202] It is nevertheless a broad approach which may, and should, encompass roles including teachers but extending beyond them to admissions and finance officers, sport coaches, and medical personnel.[203] In regard to proposing conduct unrelated to religion as a potential further limit, Alvare implicitly endorses this by noting objections to the broad approach centred around the possibility of religious institutions discriminating without impunity for reasons unrelated to religion, and then addressing these objections by pointing to *Our Lady of Guadalupe* as an exemplar for the kind of detailed factual analysis required to ascertain whether the impugned discrimination is genuinely religious:

> The majority considered all of the agreements and guidelines exchanged between the employers and employees. It looked at the theology and church law respecting the complainants' roles. It reviewed in detail the daily, weekly, and annual contents of their work. It considered what might happen to the religious institutions' missions were they forced to retain employees undermining the faith.[204]

---

[200] R Casper, 'When Harassment at Work is Harassment at Church: Hostile Work Environments and the Ministerial Exception' (2021) 25(1) *University of Pennsylvania Journal of Law and Social Change* 11, 14.

[201] H Alvare, 'Church Autonomy after Our Lady of Guadalupe School: Too Broad? Or as Broad as it Needs to Be?' (2021) 25 *Texas Review of Law & Politics* 319, 320–22.

[202] ibid 328–29.

[203] ibid 331–32.

[204] ibid 371.

Alvare also rightly points out religious institutions have a corresponding obligation to provide comprehensive evidence to support their claims regarding an employee which shows a strong connection between an employee's work and the preservation, elucidation or transmission of the religious doctrine of the institution and/or the fulfilment of its mission. For example, they would likely need to show that the employee's contract, role description and performance evaluations are mission-directed, and explain to the Court the theological grounding of the employee's role in advancing the institution's mission.[205] In short, as I have already argued, the ministerial exception should only extend to employment conduct which is related to religion, as evidenced by the religious institution, and this is entirely consistent with Alvare's position. Finally, Alvare wisely advises that consistency and integrity on the part of religious institutions will help preserve a peaceful coexistence of difference which reconciles freedom and equality:

> Religious institutions would also likely improve the odds of retaining a robust church autonomy doctrine if they fairly and consistently treated all employees' words and conduct contradicting the religion [the same] – whether racist rants on social media, or entry into a same-sex marriage. This would also assure both observers and judges that their goal is not to discriminate based upon categories such as sex, age, disability, or sexual orientation but rather to retain employees who can forward and/or role-model the institutions' religious missions.[206]

Finally, some states have also introduced model statutes which attempt to reconcile freedom and equality. Although this book focuses only on federal laws, it is instructive to briefly consider such proposals. Mutually acceptable laws which recognise same-sex rights while also accommodating religious dissenters protect the dignity of all parties and contribute to peaceful coexistence by bridging differences, 'reducing social conflict'.[207] For example, Mississippi has provided extensive protection to religious vendors who object to participating in same-sex marriages. These protections appropriately include accommodations for small businesses or closely held corporations to refuse services directly related to the affirmation of same-sex marriages. However, the protections have also been criticised as too broad, protecting 'larger businesses' offering services 'with a much looser connection' to celebrating a marriage, such as 'car rentals'.[208] The breadth of protection also means there may be access issues in rural areas.[209]

Marcossan notes the Utah Collaboration or Utah Compromise as a better example of this kind of pluralist 'compromise' which reconciles religious freedom

---

[205] ibid 371–72.
[206] ibid 373–74.
[207] T Berg, 'What Same-Sex-Marriage and Religious-Liberty Claims Have in Common' (2010) 5(2) *Northwestern Journal of Law and Social Policy* 206, 235; WN Eskridge, Jr and R Fretwell Wilson, 'Prospects for Common Ground' in WN Eskridge, Jr and R Fretwell Wilson (eds), *Religious Freedom, LGBT Rights, and the Prospects for Common Ground* (Cambridge University Press, 2018) 1.
[208] Brady (n 125) 743–44.
[209] ibid.

and equality. It was a 'deliberate strategy' which provided protections for members of the LGBT community from discrimination in housing and employment while also providing protections for religious employers and for religious expression.[210] Similar proposed provisions in Kentucky also aimed to 'demonstrate a sensitivity and respect for religious concerns'.[211] Wilson argues that the 'Utah Compromise' affirms the good and dignity of all persons and can serve as a model for reconciling freedom and discrimination.[212] The Utah compromise stemmed from the belief that courts are more likely to enforce clear, discrete and concrete accommodations. A generalised (ambiguous) exemption allows the possibility for a flood of exemptions claims, while also undermining the goodwill between parties. A legislative approach rather than a judicial approach also enables more detailed and lengthy consideration of different perspectives, interests and approaches, leading to an outcome more akin to real compromise.[213] At the initiation of the Latter Day Saints (Mormon) Church in Utah, the legislature 'gave protections to both communities in the same set of laws'.[214] By understanding the central questions of dignity and the centrality of one's faith and one's sexuality, Utah 'forged common ground' to create a product which 'rests on four pillars that provide the foundation for peaceful coexistence: respecting all people for who they are; allaying the very real fears expressed by both communities; giving clarity to parties around the immediate challenges; and honoring the non-negotiables of each community'.[215]

In regard to clarity, the legislation draws clear lines through specific protections to facilitate resolution early in litigation.[216] For the LGBT community, non-negotiable features include no undermining of existing protections, protecting all classes such as race and disability, and that the protections must be applied consistently.[217] For religious communities, non-negotiables include protections for individual belief and practice as well as groups (including associated non-profits), protection must extend to all faiths, and the protections must extend to public life. Most importantly:

> any protection for the LGBT community should not be so broadly constructed that the protections have the inadvertent consequence of washing out the religious character of religious communities, that is, of infringing on their autonomy to determine the tenets and practices of their faith.[218]

---

[210] S Marcosson, 'Masterpiece Cakeshop and Tolerance as a Constitutional Mandate: Strategic Compromise in the Enactment of Civil Rights Laws' (2020) 15 *Duke Journal of Constitutional Law & Public Policy* 139, 167–73.

[211] ibid 175.

[212] R Fretwell Wilson, 'Common Ground Lawmaking: Lessons for Peaceful Coexistence from *Masterpiece Cakeshop* and the Utah Compromise' (2019) 51(3) *Connecticut Law Review* 483.

[213] ibid 506–07.

[214] ibid 515.

[215] ibid 517.

[216] ibid 522.

[217] ibid 522–23, 527.

[218] ibid 523–25, 527.

In other words, the autonomy of religious communities should be protected in accordance with the 'respect for religious autonomy' afforded by the ministerial exception under the First Amendment.[219] Respecting all these principles are the 'articles of peace' for the Utah Compromise.[220]

For example, Utah accommodated religious objections to solemnising same-sex marriage by allowing the designation of a willing clerk or celebrant. This meant a conscientiously objecting official could step aside and allow the designated officer to solemnise. In this way the official would not be forced to violate their conscience and the same-sex couple would not be denied their legal right.[221] Specifically, the text of the Utah compromise also provides full protection from discrimination for the LGBT community without erasing the religious character of faith communities. Sexual orientation and gender identity were made protected attributes, and LGBT persons cannot be discriminated against in employment. Religious communities and small landlords operating non-commercial property can give preference to those of their own faith, and religious organisations and small businesses can give preference on the basis of religion, 'but outside these narrow areas, LGBT people cannot be penalized just for being who they are'.[222] Allaying fears of religious communities that they would not be able to associate and teach regarding same-sex marriage, the legislation protects employees for lawful and non-harassing speech. 'The Utah Compromise also preserved the ability of organizations with a unique identity to structure their affairs around that identity and populate their ranks with like-minded individuals'.[223]

The Utah Compromise has been criticised by gay-rights supporters because religious organisations are exempt and the law does not apply to employers with less than 15 employees.[224] In other words, it does not apply to the very issues gay rights advocates are agitating against: discrimination in public accommodation, religious organisations and small businesses. Wilson also notes criticisms from hard-line religious freedom advocates and social conservatives who see compromise as universal concession, a capitulation to 'LGBT orthodoxy'.[225] However, Wilson points out that argument against the Utah Compromise 'comes from individuals and organizations that remain invested in the false, zero-sum, all-or-nothing framework that has stalled progress on LGBT and religious freedom measures'.[226] Such criticisms miss that the perfect can be the enemy of the good, and it is possible that no change will result from holding out for absolutes.[227] Wilson observes the Utah Compromise leaves some issues unresolved, including

---

[219] ibid.
[220] ibid 527.
[221] ibid 534–35.
[222] ibid 536–37.
[223] ibid 521.
[224] ibid 549.
[225] ibid 550–51.
[226] ibid 549.
[227] ibid.

whether religious adoption agencies should be able to discriminate against LGBT couples in placement. The religious agency cannot in good conscience place a child with a same-sex or other household inconsistent with their faith, while the same-sex couple willing to adopt needy children into a loving home is refused. One example of a compromise is to fund parents to engage with agencies who best serve their needs, removing the tension between the positions.[228] Thus Wilson concludes with a poignant reference to how the Utah Compromise exemplifies the pursuit of peaceful coexistence in accordance with theological virtues such as patience, hope and dignity:

> Utah's success in melding LGBT protections with those for persons of faith serves as a beacon, it is striking evidence that cooperation and fair play can guide laws even as to the most divisive and seemingly intractable of questions. It is proof of principle that Americans do not have to simply accede to the forces stoking conflict. Through dialogue and good will, we can resolve conflicts and stand not just with people like ourselves, but with our neighbors, affirming the dignity of each of us.[229]

By engaging in imaginative sympathy in accordance with the golden rule, we can understand and better accommodate for the perspectives of others who we disagree with. We can, for example, accept that being refused a service by a religious vendor may impose a dignity harm on a same-sex couple. We can also accept that the religious vendor is not refusing on the basis of identity, but on the basis of message – and that equivalent services are usually readily available elsewhere. So the request to accommodate is reasonable and proportionally limited, requiring only a small sacrifice on the part of the couple. Similarly, the religious vendor has to acknowledge the rights and interests of others; they have only a narrow scope to exempt themselves from anti-discrimination requirements and cannot use their religion as a cloak for prejudice. The willingness to sacrifice, forgive and be patient with others entails the practice of the theological virtues which contribute to building a peaceful coexistence of difference. A pluralism which acknowledges the transcendent in this way is especially pertinent for the religious vendor or community which perceives the stakes as amounting to a transcendent obligation which binds conscience independent of their own or the government's preferences.[230] Even if one does not share those convictions, part of being a genuinely pluralist community which pursues the good is to admit their possibility and accommodate it in law by protecting the autonomy of religious communities.

---

[228] ibid 552–54. *Fulton v City of Philadelphia*, 593 U.S. ___ (2021) considered this question directly, with the Supreme Court holding that Philadelphia's contractual non-discrimination requirement contained a mechanism of discretionary exemptions which rendered it not generally applicable, meaning its enforcement against Catholic Social Services was hostile and unequal discrimination against religion.

[229] Wilson, 'Common Ground Lawmaking' (n 212) 557.

[230] See P Horwitz, 'A Few Grains of Incense: Law, Religion, and Politics from the Perspective of the Christian and Pagan Dispensations' (2019) 58 *Journal of Catholic Legal Studies* 125, 152–53, 160–61; see also Smith, *Pagans and Christians* (n 26) 305.

VI. Conclusion

In this chapter I have argued that secularism is not an appropriate framework to understand the relationship between church and state in the US. Secularism inappropriately and incorrectly marginalises religion and excludes the possibility of the transcendent, rendering the First Amendment ineffective to protect the autonomy of religious communities and damaging a peaceful coexistence of difference. Conversely, pluralism is the best model to conceptualise the US church-state relationship. Pluralism preserves peaceful coexistence in accordance with the theological virtues by acknowledging the possibility of the transcendent, seeking the good of neighbour by engaging with and supporting religion as part of the common good, and upholding the dignity of religious members of the community by emphasising the importance of conscience. Pluralism also reconciles freedom and equality by protecting the autonomy of religious communities to develop and deploy religion for social benefit, while simultaneously protecting the dignity of all citizens by prohibiting unlimited, unjust, arbitrary and malicious discrimination. Specifically with regard to the First Amendment, a pluralist framework recognises that the establishment clause was designed to prevent religious coercion rather than establish a wall of separation between religion and government, and the free exercise clause was designed to prevent government interference with religion in effect as well as in explicit terms. This combined approach enables the meaningful and equal participation of religion in public life so that the entire community benefits. Finally, a pluralist reading of the combined establishment and free exercise clauses in the First Amendment correctly yields the ministerial exception, which provides autonomy for religious communities to select and regulate those who develop and propagate the religion. However, a pluralism which upholds the dignity of all persons in accordance with the theological virtues cannot countenance discrimination without impunity, and consequently the ministerial exception should only protect employer conduct which occurs for religious or religion-related reasons, reconciling the freedom of religious organisations with the equality of those employed by them.

6

England: Substantive Establishment?

I. Introduction

Chapter three suggests England's legal framework requires improvement in its promotion of peaceful coexistence. Though England has extensive formal protections for the autonomy of religious communities in conjunction with equality protections, these protections are unclear in their scope and application, and deficient in their substantive and practical effect. Chapter three proposes a number of measures to address these problems. First, the European Court of Human Rights must draw on scholarly literature and its own existing thematic strands to develop a clear rationale for religious liberty and a robust jurisprudence for the autonomy of religious communities. Second, this clear rationale and robust jurisprudence ought to be explicitly incorporated into English law and judicial decision-making through the mechanism in the Human Rights Act. Third, consistently with this incorporation, the religious exemptions in the Equality Act should be clarified to provide, for example, narrow and clear exemptions for religious organisations and vendors providing public services – in conjunction with genuine allowances for religious organisations such as schools to select and preference members of their community. Undergirding these measures is a principled theoretical reconciliation which frames religious freedom and equality as good and mutually constitutive goals; rather than viewing these important imperatives as intrinsically in conflict, they enable diverse paths to seeking the common good. This will promote a peaceful coexistence of difference in accordance with the theological virtues. In this chapter, the book will analyse the theoretical model of establishment which captures England's legal framework for the autonomy of religious communities with a particular focus on articulating and defending its substantive nature and elements. I will defend English substantive establishment as not only protecting the autonomy of all religious communities (not merely the established one), but also as providing peaceful coexistence of difference in accordance with the theological virtues by facilitating a proportional, reasonable accommodation of difference. I will consequently outline more precisely how England's legal infrastructure should be reframed in this context of substantive establishment with reference to the proposed measures described above.

Part II of the chapter describes the unique features and elements of English establishment. Part III considers whether these features and elements constitute a substantive (theological) or formal (secular) establishment. It argues that although

England is becoming increasingly secular, this is merely at the social or cultural level. However, the constitutional, legal and policy features of English establishment demonstrate a substantive establishment, not merely a formal establishment. This substantive establishment shares elements of the mild establishment discussed in chapter four with regard to Australia, but goes beyond this through the features (described in Part II) which explicitly and legally establish Anglicanism as the religion of England. Part IV defends substantive establishment as preserving peaceful coexistence of difference in much the same way as mild establishment does – by appealing to universal shared virtues which provide the conceptual foundation for protecting both religious freedom and equality – yet substantive establishment further facilitates explicit reliance on a transcendent foundation which helps both the established religion and minority belief communities feel welcome and acknowledged in the public sphere. In Part V I discuss implications for how to reframe legal protection for the autonomy of religious communities in England in an establishment context. Part VI concludes that peaceful coexistence, especially in an establishment context, requires genuine attempts at reconciling religious freedom and equality which seek the good of the entire community.

II. Elements of English Establishment

A religion is established when it is recognised as the official state religion. This can take different institutional forms in different states and with different religions.[1] In England, the state provides preferential support and endorsement of a particular religion (Anglicanism or the Church of England), in conjunction with a measure of influence over the religious affairs of the religion. However, 'this collaboration between religion and state is typically viewed by the parties themselves as mutually advantageous'; the state provides the church with recognition, accommodation and support, and the church provides the state with legitimacy, shared tradition and national unity.[2] The legal establishment of the Church of England points to its securing and oversight by the Crown with the aid of Parliament.[3] This means only an Anglican can be the monarch, and in addition to being the head of state, the monarch is the head of the church: 'Supreme Governor' of the Church of England and the 'Defender of the Faith'.[4]

English establishment is legally defined by two additional primary matters. First, the Crown is involved in ecclesiastical procedures. Church law is absorbed into state law, all church law requires parliamentary approval, and the monarch

---

[1] J Rivers, *The Law of Organised Religions: Between Establishment and Secularism* (Oxford University Press, 2010) 322.

[2] R Ahdar and I Leigh, *Religious Freedom in the Liberal State,* 2nd edn (Oxford University Press, 2013) 100.

[3] Rivers, *Law of Organised Religions* (n 1) 323.

[4] R Hirschl, *Constitutional Theocracy* (Harvard University Press, 2010) 29.

appoints the Archbishop and all 111 bishops on the recommendation of the Prime Minister. Second, the Church is involved in state procedures. Any new monarch is coronated by the Archbishop in a distinctly religious anointing ritual, where the monarch pledges to be the defender of the faith and to 'preserve the laws of God, the Protestant religion, the doctrine of the church, and the rights and privileges of the church and its clergy'.[5] Furthermore, 26 Anglican bishops have designated seats in the House of Lords (the 'Lords Spiritual' as opposed to the 'Lords Temporal'), which confers an exclusive right and privilege to directly contribute to the shaping of policy and legislation; representation on the Privy Council also means the church wields significant influence on the exercise of executive powers such as that of declaring war.[6]

The Anglican Church is also directly involved with implementing many areas of state policy such as education, welfare, law and order, health and defence. Church organisations provide faith schools funded by the government and minister to the community through social support, and Anglican chaplains are attached to all branches of the armed forces, and to state prisons and hospitals.[7] These practical and constitutional arrangements demonstrate that the relationship between state and religion in England is a symbiotic 'partnership' establishment, though English law nevertheless clearly distinguishes between church and state such that the relationship is not theocratic or Erastian.[8]

III. Nature of English Establishment: Substantive (Theological) or Formal (Secular)?

The institutional and symbiotic partnership between church and state in English establishment begs the question of whether it is substantive or formal. I mean substantive in the sense that it is a distinctly theological establishment grounded on religious premises, which provides a public place for religion to facilitate a peaceful coexistence in accordance with the theological virtues, and enables diverse pursuits of the good. This contrasts with a merely formal establishment where the letter of the law prescribes an institutional relationship which is no longer normatively or descriptively relevant for how English law and policy practically functions in accordance with secular values. I argue in this part that English establishment is legally of the nature of the former, though it is clear that England is becoming more socially and culturally secular. For example, Halmai contrasts

---

[5] K O'Halloran, *State Neutrality: The Sacred, the Secular and Equality Law* (Cambridge University Press, 2021) 251–52.

[6] ibid 251. See also M Hill, *Ecclesiastical Law*, 3rd edn (Oxford University Press, 2007); Ahdar and Leigh, *Religious Freedom in the Liberal State* (n 2) 101–02.

[7] O'Halloran (n 5) 251.

[8] ibid 251–52; Ahdar and Leigh, *Religious Freedom in the Liberal State* (n 2) 101–02.

a 'weak' form of establishment with the English structure where the monarch is the supreme governor of the Church of England and the defender of the faith, implying England has a strong and substantive establishment.[9] Similarly, Kerton-Johnson claims that the public sphere cannot be a religion-free zone given that the legislature is led by this monarch and all public servants receive their authority from the monarch.[10]

Rivers engages in a detailed analysis of the question in the context of religious communities. He observes that at one level, the English law with respect to religious organisations has become neutral, which means the facilitation of broad cooperation between the state and a wide range of religious groups, and autonomy for these groups to organise themselves in accordance with their own doctrines. However, 'there is no symbolic neutrality in a State whose monarch is *ex officio* the supreme governor of a Christian church'.[11] England's version of establishment has conferred a privileged position on Christianity, and Christian concepts have influenced interpretations of religious conduct and spheres of competence.[12] Nevertheless, Rivers claims that establishment does not adequately capture the law of organised religions in England, and instead relies on the principles of neutrality (as defined above), and autonomy. Rivers defines the autonomy of religious organisations to be 'the power of a community for self-government under its own law', and 'the power to create legal effects in State law'.[13] This means the state ought not to be simply blind to the religious community, but recognise its self-governance and accommodate it through legal recognition of its autonomy; for example, law should grant rights to religious organisations to choose their leaders and members, and set belief and conduct standards in accordance with the doctrine they articulate and promulgate, as well as to establish educational, charitable and other institutions in accordance with their doctrine to have a distinctly religious presence in the public sphere (as has been explored in other chapters).[14] English law in this sense shows 'a commitment to religious autonomy over a long period of time'.[15] Rivers also explains the importance of the autonomy of religious communities as providing a link to the transcendent which can enable the pursuit of public good:

> the existence of organizations which rival the State provides in addition a social location of legitimacy and coordination that has a real chance of resisting excessive State power. This familiar argument for associational democracy, or mediating institutions, is particularly cogent in the case of religious associations. Organized religions are not like

[9] G Halmai, 'Varieties of State-Church Relations and Religious Freedom through Three Case Studies' (2017) 2 *Michigan State Law Review* 175, 180.

[10] N Kerton-Johnson, 'Governing the Faithful: A Discussion of religious freedom and liberal democracies with particular focus on the UK' (2011) 4(2) *International Journal for Religious Freedom* 77, 84.

[11] Rivers, *Law of Organised Religions* (n 1) 342.

[12] ibid 342–43.

[13] ibid 335–36.

[14] ibid 335–38.

[15] ibid 338.

any other civil society associations. In the minds of adherents, religious law can have a legitimacy superior to that of the State. By virtue of their other-worldly representation and this-worldly presence they fulfil an indispensable constitutional function in the preservation of civil liberty. If religious associations are to have a role in the preservation of civil liberty, they must to some degree compete with the institutions of the State. They cannot be purely spiritual communities, in the ethereal sense of the word, but must be expressed in the material goods common to all humankind. They must lay a claim to the proper ordering of those goods which presents itself as superior to the claims of the State. They can only do this being somewhat threatening to the authority of the State.[16]

This is augmented by establishment, which acts as a 'constitutional paradigm securing certain forms of connection', and 'ensuring the ongoing public significance of religion in a context in which it increasingly appears irrelevant'.[17] For example, the Church of England has used its influence as the established religion to broaden representation of other religions in Parliament, and pursue new forms of religious representation in communities and schools.[18]

In short, Rivers notes that establishment is not quite enough to capture the law of religious organisations in England. The concepts of autonomy (of the church) and neutrality (of the state between religions) are also necessary. However, a substantive establishment as I define it does capture and preserve the autonomy of religious communities, which incorporates the principles of autonomy (religious organisations are free to govern themselves in accordance with their own standards) and neutrality (England supports the flourishing of all religion as a function of pursuing diverse visions of the good). So there is no inconsistency here between the substantive establishment I defend and the principles of autonomy and neutrality Rivers promotes in the context of English law.

The contrast between substantive and formal establishment also begs the question of where the mild establishment articulated in chapter four fits. I defined mild establishment as the institutional facilitation or support of religion which enables beneficial interaction between religion and the state, but does not amount to state identification with a religion or legal preference of one religion over another. Mild establishment merely recognises a shared heritage or tradition and respects the importance of religion to the broader community. The recognition of God in the preamble of the Australian Constitution is a symbolic state acknowledgement of religion, but in itself has no substantive legal effect. Mild establishment in this sense is certainly a necessary condition of English substantive establishment in terms of a shared heritage, the interaction of religion and government, and legal and financial support of religion by government. Yet mild establishment is not a sufficient condition of substantive establishment. English establishment is properly substantive in the sense that Anglicanism is officially and legally endorsed as

---

[16] ibid 336.
[17] ibid 345–46.
[18] ibid 345.

the state religion, the monarch is the head of the state and the church, and there is an enmeshing of ecclesiastical and state procedures as described in Part II.

However, it is worth noting that English establishment, despite its clearly substantive nature, does not amount to a theocracy. Hirschl outlines four components which define a 'constitutional theocracy': a formal distinction between political and religious authority together with judicial review, formal endorsement and active support of a single religion, constitutional establishment of the religion as a main source of legislation and interpretation, and religious tribunals with civil jurisdiction subject to review by higher courts.[19] The English structure satisfies the first two components. In terms of the third and fourth components, Anglicanism is constitutionally established but not the main source of legislation and interpretation, and there are religious tribunals (the ecclesiastical courts) but these do not have civil jurisdiction. Thus while English establishment is substantive, it is not theocratic.

Ten Napel considers that England is an example of 'restrained establishment'.[20] This allows religion to play a role in public life. Though the Anglican Church of England is formally the established church, this does not in practice mean that the Anglican church enjoys 'all kinds of privileges over other denominations'; it also has the effect that religion is not excluded from the public sphere.[21] This, according to ten Napel, is the reason why religious minorities have generally been in favour of this 'mild or inclusive model of establishment' – as they are able to be included as well.[22] However, as has been alluded to above, categorising English establishment as restrained or mild is not quite correct. The Anglican church does have at least some privileges over other denominations as noted in Part II. The monarch is the head of the church and can only be a member of that church, and there are designated seats in the House of Lords for Anglican Bishops, for example. This more substantive establishment is also exemplified through the fact that religious schools are financed by the state, and religious education and worship are part of the curriculum of non-religious schools. Religious organisations are also active in coordination with government by providing social services, though they are subject to the Equality Act (with religious exemptions in some situations).[23] Modood and Thompson further note that Anglican establishment gives the Anglican church symbolic and material advantages not enjoyed to a proportionate degree by other faiths, such as greater school funding and greater political representation.[24] In this sense the English

---

[19] Hirschl (n 4) 2–3, 242.

[20] H-M ten Napel, 'The boundaries of faith-based organisations in Europe' in R Ahdar (ed), *Research Handbook on Law and Religion* (Edward Elgar, 2018) 236.

[21] ibid.

[22] ibid.

[23] ibid 236–37.

[24] T Modood and S Thompson, 'Othering, Alienation and Establishment' (2021) *Political Studies* 1, 10, see doi.org/10.1177/0032321720986698.

establishment is more substantive than mild, but that does not mean it is not inclusive. Indeed, the fact that the state is friendly to religion in general means that religious minorities are welcomed in a way that they would not be in a more secular state.

This claim will be substantiated in more detail in the following Part, but for now it is worth noting the significant government rhetoric regarding the need to support religion and religious organisations in society, including through the financing of diverse faith schools and interfaith dialogue.[25] Church and state have also partnered together for broader public benefit, leading O'Halloran to conclude that 'the extent of church–state entanglement is complex and though seemingly largely symbolic and ceremonial, the relationship continues in law and practice to have real depth and functionality'.[26] Despite the maintenance and continued significance of this substantive establishment, England is also becoming increasingly secular. More citizens are abandoning religion and society is becoming secularist and multicultural. Yet in its legal and constitutional arrangements, the state remains in a mutually symbiotic and supportive relationship with the church.[27] Hence, though England could be defined as becoming more secular in its cultural or social outlook, 'religion, and in particular established religion, still plays an important role in government and other institutions'.[28] Bonney suggests that this secularisation is limited to private and personal behaviour 'without having major consequences for the public sphere'.[29]

In addition to Rivers' arguments that protecting the autonomy of religious communities provides a link to the transcendent and contributes to the diverse pursuit of the common good, a substantive establishment which preserves peaceful coexistence of difference through protecting the autonomy of religious communities and reconciling freedom and equality is also religiously grounded and gains theological support through Joel Harrison's development of a post-liberal religious liberty.[30] This post-liberal vision entails forming 'a just community pursuing the common good', which means encouraging the existence and flourishing of diverse communal endeavours, and understanding religious organisations 'not as delegates providing state services or as the result of contracting individuals, but as groups exercising their own authority and co-constituting the public sphere through a life of worship, charitable care, hospitals, education, and service to the community'.[31]

[25] O'Halloran (n 5) 252.

[26] ibid 259–60.

[27] ibid 252, 306, 499.

[28] R Barker, *State and Religion: The Australian Story* (Routledge, 2019) 103.

[29] N Bonney, *Monarchy, Religion and the State: Civil Religion in the United Kingdom, Canada, Australia and the Commonwealth* (Manchester University Press, 2013) 7.

[30] See J Harrison, *Post-Liberal Religious Liberty* (Cambridge University Press, 2020). For a more concise statement of Harrison's argument, see J Harrison, 'The problem and the promise of religious liberty' in P Babie, N Rochow and B Scharffs (eds), *Freedom of Religion or Belief: Creating the Constitutional Space for Fundamental Freedoms* (Edward Elgar, 2020).

[31] Harrison, *Post-liberal Religious Liberty* (n 30) 7.

This kind of religious liberty is an 'ecclesiological account' which questions the narrative of secularisation and recognises the importance of a 'public commitment to religion' and acknowledging religious groups as sites of authority.[32] Religious liberty, then, 'protects religion' by 'encouraging the pursuit of religion within multiple groups and sites of authority', which 'secures the free creation of communities of solidarity, fraternity, and charity'.[33] Religious liberty not only protects against coercing faith, but facilitates the quest for true religion through providing autonomy to communities which seek transcendent truth for the good of the broader community, or the common good.[34] As Harrison summarises:

> The pursuit of 'true religion' then – that is, a quest to orient oneself rightly in relation to God – is also an orientation for the entire community. It is neither simply an extra-temporal good – an end outside of history – nor a single good for individual choosing. Rather, it shapes our institutions, our actions, and our communal economic and political life. As integral to the common good, true religion shapes the bringing about of recognisable social goods – hospitals, schools, institutions of care, cooperative work endeavours, and sites of worship. Civil authority is tasked with pursuing the common good, a vision of right relationship in which virtuous living is encouraged.[35]

So Harrison's theological account of religious liberty is also fundamentally aimed at creating a peaceful coexistence of difference in accordance with the theological virtues, or the peaceful pursuit of diverse endeavours which encourage virtuous living for the common good. Furthermore, such a vision of public commitment to religion, which privileges a distinct religion and/or the general pursuit of religion, is not incompatible with equality and religious diversity; indeed, it can secure it as argued in the following part. At the very least, the European Court of Human Rights has acknowledged that 'respecting and facilitating institutional autonomy' is 'consistent with the state adopting a confessional identity'; a liberal pluralist state may permissibly 'recognise religion'.[36] Halmai agrees that 'liberal democracies are compatible with … established churches'.[37]

Admittedly, conceiving religious liberty as protecting the public quest for religion does not require the kind of substantive establishment England has. A public commitment to religion could take different forms. However, as Harrison points out:

> if a public commitment to religion is foundational, then this raises the possibility that some kind of formal recognition, at the heart of the political community, is beneficial … Persons of other faiths now at times support establishment precisely because it affords recognition that the religious quest is fundamental to public life.[38]

---

[32] ibid 21–22.
[33] ibid.
[34] ibid 142–43.
[35] ibid 158.
[36] ibid 40, 127.
[37] Halmai (n 9) 178.
[38] Harrison, *Post-liberal Religious Liberty* (n 30) 235–37.

The following part argues that English substantive establishment preserves peaceful coexistence because it seeks to accommodate difference through the transcendent – to facilitate the pursuit of the true and the good in diverse ways according to the eternal virtues.

IV. Peaceful Coexistence and an Evaluation of English Establishment

To reiterate, the autonomy of religious communities is 'indispensable to shaping and sustaining democratic societies', and an 'inherited constitutional arrangement' of a substantive establishment where there is a 'close and entrenched relationship' between church and state is compliant with Article 9 of the Convention.[39] Different constitutional models do not themselves determine the status of religious rights in a polity; freedom of religion 'can also be provided by nonsecular state-church approaches'.[40] Indeed, extensive analysis by Jonathan Fox has demonstrated that 'secular' Western liberal democracies may not be the most religiously tolerant nations because of a secular-liberal ideology which can repress religion:

> Secular ideologies can cause a focus on restricting religious practices that are counter to the secular ideology in question … religious practices are limited in at least some Western liberal democracies. Thus, the secular Gods are also, in a way, jealous of those who follow ideologies, including religious ideologies that contradict their secular ideals. Thus, the liberal ideal of religious freedom is often trumped by secular ideology and beliefs.[41]

What matters is government religion policy or how governments choose by policy to address religion. Fox distinguishes between ideological neutrality, where a secular ideology demands separation but also includes other metaphysical ideologies which clash with religion, and laissez-faire neutrality where the state leaves religion alone. Some democratic states espouse secular ideologies with anti-religious elements, and 'many democratic states that have technically neutral religion policies and maintain high levels of separation of religion and state are still influenced by secular ideologies that can be intolerant of religious practices that contradict those ideologies'.[42] The laicist conception of religious freedom is the strictest because it 'bans state support for religion *and* restricts religion's presence in the public sphere'.[43]

---

[39] O'Halloran (n 5) 62, 95–96. See eg *Holy Synod of the Bulgarian Orthodox Church (Metropolitan Inokentiy) and Others v Bulgaria*, Application Nos. 412/03 and 35677/04 (2009).

[40] Halmai (n 9) 206–07.

[41] J Fox, *Thou Shalt Have No Other Gods Before Me: Why Governments Discriminate Against Religious Minorities* (Cambridge University Press, 2020) 7.

[42] ibid 8.

[43] ibid 25.

For example, a UK Appeals Court has recently ruled that a Christian foster agency cannot refuse to foster children to gay couples for religious reasons, because Parliament has chosen to prioritise religion in the private sphere and prioritise sexual orientation in a public context.[44] Putting aside the questionable diminution of religion in the public context, even religion in the private sphere is not safe – for the House of Lords has also held that the decision of a church to dismiss a minister is subject to the jurisdiction of secular courts to consider a sex discrimination claim.[45] Rivers is scathing:

> We always used to think that the courts of the Church of Scotland were free from secular judicial oversight in matters of doctrine, worship, government and discipline; apparently not in the face of equality law.[46]

So secular liberal democracies must remain wary of 'state atheism', defined as 'the denial of religious freedom by imposing a secular viewpoint [such as absolute equality in matters of sexual discrimination] in an authoritarian manner'.[47] Rivers explains this as 'secularism-as-indifference', where the state has an 'unqualified secular legal monopoly' and religious considerations 'must always give way to the secular … they have no weight'.[48] This has the effect of restricting and marginalising religion, as can be seen through the loss of special employment and legal status for ministers, and tighter regulation for charities (including exclusion of Christian adoption and fostering agencies which refuse to provide children to same-sex couples), chaplains and faith schools.[49] The statutory equality duty means 'practically all organised social life comes under the influence of a state promotion of equality' – a secular idea of equality which is 'inappropriately univocal'.[50] 'The division of domains between "church"/private and "state"/public is undermined, conscientious objection is not accommodated and the autonomy of religious groups constricted'.[51] As Rivers notes, 'an exemption would surely be preferable to this sort of ideological bullying'.[52] It has resulted in many religious organisations choosing to give priority to their beliefs and withdraw from service provision, which undermines the diversity of the public square, community choice, and the public good.[53] Excluding religion through a secular equality regime undermines

---

[44] *The Queen (on the application of Cornerstone Adoption and Fostering Services Ltd) v Her Majesty's Chief Inspector of Education, Children's Services and Skills* [2021] EWCA Civ 1390 [40].

[45] *Percy v Church of Scotland Board of National Mission* [2005] UKHL 73.

[46] J Rivers, 'Is Religious Freedom under Threat from British Equality Laws?' (2020) 33 *Studies in Christian Ethics* 179, 181.

[47] H Keller and C Heri, 'The Role of the European Court of Human Rights in Adjudicating Religious Exception Claims' in S Mancini (ed), *The Conscience Wars: Rethinking the Balance between Religion, Identity, and Equality* (Cambridge University Press, 2018) 312.

[48] Rivers, *Law of Organised Religions* (n 1) 331–32.

[49] ibid 332–34.

[50] J Rivers, 'Promoting Religious Equality' (2012) 1 *Oxford Journal of Law and Religion* 386, 399–400.

[51] ibid.

[52] Rivers, *Law of Organised Religions* (n 1) 334.

[53] O'Halloran (n 5) 473–74.

peaceful coexistence by stoking conflict; exemptions or the equivalent which recognise the importance of religion alongside equality would facilitate the flourishing of diverse pursuits of the good.

As such, the secular liberal paradigm can be limiting and problematic for the autonomy of religious communities. It does not reflect how faith is actually experienced as a matter of obligation which renders the public/private distinction meaningless.[54] Stychin asks whether a 'richer form' of liberalism could provide solutions which recognise that deeply held views may not be compatible but can be 'meaningfully accommodated in the public sphere'.[55] Ten Napel considers a 'post-liberal' alternative which acknowledges that ecclesiastical and secular authority exist together and both pursue the spiritual welfare of humanity. Religious freedom then is in service of this common goal, including to form communities – which means post-liberal religious liberty is an essential element for the autonomy of religious communities.[56] This, of course, precisely reflects Joel Harrison's theological idea of post-liberal religious liberty as protecting the quest for true religion through the formation of diverse communities, and also reflects the focus of this book which is to provide a principled framework for the autonomy of religious communities which reconciles freedom and equality by creating peaceful coexistence in accordance with the theological virtues. In the English context, substantive establishment is perfectly suited for these purposes because it explicitly enshrines the importance of religion without excluding or marginalising other communities. Hirschl agrees that 'constitutional enshrinement of religion protects and promotes religion to enhance democracy and citizenship while also providing a bulwark against the threat of religious discrimination. Establishment is an attractive … option which defuses the theocratic demands of radical religion in a nonsecularist world'.[57]

As noted in chapter four with respect to mild establishment in the Australian context, substantive establishment (in an even more concentrated way) gives principled space for religious diversity by pointing to a transcendent foundation for the eternal yet universal theological virtues which ought to characterise political community. These virtues provide solidarity through a shared heritage and encourage mutual responsibility and virtuous treatment of others as persons with unique dignity and value. This produces a peaceful coexistence of difference because other religions support establishment on the basis that it reminds all people of the importance of religion to life, rather than implying a crude, reductionist view of religion which says it is merely private.

Modood and Thompson observe that formal connection between a religious community and the state 'are appropriate when the religion thus established is

---

[54] C Stychin, 'Faith in the Future: Sexuality, Religion and the Public Sphere' (2009) 29(4) *Oxford Journal of Legal Studies* 729, 732.

[55] ibid 748.

[56] H-M ten Napel, 'Why Europe needs a more Post-Liberal theory of religious liberty' (2020) 13(1.2) *International Journal for Religious Freedom* 157, 165–66.

[57] Hirschl (n 4) 19.

closely bound up with the history and identity of that state'.[58] And Miller notes that in such a context, the nation may 'legitimately give precedence to the artefacts of a particular religion when decisions about the use of public space are taken'.[59] This exactly reflects the English situation. As Schonthal has suggested, religious constitutions are important and valid forms of ordering political community.[60] Furthermore, one advantage in England is citizens also have legal entitlements against the Church, including the Church having the legal obligation to minister to all citizens in their geographical parish, not just their own members. This obligation is further reflected in preference for Anglican chaplaincy in schools and prisons. The important national role of the church in the community through parish responsibilities, chaplaincy, and education arguably 'justifies the elements' of constitutional establishment.[61] Though England has a 'formal' legal establishment with 'substantive expression where a specific religion is identified and promoted', Anglican entitlements for ministry or representation are a relatively weak preference which does not compromise the autonomy of religious communities.[62] Rather, 'the purpose of these advantages is to enable the church to carry out a national ministry and pastoral duties that are supposedly wider than those of other religious organisations'.[63] Other religions 'suffer no formal legal disadvantage'.[64]

Modood and Thompson also point out that the alienation of religious minorities should not be assumed as a necessary result of establishment. The marginalisation of religions can also alienate.[65] More specifically, there needs to be an actual dialogue with the purportedly alienated groups to gather evidence that they are alienated because they cannot identify with their polity.[66] Modood and Thompson conclude:

> It cannot be claimed a priori that establishment is alienating to a religious minority like British Muslims … Most religious minorities do not seem to be alienated from their state due to state–religion arrangements that may be described as establishment or that approximate to it … In the case that we have discussed throughout this article – that of British Muslims and the Anglican establishment – we actually think that if political theorists were to follow up on their claims of alienation, they would not find the necessary evidence.[67]

---

[58] Modood and Thompson (n 24) 2.

[59] D Miller, 'Majorities and Minarets: Religious Freedom and Public Space' (2016) 46(2) *British Journal of Political Science* 437, 454.

[60] B Schonthal, 'The Case for Religious Constitutions: Comparative Constitutional Law among Buddhists and Other Religious Groups' (2021) *Law and Social Inquiry* 1–29, see doi.org/10.1017/lsi.2021.36.

[61] Ahdar and Leigh, *Religious Freedom in the Liberal State* (n 2) 102–03.

[62] ibid 104.

[63] ibid 106.

[64] ibid 108.

[65] Modood and Thompson (n 24) 3.

[66] ibid 3, 10–11.

[67] ibid 11, 13. See also N Perez, J Fox and J McClure, 'Unequal State Support of Religion: On Resentment, Equality, and the Separation of Religion and State' (2017) 18(4) *Politics, Religion, Ideology* 431.

In short, Modood and Thompson argue that if minority religions are alienated by establishment, then this counts against establishment in terms of peaceful coexistence. However, English establishment does not alienate – it does privilege Anglicanism specifically, but it also supports religion in general, contributing to peaceful coexistence by pursuing the common good. This is why the evidence indicates that British Muslims, for example, are not alienated by English establishment. Rather, as I have already noted elsewhere, an establishment of religion helps religious minorities feel at home and a genuine part of the state and policy discussions. Modood and Thompson even suggest that genuine dialogue with religious minorities may reveal they find establishment more congenial than secular or separationist alternatives.[68]

No doubt Anglicanism has a special privilege in England. Yet despite the claim that this 'special privilege' may disrupt the object of equality, states such as England with an established church 'usually do more to fulfil the needs of other religious communities and therefore standards of religious freedom are even higher than might appear at first sight'.[69] The presence of the majority religious community makes minority communities more comfortable in the public domain.[70] To expand upon this objection and its response, O'Halloran argues that 'the freedom of association is predicated on the autonomous existence of religious communities, which is clearly compromised by the concept and role of an "established" church'.[71] And again:

> The right to form associations constitutes a hallmark of democracy … The autonomous existence of religious organisations or communities is considered to be a fundamental aspect of the freedom of association … pluralism and the right to religious freedom in a democratic society are dependent upon such autonomy. Thus, on the face of it, the retention of an 'established' Church as in England, must be viewed as seriously compromising that autonomy and as non-compliant with the freedom of association.[72]

However, O'Halloran provides no reasoning which explains why freedom of association is 'clearly compromised' by establishment. Presumably the unarticulated assumption is that an established church is more susceptible to state interference, and therefore religious communities are not autonomous. But in fact the nature of English establishment supports the autonomy of religious communities by reminding citizens of the transcendental and eternal nature of humans and citizenship, providing a basis for the acknowledgement of dignity and virtuous treatment. Religious communities have an essential role in developing and deploying theological resources which bolster broader understanding of these

---

[68] Modood and Thompson (n 24) 2–3.

[69] V-I Savic, 'It works better if it is not too secularised: the Croatian constitutional model for regulating state-church relations' in P Babie, N Rochow and B Scharffs (eds), *Freedom of Religion or Belief: Creating the Constitutional Space for Fundamental Freedoms* (Edward Elgar, 2020) 275.

[70] ibid.

[71] O'Halloran (n 5) 114.

[72] ibid 460–61.

principles and enhance peaceful coexistence in a diverse democracy. In addition, there is nothing preventing non-established religions from exercising religious freedom or forming autonomous associations. This objection is overstated and unsubstantiated.[73]

Furthermore, as Rivers discusses, the dismissal of establishment as a breach of the autonomy of religious communities is 'too simple':

> There is no necessary incompatibility between State recognition and self-government. Indeed, in a legal context in which the norm for other religions and non-religious bodies is a certain degree of accountability to Government, establishment in the sense of special legal regulation may be necessary to secure greater levels of autonomy … The established position of the Church of England has been combined with an expectation that its rights and privileges should, where possible, be available more widely. Part, at least, of the legitimacy of its position has been derived from its willingness to argue for widening access for others.[74]

The existence of faith schools in England demonstrates this. The schools have autonomy as religious associations to defend themselves against disproportionate state intervention. Faith schools are popular in the community and thought to produce higher standards of educational attainment. So in an establishment context where faith schools are 'deeply embedded in the cultural and religious history' of England, they nevertheless retain their autonomy and facilitate freedom of choice for parents to educate in accordance with their faith convictions.[75] Even O'Halloran later concedes that 'in practice, despite its entrenched commitment to an "established church", the state has a decidedly relaxed approach towards religion and promotes religious pluralism'.[76]

Thus, in a context of established religion, England supports the autonomy of religious communities on the basis that respecting the religious beliefs of others facilitates peaceful coexistence. The state should only intervene where peaceful coexistence is undermined by unmoderated religious passions.[77] Reasonable accommodation as part of a peaceful coexistence of difference is also a way of 'enhancing' the theological virtue of 'human dignity', which itself 'provides an important normative link with legal protection of religion or belief'.[78] As Harrison discusses, dignity is 'integral to pursuing true religion', which is the purpose of religious liberty; 'to act contrary to dignity is to act contrary to religion'.[79]

---

[73] For example, for arguments that establishment can be consistent with religious freedom, see generally R Ahdar and I Leigh, 'Is Establishment Consistent with Religious Freedom?' (2004) 49 *McGill Law Journal* 635; R Ahdar and I Leigh, *Religious Freedom in the Liberal State* (Oxford University Press, 2005) ch 5.

[74] Rivers, *Law of Organised Religions* (n 1) 344.

[75] ibid 266–67.

[76] O'Halloran (n 5) 493.

[77] C McCrudden, *Litigating Religions: An Essay on Human Rights, Courts, and Beliefs* (Oxford University Press, 2018) 66.

[78] M Gibson, 'The God "Dilution" Religion, Discrimination and the Case for Reasonable Accommodation' (2013) 72 *Cambridge Law Journal* 578, 592–93.

[79] Harrison, *Post-liberal Religious Liberty* (n 30) 239–40.

Part of acknowledging human dignity with respect to religion is emphasising the collective dimension of the religious domain, and reflecting this through protection for the autonomy of religious communities rather than merely individuals (and then individual protections flow from the protection of communities).[80] Simply characterising the group as a vehicle for individual interests implies state interference is justified if there is sufficient aggregate interests. This conception, according to Harrison, 'misconceives the nature of the group' and 'religious difference is flattened in favour of abstraction' because it omits the distinct and unique transcendental purpose of the group to 'pursue virtuous ends' and 'reconcile the good of the individual with the common good'.[81] It is not about theocratic rule, but the instantiation of a 'culture of love' which seeks the good of neighbour as self, the law of love.[82] So then 'religious liberty protects the free creation of communities of solidarity, fraternity, and charity, or what we may call "right relationship"'.[83]

The theological grounding of substantive establishment conducive to this process in England is nevertheless 'hospitable to difference' because the pursuit of universal goods such as education, work, charity and community in accordance with theological virtues such as love, kindness, humility and patience is possible for all communities, not just Christians.[84] Christianity also recognises 'parallel communities of common endeavour' which seek the good and right relationship, 'the possibility of harmony – precipitated by some real affinities between different groups, an emphasis on the integrity of civil society as a space of solidarity, and the hope that we are pursuing some shared goals'.[85] Harrison concludes:

> If religion entails reaching out to a God who has condescended to us, a God whose life is love, then this necessarily flows into a life of solidarity, fraternity, and charity. In other words, religious liberty only reaches the heights of true liberty when it is rightly oriented to manifesting this end, reflecting what it means to be human.[86]

McCrudden agrees, also concluding that protecting the autonomy of religious communities is 'indispensable for developing an understanding of human rights and human dignity', because it helps humans make sense of their lives through a transcendent source.[87] 'The importance of religious freedom for those who are not religious is the possibility it offers to engage with alternative views on the world and our place in it', which is a 'condition for self-understanding'.[88] In other words, protecting the autonomy of religious communities contributes to the cultivation of the theological virtues of dignity, patience and humility, and therefore enhances

---

[80] Gibson (n 78) 609–10; Rivers, *Law of Organised Religions* (n 1) 318–22, 396.
[81] Harrison, *Post-liberal Religious Liberty* (n 30) 52–56.
[82] ibid 144.
[83] ibid 172.
[84] ibid 203.
[85] ibid 205–06.
[86] ibid 239.
[87] McCrudden (n 77) 139.
[88] ibid 140.

peaceful coexistence. Human dignity underpins the claims of both those who seek to manifest religious belief and those who seek to restrict religious practices. This use of shared virtue helps build common ground and provides common language in the event of disputes.[89] However, both equality and religious freedom rights 'carry significant weight. They should therefore be protected to the greatest extent possible, and this requires that each be accommodated to the greatest extent possible by the other. Only by each side backing off from making claims that assert its interests to the limit, can this be accomplished'.[90]

In this respect, Ahdar and Giles suggest the political process will be more productive, because this can facilitate a generous and collaborative approach to living together. For example, faith communities and LGBT communities can emphasise the dignity and good of each other, and seek common ground as discussed in more detail in the previous chapter. Members of the LGBT community are entitled to protection from discrimination, and religious communities are also entitled to associational protections. There should be 'space for both communities', and 'the question is how to contour the public sphere so as to enable each community to adhere to beliefs and values which its members regard as inseparable and integral to their identity and very being'.[91] These suggestions will be explored further in the next part in the context of framing religious freedom and equality as mutually supportive goals to enable the peaceful coexistence of diverse conceptions and pursuits of the good.

V. Implications for the English Legal Framework

As noted in the introduction of this chapter, chapter three indicated a number of measures to better facilitate peaceful coexistence in accordance with the theological virtues, or a reasonable accommodation of difference in the context of a substantive establishment. First, the European Court of Human Rights must develop a clear rationale for religious liberty and a substantive jurisprudence of the autonomy of religious communities. As canvassed in chapter three, the resources already exist in the case law. The ECtHR has recognised that religious communities exist in organised structures which follow divine obligation, and states should not underestimate the importance of this community dimension of freedom of religion. Such freedom is in the interests of the common good because it contributes to the pluralism which is a necessary component of a democratic society. This emphasises the 'public nature of the association and the perceived value of the diversity of expression that is protected'.[92] At times the ECtHR has placed special emphasis on

---

[89] ibid 144.
[90] ibid 144–45.
[91] R Ahdar and J Giles, 'The Supreme Courts' Icing on the Trans-Atlantic Cakes' (2020) 9(1) *Oxford Journal of Law and Religion* 212, 223–24.
[92] McCrudden (n 77) 68–69.

the autonomy of religious bodies, promoting the ability of organisations to internally organise themselves to ensure the effective enjoyment of religious freedom by their members, and defending organisations against state encroachment. This includes upholding the rights of religious groups to acquire legal personality, operate places of worship and publish literature, and establish charities, educational institutions and welfare groups in accordance with the doctrines of the organisation. Most importantly, the ECtHR has supported the ability of religious groups to select their leaders and members (and by implication, exclude those who reject the doctrines or conduct of the religion). 'So long as the group respects the individual's right to leave without impediment or interference, the group's internal authority trumps the individual's right to participate as a member of that group'.[93]

Second, this clear rationale and substantive jurisprudence should be incorporated into English law by the Human Rights Act. British cases have typically treated religion as a matter of choice and conduct rather than identity, and as private rather than public. This has resulted in religion having an aberrant place in the equality hierarchy. In effect other types of equality are privileged.[94] For Rivers, it is concerning that this autonomy of religious communities has been 'eroding' in English society, particularly in the context of a provision in the HRA which was specifically designed to assure religious communities their autonomy would be respected.[95] Unfortunately, there is no evidence the provision has had any effect on protecting the autonomy of religious communities in England; it has coincided with a decline in religious freedom.[96] However, the law should in principle side with the religious community rather than an aggrieved individual in the event of conflict. Rivers explains:

> If the law sides with the individual, there is no way of protecting collective freedom to unite around a given conception … but if the law sides with the collective body, there is always the option of exit and founding a new organization … While the State may legitimately adopt a particular, more-or-less controversial, conception of equality, it should not impose such a conception uniformly on the whole of civil society. Protection from uniform State ideologies is one of the main points of collective religious liberty.[97]

Third, religious freedom and equality must be framed as good and mutually supportive goals rather than intrinsically in conflict. Preserving equality in conjunction with accommodations for religious communities enables diverse paths to seeking the good. This entails clarifying the exemptions in the Equality Act. As noted in chapter three, this may be done through making the preservation of religious ethos a legitimate aim in employment practices, reasonable deference to a religious body as to how they seek to preserve that ethos, and building

---

[93] See J Witte and A Pin, 'Faith in Strasbourg and Luxembourg: The Fresh Rise of Religious Freedom Litigation in the Pan-European Courts' (2021) 70 *Emory Law Journal* 587, 640, 657.

[94] McCrudden (n 77) 82–84.

[95] Rivers, *Law of Organised Religions* (n 1) 338–39. The provision was discussed in ch 3.

[96] ibid.

[97] ibid 135–36.

religious perspectives into the structure of determining what is reasonable and appropriate so that genuine abilities to select members and leaders (such as requiring a priest to a man) are not considered as discrimination. This provides principled consideration of how to reconcile freedom and equality rather than a crude utilitarian calculus of what is in the 'public interest' as a composite of aggregative individual interests.[98]

Individualising rights claims undermines the autonomy of religious communities because of a growing assumption that anyone who wants to join a religious group can decide whether they qualify for membership, rather than the decision being in the hands of the group. This assumption wields individual rights against the religious group and implies the group should adjust for the individual, despite the fact the individual has a right of exit (not to mention the impact this would have on the other individual members of the group).[99] So Rivers notes that this conception 'fails to capture central parts of the subject-matter', 'distorts the underlying social reality', is 'inherently weak', and 'risk[s] capture by a statist agenda that subjects all of civil society to its own ethos'.[100] In other work, Rivers also identifies the fact that current equality law confines religion to the private sphere, with the fear that equality is or will become its own comprehensive doctrine which will be imposed by the state in the private sphere as well.[101] Rivers concludes that English equality law 'puts pressure on religious liberty in four specific ways':

> (1) it confines the relevance of 'religion' to limited social contexts; (2) it creates a priority for equality-perspectives over liberty-perspectives on social conflict; (3) it generates new social assumptions about what individuals have to believe and say (or refrain from saying) if they are to be trusted to uphold the law; (4) it provides legitimation for the imposition of contested comprehensive equality doctrines, some of which are inimical to civil liberty.[102]

These pressures are linked with equality becoming an active policy for public bodies and employers, and equality acquiring a privileged status 'from which no reasonable person would dissent' which therefore 'enables it to limit other human rights' such as religious freedom.[103]

However, this approach 'corrodes any idea of genuine pluralism' and 'ignores the fact that liberal rights were intended to be founded on a vision which recognises' that the religious quest is special and 'deserves special protection'.[104] Since religious liberty is the 'desirable' quest for the pursuit of true religion which shapes our good life, Harrison suggests that religious claims should be generously

---

[98] ibid 321.
[99] ibid 320–22.
[100] ibid 322.
[101] Rivers, 'Religious Freedom under Threat' (n 46) 184–85, 189–91.
[102] ibid 179.
[103] ibid 187–88.
[104] Stychin (n 54) 749.

accommodated.[105] For example, with respect to faith-based welfare providers, the 'grudging exceptions in non-discrimination law' have the potential of undermining 'The Government's avowed policy of welfare pluralism and partnership' by having the effect of 'imposing alien [secular equality] values' on those providers.[106] A genuinely religious body providing welfare 'may be religiously distinctive, setting faith-specific tests for membership, office-holding, and standards of behaviour ... Applying norms of non-discrimination to a faith-based welfare provider may ... be destructive of the very diversity equality-norms are supposed to protect' because it damages peaceful coexistence of difference, or the ability of diverse welfare providers to help people in accordance with their religion.[107] Rivers articulates 'a more pluralistic conception of equality':

> which sees the value of the voluntary sector precisely in its diversity of ethos and provision. Equality on this account does not require the imposition of a single secular ethos on all organizations which occupy the domain of the State's activity, but even-handed partnership with religiously-distinctive bodies. This not only allows for greater integration between motivation and activity on the part of these organizations, it also contributes to State legitimacy.[108]

In other words, this more pluralistic conception of equality frames equality and religious freedom as good and mutually supportive goals which uphold the importance of religious diversity in a substantively established state for the purpose of augmenting the common good. It contributes to a peaceful coexistence of difference through reasonable accommodations which uphold the theological virtues such as dignity, patience, love and kindness. Similarly, with respect to religious vendors, the decision in *Asher's Baking* indicates that religious freedom 'need not be interpreted so as to imperil the viability of laws prohibiting discrimination in the market for goods and services'.[109]

In particular, Reyes notes that the UK Supreme Court did not hold that religious vendors are entitled to an exemption from anti-discrimination law. It was an objection to the explicit written message ('support gay marriage'), not the messenger (customers). The owners were apparently prepared to provide the wedding cake without the written message, were unaware of the sexual orientation of the customers, and would have refused to provide a cake with such a message to anyone regardless of sexual orientation. The decision therefore 'preserves protections for LGBTQ customers and does not license religiously-motivated discrimination'.[110] Reyes also notes this is a distinction from *Masterpiece Cakeshop* in the sense that the refusal there was 'directly dependent

---

[105] Harrison, *Post-liberal Religious Liberty* (n 30) 23–24.

[106] Rivers, *Law of Organised Religions* (n 1) 287–88.

[107] ibid 276.

[108] ibid 287–88.

[109] R Reyes, '*Masterpiece Cakeshop* and *Asher's Baking Company*: A Comparative Analysis of Constitutional Confections' (2020) 16(1) *Stanford Journal of Civil Rights & Civil Liberties* 113, 115–16.

[110] ibid 135.

upon the sexual orientation of the customers'.[111] But this is not quite right. Phillips would have refused supply to any customer who requested a cake for the purposes of a same-sex wedding, regardless of the customer's sexual orientation. The issue for Phillips was the purpose of the cake, not who was requesting it. This does raise more difficult issues concerning the divination of the purpose of a product and whether it is permissible to refuse on such a basis (and how clear a message of support is expressed by creating a cake as opposed to an explicit message on a cake). However, fundamentally, like *Asher's Baking*, refusing to supply a uniquely created cake for a purpose which violates the conscience of the vendor is not discrimination on the basis of sexual orientation. The laudable goal of non-discrimination can be preserved, and the religious freedom of the vendor can be simultaneously protected.

Hornby suggests a way forward to achieve 'accommodation and compromise' through 'respectful dialogue (the commitment to an independent recognition of different beliefs on the part of the state)', bearing in mind the nature of entrenched religious beliefs.[112] 'Common unity' is required to 'accommodate', and conflict will only intensify until society learns that compelling the violation of religious conscience is 'untenable'.[113] Religious vendors are not asking for the destruction of equality law or a general right to discriminate, but as Hornby outlines, 'certain practical exemptions are necessary' where there is a direct connection to celebrating a wedding:

> … while a baker cannot refuse to serve a cake that is sold to all to a gay couple, small business owners should not have to violate their moral integrity-no matter how retroactive or unpopular those moral norms are-in the marketplace. This protection cannot be afforded to indirect connections to a wedding, but for those personally involved in ensuring that the wedding is the best it can be through their own creative efforts and artistry, protection must be afforded for that person's conscience. In return, same-sex marriage and the rights of gay participants can surely be left alone. Any refusal of accommodation in the marketplace will be limited to a very few instances-such as a custom-designed wedding cake from a small businessowner-but any discrimination against the gay people themselves will be prohibited, i.e., a refusal to sell a cake featured in the window.[114]

These exemptions are narrow and clear, as I have discussed in more detail in previous chapters. If democratic society is truly committed to freedom and equality, exemptions for 'religious groups' are necessary to achieve 'peace, equality and cohesion' – otherwise religious groups 'will likely be crushed by the weight of majoritarian law and culture'.[115] Rather than the state taking the 'invasive'

---

[111] ibid.
[112] G Hornby, 'Let Them Eat Cake: A Comparative Analysis of Recent British and American Law on Religious Liberty' (2020) 58 *Duquesne Law Review* 377, 404–07.
[113] ibid.
[114] ibid.
[115] ibid.

approach of imposing a requirement on groups to cater to individuals, 'we should instead seek to be a community of communities, pursuing ends of right relationship, virtue, or solidarity, fraternity, and charity, and consequently accommodating difference within that shared quest'.[116] This approach therefore upholds both religious freedom and equality as goods which ought to be pursued, and adheres to the principled framework for the autonomy of religious communities which entails peaceful coexistence of difference and reasonable accommodation in accordance with the theological virtues.

VI. Conclusion

In this chapter I have argued that England has a substantive establishment. Despite superficial objections that a substantive establishment undermines pluralism and religious diversity, English substantive establishment points to the eternal foundations of citizenship and the theological foundation for the virtues which facilitate acknowledgement of dignity and mutual political responsibility. In doing so, substantive establishment avoids the crude secularist marginalisation of religion and actually encourages pluralism and religious diversity because the Church of England uses its unique privilege to welcome majority and minority religions to the public table, in conjunction with helping both religious and non-religious society more broadly through providing welfare, education and other kinds of charitable assistance. This flourishing diversity also manifests with respect to religious freedom and equality; substantive establishment supports both the autonomy of religious communities and equality between citizens in accordance with the theological virtues of dignity, love and patience, accommodating and facilitating diverse pursuits of the good to produce a peaceful coexistence, and ultimately providing a principled framework which reconciles freedom and discrimination.

However, as noted in previous chapters, different jurisdictions may require different approaches. In this sense the principled framework is not a uniform framework, but rather embraces flexibility and diversity as part of pursuing a peaceful coexistence of difference which reconciles the autonomy of religious communities with equality as mutually beneficial goods in accordance with the theological virtues. Therefore, in the final chapter, I conclude by re-examining the tensions between religious freedom and equality which I identified in the Introduction, articulating principles for engaging with them in light of the preceding analysis of the book. Finally, based on the findings of this book, I will provide legal and policy recommendations for Australia, the US and England to more effectively pursue the peaceful coexistence of difference in their communities.

---

[116] Harrison, *Post-liberal Religious Liberty* (n 30) 161, 224.

PART IV

A Principled Framework

7

Reconciling Religious Freedom and Equality in a Principled Framework

I. Introduction

In this book I have attempted to develop a principled framework for the autonomy of religious communities which reconciles religious freedom and anti-discrimination. To do this, I have applied the idea of a peaceful coexistence of difference in accordance with the theological virtues as a standard to evaluate the theoretical assumptions and legal structures which undergird Australia, the US and England. This has revealed several elements of a principled framework. First, a principled framework must be flexible and diverse to properly reconcile freedom and equality in religiously pluralist societies, and between different kinds of societies. For some polities, various types of establishment may be appropriate to best protect the autonomy of religious communities and equality for peaceful coexistence. For others, pluralism may be suitable. Secularist separationism should be rejected due to its marginalisation of religion and the consequent impossibility of enabling difference through the autonomy of religious communities. Equality is also undermined by the discriminatory treatment of religion. Second, a principled framework should, in accordance with the theological virtues, acknowledge the intrinsic dignity and value of all people among, between and outside religious communities and LGBT communities. Framing religious freedom and equality as mutually constitutive though diverse means which ultimately pursue the public good is essential to building the trust and common ground which is necessary for a peaceful coexistence of difference which protects both religious freedom and equality.

Finally, protecting the autonomy of religious communities alongside equality necessarily entails the preservation of difference, or diverse pursuits of the good. This protection may come in different legal forms, such as positive associational rights for religious bodies, or religious exemptions from anti-discrimination law. Different forms may be appropriate for different contexts. What matters is that the forms of protection consistently frame religious freedom and equality as important goods to be pursued together, but in diverse ways – rather than entering a zero-sum game where one always dominates the other. In areas of tension, reasonable accommodations of difference are almost always possible without undermining the fundamental goals of freedom and equality, as supported by the cultivation and practice of theological virtues such as kindness, patience, humility and love. Against such virtues there is no law, for they are the path to living peacefully together despite intractable moral difference.[1]

In this chapter I further explore the tensions between religious freedom and equality identified in the Introduction, and articulate some general principles for reconciling them in accordance with the elements of a principled framework. I then draw on these general principles to provide legal and policy recommendations for Australia, the US and England to create a peaceful coexistence of difference in accordance with the theological virtues which simultaneously reconciles freedom and equality.

II. Reconciling Religious Freedom and Equality

A. Individual and Collective Approaches to Religious Freedom

The first tension identified in the Introduction of this book was whether religious freedom is intrinsically a group or associational right where the group is a separate or distinct entity possessing its own authority, or whether the group is merely a vehicle for the religious rights of individuals and is merely an aggregate of individual interests. This tension was not considered in significant depth in the book, but it is relevant to a principled framework because if religious groups are merely an aggregate of individuals, the right of an individual to participate in a group is given far more weight. A religious community would not truly have its own autonomy, but would be beholden to the individual. As discussed in chapter six, if the law prioritises individuals over groups, this undermines the ability of a community to unite around a common purpose. The group would cease to have its own identity and be subject to the whims of any individual who purports to join. Such an approach utterly fails to reconcile freedom and equality because it does not protect the autonomy of religious communities, not to mention the impact such interference with the internal mechanisms of a group would also have on the individuals of the group who have united for a common purpose which is now being damaged by rogue individuals.

Conversely, if the law prioritises the group over the individual, the group is able to maintain its autonomy and can continue to unite around a common purpose. The individual is then free to exit the group and, if they desire, join another group with a consistent purpose or form a new group. Respecting religious freedom as an associational right therefore ensures the protection of both freedom and equality. For example, David has recently articulated a Christian approach to corporate religious liberty which recognises the group or community as an entity in itself

---

[1] *cf* Galatians 5:22.

through its actions rather than taking a secular atomistic individualist approach which sees the group as merely the aggregation of individuals.[2] This is also a more empathic approach which sees the autonomy of religious communities from their own perspective, providing a more robust basis for protection in accordance with the theological virtues. It entails recognising groups as involving coordinated action in the group pursuit of truth and the good. Thus, religious freedom ought to be viewed as an associational right which grants religious communities their own autonomy and internal authority separate from the autonomy and authority of individuals within the group. A principled framework for protecting the autonomy of religious communities and reconciling freedom and equality entails recognising that religious groups are more than the sum of their parts, and no individual is more important than the group.

B. Religious Vendors as Religious Bodies

The second tension identified in the Introduction is whether religious vendors should be understood as religious bodies, or whether the fact they are ostensibly 'secular' organisations providing 'secular' services in the public sphere should exclude vendors from being categorised as religious. In this book, I have consistently argued that religious vendors are genuinely religious bodies. This is not surprising since I have explicitly taken this position previously.[3] In my earlier article, I simply argued by analogy with other religious bodies (such as churches and schools) that religious vendors are religious bodies. However, in this book I have adopted a more principled rationale for that position, consonant with my broader purposes. The reason why religious vendors are religious and practicing their religion in performing their duties (just as much as churches or schools) is because for many religious people, religion is not just a discrete compartment of their life that they display only on special occasions. For many religious people, their religion constitutes their beliefs, character and actions – their very identity. It is practised through and entailed in everything they do. There is nothing intrinsically anti-religious about engaging in commercial ventures. The only reason a contrary view has become prominent is due to secular separationist tendencies which assume a spurious and damaging public/private divide for religious people and religious practice, which in effect marginalises religion by relegating it to an imaginary private sphere. Creating a peaceful coexistence of difference in accordance with the theological virtues such as love, humility and the golden rule entails acknowledging the genuinely religious status of religious vendors.

Even David falls into this secular trap in places. While acknowledging that the state should respect religious groups to carry out their mission and defer to

---

[2] E David, *A Christian Approach to Corporate Religious Liberty* (Palgrave Macmillan, 2020) 3.
[3] See A Deagon, 'Religious Schools, Religious Vendors and Refusing Services After Ruddock: Diversity or Discrimination? (2019) 93(9) *Australian Law Journal* 766.

a group as to the articulation of their mission, he argues there are 'categorical differences' in the actions of different religious groups, which implies 'more robust protections for more inward-focused religious groups' (as opposed to 'for-profit corporations').[4] Specifically, he distinguishes between ends which are 'distinctly religious, thus suggesting a theory of church freedoms', and ends which are 'religiously motivated yet secular in nature, thus suggesting a theory of non-church organizational exemptions'.[5] So while David correctly calls for a theory of group exemptions covering all religious communities, including vendors, he limits the potential scope of exemptions for so-called ends which are secular in nature, claiming that the pursuit of religious truth through such ends is 'attenuated'.[6] This has significant consequences; it allows the state more power over 'secular actions'.[7]

However, what David fails to acknowledge, and what I have consistently argued in this book, is that for many religious people no action is truly secular. In the Christian tradition, this is summed up by the Apostle Paul saying 'So, whether you eat or drink, or whatever you do, do all to the glory of God'.[8] What could be a more mundane secular action than eating or drinking? And what is a greater religious end than bringing glory to God? Yet in Christianity, as just one example, these are brought together, and in fact extended to whatever you do. There are no secular actions from this perspective, and categorising the actions of religious vendors as a lesser form of religious action compared to those of churches is problematic. David is nevertheless right that any regime of exemptions must be 'carefully handled' and will often turn on particular circumstances; religious motivations cannot be simply overridden by any harm, nor will religious vendors always win.[9] Of course, what all this demonstrates is the main issue at stake here is not whether religious vendors are genuinely religious, but whether their status as genuinely religious entitles them to exemptions from anti-discrimination law. This leads into the third tension.

C. The Scope of the Autonomy of Religious Communities

The third tension considers how far the autonomy of religious communities extends, and in particular whether religious freedom is public or private, and whether the state should intervene in the autonomy of religious communities where the exercise of this autonomy may involve discrimination against members of the community or discrimination against members of the public seeking the services of the community. This incorporates aspects of the first two tensions.

---

[4] David (n 2) 16–18.
[5] ibid 21.
[6] ibid 138.
[7] ibid 140.
[8] 1 Corinthians 10:31.
[9] David (n 2) 140.

As discussed above, religious freedom collapses the spurious secular distinction between public and private; the practice of religion permeates all parts of life. In addition, where there is a conflict between the doctrines or practices of a religious group, and the doctrines or practices of an individual within that group or seeking to be part of that group, the intrinsic internal freedom of the group prevails, providing the individual with the freedom to leave the group and join or form another group. This principle would apply to churches and faith schools, for example.

This just leaves the exercise of autonomy which may involve discrimination against members of the public seeking the services of the community. This is the religious vendors situation. In this book, I have argued that religious vendors are entitled to exercise their religious conscience in their commercial pursuits, but only in very limited situations. I have articulated narrow and clear exemptions. The religious vendor must be genuinely religious, and must object to participating in a significant moral act due to religious conscience, and there must be a direct connection between the act and the issue of conscience, and there must be an equivalent alternative reasonably available. The religious vendor should clearly outline their policy, perhaps in website terms and conditions. This is a set of cumulative requirements which are difficult to meet. There will not be many exemptions granted on this basis. Therefore, equality will be upheld while simultaneously providing genuine religious objectors, such as those vendors who were the subject of the Masterpiece and Ashers cases, with the freedom to participate in and benefit society without compromising their religion.

Conversely, David claims:

> (i) if the relevant gay rights are accounted for in public-accommodations laws; and (ii) if public-accommodations laws help secure the public peace over which the state has charge; then (iii) it may not be prudent to assert the free exercise of religion in (many) public-accommodations contexts. Doing so would presumably disrupt public peace, inciting animosity towards those seeking organizational exemptions.[10]

However, as already seen, David falsely distinguishes between ends which are distinctly religious versus ends which are secular in nature. For many religious people all ends are religious, and to categorise some ends as non-religious is itself imposing a secular distinction. David consequently differentiates too starkly between church bodies (said to be engaging in religious ends) and religious vendors (said to be engaging in secular ends). For many religious people, all ends are religious, and therefore religious vendors should be entitled to religious freedom protection as part of a principled framework. Furthermore, as discussed in chapters five and six, failing to accommodate religious vendors does not preserve social peace. It stokes conflict through the marginalisation of religion. Narrow and clear exemptions which enable a reasonable accommodation of difference preserves both virtue and peace, and also upholds the value of pursuing true religion.

---

[10] ibid 232–33.

D. Balancing Religious Freedom and Equality

The final tension is in a sense a culmination of the other three tensions: what is the relative weight of religious freedom versus equality, and which should prevail in the event of conflict? What this book has argued is seeing religious freedom and equality as dichotomous is counterproductive. Asking how to balance the tense relationship between religious freedom and equality is actually the wrong question. We should be seeking ways to support both through reasonable accommodations of difference, which will in turn create peaceful coexistence in accordance with the theological virtues. This book has discussed the ideas of exemptions from equality law and positive associational rights for religion. As argued in chapter four, positive associational rights provide a better framing of the issues for the purposes of reconciling freedom and equality. Where exemptions give the perception of religious freedom challenging or undermining equality, positive associational rights for religious freedom support freedom without directly challenging equality, and in fact positive associational rights frame the religious rights of public participation and association as part of a general pursuit of equality which upholds the intrinsic and holistic dignity of all people.

For example, with respect to churches, faith schools, and other like religious associations, these communities should have their autonomy protected through the legislation of positive associational rights which enable these communities to select and preference their leaders and members in accordance with the doctrines and practices of the religious community. With respect to religious vendors, the narrow and clear exemptions discussed above can be alternatively framed as narrow and clear positive rights for religious vendors not to creatively participate in significant moral acts (such as same-sex marriage). In the following part, I provide more specific legal and policy suggestions for Australia, the US and England to implement a principled framework for the autonomy of religious communities which reconciles freedom and equality along these lines.

III. Recommendations

A. Australia

I critiqued Australia's theoretical framework and legal infrastructure in chapters one and four, offering a number of legal and policy recommendations. The first is to embrace the conceptual overlay of mild establishment or Christian Democracy, which entails the general institutional support of religion in accordance with the theological virtues. This is consistent with section 116 of the Constitution because it does not amount to a substantive identification of the state with religion, but rather implements the proper interpretation of section 116 as a pluralist provision which facilitates the beneficial interaction between religion and government. It also contributes to a peaceful coexistence of difference through cultivating the virtues of love, kindness, humility and patience, acknowledging the dignity of all people and encouraging mutual responsibility towards all citizens as transcendentally linked to the eternal. This is possible because the eternal virtues are also universal and can be implemented by all people of all beliefs. As part of implementing the first recommendation, the second recommendation is to broaden the interpretation of the free exercise clause in particular to implement it as a provision which promotes the beneficial interaction of government and religion, and the protection of the exercise of religion in public and group contexts.

The remaining Australian recommendations pertain to Commonwealth legislation. The religious exemptions in the Sex Discrimination Act should be removed because they undermine peaceful coexistence by unfairly and unnecessarily targeting sexual minorities. They should be replaced by positive associational rights which uphold the autonomy of religious communities without undermining equality. These positive associational rights entail the ability for religious groups such as churches, schools and charities to select and regulate their leaders and members in accordance with their doctrines and practices. If these doctrines and practices entail rejecting some members or applicants for reasons of incompatibility with the group, then the group should have a publicly available policy outlining the criteria and rationale for those selective policies, which minimises the imposition of dignity harm and upholds the virtue of honesty. Providing religious schools with alternative legal infrastructure to operate in accordance with a religious ethos is loving because it promotes diverse approaches to the good and upholds the virtues of humility, patience and tolerance, while also avoiding the unkind nature of the current exemptions. For the same reasons, narrow and clear rights should also be provided for religious vendors to not creatively participate in significant moral acts in accordance with the requirements outlined in the previous part.

As for the specific legal mechanism for these positive rights, for the reasons discussed in chapter four a bill of rights is unlikely to be an appropriate candidate. Alternatives include amending the Fair Work Act to provide employment rights to organisations established for religious purposes, affirming their autonomy to choose or prefer members in accordance with those purposes. The Religious Discrimination Bill could be another method of providing positive associational rights for religious groups to select and regulate leaders and members in accordance with the beliefs and acceptable conduct of the religion. However, the Bill would need to be altered to ensure that there are no exclusions on the basis of commercial activities (which, as noted above, assumes a problematic secular distinction between specific religious actions), and to ensure that secular courts must defer to the religious group's own understanding of its doctrinal and conduct requirements. By demonstrating humility and patience towards religious communities in these ways, peaceful coexistence of difference can be more effectively implemented.

B. United States

I critiqued the theoretical framework and legal infrastructure of the US in chapters two and five, offering a number of legal and policy recommendations. The first is to reject separationist readings of the US religion-state relationship and the First Amendment. Secularist separationism marginalises religion and damages peaceful coexistence of difference by hindering the autonomy of religious communities. Instead, I argued that the US should adopt a pluralist framework which protects the autonomy of religious communities through the ministerial exception, facilitates religious freedom and diversity through the free exercise clause, and simultaneously prevents government coercion of religion through the establishment clause. Such a framework is the most plausible interpretation of the history and jurisprudence of the First Amendment. In this way, pluralism preserves the peaceful coexistence of difference in accordance with the theological virtues, and reconciles freedom and equality by enabling religious communities to develop and deploy religion for social benefit, while simultaneously protecting the dignity of all citizens by prohibiting unlimited, unjust, arbitrary and malicious discrimination. Emerging scholarship suggests 'covenantal pluralism' as an appropriate means of adopting pluralism, because it explicitly assumes the theological virtues of dignity, humility, patience and compassion to seek common ground and peaceful coexistence with our neighbours even in the face of deep difference.[11]

With respect to the establishment clause specifically, the secularist wall of separation metaphor should be rejected. Analysis of the history and jurisprudence of the clause reveals that it was designed to prevent religious coercion. Adopting a coercion test fulfils the function of the establishment clause while also properly protecting the ability of religious communities to financially and practically cooperate with government in the provision of community services, whilst retaining their autonomy. This interpretation would consequently contribute to loving our neighbour by exhibiting humility, forgiveness and patience towards different views, by a willingness to accept genuine diversity by not excluding any perspectives, and by enabling the peaceful coexistence of diverse religious communities without government favouritism.

With respect to the free exercise clause, as argued in chapter five, free exercise jurisprudence should facilitate the autonomy of religious communities to meaningfully and equally participate in public life by explicitly overruling the *Smith* requirement that such communities are necessarily subject to generally applicable

---

[11] See WC Stewart, C Seiple and DR Hoover, 'Toward a Global Covenant of Peaceable Neighborhood: Introducing the Philosophy of Covenantal Pluralism' (2020) 18(4) *The Review of Faith & International Affairs* 1–17. See also eg RJ Joustra, 'The Coordinates of Covenantal Pluralism: Mapping Pluralist Theory in the 21st Century' (2020) 18(4) *The Review of Faith & International Affairs* 18–34; C Seiple and D Hoover (eds), *The Routledge Handbook of Religious Literacy, Pluralism, and Global Engagement* (Routledge, 2022).

laws which may have the incidental effect of targeting religion. This reconciles freedom and equality by graciously welcoming religion to public life and confirming the equal dignity of religious citizens by recognising that government cannot discriminate against religious communities. In addition, clearly limited and stringent exemptions for religious vendors protect the dignity and life of both religious communities and those who may be discriminated against. Though the US typically relies on the language of exemptions, it should be possible to reframe this language into positive rights as recommended above, given the reliance on the First Amendment right of free exercise. Such positive rights must be narrow and clear as outlined above, which upholds the dignity of religious vendors by not compelling them to violate their conscience, and upholds the dignity of those seeking services by minimising the potential of rejection and providing reasonable alternatives. As Rienzi has recently pointed out, the Supreme Court appears to be recognising the importance of promoting pluralism through the First Amendment, resulting in a peaceful coexistence of difference: 'The Court has thus emphatically demonstrated that it views the Religion Clauses as important and enforceable protectors of religious liberty and peaceful pluralism'.[12] The blessing of religious freedom is 'built on the First Amendment's Religion Clauses, including the constitutional promise of free exercise, which the Court recently recognised as "the heart of our pluralistic society"'.[13] 'Serious enforcement of free exercise is a crucial component of the Constitution's ability to promote social peace in a pluralistic society ... the most logical result of a pluralist approach to the Free Exercise Clause is not Smith but religious exemptions'.[14] Thus, in divided times, a pluralist approach to the First Amendment 'allows free people with divergent views to live and work together in peace'.[15]

With respect to the ministerial exception, a pluralist reading of the combined establishment and free exercise clauses in the First Amendment correctly yields the ministerial exception, which provides autonomy for religious communities such as churches, schools and like associations to select and regulate those who develop and propagate the religion. This enables religious communities to cultivate and articulate their own versions of the good, loving neighbour and enhancing the virtues of honesty, patience and forgiveness by allowing religious citizens the dignity of their own autonomous groups, and motivating considered debate outside of those groups in areas of profound disagreement with the mutual aim of good for all. However, a pluralism which upholds the dignity of all persons in accordance with the theological virtues cannot countenance discrimination without impunity. An extremely broad approach may provide an unconstrained

---

[12] M Rienzi, 'Religious Liberty and Judicial Deference' (2022) *Notre Dame Law Review* 36 (forthcoming).
[13] ibid 58; *Bostock v Clayton Cty., Georgia*, 140 S. Ct. 1731, 1754 (2020).
[14] Rienzi (n 12) 59.
[15] ibid 60. See also *American Legion v Am. Humanist Ass'n*, 139 S. Ct. 2067, 2074 (2019).

licence to discriminate. Consequently the ministerial exception should only protect employer conduct which occurs for religious or religion-related reasons, reconciling the freedom of religious organisations with the equality of those employed by them.

Finally, with respect to federal legislation, existing provisions largely preserve the peaceful coexistence of difference by reconciling the autonomy of religious communities with equality. Protection of small businesses and closely held corporations under RFRA recognises the intrinsic dignity of religious people in terms of their holistic identity. More broadly, RFRA, RLUIPA and the Title VII exemptions appropriately prevent government from imposing substantial burdens on religious exercise, and enable religious employers to select and regulate staff on limited religious grounds. There is a need for further clarity around central terms such as substantial burden, and more generally, for affected parties to cultivate the theological virtues to facilitate reasonable compromises. However, the proposed *Equality Act* is an example of opposing religious liberty without compromise. It could be used to severely damage the autonomy of religious communities including churches, schools, charities and businesses, and should be rejected. The *Fairness for All Act* proposes to expand LGBT protections while simultaneously enabling religious communities to operate according to their religious ethos through strengthening reasonable accommodations along the lines of the relatively successful Utah Compromise. This proposal seems to more effectively underscore that all people, religious and/or LGBT, are created in the image of God and therefore possess intrinsic dignity and worth. It appears to promote peaceful coexistence in accordance with the theological virtues such as love of neighbour and forgiveness, contributing to a society where people with profound moral differences can live together in peace.

C. England

I critiqued England's theoretical framework and legal infrastructure in chapters three and six, offering a number of legal and policy recommendations. First, I argued that England has a substantive establishment, and this ought to be retained because it actually facilitates peaceful coexistence in accordance with the theological virtues. Substantive establishment explicitly acknowledges the transcendent foundations of human dignity and citizenship, and grounds them in the eternal virtues which enable the reconciliation of religious freedom and equality. For example, David argues that the state should recognise religious truth and the 'distinct moral value of collective religious action', encouraging a government response which protects the autonomy of religious communities 'through an establishment whereby the government engages in, or directly supports, ecclesial activity' – as is the case in England.[16] Substantive establishment also avoids the

---

[16] David (n 2) 130–31.

marginalisation of majority and minority religions by welcoming religion in the public sphere, and the Church of England uses its privilege to provide spiritual, educational and charitable support to both the state and civil society.

In addition, the European Court of Human Rights must draw on scholarly literature and its own existing thematic strands to develop a clear rationale for religious liberty and a robust jurisprudence for the autonomy of religious communities. As a corollary of substantive establishment, this clear rationale and robust jurisprudence subsequently ought to be explicitly incorporated into English law and judicial decision-making through the mechanism in the Human Rights Act. Finally, consistently with this incorporation and the above arguments regarding the problem of 'exemptions', the religious exemptions in the Equality Act ought to be reframed (perhaps in a separate Act) as positive associational rights for religious communities such as churches, schools and charities to select and regulate members of their community. Similarly, narrow and clear positive rights should be provided for religious vendors to choose not to creatively participate in significant moral acts as articulated above. Undergirding these measures is a principled theoretical reconciliation which frames religious freedom and equality as good and mutually constitutive goals; rather than viewing these important imperatives as intrinsically in conflict, they enable diverse paths to seeking the common good. This will promote a peaceful coexistence of difference in accordance with the theological virtues.

For these endeavours to succeed, there must be genuine attempts to reconcile, understand and compromise with respect to religious freedom and equality, with both perspectives seeking the maximum protection for each other. For example, secular courts should seek to understand and defer to the self-understanding of a religious organisation regarding what is required for them to fulfil their mission, rather than imposing a hostile secular perspective upon them. Religious organisations need to be prepared to co-exist with and protect the dignity of those who they have moral disagreement with. Doctrinal and conduct preference by religious organisations and conscientious objections from religious vendors can usually be accommodated with limited adverse effects if there is a genuine engagement with practical solutions which protect both religious freedom and equality, rather than simply allowing one concern to override and marginalise the other. This will not mean everyone always gets what they want. But it will hopefully produce productive dialogue characterised by the theological virtues of patience, humility and kindness, affirming the intrinsic dignity of all parties. This enables the pursuit of unity in diversity through diverse paths to the common good: a peaceful coexistence of difference which reconciles freedom and equality through reasonable accommodations.

INDEX

Ingram Content Group UK Ltd.
Milton Keynes UK
UKHW020026050523
421270UK00003B/158